GCSE 9-1 GEOGRAPHY EDEXCEL B REVISION & EXAM PRACTICE

Dan Cowling,
Philippa Conway-Hughes,
Natalie Dow and
Lindsay Frost

Authors
Dan Cowling, Philippa Conway-Hughes, Natalie Dow:
Hazardous Earth
Challenges of an urbanising world
The UK's evolving physical landscape
The UK's evolving human landscape
Geographical investigations

Lindsay Frost:
Development dynamics
People and the biosphere
Forests under threat
Consuming energy resources
People and environment issues: Making geographical decisions

Editorial team Aidan Gill, Turnstone Solutions Limited, Lynette Woodward, Sarah Christopher
Series designers emc design ltd
Typesetting Couper Street Type Co.
App development Hannah Barnett, Phil Crothers and Haremi Ltd

Designed using Adobe InDesign
Published by Scholastic Education, an imprint of Scholastic Ltd, Book End, Range Road, Witney, Oxfordshire, OX29 0YD
Registered office: Westfield Road, Southam, Warwickshire CV47 0RA
www.scholastic.co.uk

Printed by Bell & Bain Ltd, Glasgow
© 2018 Scholastic Ltd
1 2 3 4 5 6 7 8 9   8 9 0 1 2 3 4 5 6 7

British Library Cataloguing-in-Publication Data
A catalogue record for this book is available from the British Library.
ISBN 978-1407-18241-4

All rights reserved. This book is sold subject to the condition that it shall not, by way of trade or otherwise, be lent, hired out or otherwise circulated without the publisher's prior consent in any form of binding or cover other than that in which it is published and without a similar condition, including this condition, being imposed upon the subsequent purchaser.

No part of this publication may be reproduced, stored in a retrieval system, or transmitted, in any form or by any means, electronic, mechanical, photocopying, recording or otherwise, other than for the purposes described in the content of this product, without the prior permission of the publisher. This product remains in copyright.

Due to the nature of the web, we cannot guarantee the content or links of any site mentioned.

Every effort has been made to trace copyright holders for the works reproduced in this book, and the publishers apologise for any inadvertent omissions.

Note from the publisher:

Please use this product in conjunction with the official specification and sample assessment materials. Ask your teacher if you are unsure where to find them.

How to use this book

Inside this book you'll find everything you need to help you succeed in the new GCSE 9–1 Edexcel Geography B specification. It combines revision and exam practice in one handy solution. Broken down into topics and subtopics, it presents the information in a manageable format. Work through the revision material first or dip into the exam practice as you complete a topic. This book gives you the flexibility to revise your way!

DO IT!

Activities to embed your knowledge and understanding and prepare you for the exams.

SNAP IT!

Use the revision app to take a picture of key concepts and information. Great for revision on the go!

NAIL IT!

Tips written by a subject expert to help you in the revision process.

Case study

Case studies that illustrate the ideas that you have learned.

Geographical skills

Tasks to develop your geographical, practical, numerical, statistical and mapwork skills.

STRETCH IT!

Concepts and questions that stretch you further, so as to access the higher grades.

REVIEW IT!

Consolidate your revision with questions at the end of every topic.

CHECK IT!

Check your knowledge at the end of a subtopic.

★ STAR RATING ★

A quick visual guide to question difficulty, from 1 star (least demanding) to 5 stars (most demanding).

PRACTICE PAPERS

Full mock-exam papers to practise before you sit the real thing!

FREE REVISION APP

- The **free revision app** can be downloaded to your mobile phone (iOS and Android), making **on-the-go revision** easy.

- Use the revision calendar to help map out your revision in the lead-up to the exam.

- Complete multiple-choice questions and create your own **SNAP IT!** revision cards.

www.scholastic.co.uk/gcse

Revision Guide Contents

Topic 9

Topic 10

5

Practice Book Contents

HOW TO REVISE!

PLAN YOUR REVISION

Get ahead by planning your revision!

Work out the **time** you have available for revising.

Think about when you work at your best. Are you a morning or an evening person?

Allocate **MORE TIME** for the topics you struggle with.

Revision works best in **SMALL BURSTS**, so keep sessions **SHORT AND SWEET**!

Remember to allow time to **PRACTISE** applying what you have revised.

Use your **revision app** to put together a revision timetable.

LOOK AFTER YOURSELF

Help your brain by looking after your whole body!

Take regular **breaks** from revising – your brain needs time to digest information in order to retain it.

HOTEL

Keep **hydrated** by drinking plenty of water – dehydration stops your brain from working at its full capacity.

Regular **exercise** helps stimulate the brain and will help you relax.

Get plenty of **sleep**, especially the night before an exam.

EAT WELL and limit unhealthy snacks – your brain needs fuel for memory and concentration.

Find methods of **relaxation** that work for you throughout the revision period.

BE PREPARED!

Limit potential stress on the day of an exam by getting everything you need ready the night before.

30

Highlight key pieces of written information and use different colours to classify it.

DO IT!
Take an active approach to revision. Create **revision cards**, **lists**, **mind maps**, **flow charts** and **infographics** like this one.

Annotate and summarise your class notes and revision pages.

Revise in pairs or small groups and deliver presentations on topics to each other.

SNAP IT!
Use your phone to take pictures of your revision material so that you can **revise on the go!**

REMEMBERING INFORMATION

Use different methods to digest information!

Create a safe place to **store** all of your revision notes and keep everything together.

Use **mnemonics** or songs to help learn tricky bits of information.

RETRIEVING INFORMATION

Use the information you have remembered!

REVIEW IT!
Revisit the content you have already revised to confirm your understanding.

CHECK IT!
Make sure you know the material using simple **recall** questions.

Practise *applying* your knowledge using *exam-style questions*.

READ THE QUESTION CAREFULLY!
Make sure you understand what you are being asked to do.

Mark your work to help you see where you can **improve**.

FOR HIGH-MARK QUESTIONS, SPEND TIME **PLANNING** YOUR ANSWER!

Stick to the **TIME LIMITS** you will need to in the exam.

FINISH

1 Hazardous Earth

1.1 The world's climate system

THE EXAMINATION!

- This section is tested in Paper 1 Section A.
- You must know Global circulation of the atmosphere and changing climate, Tectonic hazards and Weather hazards.
- You must know two in-depth studies of tropical cyclones and tectonic hazards at contrasting locations.

OUTCOMES

By the end of my revision I will be able to:

- Explain how global atmospheric circulation and ocean currents affect patterns of weather and climate.
- Explain how climate has changed in the past due to natural causes, and that climate is currently changing as a result of human activities.
- Analyse the extent to which there is uncertainty about future climates.

Global atmospheric circulation

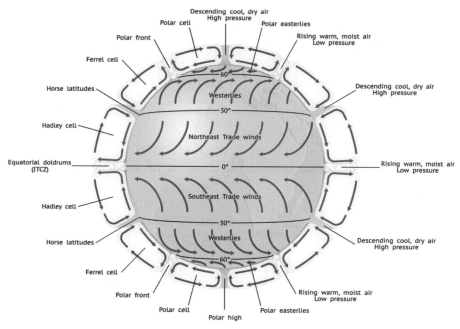

Figure 1 Global atmospheric circulation

Global atmospheric circulation helps us to understand the world **climate** zones and the pattern of global weather hazards.

1. Areas of high pressure and dry (arid) conditions are found where the air is sinking towards the ground. Winds on the ground move outwards from areas of high pressure.

2. Areas of low pressure and high rainfall are found where the air is rising. Winds on the ground move towards areas of low pressure.

3. Winds on the ground transfer heat and moisture between areas.

Patterns of pressure belts and winds are affected by seasonal change and the tilt and rotation of the Earth.

SNAP IT!

Make your own simple diagram based on Figure 1. Snap a picture of it and use it to help you recall where the low- and high-pressure systems are.

Ocean currents

Ocean currents are permanent or semi-permanent large-scale horizontal movements of the water in the oceans.

- The Gulf Stream is an example of an ocean current.
  - In the North Atlantic the water is dense due to it being cold and salty, causing it to sink.
  - A current is set up, which drags surface water down.
  - The current draws warmer salty water over the ocean surface from areas near the equator.

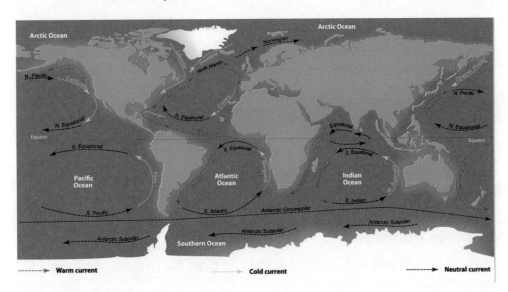

Figure 2 The world's ocean currents

Natural causes of climate change

1 Orbital changes

The Earth's orbit changes over time due to its:

- **eccentricity**: the path of the Earth around the Sun. The Earth's orbit follows different elliptical paths, on a 100 000 year cycle. A more elliptical path may cause ice ages.

- **precession**: the natural wobble of the Earth on its axis, which is on a 26 000 year cycle.

- **tilt**: the Earth being currently at a tilt of 23.5 degrees. Over a period of 41 000 years, the Earth's tilt moves between 21.5 and 24.5 degrees.

Eccentricity   Precession   Tilt

Figure 3 Milankovitch Cycles: changes in the Earth's movements that affect its climate

DO IT!

Draw a sketch to show:
- why it is hot and wet at the equator
- why it is hot and dry in the desert.

Hint: think about what weather you find at low- and high-pressure systems.

STRETCH IT!

Research what the ITCZ is, where it can be found and how it influences the weather.

SNAP IT!

Snap a picture of Figure 2. Cover up sections to test your recall of how warm and cold currents circulate in the Earth's oceans.

SNAP IT!

Snap an image of Figure 3 and use it to help you create a podcast to explain why orbital changes affect the Earth's climate.

2 Solar output

There are cyclical changes in solar energy linked to sunspots.

- A sunspot is a dark area that appears on the surface of the Sun.

- The number of sunspots increases from a minimum to a maximum and then back over an 11-year period.

- The more sunspots there are, the more heat is given out (solar output). The fewer sunspots there are, the less heat is given out. This can reduce the Earth's temperatures.

3 Volcanic activity

- Volcanic ash can block out sunlight and so temperatures are reduced.

- When sulfur dioxide mixes with water vapour it forms sulfuric acid. This reflects the Sun's radiation, reducing temperatures.

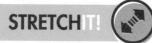

STRETCHIT!

The Mount Pinatubo eruption in 1991 had a short-term impact on the climate. Research the effect of this eruption on the climate.

4 Asteroid collisions

- Large asteroids colliding with the Earth can blast out millions of tonnes of ash and dust into the atmosphere.

- This can block out the sunlight and cause similar effects to those of a large volcanic eruption.

Evidence of climate change

Ice cores

- These contain layers of ice: oldest at the bottom and newest at the top. Each layer is a year of snowfall.

- Air bubbles are trapped in the ice layers, which preserve air from the time the snow fell to ground.

- Carbon dioxide (CO_2) is trapped in the air bubbles, which helps climatologists to reconstruct past temperatures, including during ice ages (glacial times) and between ice ages (interglacial times).

Tree rings

- Tree rings show the history of a tree's growth. Each ring represents the tree's growth for a single year.

- Trees grow more in warmer, wetter climates, so their rings are further apart.

- When the climate is colder and drier, tree rings will be closer together.

- Living trees show the effects of more recent climate changes. Fossilised tree remains show glacial and interglacial changes.

DOIT!

Create a revision poster showing the evidence for climate change.

NAILIT!

Make sure that you understand the three natural factors that affect climate change and whether they have a short- or long-term impact on the climate.

Historical sources

More recent climate change can be seen in:

- old photos, drawings and paintings
- written records
- recorded dates of regular events (for example, harvests, arrival of migrating birds).

These records are not very accurate.

Human causes of climate change

Figure 4 The greenhouse effect

Greenhouse gases include carbon dioxide (CO_2) and methane. People adding more and more greenhouse gases to the atmosphere has led to the **enhanced greenhouse effect**. Most scientists believe this is the cause of recent global warming.

Fossil fuels

- Burning fossil fuels releases carbon dioxide into the atmosphere.
- **Fossil fuels** are used in transport, industry and power stations.
- As population increases and people are becoming wealthier, more energy is used, which means more fossil fuels are burnt.

Agriculture

- Produces large amounts of methane, especially cattle and rice farming.
- As population increases, more food is required, especially in Asia where rice is a main part of the diet.

Deforestation

- Deforestation means there are fewer trees to take in carbon dioxide.
- Forests are carbon stores. When they are burned to clear an area, the carbon dioxide that has been stored is released.

Draw your own diagram of the **greenhouse effect**. Snap an image of it and use it to remind yourself of how it works. Can you explain how it affects the climate?

Plan an answer to a question that asks you about how humans have contributed to climate change.

Human and natural causes

Make sure that you understand the difference between **human** and **natural** causes of climate change.

Recent evidence for climate change

- Shrinking glaciers and melting ice.
- Rising sea levels: sea levels rose by 210 mm from 1870 to 2010 due to melting ice and thermal expansion; warmer water takes up more volume.
- Seasonal changes.

Effects of climate change

- An increase in flood risk due to increased levels of heavy rainfall.
- Rising sea levels may breach sea defences and increase coastal flooding.
- An increase in extreme weather events, such as drought in the UK.
- An increase in crop yields in Europe, but a decrease in South-East Asia.
- Less heating needed in Northern Europe.
- Less ice in the Arctic, which could open up shipping routes.
- Declines in wildlife numbers, such as polar bears and seals in the Arctic.
- Warmer oceans are causing coral bleaching and reducing biodiversity in the Great Barrier Reef.

Uncertainty about future climate

- It is uncertain how global warming may affect the Earth in the future.
- Scientists estimate that by 2100:
  - Temperatures will rise between 1.1 and 6.4 degrees Celsius.
  - Sea levels will rise by between 30 cm and 1 m.
- Predicting future climate is difficult because there is uncertainty about:
  - World future population growth.
  - The use of fossil fuels.
  - How much people will change their lifestyles (for example, recycling, use of public transport).

DO IT!

Look at the effects of climate change. Are the effects of climate change going to be the same for people everywhere in the world? Explain your answer.

✓ CHECK IT!

1 Describe what low- and high-pressure systems are.

2 Describe the three causes of natural climate change.

3 Explain how volcanic activity affects the global climate in the short term.

4 Describe how tree rings and ice cores provide evidence for climate change.

5 Define the greenhouse effect.

6 Explain the difference between the greenhouse effect and the enhanced greenhouse effect.

7 Explain two ways in which humans have contributed to climate change.

8 Explain how the effects of climate change may differ around the world.

9 State and explain two reasons why the predictions for future global temperatures are uncertain.

1.2 Extreme weather events

OUTCOMES

By the end of my revision I will be able to:

- Explain how tropical cyclones are caused.
- Explain how tropical cyclones are natural hazards to people and places.
- Explain the impacts of tropical cyclones.
- Analyse the extent to which people can prepare for and respond to tropical cyclones in developed and developing countries.

Tropical cyclones

Global distribution of tropical cyclones

Tropical cyclones develop in the tropics where there are areas of intense low pressure. They have different names depending on where they develop:

- **Hurricanes** in the USA and the Caribbean.
- **Cyclones** in South-East Asia and Australia.
- **Typhoons** in Japan and the Philippines.

TD | TS | 1 | 2 | 3 | 4 | 5

Saffir-Simpson hurricane intensity scale (TD = tropical depression; TS = tropical cyclone)

Figure 5 Global distribution and track of tropical cyclones, with intensity according to the Saffir-Simpson scale

DOIT!

Write a paragraph describing the distribution of tropical cyclones. Use the following words in your notes:

- 5–15°
- equator
- north
- tropics.
- south

NAILIT!

When asked to describe a map or data in geography examinations, always look for the overall pattern. Are there any anomalies? Include data to support your description.

Formation of a tropical cyclone

Draw a revision poster to show the formation of a tropical cyclone. Include an annotated diagram.

STRETCHIT!

Research the Coriolis effect. How does the Coriolis effect influence the formation of tropical cyclones?

1 Air is heated above the warm tropical oceans (26–27°C or above), causing it to rise rapidly.

2 Upwards movement of air draws up water vapour from the ocean's surface.

3 Evaporated air rises and cools, causing it to condense to form large cumulonimbus clouds.

4 As air condenses, it releases heat that powers the storm, causing more and more water to be drawn up from the ocean.

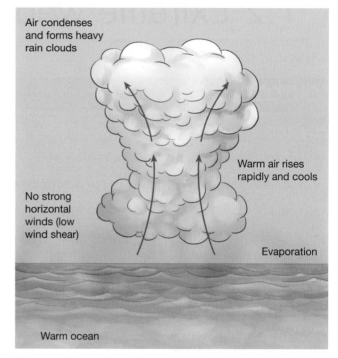

Figure 6 Formation of a tropical storm

5 Several thunderstorms join together to form a giant spinning storm. It officially becomes a tropical cyclone when winds reach 63 km/h. Tropical cyclones are formed in part due to air circulation caused by the Coriolis effect, which is caused by the rotation of the Earth. The Coriolis effect is weakest near the equator – one reason why tropical cyclones do not form there.

6 The eye of the cyclone is created at the centre, where air descends rapidly.

7 As the cyclone moves across the ocean directed by prevailing winds, it gains strength.

8 When the cyclone hits land it loses its energy source (evaporated water), and friction with the land causes it to slow down and weaken.

Structure of a tropical cyclone

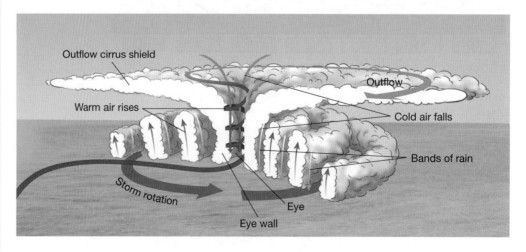

Figure 7 Structure of a tropical cyclone

Impacts of a tropical cyclone on people and places

- Strong winds can bring down trees, power lines, lift roofs and destroy entire houses.

- Storm surges cause flooding due to high tides. Tides are higher than normal because tropical cyclones bring areas of low pressure, which cause the sea level to rise because the air holding it down is less dense.

- Intense rainfall: 1000 m of rainfall can fall in one cyclone.

- Landslides: heavy rainfall causes land to become saturated, which makes it heavy and can cause it to slump.

The effects of and responses to a tropical cyclone

Figure 8 Track of Cyclone Alia

Example

Cyclone Alia, May 2009

Primary effects

- Approximately 190 people died, mainly due to storm surge.
- 750 000 people were displaced: 90 per cent of these people suffered from high levels of poverty.
- Land was flooded with salt water, killing crops.
- 59 000 animals were killed.
- There was widespread flooding.

Secondary effects

- 3.5 million people were affected.
- People were forced to move to cities to find work.
- Water was contaminated by flood waters, which increased the number of diseases such as typhoid and malaria.

DO IT!

Will climate change bring more tropical cyclones? Explain your answer.

DO IT!

1 Sort the primary and secondary effects of Cyclone Alia, or the tropical cyclone you have studied, into: social, economic and environmental.

2 Rank the effects, starting with the one you think is the worst effect.

3 Explain why Bangladesh is vulnerable to tropical cyclones.

Practical skills

Tracking Cyclone Alia

1. Find a blank map of South-East Asia.

2. Plot out the path of Cyclone Alia onto the map using the longitude and latitude coordinates.

3. Label the countries on the map that were affected.

4. Describe the path of Cyclone Alia.

DOIT!

1 Draw a spider diagram to explain the ways in which the effects of a tropical cyclone could be reduced in a developing country.

2 What are the challenges that developing countries face in preparing for tropical cyclones?

Date	Time (GMT)	Latitude (°N)	Longitude (°E)
23 May	0600	16.5	88.0
23 May	1800	17.0	88.5
24 May	0600	18.0	88.5
24 May	1800	19.0	88.5
25 May	0600	21.5	88.0
25 May	1800	23.5	88.0
26 May	0600	27.0	88.5

Table 1 The path of Cyclone Alia, 2009

Reducing the effects of a tropical cyclone

There are four main strategies used to help manage the risk of tropical cyclone: weather forecasting, satellite technology, warning and evacuation strategies, and storm-surge defences.

Example

Bangladesh: A developing country

Weather forecasting

- Bangladesh Meteorological Department issues weather forecasts on TV and radio.

- Outside major cities, many people do not have access to TV or radio.

- Households with radios had lower death rates than those without.

Satellite technology

- Weather forecasting is expensive.

- In 2012, Bangladesh announced it was going to spend $150 million on developing its own space satellites.

Warning and evacuation strategies

- Bangladesh has developed early warning systems to help protect and evacuate coastal communities.

- They run awareness campaigns to help people prepare for cyclones, including village meetings, posters and demonstrations.

- There are 45 000 cyclone warning volunteers in Bangladesh.

Storm-surge defences

- Bangladesh has invested in coastal embankments to protect against storm surges.

- There are 3500 coastal shelters. They have been effective for those people who can access them.

Example

The USA: A developed country

Weather forecasting and satellite technology

- The USA has over 20 weather satellites.

- All warnings are issued on TV and radio. Almost everyone has access to media and there are 103 mobile phones per 100 people.

- In Miami, there is the National Hurricane Centre that issues warnings and educates people about tropical cyclones.

- Satellites are ageing and so are not always accurate.

Warning and evacuation strategies

- The USA has cyclone warning and evacuation systems in places.

- Areas are assessed for risks between Extreme and Low and so people who need to evacuate are informed.

Storm-surge defences

- Beach nourishment, artificial reefs and wetlands absorb water and wave energy.

- Protection systems were destroyed during Hurricane Katrina in 2005.

DO IT!

1 Draw a revision poster to show how developed countries prepare for tropical cyclones.

1 Does the USA or Bangladesh protect people better against tropical cyclones? Explain your answer.

CHECK IT!

1 Describe the global distribution of tropical cyclones.

2 Explain why tropical cyclones do not occur at the equator.

3 Explain the formation of a tropical cyclone.

4 What is the difference between a primary and a secondary effect?

5 Using a named example, explain the immediate and long-term responses to a tropical cyclone.

6 Evaluate the different methods of reducing the effects of a tropical cyclone.

1.3 Tectonic hazards

OUTCOMES

By the end of my revision I will be able to:

- Explain the structure of the Earth and its physical properties.
- Explain the physical processes that result in earthquakes and volcanic eruptions.
- Analyse the effects and responses of tectonic hazards in countries of contrasting wealth.
- Explain how management can reduce the effects of tectonic hazards.

Structure of the Earth

DO IT!

Study Figure 9 that shows the structure of the Earth. Create a revision poster of the structure of the Earth, including:

- composition
- temperature
- density
- physical state.

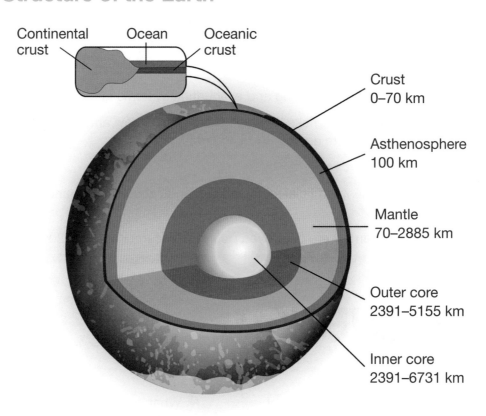

Figure 9 Structure of the Earth

STRETCH IT!

Research how earthquakes and meteorites provide evidence for the different layers of the Earth.

Convection currents

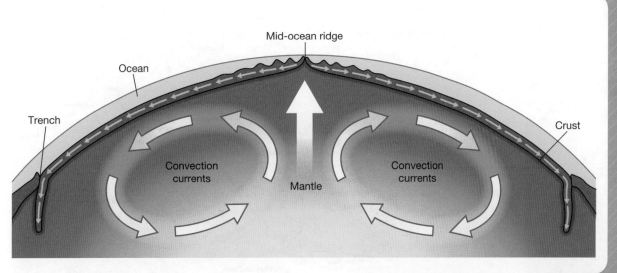

Figure 10 Convection currents

- Heat from inside the Earth is produced by radioactive decay.

- This raises the temperature to 5000 °C.

Plate tectonic theory

1. The Earth's crust is split into a number of plates.

2. There are two types of crust: oceanic and continental.

3. Plates move due to heat deep within the Earth's core causing convection currents in the mantle, or due to slab pull and ridge push.

4. Tectonic activity at plate margins causes earthquakes and volcanoes.

SNAPIT!

Snap a picture of Figure 10. Use it later to identify and write notes about the different types of plate margins shown in Figure 10.

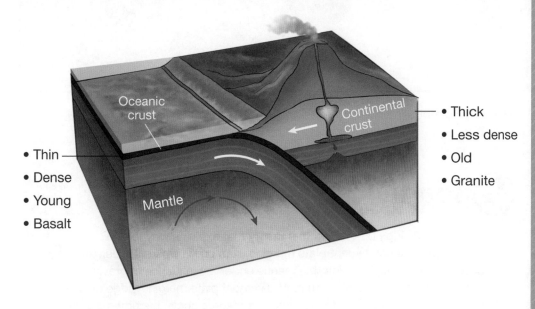

- Thin
- Dense
- Young
- Basalt

- Thick
- Less dense
- Old
- Granite

Figure 11 Oceanic and continental crust

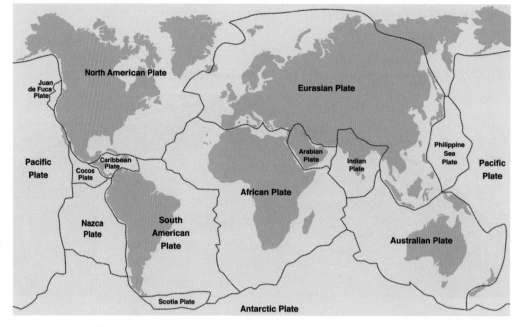

Figure 12 Earth's tectonic plates

Figure 13 Distribution of earthquakes and volcanoes

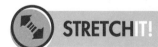

Study Figure 13, which shows the distribution of earthquakes and volcanoes. Plan an answer to explain why earthquakes and volcanoes occur at the edge of plate margins.

STRETCH IT!

Slab pull and ridge push is another theory that explains why tectonic plates move. At convergent plate margins, slab pull is where the denser oceanic plate sinks back into the mantle under the influence of gravity, pulling the rest of the plate with it. At divergent plate margins, ridge push is where magma rises at plate margins. The magma cools, becomes denser and slides down, resulting in the plates moving away from each other.

Physical processes at plate margins

Divergent plate margins

At a divergent plate margin, two plates are moving away from each other.

- As the two plates move apart, magma breaks through the crust, causing earthquakes and volcanoes.

- The magma is very thin and runny, which allows the lava from an erupting volcano to travel long distances before cooling.

- This creates gently sloping shield volcanoes.

Sometimes the magma never reaches the surface, but can push up the crust to form ridges on the Earth's crust.

Figure 14 Divergent plate margin

Convergent plate margins

At a convergent plate margin, two plates are moving towards each other.

- When an oceanic and a continental plate meet, the denser oceanic plate is subducted underneath the lighter continental plate. This creates deep ocean trenches and fold mountains.

- The sudden release of built-up pressure causes strong earthquakes.

- As the plate is being subducted, it allows magma to rise, resulting in very explosive volcanic eruptions.

- The magma is thick and forms steep-sided composite volcanoes.

When two continental plates meet, the crust is folded and uplifted to create fold mountains. This movement creates earthquakes but no volcanic eruptions.

Figure 15 Convergent plate margin where an oceanic and a continental plate meet

Conservative plate margins

At a conservative plate margin, two plates are moving past each other. Pressure builds up over many years. When the plate slips, strong, destructive earthquakes occur.

Figure 16 Conservative plate margin

SNAPIT!

Snap images of Figures 14, 15 and 16. Use them to learn about what happens at plate margins.

DOIT!

Create a table summarising the differences between the three types of plate margin. Include:

- direction of plate movement
- tectonic activity (earthquake and/or volcanoes)
- type of plate (continental or oceanic)
- an example.

Hotspots

- Hotspots are volcanoes that occur away from plate boundaries.
- They are created by a plume of magma rising through the mantle.
- When the magma reaches the upper mantle, it causes the asthenosphere and base of the lithosphere to melt.
- Magma rises through weaknesses in the crust (for example, the Hawaiian hotspot).

NAILIT!

Plate margins and tectonic activity

Make sure you can describe and explain the relationship between plate margins and tectonic activity, such as why earthquakes and volcanoes occur at convergent plate margins.

Types of volcano

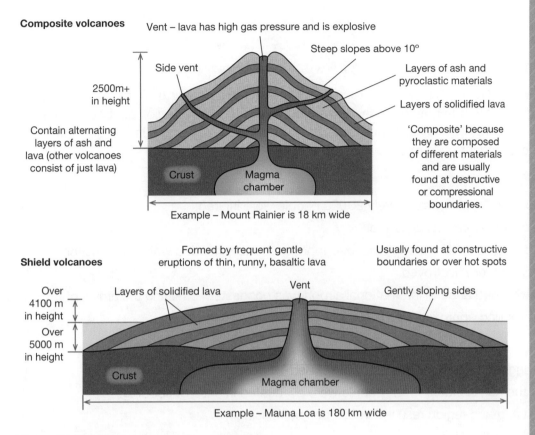

Composite volcanoes

Vent – lava has high gas pressure and is explosive

Side vent

Steep slopes above 10°

Layers of ash and pyroclastic materials

Layers of solidified lava

2500m+ in height

'Composite' because they are composed of different materials and are usually found at destructive or compressional boundaries.

Contain alternating layers of ash and lava (other volcanoes consist of just lava)

Crust

Magma chamber

Example – Mount Rainier is 18 km wide

Shield volcanoes

Formed by frequent gentle eruptions of thin, runny, basaltic lava

Usually found at constructive boundaries or over hot spots

Over 4100 m in height

Layers of solidified lava

Vent

Gently sloping sides

Over 5000 m in height

Crust

Magma chamber

Example – Mauna Loa is 180 km wide

Figure 17 Shield and composite volcanoes

DO IT!

Create a table comparing composite and shield volcanoes. Include where they are formed, how they are formed and their characteristics.

Tsunami

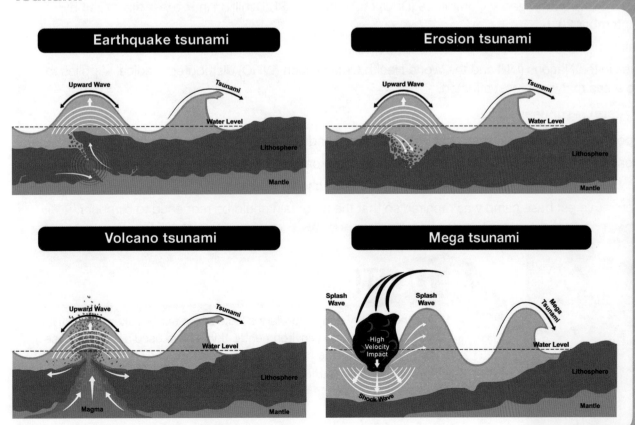

Earthquake tsunami

Upward Wave

Tsunami

Water Level

Lithosphere

Mantle

Erosion tsunami

Upward Wave

Tsunami

Water Level

Lithosphere

Mantle

Volcano tsunami

Upward Wave

Tsunami

Water Level

Lithosphere

Magma

Mantle

Mega tsunami

Splash Wave

Splash Wave

Mega Tsunami

High Velocity Impact

Water Level

Lithosphere

Shock Wave

Mantle

Figure 18 Formation of different types of tsunami

The effects of and responses to tectonic hazards

Example

An earthquake in a developing country: Nepal earthquakes, 2015

An earthquake happened in Nepal on 25 April 2015, measuring a magnitude of 7.8. The epicentre was 80 km north-west of the capital, Kathmandu. A second earthquake in the same region occurred some days later on 12 May. The earthquakes happened because the Indo-Australian plate is colliding with the Eurasian plate – a convergent plate margin.

Primary effects

- Nine thousand people died and approximately 20 000 people were injured.
- Nearly three million people were left homeless.
- Following the earthquake, 1.4 million people needed food; even more needed water and shelter.
- Seven thousand schools were destroyed.
- Hospitals were overwhelmed and the international airport was congested, affecting the arrival of aid.
- The cost of damage totalled approximately US$5 billion.

Secondary effects

- An avalanche was triggered on Mount Everest, which killed 19 people.
- A landslide blocked the Kali Gandaki River; people were evacuated in case of flooding.
- An avalanche in the Langtang region resulted in 250 people missing.

Immediate responses

- The UK, India and China provided rescue teams, water and medical support.
- The Disasters Emergency Committee (DEC) had raised US$126 million in international aid by September 2015.
- Half a million temporary shelters were set up.
- The United Nations (UN) and the World Health Organisation (WHO) distributed medical supplies to the areas that were most affected.

Long-term responses

- A post-disaster needs assessment was carried out and buildings were built to stricter codes.
- Areas where there were landslides were cleared and roads were repaired.
- People left homeless had to be rehoused and 7000 schools were rebuilt.
- Mount Everest base camp was repaired so that the mountain could be reopened to climbers.

DOIT!

1 Sort the primary and secondary effects of the earthquakes in Nepal into social, economic and environmental. If you have used a different case study, use that as the basis for your answer instead.

2 Rank the effects, starting with the one you think is the worst.

Example

An earthquake in a developed country: L'Aquila, Italy, 2009

An earthquake happened in central Italy on 6 April 2009, measuring a magnitude of 6.3. The epicentre was 7 km north-west of L'Aquila.

Primary effects

- More than 300 people died and 1500 people were injured.
- 67 500 people were left homeless.
- 10 000–15 000 buildings collapsed, including many churches and medieval buildings.
- The hospital was severely damaged.
- The cost of damage totalled approximately US$16 billion.

Secondary effects

- Landslides and rock falls caused damage to transport.
- The number of students at the University of L'Aquila has declined.
- People were stopped from entering some areas of the city due to unsafe buildings.

Immediate responses

- Hotels and tents were provided for those who were homeless.
- The Italian Red Cross searched for survivors – they also gave out water, tents, blankets and hot meals.
- The British Red Cross raised £171 000.
- Mortgages and bills for those affected were suspended.
- The EU granted US$552.9 million from its fund for major disasters to help L'Aquila straight away.
- The DEC did not provide aid, as Italy is a developed country.

Long-term responses

- A remembrance day procession is held on the anniversary of the earthquake.
- Residents paid no taxes during 2010.
- Students were exempt from university fees for three years.

STRETCH IT!

Research shows that countries that are wealthier often suffer fewer impacts than developing countries. What evidence is there that the wealth of a country influences the extent to which it is affected by an earthquake?

DO IT!

1 Sort the primary and secondary effects of the earthquake in Italy into social, economic and environmental.

2 a Rank the primary effects, starting with the one you think is the worst.

   b Rank the secondary effects, starting with the one you think is the worst.

NAIL IT!

Earthquakes can have very different effects depending on what type of country they happen in. Remember why you often have worse impacts in a developing country.

Draw a revision poster showing the costs and benefits of living in an area that is prone to hazards.

Reducing the risk from tectonic hazards

There are four main strategies used to help manage the risk of tectonic hazards.

1. **Monitoring**: scientists use equipment to help detect the warning signs of a volcanic eruption or tsunami wave.

2. **Prediction**: scientists look at historical evidence and use monitoring equipment to help them make predictions about when and where a tectonic hazard may happen.

3. **Protection**: buildings are designed to withstand a tectonic hazard. This is more easily done for earthquakes than for volcanic eruptions.

4. **Planning**: authorities identify areas most at risk from a hazard.

Monitoring

- **Volcanoes**: scientists monitor volcanoes in a number of ways. They use remote sensors to detect changes in the volcano's heat and shape, seismometers to record any earthquake activity, tiltmeters to measure changes in the shape of the volcano as magma rises to the surface and instruments to measure the gases being released.

- **Earthquakes**: these usually occur without any warning.

Prediction

- **Volcanoes**: prediction is based on monitoring the volcano. For example, before an eruption there is sometimes an increase in earthquake activity.

- **Earthquakes**: it is impossible to make accurate predictions, but scientists do use historical evidence to predict where an earthquake may be overdue.

Protection

- **Volcanoes**: it is harder to protect against violent volcanic explosions. Often, people will have to evacuate if a volcanic eruption occurs.

- **Earthquakes**: it is possible to create buildings that will withstand some earthquakes. In many countries there are regular earthquake drills so that citizens know what to do.

Planning

- **Volcanoes:** hazard maps are created for volcanoes to show the areas likely to be affected. This helps people to know which areas should be evacuated in the event of a volcanic eruption.

- **Earthquakes:** maps can be produced to show critical buildings, such as hospitals, in areas that are at high risk, so these areas can be protected.

Rolling weight

Strong framework

Reinforced walls

Shock absorbers
Reinforced foundations

Figure 19 An earthquake-proof building

DO IT!

1 Plan an answer to explain which method of risk management is the most effective.

2 How would hazard management be different between developing and developed countries?

SNAP IT!

Snap an image of Figure 19. Use this to help you remember how to make a building earthquake-proof.

CHECK IT!

1 Describe the pattern of earthquakes.

2 Describe two differences between the oceanic and the continental crust.

3 Explain why earthquakes and volcanoes happen at plate margins.

4 Name the three different plate margins.

5 Explain why you do not get volcanoes when two continental plates meet.

6 Explain the processes happening at a convergent plate margin.

7 Give a definition of primary and secondary effects.

8 Describe the effects of the L'Aquila earthquake.

9 'Earthquakes cause more damage in a developing country.' To what extent is this statement true?

10 Describe the benefits of living near a volcano.

11 Explain how buildings can be made earthquake-proof.

REVIEW IT! Hazardous Earth

1 What is global atmospheric circulation?

2 Give two natural causes of climate change.

3 Give two ways to reduce the effects of tropical cyclones.

4 Describe the distribution of earthquakes and volcanoes.

5 Describe how a developing country can prepare for a tropical cyclone.

6 Describe the formation of a tropical cyclone.

7 Describe why some countries are more vulnerable to tropical cyclones than others.

8 Explain why volcanoes are formed at convergent plate margins.

9 Explain how solar activity can affect global climate change.

10 Explain how humans contribute to an increase in carbon dioxide in the atmosphere.

11 Using a named example, explain the effects of an earthquake.

12 Explain why there is uncertainty about future climates.

13 'A developing country is likely to be more affected by a tectonic hazard than a developed country'. To what extent do you agree with this statement?

2 Development dynamics

2.1 Development and inequalities

OUTCOMES

By the end of my revision I will be able to:

- Describe and use ways of defining and measuring development.

- State the limitations of economic, social and political measures of development.

- Explain global inequalities in development and the theories associated with development.

- Describe and explain rapid economic growth and its consequences in a named developing country.

THE EXAMINATION!

- This section is tested in Paper 1 Section B.

- You must know all parts of this topic.

Ways of defining and measuring development

Economic development is the making of money through jobs and businesses, so is classified by amounts of money. It is commonly measured by **gross domestic product (GDP)** per person and by **gross national income (GNI)**.

You might expect that, the wealthier the people and the more successful the businesses, the more a country would develop and the higher the quality of life would be there. **Quality of life** can be judged by social factors such as education, health care, happiness, freedom and gender equality, as well as how much money people have to spend. However, economic development does not always lead to a better quality of life for everyone in a country straight away, which leads to inequalities.

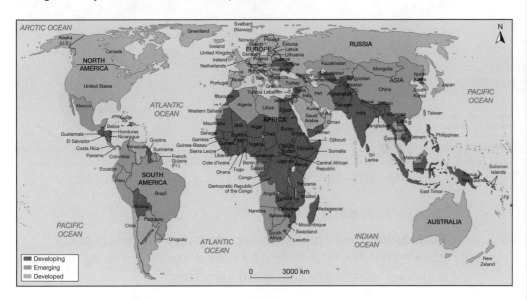

Figure 1 Economic classification of countries as developing, emerging and developed

DO IT!

Copy and annotate Figure 1 to summarise the characteristics of the three development categories of country:

- **developing**

- **emerging**

- **developed**.

Measures of development

Economic measures

- **Gross national income (GNI)** per person (per capita): takes all of the money made within a country and from investments overseas, minus any debts, and divides it by the total population to find an average of how much each person makes in a year.

- **Gross domestic product (GDP)** per person: takes all the money made within a country and divides it by the total population to find an average of how much each person makes in a year.

Social measures

- **Adult literacy rate** shows percentage of adults in a population who can read and write. This reflects the level of education.

- **Infant mortality**: measures the number of deaths of babies under one year of age per 1000 live births (see Table 1). This reflects living conditions and the level of specialist health care available.

- **Life expectancy**: measures how many years a new-born child can be expected to live for. This reflects access to health care and living conditions in the country.

Economic and social measures

- **Human Development Index (HDI)**: measures economic and social factors to give an overall measure of development (Figure 2). It includes life expectancy, literacy levels and GDP.

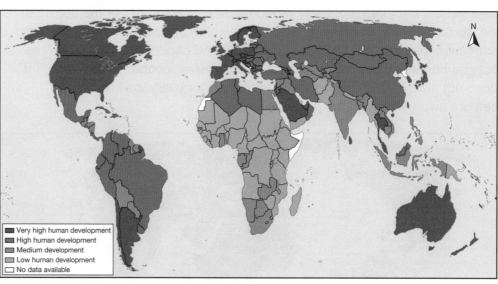

Very high human development
High human development
Medium development
Low human development
No data available

Figure 2 HDI scores for 2015–16

Political measures

Corruption Perceptions Index: measures the quality of the government of a country and fairness of decision making, grading countries from 'highly corrupt' to 'very clean'.

NAILIT!

There are several ways of looking at 'development', but perhaps the most important is people's quality of life. This includes having access to the basics needed to stay alive: clean water, enough food and a balanced diet, and shelter from the weather and for safety. In the modern world, you might add having a job to make money and services to help you stay healthy, such as sanitation, health care and education so that you can improve your life. Very few people in developing countries are likely to think about fashion clothing and the latest electronic gadgets!

NAILIT!

Make sure that you can define each measure of development. Most people think the HDI is the best composite measure available as it covers social and economic factors.

Limitations of development measures

Each measure of development has strengths and weaknesses:

- **Economic**: GNI per person is a strong measure of wealth within a country and of the country's role in international business (see Table 1). However, using an average hides the difference between the very rich and the very poor. GNI does not consider the fact that the 'cost of living' varies between countries, or that currency values change.

- **Social**: in developing or emerging countries, data collection by governments is difficult (due to lack of money, the remoteness of many rural areas and the overcrowding of some urban areas) so the accuracy of data varies.

- **Economic and social**: HDI has been used by the United Nations (UN), a trusted organisation, since 1990, so is a reliable way of measuring a combination of social and economic development. However, it does not consider measures of the natural environment that are also important to long-term sustainable development. It also leaves out measures of human rights (e.g. gender equality).

- **Corruption**: This is difficult to obtain data for because governments deny that there is corruption, and don't record it. The index may not be entirely accurate, but it is useful because decisions or deals that are corrupt lower quality of life and create instability within a country.

> **DO IT!**
>
> Plan an answer to a question that asks you to suggest the most reliable way of measuring development.

Country		GNI (US$'000s per capita)	Infant mortality rate (per 1000 live births)
Developed	Chile	21.74	7
	Japan	38.87	2
	Saudi Arabia	54.73	13
	UK	40.55	4
	USA	56.43	6
Emerging	Brazil	15.02	15
	China	14.16	9
	India	6.02	38
	Mexico	17.15	11
	South Africa	12.83	34
Developing	Afghanistan	1.99	66
	Chad	2.11	85
	Ethiopia	1.62	41
	Haiti	1.76	52
	Nepal	2.50	29

Source: World Bank

Table 1 GNI and infant mortality data for selected countries in 2015

STRETCH IT!

The Gini index looks at how wealth is distributed among a population. It is used to compare this distribution between countries.

Purchasing power parity (PPP) can be calculated to compare how much US$1 would buy in different countries to consider 'cost of living' differences. (The BigMac index works in a similar way.)

Graphical skills

Comparing GNI to infant mortality (scattergraph and line of best fit)

Using the data in Table 1, complete the following steps.

1. Draw two axes on graph paper: one for GNI (from 0 to 60) and one for infant mortality (from 0 to 90).

2. Plot the position of each country with a cross on the graph to create a scatter of points.

3. Draw a line of best fit. Judge where the middle is between the points as you move from left to right across the graph, so that there is an equal number of points either side of your line when you have drawn it.

4. What pattern or trend do you notice from your completed graph?

5. Compare the rank positions of countries produced by single indicators of development, such as GNI or IMR (Table 1), with the positions produced by a composite indicator, such as HDI (Figure 2).

SNAPIT!

Snap an image of Figure 3. There are quite a few linked ideas here.

Study the image a few times during your revision and test yourself on what happens in each stage of the **demographic transition model (DTM)**.

Population characteristics and levels of development

As a country develops economically and people and governments have more money, the culture of the country begins to change. For example, in the past, as countries developed they became more

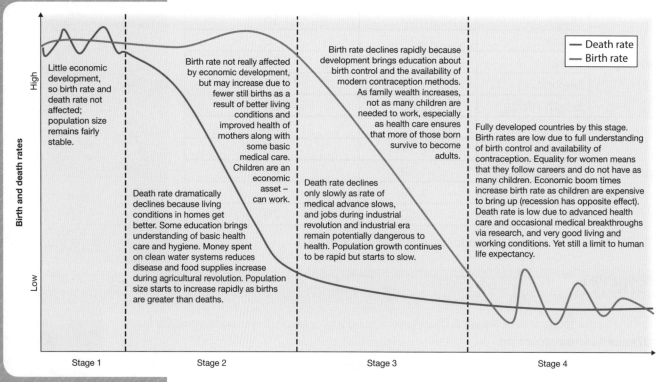

Figure 3 Links between level of development and demographic transition

democratic – people had greater freedom, such as free elections and freedom of speech. They also had more to spend on education, health care and welfare systems, which changed birth and death rates (Figure 3).

Countries that are overpopulated have difficulty providing resources, services and jobs for everyone, so their development is slower (for example, in Chad). However, underpopulation can also be a problem, as there are not enough people to do the work that needs doing (for example, in Japan with its ageing population). These features are part of the population structure of a country as shown by population pyramids (Figure 4).

DO IT!

Describe and explain the shape of each population pyramid shown in Figure 4.

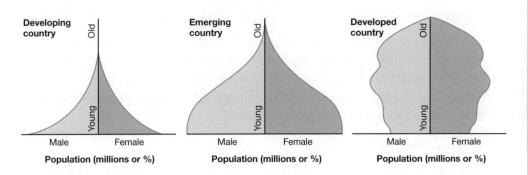

Figure 4 Population pyramids at different stages of development

Causes of inequality

Inequalities can be found on a world scale and also within countries. There is some disagreement about the strength of the causes of uneven development, and there may be a difficult transition time within the development process.

Environmental geography

1. Climate has had a long-term influence on the development of countries. Low temperatures (temperate climate) allow a wider variety of crops to grow and livestock farming to take place, so there is a plentiful and reliable food supply; there are fewer fatal diseases and working is much easier as it does not get too hot for the human body. In contrast, extremely hot or cold places are more difficult areas to develop.

2. Natural resources are found in certain places (for example, fertile soils and coal in temperate areas; oil in hot areas such as the Middle East and cold areas such as the Arctic). Areas with more natural resources have developed faster than those without.

3. Location provides access to other areas for trade around the world. The sea has long been the best way of transporting heavy and bulky goods, so countries or regions with access to the sea have developed faster than those without.

4. Natural hazards may slow rates of development. It is not yet known how climate change may increase the frequency of weather-related hazards such as floods, droughts and tropical storms.

Economic geography

NAILIT!

Quintiles

A quintile is a fifth (20%) of something. When applied to the sharing of wealth within a country it helps to show inequalities. If wealth is shared equally in a country each quintile of population will have a fifth of the wealth. But often the top quintile has a much larger share, and the bottom quintile a smaller share. For example, in 2016 the USA's top quintile had 47 per cent of the wealth and the bottom quintile only 5 per cent.

① **Trading** helps countries develop: they can get the resources they need and sell the products they make. However, not all countries have resources or the ability to make products, so they stay poorer than those that can trade. Not all trade is 'fair': developed countries often gain and developing countries lose in trade agreements.

② **Foreign direct investment (FDI)** helps countries because businesses from other countries spend money building factories and bringing machinery and new ideas.

③ **Spending on education and health** improves the skills and abilities of workers, helping businesses to be more efficient and make more money.

④ **Government policies** based on a 'free market' (where businesses compete and the best survive) have tended to bring more sustained development than in countries with heavily supported old inefficient industries. Corruption in some developing and emerging countries has stopped benefits reaching poor people.

Historical geography

① **Colonial expansion** (18th century to 1945) led to many poor parts of the world being politically controlled and economically dominated by rich European countries. Some say that the rich countries became richer and the poor countries became poorer because of an unequal relationship in terms of trade and exploitation of resources. There was a lack of investment in colonies and after independence these countries had trouble developing. This was often made worse by internal conflicts because borders did not match ethnic areas.

② **Aid** was given by government organisations and **non-governmental organisations (NGOs)** or charities to many poorer countries from 1945 to help them develop. This included foreign direct investment, medical and education help, farming and clean water aid, trading agreements and loans for expensive schemes. Some believe that this made the poorer countries dependent on help, instead of allowing them to develop themselves.

Consequences of inequality

Inequality may mean that some people have what they need for life and others do not. Some aspects of development may happen faster than others, such as economic development happening before social development.

Inequalities in wealth

- Development has not spread wealth evenly. About 13 per cent of the world's population live on less than US$1.90 a day, but in sub-Saharan Africa the figure is about 43 per cent. In 2012, India (emerging) had 22 per cent of its population on less than US$1.90 a day and South Africa (emerging) had 17 per cent. Even China (emerging) had 11 per cent.

- Many people in developing and emerging countries are stuck in a cycle of poverty (see Figure 5).

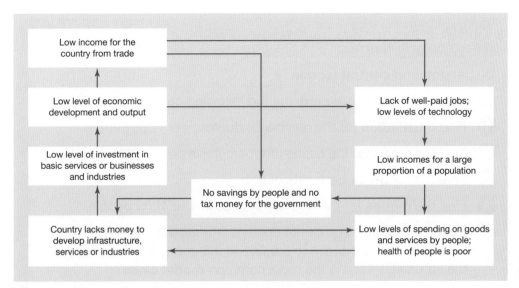

Figure 5 A cycle of poverty

Inequalities in health

- In 2015, about 9 per cent of the world's population had no access to safe, clean water and about 32 per cent did not have basic sanitation. These people are more likely to get life-threatening diseases. In 2015 in developing countries, 66 per cent of people had access to improved water but only 28 per cent had improved sanitation. Developed countries do not face these problems. Many developing or emerging countries can neither provide health care in remoter areas nor afford modern medicines. The results of this are reflected in high infant mortality rates (Table 1, page 33) and other health data (Table 2).

Country		Doctors (per 1000 people)	Incidence of tuberculosis (per 100 000 people)
Developed	Chile	1.0	16
	Japan	2.3	18
	Saudi Arabia	2.5	12
	UK	2.8	12
	USA	2.5	3
Emerging	Brazil	1.9	44
	China	1.9	68
	India	0.7	167
	Mexico	2.1	21
	South Africa	0.8	834
Developing	Afghanistan	0.3	189
	Chad	na*	159
	Ethiopia	0.0	207
	Haiti	na*	200
	Nepal	na*	158

*data not available (likely to be very low)

Table 2 Health data for selected countries, 2014

Ten causes of global inequalities in the world are listed here. Discuss these with a friend then rank them, starting with the cause you think was the most important in creating today's worldwide gap between rich and poor countries.

Keep your notes to use in your revision.

Statistical skills

Dispersion and central tendency

Use the data in Table 2 to carry out the following calculations.

1. Find the **median** for the number of doctors per 1000 people.

2. Find the **mean** for the cases of tuberculosis per 100 000 people.

3. Give the **range** for both sets of data.

4. Find the **modes** for the number of doctors per 1000 people.

5. Place the data for number of doctors into **modal classes** 0 to 0.5, 0.6 to 1.0, 1.1 to 1.5, 1.6 to 2.0, 2.1 to 2.5 and 2.6 to 3.0 (ignoring the na data). Which is the most common **modal class**?

6. Plot the data for cases of tuberculosis on a single-axis scattergraph. Use this to calculate the upper and lower **quartiles** and **inter-quartile range**.

7. Use the data and all the calculations to make conclusions about the quality of life in the three different types of country.

STRETCH IT!

The World Bank uses the categories 'high income' and 'low income' for countries in its World Development Indicators database, and divides the emerging economies into 'lower middle income' and 'upper middle income'. Countries are not fixed in these categories and may move between them. For example, India is placed in the lower middle income category, but has an income per person about half that of the other emerging countries, and more than 20 per cent of the population live on less than US$1.90 a day.

Environmental inequality

- Overuse of natural resources, such as soils by farming or metal ores by mining, has led to degradation of environments in developing and emerging countries. Many developed countries are now repairing this damage.

- Economic activities in developing or emerging countries have fewer enforced controls, which can lead to pollution. Controls in developed countries are much stricter.

- Developing and emerging countries are less able to cope with natural disasters, especially those that are a result of climate change.

International migration

- Globalisation processes such as fast transport and instant communication, as well as the spread of 'Western' culture, have increased awareness of the possibility of a better quality of life. This has made many people in poorer countries want a new and better life, which has encouraged both skilled and unskilled people to move (see Figure 6).

- Many people around the world are wealthier than in previous generations, and transport methods are more easily available, so the pull to richer countries and the push from poor countries has increased migration. Refugee numbers in particular have grown, as have illegal migrations in places.

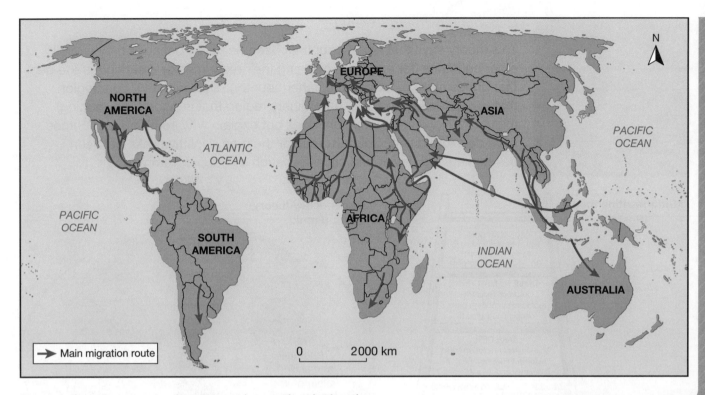

Figure 6 Flow line map to show recent international migration

STRETCH IT!

Developing and emerging countries can benefit or lose because of emigration to developed countries. If the most educated and skilled people leave (brain drain) for higher-paid jobs in developed countries, the poorer countries lose the very people who could help them most to develop the country. However, all types of migrants earn more money in the developed countries and usually send money (remittances) back to their families, helping to break the cycle of poverty and stimulating development by increasing local spending.

Development theories

There are several theories to help explain how global development has taken place. Two of these were devised in the 1960s when a lot of economic change was taking place in the world.

Modernisation theory (Rostow)

This theory says that all countries will go through the same stages of economic development, but at different times. Developing countries will be at the 'pre-conditions for take-off' stage; emerging countries will be at the 'take-off' stage; and developed countries will be at the stage of 'high mass consumption' (Figure 7). However, this theory does not fully explain how a country moves from one stage to the next, or why some countries are still extremely poor in the 21st century.

DO IT!

Draw a diagram to show how the push factors in a poor country and the pull factors in a rich country combine to produce international migration.

Dependency theory (Frank)

This theory says that some countries become richer because they exploit other countries (for example, by using their resources or creating a trade deal that brings more money to the richer country). This creates a core region that is rich (developed) and a periphery region that is poorer (developing) (Figure 7). However, this theory does not explain why some poor countries have developed (e.g. South Korea), or the many positive links between developing and developed countries such as aid programmes.

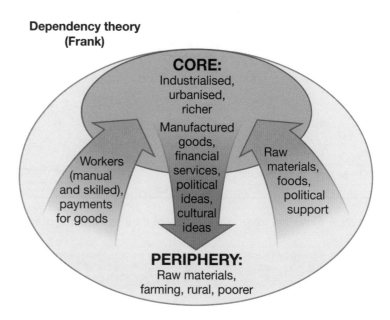

Figure 7 Modernisation and dependency theories

CHECKIT!

1 Give a definition of the term 'inequality'.

2 Explain one economic, one social and one political measure of development.

3 Using any measures of development, state two differences between developing and emerging countries.

4 a Give the characteristics of the birth rate and death rate in a developing country.

   b Explain the state of economic development of a developing country.

5 Compare the development problems created by overpopulation and underpopulation.

6 Describe two physical geography and two human geography causes of global inequality.

7 Describe a cycle of poverty.

8 Give two reasons why people in developing or emerging countries often face health problems.

9 Suggest whether push or pull factors are more important in encouraging international migration.

10 a Name the theory that suggests that all countries will go through stages of development.

   b Outline one weakness of the dependency theory.

2.2 Development strategies

OUTCOMES

By the end of my revision I will be able to:

- Describe different approaches to development.
- Explain which factors help development.
- Explain the advantages and disadvantages of different development strategies.

Characteristics of development strategies

Strategies are often in the form of projects or schemes. These can be large, expensive and government-led (top-down) involving foreign experts, or small, relatively cheap and community-led (bottom-up) involving non-governmental organisations (NGOs). All aim to promote development through a multiplier effect (see Figure 8).

Figure 8 A multiplier effect cycle

Investment

This strategy involves putting money into a project. The money could be:

- a loan from the World Bank to build infrastructure that would help to increase exports, such as better port facilities
- from foreign direct investment (FDI), where transnational corporations (TNCs) build factories and develop links with local businesses
- from international migrants working abroad who send remittances back to their families.

NAILIT!

'Infrastructure' refers to all of the things that need to be in place before a business or industry can operate. The site of a business or factory will need energy and water supplies, a waste disposal and sewerage system and roads. Away from the site, long-distance roads or railways and ports and airports may be needed.

DOIT!

Think about how each development strategy would help development take place. For example, explain how giving aid to a developing country would help it to develop. Write down your ideas.

Industrial development and tourism

This strategy involves a developing or emerging country finding something it has that is unique, which people in other countries would want to buy. Advantages may be climate, physical resources or natural landscape.

- This could lead to the development of industries based on the resource or the development of tourism based on a sunny climate, scenery, tropical beaches or wildlife.

- However, tourist trends change and resources may be used up, creating uncertainties on the path of development.

Aid

This strategy involves a developing or emerging country getting help from other countries, either directly from governments or from NGOs (international aid).

- The UN has set a target of developed countries donating 0.7 per cent of their annual wealth to help developing or emerging countries. Few countries reach this target. The aid is usually tied to specific major projects or schemes (top-down approach) with long-term benefits, but some criticise this for not helping the poorest people enough. There may also be corruption in the developing or emerging country, which stops a lot of the money being spent on the project or scheme.

- NGOs such as Oxfam, WaterAid or Practical Action collect donations from people in developed countries and use the money in smaller projects and schemes directly linked to poorer people, such as health projects (bottom-up approach). Some see this as a more sustainable approach, but a criticism is that it does not help many people.

Intermediate technology

- The most advanced technologies (high-tech) are often expensive, so are not suitable for developing or emerging countries. Many think that improvements to the technology found in poorer countries should be through intermediate technology. This is more appropriate because it is affordable, does not use expensive energy sources, and is easy to understand, maintain and repair.

- Intermediate technology can be applied to villages and communities or to industry and businesses to make small but significant improvements. Examples include sustainable energy sources and water pumps, such as the Afridev hand pump or the Playpump roundabout.

Fair trade

- In a normal trading situation, a developed country usually gains and a developing or emerging country loses. For example, often a developing country will sell raw materials (metal ores, crops), of relatively low value, to a developed country, but will buy back relatively expensive machinery and energy. The poorer country actually loses money. Many see this as unfair.

- Fair trade is about obtaining better prices, better working conditions and fair terms for trade for farmers and workers in developing or emerging countries. It supports farmers and workers in gaining more from trade. Through this they can take more control of their lives.

STRETCH IT!

The involvement of Trans-National Corporations in development is controversial. They bring benefits to a developing or emerging country, such as providing paid jobs, introducing new technologies and training, and increasing wealth in communities through linked jobs and services. However, they also bring issues such as their political power over poor governments, exploiting the workforce by paying low wages and avoiding tax. While many TNCs are from developed countries in Europe, Japan and USA, an increasing number are from emerging countries, such as India and China.

- Small-scale producers often form a cooperative to share costs and coordinate selling. The more money they receive helps all members to invest in their farms and businesses and improve the quality of life for their families.
- The UK is the largest buyer of fair trade products (Figure 9).

STRETCH IT!

- The Fairtrade Foundation is an independent, non-profit organisation that licenses use of the FAIRTRADE Mark on products in the UK. For products with the FAIRTRADE Mark, the ingredients in the product have been produced by small-scale farmer organisations or plantations that meet Fairtrade Foundation social, economic and environmental standards. These include protection of workers' rights and the environment, payment of the Fairtrade Minimum Price and an additional Fairtrade Premium to invest in business of community projects.
- More than 1.65 million farmers and workers in 74 countries benefit from Fairtrade certification for their products.

Figure 9
FAIRTRADE Mark

Debt relief

- Many developing or emerging countries borrowed money from the World Bank and others from the 1960s on, to help them build projects to help them develop. However, the economic recession of the 1980s slowed development to a point where they could not keep up repayments and interest payments. By the 1990s they had very large debts, many of which continued into the 21st century.
- Debt-for-nature swaps have been used to reduce the debt of developing or emerging countries. Here the poorer country agrees to protect part of its natural environment in return for some of the debt being 'wiped out'. One example is a US$21 million swap between the USA and Brazil to protect an area of rainforest.
- The World Bank and the International Monetary Fund (IMF) introduced the Heavily Indebted Poor Countries Initiative (HIPC) in 1996. This defers repayments until a later date when the poor countries have developed and can afford to repay.

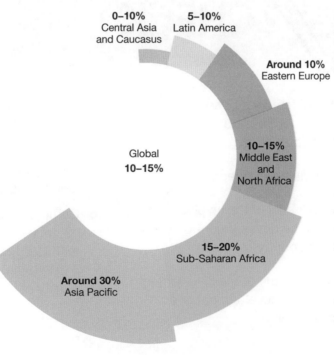

Figure 10 Development and growth trends across the world's microfinance markets in 2016

DO IT!

Next time you visit a supermarket, look out for Fairtrade products for sale with the FAIRTRADE Mark (see Figure 9) and study their labels. Make a note of each product and the country it came from.

DO IT!

Create a podcast to bring the problems of loaning money to countries to the attention of the World Bank and IMF.

Microfinance loans

- **Microfinance loans** are small amounts of money lent to poor people by local banks or non-profit organisations to help break the cycle of poverty (Figure 10). The money must still be repaid with interest, but dependency on aid is avoided.

- Microfinance loans could be used for home improvements, business improvements or education. Loans could be taken out by a group of people or individuals. However, the interest payments could still be too high for poor people and some require a guarantor (someone to pay in case the person receiving the loan cannot), which is not easy to find in communities where everyone is poor.

- The growth of mobile phone use even in sub-Saharan Africa (through the donation of second-hand ones from developed countries) now means that small businesses, including farmers and fishermen, can get micro-insurance and microfinance loans to improve their business.

DO IT!

All development strategies have advantages and disadvantages. Create a revision card with sentences for each development strategy:

- the main characteristic of the strategy

- the main advantage that helps a country develop

- the main disadvantage that causes development problems.

STRETCH IT!

Many developing and emerging countries face obstacles to development but don't publicise them, as they may reduce tourist numbers. For example, natural hazards such as tropical cyclones (hurricanes) cause considerable damage with storm surges, heavy rain and strong winds – as in the Caribbean in the autumn of 2017. Crime rates may also be high, which reduces a country's ability to carry out its usual economic activities.

CHECK IT!

1 What are the differences between a top-down and a bottom-up development approach?

2 Describe the multiplier effect.

3 a Give two benefits of the involvement of a TNC in the development of a developing country.

   b Give two problems of the involvement of a TNC in the development of a developing country.

4 a Explain how giving aid to a country can help it to develop.

   b Compare the suitability of fair trade and debt relief for helping a developing country to develop.

   c Compare the suitability of microfinance loans and intermediate technology for helping poor people in a developing country to improve their quality of life.

2.3 Rapid economic development and change in an emerging country

OUTCOMES

By the end of my revision I will be able to:

- Give the meanings of economic change, social change, environmental change and cultural change.
- Explain why rapid economic development can take place.
- Give information about an emerging country to show the economic, social, cultural and environmental changes taking place.
- Explain the causes and effects of the changes in the emerging country.

Case study

Change in an economically emerging country: India

Location and world context

Site, situation and characteristics

India is in South Asia (Figure 11). It has a coastline on the Indian Ocean and borders with six countries, including Pakistan to the west, Bangladesh to the east and Nepal to the north. India extends from 10°N to 30°N of the equator, with the Tropic of Cancer passing through the country. It is made up of 29 states and seven territories under a parliamentary democracy with a president and state governors.

India is the seventh largest country in the world, stretching mostly north to south from the Himalayan Mountains to the River Ganges floodplain to the Deccan Plateau, with the Thar Desert in the west and some jungles in the east. It has a range of climatic conditions, including desert, tropical in the south and mountainous in the far north. It experiences a monsoon climate with distinct wet and dry seasons, which is important to farming but can also bring serious flooding in the wet season or drought in the dry season.

India is considered an emerging economy and one of the economic leaders in Asia. According to the International Monetary Fund (IMF), India was ranked seventh in the world in terms of its GDP in 2016. It is predicted to increase its GDP by 350 per cent by 2030 and rise to third position, behind China and the USA. Many Indians have migrated to other countries but retain strong links with India; according to the World Bank, it is the top nation for receiving remittances (US$62.7 billion in 2016). In 2016 India had a population of over 1.3 billion; it will soon have the largest population in the world, overtaking China, due to a very high birth rate. Most people live on the northern plains, which is also the location of some of the poorest states.

With such a large population, it is not surprising that there are socio-cultural contrasts. Hindi and English are the two official languages but there are over 1500 different local languages or dialects. There are several religions besides Hinduism, such as Islam, Buddhism and Sikhism. A controversial legacy is the 'caste system' where social position in Indian society is determined by which caste a person is born into, mainly based on employment. At the top are priests and teachers (Brahmins), much lower are labourers (Shudras), then lower still are cleaners (Dalits). The caste system persists despite the Indian constitution stating that everyone is equal. Only 12 per cent of Indian MPs are female.

India's infant mortality rate is nearly 10 times higher than that of the UK; the adult literacy rate is only 69 per cent and the GNI per capita is only 15 per cent of that of the UK. It is estimated that 20 per cent of India's population lives in poverty (earning less than US$1.90 a day). Things are improving: the infant mortality rate and poverty have more than halved since 1990.

World links

India was a UK colony, becoming independent in 1947. Independent India was split into two countries based on religion; India is primarily Hindu (80 per cent) with Pakistan (west and east) being Muslim. Like several former colony countries, it suffered from civil conflict between different factions, and there was mass migration between India and Pakistan on a religious basis. There have been four 'wars' between India and Pakistan over the disputed territory of Kashmir, and tensions still exist. In 1971, the eastern part of Pakistan became the new country of Bangladesh.

Politically, India is a member of the United Nations, a key member of the Commonwealth (the UK and its former colonies) and a member of the South Asian Association for Regional Cooperation (SAARC). India has a key position between East Asia and Europe and the Middle East, and should benefit from increased trade between these world regions.

Culturally, Indian cinema (Bollywood) and sport (notably cricket) are all well known globally.

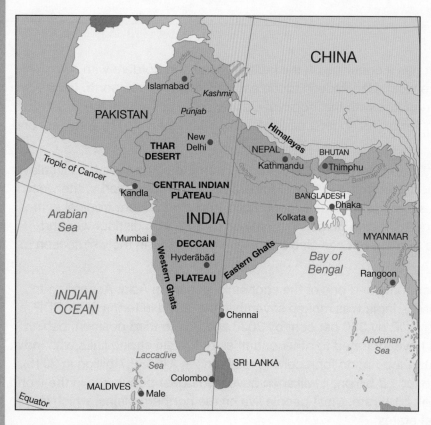

Figure 11 The location of India

Economic change and globalisation

Industrial structure and trade

Traditionally, India traded in agricultural products, which were the most important sector of the economy after independence until the mid-1970s. More than half the population still work in agriculture, and farm products are still an important export. However, there has been a steady decline in the importance of agriculture in the economy since industrialisation increased the contribution of manufacturing (especially between 1980 and 2008) and services (especially since 2000) (Figure 12). Now India has technology and manufacturing sectors as advanced as any in the world. There is a small, but important, tourist industry, with famous sites such as the Taj Mahal. Since 1990 the Indian government has had a policy of promoting exports and has offered subsidies to companies selling goods and services abroad. It encourages foreign trade (Table 3) to create a positive trade balance, and in 2015 set a target of doubling export value by 2020. Seventy per cent of India's trade (by value) passes through its sea ports (e.g. Kandla at Kutch, Gujarat). In 2015/16 India exported US$262 billion in goods and services. However, this was a decrease of 15.6 per cent on the previous year due to the recession slowing down the global economy. India's share of world exports has stabilised at around 1.3 per cent for goods and 3.3 per cent for services. The main export destinations are the USA, UAE, China, UK and Singapore. In 2015/16 India had a trade deficit of US$118 billion, so it has a long way to go to meet its target. In 2017 India ranked 143rd on the Economic Freedom Index, placing it in the 'mostly unfree' category, due to poorer financial health, too much government control of investment and finances, undeveloped infrastructure, corruption and weak enforcement of regulations.

Import goods	% of total value	Export goods	% of total value
Mineral fuels, oils, distilled products	25	Pearls, precious stones, metals, coins	16
Pearls, precious stones, metals, coins	13	Mineral fuels, oils, distilled products	11
Electrical, electronic products	10	Vehicles (excluding railway)	5.8
Machinery, nuclear reactors, boilers	9.1	Machinery, nuclear reactors, boilers	5.2
Organic chemicals	4.1	Pharmaceutical products	5

Table 3 Top five Indian imports and exports (by value), 2016

The GDP and GNI per capita data show that India is an emerging economy (Table 4), with both doubling despite the world economic collapse of 2008. Growth is predicted to continue faster than most other countries in the future.

 Graphical skills

Using Table 4, choose a suitable graphical method to present both the GDP and GNI data. Why is your choice the best one?

	1990	1995	2000	2005	2010	2015	2020
GDP per capita $	385	391	463	749	1430	1616	2358
GNI (PPP) per capita $	1120	1470	1960	2810	4270	6050	9160

Table 4 Indian GDP per capita and GNI (PPP) per capita 1990–2020

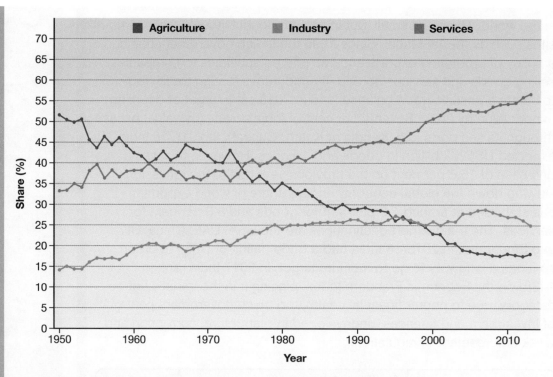

Figure 12 Contribution of industrial sectors to India's GDP (1950–2014)

FDI, TNCs and aid

India has good connections with many other countries because its official language is English. Modern phone and internet connections have also helped attract outsourcing (e.g. call centres). While Indian FDI abroad has varied, it reached a peak in 2010 at US$16 billion. The top countries to receive Indian FDI were Ireland, Netherlands, Belgium and Canada. India has its own large TNCs including Tata Steel, which employs nearly 46 000 people abroad and made US$15 billion from its foreign operations in 2013. Figure 13 shows the pattern of FDI into India, which was very low until 2007. US TNCs invest most in India with over 1100 business deals; TNCs include Lockheed Martin, Coca-Cola, General Electric, Ford Motor Company and Cisco Systems.

As India has emerged economically now, it receives less official aid from abroad, although the links to the UK remain strong and NGOs, such as Practical Action, work in areas of poverty. India now provides aid to other South Asian countries such as Sri Lanka and Nepal (for example, to the latter after the major earthquake there in 2015).

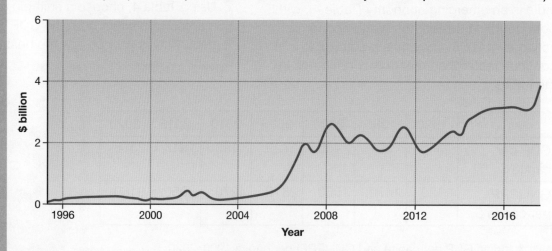

Figure 13 Monthly Foreign Direct Investment into India 1995–2017 (line of best fit)

Economic change and people and the environment

People

As economic development has taken place, there has been a steady population change with high fertility rates leading to India's population doubling between 1960 and 2000. This growth has slowed in the 21st century (for example, there was a 4 per cent drop in the growth rate between 2001 and 2011). This is because the fertility rate has fallen to an average of 2.5 children per female of child-bearing age. However, there are regional differences, with wealthier regions such as Punjab having below average fertility rates and poorer regions such as Uttar Pradesh having higher rates.

Positives arising from population change include a larger workforce – especially scientific and technical workers – to help the economic development of the country. Life expectancy has increased, bringing work and family benefits. There is a growing middle-class with money to spend, these consumers help Indian businesses by buying their goods and services. The government has invested in urban areas and the transport and communications links between them.

Negatives arising from population change include a future ageing population as the large numbers of young people live longer and become the elderly age group (Figure 4), increasing the strain on the healthcare system. There are so many children that they suffer from under-nutrition and are vulnerable to exploitation. To create a future educated workforce, schooling and nutrition need to improve, as does the role and status of women in Indian society. A gender imbalance has arisen, with more boys than girls (up to 10 per cent in some areas), especially among richer people who can afford to find out the gender of the foetus and choose to have an abortion. Population growth, industrialisation and irrigation have increased the use of groundwater by 70 per cent since the 1990s, causing concerns about water supply.

The difficulties in rural areas (no toilets, lack of electricity) and the location of new jobs in the cities has encouraged a large rural to urban migration. In 1990, about 25 per cent of India's population lived in urban areas; by 2020, this is predicted to reach over 35 per cent. Over 60 per cent of the migrants arriving in Delhi and Mumbai are from rural areas. In 2011, about 17 per cent of the Indian urban population lived in slums ('bustees'). In Mumbai the population density is over 20 400 people per km^2, and 41 per cent of the population live in slum conditions. However, even slums offer possibilities, providing access to education (primary school age literacy improved by 9 per cent between 2001 and 2011) and jobs for women (which help to reduce fertility rates) access to healthcare and the chance of equality for people from lower castes.

Graphical skills

Study Figure 13. Describe the trends of foreign direct investment into India between 1995 and 2017. Suggest reasons for the trends that you identify.

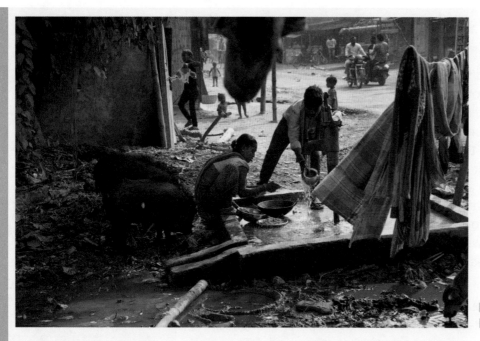

Figure 14 Poverty in Patna, Bihar, India

Quality of life

Statistics show that there has been a slow improvement in the quality of life for the average Indian since 1990: life expectancy has increased, mortality rate has fallen and enrolment in secondary school has doubled. The Human Development Index has increased slowly – from 0.428 in 1990 to 0.494 in 2000, then a little faster from 0.536 in 2005 to 0.624 in 2015 – but with a recent decline in rank position (to 131st). India is in the 'medium human development' category despite its economic improvements. The decline in rank position is due to regional disparities within the country, especially variations in education, health and living standards. In 2017, it was reported that India has more people in rural areas (over 63 million) living without access to clean water than any other country due to contamination by salts, iron and arsenic. Kerala is the best Indian state with a HDI score of 0.712; Bihar is worst with a score of 0.536 (Figure 14). The Indian government is struggling to find a development path that reduces inequalities and includes of all parts of the diverse population. Many believe that the government needs greater emphasis on solving these internal issues.

Environment

India has 2.4 per cent of the world's land area but 18 per cent of the population. This means that the environment is under considerable pressure, especially when rapid industrialisation and lack of enforced regulations are added. As well as the natural environment being damaged, there are costs to people as it degrades (estimated at up to US$80 billion a year).

- Urban areas have bad air pollution (e.g. Delhi – vehicles and industries), which reduces life expectancy by over three years and is the fifth biggest cause of death.

- Water supplies are reduced, especially as groundwater is used up and rivers are polluted by untreated sewage, industrial waste and chemicals from fertilisers.

- Deforestation has removed wooded areas used for timber and living space, increasing run-off, soil erosion and flooding, as well as reducing biodiversity.

- A quarter of India is suffering from desertification due to reduced water availability and half of lakes and wetland areas have disappeared in the last 100 years.

- India is the third highest producer of CO_2 emissions, mainly from burning coal. Climate change has altered the monsoon cycle, and fragile areas such as the Sundarbans mangroves are threatened by sea-level rise.

Changing international role

India has increased its geopolitical influence recently due to its economic growth and potential.

- It jointly set up the New Development Bank (fully operational from 2016) with Brazil, Russia, China and South Africa with the aim of helping other developing countries. The NDB provides loans for green or renewable technology and transport projects.

- It is a member of the G20 economic group of countries, which discusses and tries to resolve economic issues in a globalised world.

- It is regarded as representing the interests of developing and emerging countries and is pushing to be a permanent member of the UN Security Council.

- It is becoming more environmentally aware, especially at international level.

- It has created stronger links with the USA, especially in defence cooperation.

DO IT!

There are four main sections to know about for the development and change in India.

For each section produce a revision card with six to eight bullet points to learn, ready for an eight-mark exam question. Make sure that you include some case study facts in your bullet points.

NAILIT!

Remember that in a large country with a varied physical geography, like India, there will probably be significant differences between parts of the country in terms of human geography. Inequalities may exist because some regions are more economically developed and some people have a higher quality of life than others. HDI scores suggest that Kerala State is similar to the country of Libya, Himachal Pradesh State to South Africa, Uttar Pradesh State to Swaziland and Bihar State to Angola.

CHECKIT!

1 a Give a definition of the term 'economic change'.

  b Give a definition of the term 'environmental change'.

2 For a developing or emerging country that you have studied:

  a List the advantages that the country has to help it develop economically.

  b Describe the cultural characteristics of the country.

  c Explain the socio-cultural challenges that exist in the country.

  d Describe and explain the global influence the country has on political and economic matters.

3 Assess the extent to which quality of life has changed in India, or the country you have studied, as the economy has developed.

Development dynamics

Development and inequality

1 Outline four ways of measuring development.

2 a Name two developing countries.

b Name two emerging countries.

c Explain the differences between a developing country and a developed country.

3 a Give a definition of the term 'gross national income'.

b Explain how data on infant mortality can be used to measure development.

c Explain the strengths and weaknesses of using HDI to measure development.

4 a Describe the trends of the birth rate and death rate in an emerging country.

b Explain how changes to the birth rate in an emerging country are linked to the country's development.

5 a Explain how climate may be a cause of global inequalities.

b Explain how international trade may lead to global inequalities.

c Explain how social factors may be responsible for some of the global inequalities.

6 a Describe the wealth disparity in one country or world region.

b Give one reason for the health disparities in developing countries.

c Explain how a cycle of poverty in a developing country keeps people poor.

7 a Give a definition of the term 'refugee'.

b Explain the push and pull factors involved with international migration from a developing country to a developed country.

8 Compare the Modernisation theory of development with the Dependency theory.

Development strategies

1 Describe the features of a bottom-up development scheme.

2 a Give a definition of the term 'remittances'.

b Give a definition of the term 'infrastructure'.

c Explain how improvements to infrastructure in a country can help it to reduce the development gap.

d Explain why a multiplier effect can be considered to be self-sustaining.

3 a Give a definition of the term 'NGO'.

b Describe the types of development project that an NGO usually supports.

c Explain why some international aid may not help to reduce the development gap.

4 Give two reasons why intermediate technology should be used in development projects.

5 Explain why fair trade may be better at reducing the development gap than normal trade between countries.

6 a Name two schemes for reducing the debts of developing or emerging countries.

b Explain why microfinance loans from local banks to people in developing countries may be better for reducing the development gap than loans to a country from the World Bank.

Rapid economic development and change

1 **a** Give a definition of the term 'environmental change'.

   b Outline the differences between economic change and socio-cultural change.

2 For an emerging country that has experienced rapid economic development and change:

   a Give two advantages that the country has to help it develop economically.

   b Outline two obstacles that the country faced inorder to successfully develop.

3 For an emerging country that has experienced rapid economic development and change:

   a Describe one political change that has taken place.

   b Describe one economic change that has taken place.

   c Describe one environmental change that has taken place.

   d Describe one socio-cultural change that has taken place.

   e Suggest whether these changes have been positive or negative. Explain your answer.

4 For an emerging country that has experienced rapid economic development and change:

   a Describe how the country's industrial structure has changed.

   b Explain whether foreign direct investment (FDI) and aid have been beneficial to the country.

   c Describe the country's political and trading links with the rest of the world.

   d Explain why quality of life in the country has not increased as rapidly as expected.

3 Challenges of an urbanising world

3.1 Trends in urbanisation

THEEXAMINATION!

- This section is tested in Paper 1 Section C.
- You must know all parts of this topic.
- You must know an in-depth study of a megacity in a developing or emerging country.

OUTCOMES

By the end of my revision I will be able to:

- Explain patterns of urbanisation around the world.
- Describe reasons for urbanisation, including the impact of migration and economic change.

Urbanisation

Urbanisation is the growth in the proportion or percentage of the population who live in urban areas compared to rural areas.

Urbanisation has taken place at different times and at different rates across the globe. Urbanisation occurred in Europe and North America during the Industrial Revolution in the 18th and 19th centuries. Urbanisation has occurred at a rapid rate in Asia and Latin America since the 1970s and 1980s. Africa has been experiencing rapid urbanisation since 2000.

Why do cities grow?

There are two main reasons why cities grow:

- **Natural increase**: when the birth rate exceeds the death rate.
- **Rural–urban migration**: when people move from the countryside to the city.

DO IT!

Describe and compare the different rates of urbanisation globally, as shown in Figure 1.

DO IT!

Calculate the rate of urban population growth in Asia and Europe between 1950 and 2011.

How much is the population predicted to increase by 2050?

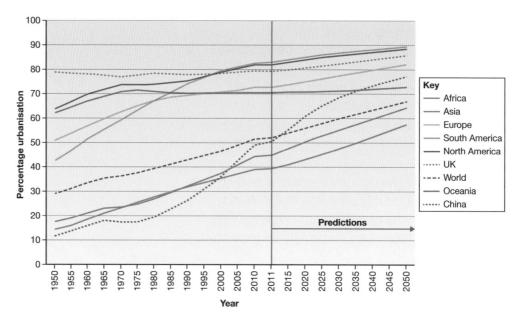

Figure 1 Rates of urbanisation

Megacities and world cities

Million cities house more than one million people; **megacities** more than ten million.

Until the 1970s, most of the world's biggest cities were located in developed countries. Now the majority of megacities are located in emerging countries such as China, India and Brazil.

Figure 2 The world's largest cities in 2015

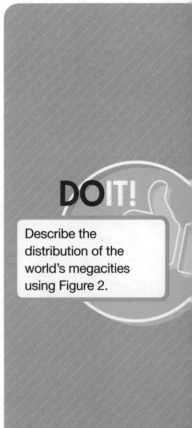

DO**IT!**

Describe the distribution of the world's megacities using Figure 2.

World cities are the most important cities in the world and have a disproportionate role in global current affairs. **Primate cities** are world cities that are at least twice as big as the next largest city in their country.

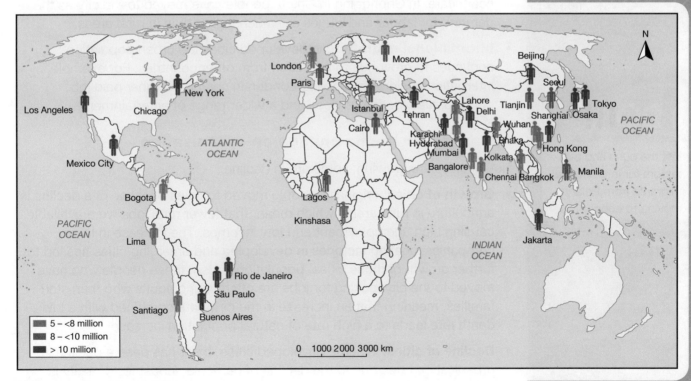

Figure 3 World cities in 2002

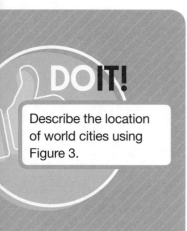

Describe the location of world cities using Figure 3.

World cities are so important for many reasons, including:

- **Investment flows** – London, New York and Tokyo are the world's most important financial centres.

- **Air traffic flows** – world cities have hub airports with the largest flows of passengers and goods.

- **Decision makers** – 80 per cent of transnational corporations, TNCs are headquartered in world cities in Europe, the USA and Japan.

- **political decisions** – governance in the biggest cities affects global politics.

Reasons for urbanisation

Impact of migration on urbanisation

The rate of urbanisation is affected by 'push' and 'pull' factors.

- **Push factors** make people want to leave a place: for example, no jobs, poor health care or lack of education opportunities.

- **Pull factors** attract people to a place: for example, better job opportunities, services or infrastructure.

The movement of people into cities occurs at a national level and globally.

- **National migration**: in developing cities and emerging cities urbanisation has increased due to national migration (movement within a country). People move from rural areas to cities to find better jobs, education and healthcare. In Chongqing in China, people have moved to the city as the demand for labour and wages are much higher than in rural areas.

- **International migration**: in developed cities the urban population continues to grow due to migration from other countries. For example, international migrants move to London in search of higher paid job opportunities, better services and a wider range of entertainment.

Impact of economic change on urbanisation

Not all cities are growing; some are in decline.

- **Growth of cities**: originally, people moved to cities because of a decline in agriculture in rural areas, which meant that fewer rural jobs were available, causing high unemployment and low incomes. The increase in large companies locating factories in developing and emerging cities has led to further growth of those cities' populations. Also, those people who have moved to the city looking for jobs are often young adults who then start families, meaning that an increase in the birth rate combined with a low death rate leads to a high rate of natural population increase.

- **Decline of cities**: in some developed cities, there has been a decline in urbanisation rates due to the decline of particular industries. If a city is reliant on one dominant industry and that industry goes into decline, it can lead to people leaving. For example, Detroit in the USA experienced a decline in the car industry due to increased competition from abroad. As factories closed, people lost jobs and therefore left Detroit.

List the push and pull factors for international migrants from Poland moving to London.

Differences in urban economies

Jobs are classified as either formal or informal.

- In formal employment, employees receive a regular wage, pay taxes and have employment rights (for example, work in factories or shops).

- In informal employment, people work for themselves, pay little or no taxes and have no workers' rights (for example, street sellers or shoe shiners).

The type of work people do varies depending on whether the city where they work is developed, emerging or developing. Cities change their employment as their economic development changes. The three-stage Clark–Fisher model shows this (Figure 4):

- pre-industrial – jobs mostly in farming, fishing and mining

- industrial – manufacturing industry dominates, and tertiary industry develops

- post-industrial – tertiary industry becomes the most important, with services growing.

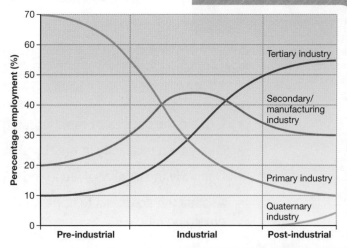

Figure 4 The Clark–Fisher model of urban employment

Type of city	Developed cities	Emerging cities	Developing cities
Examples	London, New York	Mumbai, Rio de Janeiro	Kampala, Lagos
Types of industry	<ul><li>No primary industry.</li><li>Some secondary industry.</li><li>Mostly tertiary industry in the sectors of tourism, education, finance, etc.</li><li>Quaternary industries such as IT, media and culture.</li><li>Mostly formal sectors.</li></ul>	<ul><li>Little primary industry.</li><li>Some secondary industry, processing primary goods, e.g. clothes.</li><li>Much tertiary industry, e.g. transport, retail.</li><li>Some quaternary industry, and growing.</li><li>Formal and informal.</li></ul>	<ul><li>Little primary industry.</li><li>Growing secondary industry producing primary products.</li><li>Plenty of tertiary industry, e.g. transport, retail, tourism, etc.</li><li>Many people work in the informal sector, but the formal is growing.</li></ul>

Table 1 Comparing urban economies

CHECKIT!

1 Define the term 'urbanisation'.

2 Explain why there are more megacities in emerging and developing cities.

3 Suggest why London is an important world city.

4 State examples of formal and informal sector jobs.

5 Describe the difference between the economies of developed, emerging and developing cities.

6 Make a copy of the Clark–Fisher model and annotate it to show the economic features at each stage. Add examples of countries at each stage.

3.2 Changing cities over time

OUTCOMES

By the end of my revision I will be able to:

- Explain the causes of rapid urban change and the challenges it creates.
- Describe a megacity in the developing or emerging world.
- Describe the quality of life in a developing or emerging megacity.
- Assess the solutions to improving quality of life in a megacity in a developing or emerging city.

Stages of urbanisation

Over time, cities in the developed world have changed shape and changed population, moving through a number of stages.

Stage	Description	Example
Urbanisation	Cities grew due to the industrial revolution and improvements to transport networks. Factories attracted workers and people moved from rural areas and beyond.	New York: attracted immigrants from Europe as the port and harbour developed. Food and clothing industries developed. Ethnic enclaves of similar ethnicity were created, e.g. Little Italy.
Suburbanisation	During the early 20th century, the cities became too noisy, crowded and polluted. People moved out of the inner city to the suburbs on the edge of the city.	New York: became very overcrowded and expensive with high crime rates. The development of the subway and railway meant people could move out to the suburbs but still commute to work in the city. Quality of life was better in the suburbs: it was quieter, cheaper, safer and the houses were bigger.
De-industrialisation	The decline of manufacturing industries due to technology and increased mechanisation meant high unemployment. People then moved out of the city.	Detroit: the decline of the car industry (due to imports from abroad and technology being used instead of people) meant a decline in the economy, so people moved out.
Counter-urbanisation	People started to move out of the city into more rural areas and commuter towns beyond the city. Rising car ownership and road and motorway development meant people could commute to the city for work. Also technology meant more people could work at home using the internet.	New York: people moved out beyond the suburbs into the surrounding towns in upstate New York, New Jersey and Connecticut. This was known as the 'white flight' because the wealthier white people moved out, leaving behind the poorer migrants and black Americans.

| Re-urbanisation | Run-down inner city areas have been regenerated to attract people back into the city. New apartments, retail areas and leisure facilities are built on brownfield sites (former industrial sites that have been developed before). | London: re-development of the London Docklands area saw the old buildings turned into apartments, new office buildings built like Canary Wharf Tower, retail, entertainment and leisure facilities and a clean-up of the environment. Young people have now moved back into the area. |

Table 2 Changes in urbanisation over time

Urban land use

Land use describes what the land in cities is used for. The land use in cities often follows a pattern that divides each city into distinct areas (Figure 5).

- **Central Business District (CBD):** found at the centre of the city where you often get financial offices, government offices, retail outlets and entertainment centres. It is the commercial part of the city. The land use is very high density, with tall modern buildings. Land prices are highest in the city centre. This is the most accessible part of the city as railway and bus stations are there and most major roads meet in the centre.

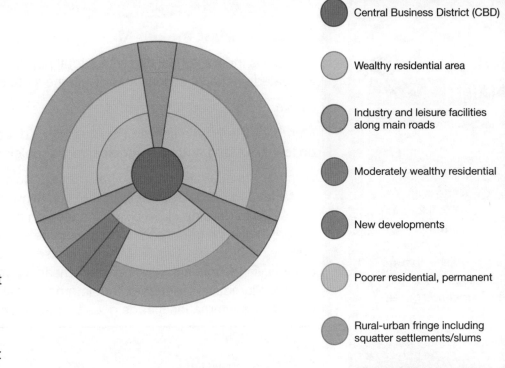

- Central Business District (CBD)
- Wealthy residential area
- Industry and leisure facilities along main roads
- Moderately wealthy residential
- New developments
- Poorer residential, permanent
- Rural-urban fringe including squatter settlements/slums

Figure 5 Land use patterns in cities

- **Inner city:** the area around the CBD where you find a mix of property types, such as old industrial buildings, older terraced housing and some areas of newer high-rise apartments. Industry in this area is located along roads, railways, rivers or canals. The land is still expensive in this area so land use is still high density.

- **Suburbs:** lower population density residential areas with larger detached and semi-detached houses, wider roads and some areas of retail and leisure, plus more green, open spaces. Land is cheaper here, allowing for more space between houses.

- **Rural–urban fringe:** the area around the edge of the city with lots of open space. Often there are low-rise retail parks and business parks. This is where land prices are lowest.

DO IT!

Give two features for each of:

- the Central Business District
- the inner city
- the suburbs
- the rural–urban fringe.

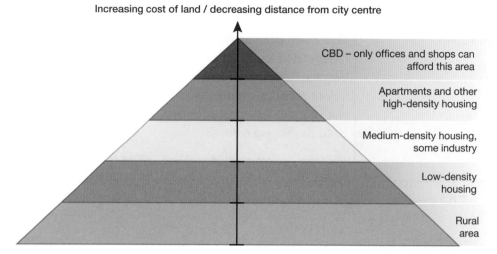

Increasing cost of land / decreasing distance from city centre

CBD – only offices and shops can afford this area

Apartments and other high-density housing

Medium-density housing, some industry

Low-density housing

Rural area

Figure 6 Cost of land in cities

NAILIT!

Make sure you understand the difference between site and situation. A city's **site** is its geographical location. A city's **situation** includes the reasons a place develops and its location relative to the surrounding area.

Case study

Mumbai: what makes Mumbai a megacity?

Mumbai is India's largest city with a total population of over 12 million. It is located on the west coast of India in the state of Maharashtra.

Mumbai's site and situation

Mumbai's site is on a series of islands with a deep water harbour. It is on low-lying land and has a tropical monsoon climate.

Mumbai's deep-water situation has made it India's largest container port with a long 10 km waterfront that has allowed manufacturing industries to develop close by. Its location on the west coast of India (Figure 7) gives it prime access to the markets of the Middle East and Europe (via the Suez Canal). Mumbai is also well connected to the rest of India via the extensive rail network, meaning goods can travel across India to Mumbai to be shipped out internationally. Twenty-five per cent of all India's international trade goes through Mumbai.

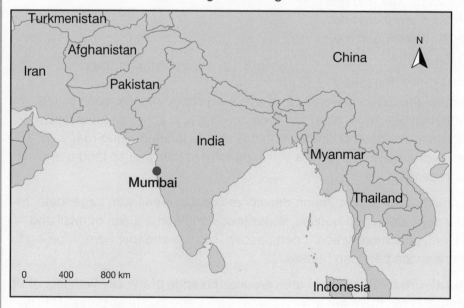

Figure 7 Mumbai's location

Mumbai's structure

CBD (central business district)

- Oldest part of Mumbai.
- Includes all the important business headquarters.
- Built around the harbour at the southern tip of the island.
- Expensive retail developments and most expensive housing.

Inner suburbs

- Located just outside the CBD.
- Where old textile mills and old housing for the textile mill workers were found.
- Now the location of squatter settlements, including Dharavi.

Outer suburbs

- Second area of suburbs located along the railways.
- New Mumbai (Navi Mumbai) – a planned residential development.
- New industries located here, where the land is cheaper and closer to an available workforce.

Urban–rural fringe

- The edge of Mumbai where it merges with the countryside and other smaller towns.
- Poorest new arrivals living in squatter settlements on the outskirts of the city; sixty per cent of the population of Mumbai live in squatter settlements.

Land uses in Greater Mumbai

- Commercial and mixed-use zones
- Residential areas and suburbs
- Industrial landscapes
- Esplanade, maidans and parks
- Defence and military

Figure 8 Land use in Mumbai

SNAPIT!

Snap an image of Figure 8 showing the land use in Mumbai. Use it to help you write a description of each land-use zone.

Why has Mumbai's population grown so rapidly?

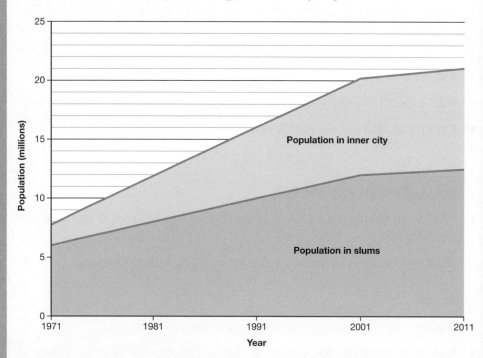

Figure 9 Mumbai's population growth

The population in Mumbai has grown rapidly, at a rate of 3 per cent per year (Figure 9). This fast rate of growth is called hyper-urbanisation. The population has grown for two main reasons:

1. migration
2. natural increase.

Rural–urban migration

People from the rural areas of India moved to Mumbai due to a series of push and pull factors.

SNAPIT!

Snap an image of the push and pull factors table. Highlight the economic reasons and the social reasons. Which do you think are most important?

Push factors: reasons people left the countryside	Pull factors: things that attracted people to Mumbai
Poor farmland and uneven climate conditions making farming difficult, providing people with very low wages.	Economic growth bringing high number of job opportunities in Mumbai, including a range of high- and low-skilled work.
Poor access to services: lack of schools, healthcare facilities.	More services available including educational opportunities and healthcare facilities.
Fewer jobs in farming due to increased mechanisation.	Higher wages in Mumbai, even in the lower-skilled jobs.
High levels of rural poverty that are impossible to escape from.	Still poverty in the city, but more opportunities for people to better themselves.

Table 3 Push and pull factors affecting Mumbai

Natural increase

Natural population growth can be summarised using a simple equation:

natural increase = birth rate − death rate

So when the birth rate exceeds the death rate, the population grows.

The migrants that arrive in Mumbai are typically people in their 20s and 30s, meaning they are likely to settle down, get married and have children.

Economic opportunities of living in Mumbai

Opportunities in the service sector

For higher-skilled and educated people, there are many opportunities opening up in the growing financial and IT sectors thanks to outsourcing by large companies (TNCs).

Lower-skilled service jobs are also created to support these large companies, such as cleaners, mechanics, taxi drivers and recycling operatives.

Opportunities in industry

Dharavi, Mumbai's largest slum, is home to over 5000 small-scale businesses and factories that provide employment for the lower-skilled residents. These businesses can be bring a lot of money into the city, estimated to be worth £350 million per year to the economy.

Opportunities in infrastructure

Even people living in slums have access to water, electricity and televisions. The large market for people needing these services means the creation and maintenance of infrastructure, bringing lots of job opportunities.

Challenges of living in Mumbai

DO IT!

List ten different employment opportunities found in Mumbai. Identify which are informal and which are formal.

Figure 10 Challenges of living in Mumbai

Study Figure 10. Recreate the diagram and add an explanation of the challenges to each branch.

Housing shortages and slums

- Limited space means there is limited housing and rents are high.

- Poorest people end up living in **chawls**, poorly maintained old tenement buildings that lack basic facilities and which are very unsafe.

- Squatter settlements containing makeshift huts have been built on the edges of the city, lacking water, sewerage and sanitation.

- Some people live rough, under bridges or wherever they can find.

Water supply

- Water is supplied by standpipes shared by large numbers of families.

- Shortages mean water is only available for two hours every morning.

- People use the rivers, polluted with waste, for washing clothes.

Waste disposal

- Waste from factories is dumped untreated into the Mithi river, which can lead to disease for the people who use the river for washing.

- Eight hundred million litres of untreated sewage are dumped into rivers daily.

- Eighty percent of all rubbish is recycled, creating an industry worth US$1.5 million a year and employing 10 000 people.

Traffic and congestion

- A rise in car ownership has led to massive congestion on the roads.

- Ninety per cent of people travel by train and bus; high-demand services are overcrowded and can be dangerous as passengers hang from doors or travel on the train roof.

- Traffic levels have caused high amounts of air pollution.

Working conditions

- Lots of people work in the informal sector with poor working conditions, no protection for workers and long hours.

- Informal sector work is often very low paid.

- Some of the jobs in heavy industries are dangerous, with toxic fumes and a lack of safety equipment.

Inequalities in the city

- There are increasing numbers of people in the middle class in Mumbai.

- There is increasing wealth due to employment in technology and tertiary sectors, where wages are higher.

- Wealthy areas of the city are growing, where there are gated communities, with electricity, sanitation and running water.

- Mumbai has become a city of contrasts, with a growing division between the rich and the poor.

Sustainable development in Mumbai

Sustainable development involves meeting the needs of the present without compromising the ability of future generations to meet their own needs.

Sustainable development needs to incorporate three main strands: the environment, society and the economy. The theory is that sustainability can be seen as a 'three-legged stool' (Figure 11), with the legs of the stool being the three main strands of sustainability. All three strands need to be linked together for a successful sustainability strategy.

Figure 11 The 'three-legged stool' of sustainable development

Top-down development strategy: Vision Mumbai

Vision Mumbai was an ambitious plan to redevelop and transform Mumbai. It was a top-down scheme involving a large-scale, high-cost plan with investment and decision-making from government and investors.

The aims of the scheme were to:

- build a million low-cost homes
- demolish Dharavi to make way for cheaper housing and offices
- improve and widen roads
- improve rail transport by increasing train capacity and safety
- boost economic growth
- improve air and water quality.

Did Vision Mumbai work? Opinions on the effectiveness of Vision Mumbai are mixed.

Yes, it was a success because...	No, it wasn't a success because...
<ul><li>200 000 dwellers were rehomed</li><li>45 000 slum houses were demolished</li><li>New flats were built with piped water and waste disposal</li><li>Improved platforms reduced deaths</li><li>Air quality measures were introduced</li></ul>	<ul><li>Slum dwellers would have preferred the slums to be improved rather than demolished</li><li>It affected local communities and broke them up</li><li>Small businesses pushed out of the slums closed down</li><li>Water quality is still not improving</li><li>Slums keep growing regardless</li></ul>

Table 4 Pros and cons of Vision Mumbai

DO IT!

Summarise the key aims of Vision Mumbai plans under these headings:

- Water
- Waste
- Housing
- Transport

Explain why the project was not a success according to the local communities in Dharavi.

Bottom-up development strategy: Lok Seva Sangam

The Lok Seva Sangam (LSS) health charity aims to improve health care in the slums. It was originally set up to control leprosy but now it has expanded its services to check for skin conditions, run skin clinics, dispense drugs from pharmacies and run education projects.

The health projects:

- Have reduced the number of leprosy cases from 4000 to 219 over 30 years and cured 75 per cent of patients.
- Work to treat people with tuberculosis.
- Employ medical staff to work in the slums.

The education projects:

- Employed five teachers to educate people about the symptoms of leprosy and TB.
- Teach people about care and treatment of skin diseases.
- Teach people about treatments and follow up with them to make sure they take their medication.

The community projects:

- Work in communities to teach them about good health and hygiene.
- Work with women to improve sanitation to improve health.
- Help women to come up with ways to make money for making and selling things.

The LSS has been very successful, but it only works in two districts of the Dharavi slum and does not cover the rest of Mumbai's slums.

 # CHECKIT!

1 State two reasons why New York developed as a megacity.

2 Explain why Detroit experienced deindustrialisation.

3 Explain how London Docklands changed after reurbanisation.

4 Draw a sketch of urban land use and annotate it to show the different features of each zone, and add case study detail to each zone.

5 Describe the rate of population growth in Mumbai.

6 Explain why the population has grown so rapidly in Mumbai.

7 Give three push factors and three pull factors to show the reasons for rural–urban migration to Mumbai.

8 Explain how rapid population growth has led to the creation of so many opportunities for people in Mumbai.

Challenges of an urbanising world

Trends in urbanisation

1 Define the terms 'megacity' and 'primate city'.

2 Describe the rate of urban growth in:

 a the developed world

 b the developing world.

3 State two push factors and two pull factors that have led to urban growth.

4 Explain the difference between the formal and the informal economy.

5 Describe the main features of urban economies of:

 a developed world cities

 b developing world cities.

Changing cities over time

1 Describe the Central Business District.

2 Explain what is meant by counter-urbanisation.

3 Give reasons why suburbanisation has occurred.

4 Explain why the city centre might have experienced decline.

5 For a city you have studied, explain how it has changed over time.

Megacity in a developing country: Mumbai

1 Give reasons why Mumbai's site and situation were important in its development as a megacity.

2 Explain why an emerging city like Mumbai has experienced urban sprawl.

3 Describe some of the challenges of living in a squatter settlement.

4 Explain why so many people in emerging cities like Mumbai work in the informal economy.

5 Explain the impact of two urban environmental problems on the people of an emerging city.

Sustainable development

1 Define 'top-down' and 'bottom-up' development.

2 Give three advantages and three disadvantages of a top-down development project in an emerging city like Mumbai.

3 Give three advantages and three disadvantages of a bottom-up development project in an emerging city like Mumbai.

4 Assess whether a top-down or a bottom-up development project is more effective in emerging cities.

4 The UK's evolving physical landscape

THE EXAMINATION!

- This section is tested in Paper 2.
- You must know about UK physical landscapes, Coastal change and conflict and River processes and pressures.

DO IT!

Study Figure 1. Describe the pattern of the UK's:

a upland areas

b lowland areas.

SNAP IT!

Snap an image of Figure 1. Use it to help you recall the UK's:

- areas of uplands and lowlands
- extensive river system.

4.1 UK physical landscapes

OUTCOMES

By the end of my revision I will be able to:

- Explain how geology and past processes have influenced the physical landscape of the UK.
- Explain how physical and human processes work together to create distinct UK landscapes.

Geology

- Scientists use carbon dating to find out the age and characteristics of rocks.
- Upland areas in the UK are formed by mainly igneous, metamorphic and some sedimentary rocks.
- Lowland areas of the UK are mainly formed by younger, less resistant sedimentary rocks.

Tectonic processes

300 million years ago, tectonic processes affected landscapes in the UK.

- The plate that the UK sits on moved away from the tropics.
- Convection currents underneath the plate uplifted rocks from below the sea, creating land.
- When the plate was uplifted some rocks some rocks snapped, causing strata to become tilted.

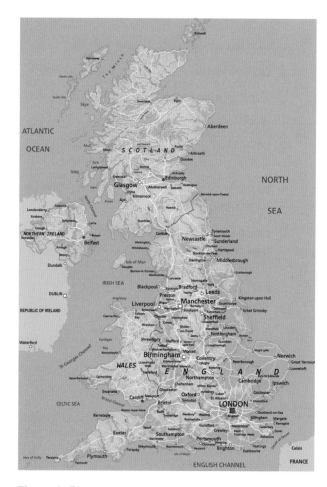

Figure 1 Physical map of the UK

Glaciation

- The most recent ice age to cover the UK was over 10 000 years ago.

- Glaciation changed river valleys from V-shaped valleys to U-shaped valleys by deepening and widening them.

- When the glaciers melted and retreated, they left features behind such as waterfalls.

Types of rock

Sedimentary rocks are formed of small particles that have been eroded and deposited in layers, or from the remains of plants and animals. Examples: limestone and chalk.

Igneous rocks are formed from volcanic activity. When magma or lava cools it forms rocks made of large crystals. Example: granite.

Metamorphic rocks are existing rocks that are formed when changed under extreme pressure or heat. Example: slate.

The **relief** of the land is determined by its geology. Hard rocks such as granite form mountain ranges; soft rocks such as clay and limestone form more low-lying landscapes.

Physical processes in the landscape

Weathering is the breakdown of solid rock by the action of the weather or plants. **Freeze-thaw weathering** is where repeated freezing, expanding and thawing of water causes fragments of rock to become detached. This can affect exposed granite. The movement of rocks and soil is caused by **slope processes** including rockfall, landslides, soil creep (where soil moves slowly down gentle slopes) and mudflow (caused by heavy rainfall).

Upland landscapes (for example, the Lake District)

- Upland areas can be rough, with large rock fragments (scree) that are created by freeze-thaw weathering.

- Scree is unstable and easily moves during rockfalls.

- Landslides are common in upland areas due to the high amount of rainfall.

- Glaciers created U-shaped valleys in the Lake District.

Lowland landscapes (for example, the Weald)

- Chemical weathering affects chalk landscapes because acidic rain reacts with chalk (it contains calcium carbonate, which is an alkali).

- Trees and shrub roots break up rocks through biological weathering.

- Chalk is porous, so rivers are not common in chalk landscapes.

- **Soil creep** occurs in lowland areas.

DO IT!

Draw a mind map to explain how geology, glaciation and tectonic processes can create different landscapes.

NAIL IT!

Make sure you can explain how different rock types have determined the UK's landscape.

DO IT!

Create a table comparing weathering, slope processes and river processes in upland and lowland areas.

Human activity creating distinctive UK landscapes

Agriculture

- Chalk grassland is ideal for grazing sheep because the grass is short and rich in nutrients.
- Clay grassland is suitable for cattle farming because the grass grows to a longer length.

Advantages	Disadvantages
• Farming supports the local economy • Arable farming supports bird species on the South Downs	• Decline of the traditional practice of sheep grazing has led to scrub encroachment • Decline in chalk grassland due to use of chemicals in farming

Forestry

- The South Downs National Park consists of 23.4 per cent woodland.
- Human activity in woodland areas has increased.

Advantages	Disadvantages
• A large amount of ancient trees in the South Downs National Park • Timber from the South Downs National Park is a sustainable product	• New building developments are threatening woodlands • Traditional management of woodlands has decreased, reducing biodiversity

Settlement

- The South Downs National Park is the most populated national park in the UK.
- New settlements have been created in the South Downs that do not always reflect the traditional settlements.

DOIT!

1 Explain how humans have affected UK landscapes.

2 In your opinion, have humans had a positive or negative effect on UK landscapes?

NAILIT!

Make sure you can explain how human factors have combined to produce distinctive landscapes.

CHECKIT!

1 Describe the physical evidence that suggests harder rocks may be found to the north and west of the UK, and softer rocks may be found to the south and east.

2 Describe the course of the River Thames from source to mouth.

3 Explain how different rock types affect the landscape.

4.2 Coastal landscapes

OUTCOMES

By the end of my revision I will be able to:

- Explain how coasts are shaped by a number of physical processes.
- Explain how coastal landscapes are changed by human activity.
- Analyse a range of management strategies used to protect coastlines.

The coastal zone

- **Hard rock coasts** consist of resistant rocks, such as igneous granite and resistant sedimentary rocks, and erode at a slower rate.

- **Soft rock coasts** consist of less resistant rocks, such as clay, and erode at a much faster rate.

Figure 2 Discordant coastline

Figure 3 Concordant coastline

SNAPIT!

Snap an image of Figures 2 and 3 and use it to remind yourself of the differences between concordant and discordant coastlines. Think about why they are different.

Wave types

Waves are formed by the wind blowing over the sea. The size of a wave is affected by:

- speed of the wind

- length of time the wind has been blowing

- distance the wind blows across the water – the fetch.

Figure 4 When waves reach the coast

There are two main types of waves: constructive and destructive waves.

Constructive waves

- gently sloping

- strong swash

- weak backwash

- long wavelength

- deposit large amounts of sediment

Destructive waves

- steep wave

- weak swash

- strong backwash

- short wavelength

- remove large amounts of sediment

DO IT!

Draw an annotated diagram to show the difference between a constructive wave and a destructive wave.

SNAP IT!

Snap an image of Figures 5 and 6. Use them to remind yourself of the differences between a constructive wave and a destructive wave. Think about why they are different.

Figure 5 Constructive waves

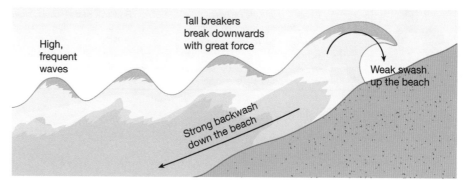

Figure 6 Destructive waves

Coastal processes

Weathering processes

There are three types of weathering.

1 **Chemical weathering**: caused by chemical changes. For example, slightly acidic rainwater can dissolve certain rock types.

Figure 7 Freeze-thaw weathering

2 **Mechanical weathering**: causing the break-up of rocks. For example, freeze-thaw weathering.

3 **Biological weathering**: caused by the action of plants (flora) and animals (fauna). For example, plant roots growing into cracks in the rock.

Mass movement

Mass movement is the downward movement of surface material, such as rock or soil, under the influence of gravity. The main types of mass movement at the coastline are:

- **rock fall** – when rocks break away from the cliff

- **landslides** – when blocks of rock slide down the cliff face

- **mudflows** – weak rock and saturated soil flow down a slope

- rotational slip – a slump of saturated soil and weak rocks move along a curved surface.

A. Rockfall

B. Landslide

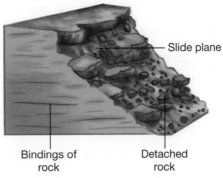

C. Mudflow

D. Rotational slip

Figure 8 Mass movement

DO IT!

Chemical weathering

Research two types of rock affected by chemical weathering.

Mechanical weathering

Draw a set of annotated sketches to show the process of freeze-thaw weathering.

Biological weathering

Research an image from the internet to show an example of biological weathering.

NAIL IT!

Make sure that you understand the different forms of weathering and how they can influence cliff collapse. Freeze-thaw weathering weakening a cliff face over time may result in rock fall.

DO IT!

Draw a revision poster to show the different types of mass movement. Try to include annotated sketches to help you understand the different types of mass movement.

NAILIT!

Remember the different types of erosion, transportation and deposition. You will need to know these to understand why we get different landforms along the UK coastline.

Figure 9 Coastal transportation

Coastal marine processes

Coastal erosion

Erosion is the removal of sediment and rocks. There are three types of coastal erosion.

DOIT!

Create a revision card for each type of coastal erosion. Include an annotated sketch to explain how each works.

1. **Hydraulic action**: the power of the waves smashing into a cliff. Trapped air is forced into holes and cracks in the rock again and again with explosive release, eventually causing it to break apart.

2. **Abrasion/corrasion**: the wearing away of the cliffs by sand, shingle and boulders being hurled against them by waves.

3. **Attrition**: rocks in the sea knock against each other, causing them to become smaller and rounder.

Transportation

There are four ways in which sediment can be transported:

1. Solution – dissolved minerals in the water.

2. Suspension – small particles that are carried with the water.

3. Saltation – particles that are too heavy to be suspended are bounced along the sea floor.

4. Traction – large particles that are rolled along the sea floor.

Longshore drift is the process by which sediment is moved along a beach.

SNAPIT!

Snap an image of Figure 10. Use it to remind you of how longshore drift happens. Remember that swash always moves in the direction of the prevailing wind and backwash is always at 90 degrees to the coastline.

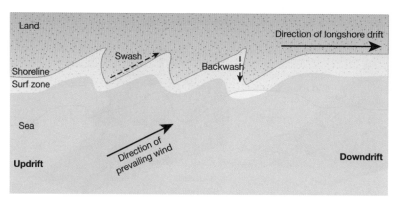

Figure 10 Longshore drift

Deposition

When water loses its energy, sediment can no longer be carried or transported and so it is deposited. Deposition can occur:

- In sheltered bays where constructive waves are dominant.
- Where there are large expanses of flat beach.
- Where material is trapped behind a spit.
- Where structures, such as groynes, trap sediment.

Coastal landforms

Factors affecting coastal landforms

- **Geological structure**: this is the way that rocks are folded or tilted. This is an important factor affecting the shape of cliffs.
- **Rock type**: harder, more resistant rocks such as granite and limestone are more resistant to erosion; softer rocks such as clay and sandstone are more easily eroded.

Coastal erosion landforms

Headlands and bays

- Soft rock and hard rock are eroded at different rates.
- Weaker bands of rock erode more easily to form bays.
- More resistant bands of rock erode more slowly and stick out to form headlands.

Coastline changes over time

Figure 11 Formation of headlands and bays

There is a range of UK coastal landforms. Remember they are all formed by the processes of erosion, transportation and deposition.

Study Figure 11 and the information about coastal marine processes. Draw a sequence of diagrams to show the formation of headlands and bays. Remember to annotate your diagrams.

STRETCHIT!

1 a Research an area of coastline in the UK with headlands and bays.

   b Find a map or photo of this coastline and label the coastal landforms.

   c Explain how the landforms could have been created.

DO IT!

Study Figure 12 and the information on how wave cut platforms are formed. Create a flow diagram to show the process of how a wave cut platform is created. You may want to include diagrams to help you remember the formation.

Cliffs and wave cut platforms

① Weathering processes weaken the rock face.

② Marine erosion processes, such as hydraulic action and abrasion erode the base of the cliff.

③ The base of the cliff starts to wear away and destructive waves remove this material. A wave cut notch is formed, which results in the cliff above being unsupported.

④ The notch will become bigger and bigger due to erosional processes, resulting in the cliff above eventually breaking away.

⑤ This process continues to happen over time, leaving behind the former base of the cliff as a wave cut platform (see Figure 12).

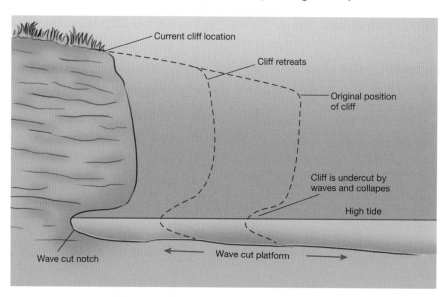

Figure 12 Cliff retreat and formation of a wave cut platform

SNAPIT!

Snap an image of Figure 13. Use it to learn the formation of a stack.

Caves, arches and stacks

1   There is a large crack/line of weakness in the headland.

2   The crack is enlarged by the process of hydraulic action and abrasion to form a notch.

3   Waves make the notch larger over time, forming a cave.

4   Two caves form back-to-back and eventually cut through the headland to form an arch.

5   Weathering processes weaken the top of the cliff. It becomes too heavy and collapses, leaving a stack.

6   The stack is eroded over time and collapses, leaving a stump.

Figure 13 Here, a notch formed and steadily enlarged to become a cave. This then joined another cave forming on the other side of the headland to form the arch we see today.

Coastal deposition landforms

Beaches

A beach is the deposit of sand and shingle – materials that are found in sheltered bays. Beaches are formed due to constructive waves, which have a strong swash, carrying the material up the beach and depositing it.

Spits and bars

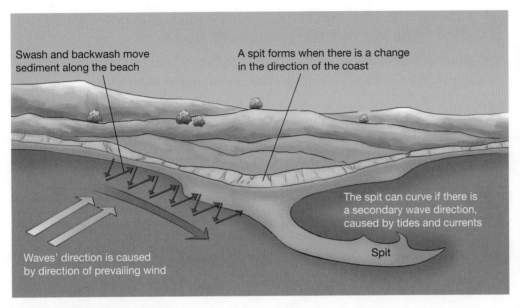

Swash and backwash move sediment along the beach

A spit forms when there is a change in the direction of the coast

The spit can curve if there is a secondary wave direction, caused by tides and currents

Spit

Waves' direction is caused by direction of prevailing wind

Figure 14 Formation of a spit

A spit is a long finger of sand or shingle that sticks out from the land into the sea. Spits are formed due to longshore drift, where the coastline changes direction and bends sharply, resulting in sediment being deposited out to sea. Over time, this sediment builds up, forming an extension from the land. As the process continues, the spit grows further out into the sea. If a spit grows across a bay, trapping a freshwater lake behind it, this then forms a bar. In the sheltered area behind the spit, a saltmarsh may form.

Influence of human activities on coastal landscapes

- **Settlements**: over 20 million people in the UK live along the coastal zone. Settlements are lost due to erosion: for example, 29 villages have disappeared along the Holderness coastline in the past 1000 years.

- **Tourism** is important for coastal settlements economies. Groynes are used to trap sediment for tourist beaches, but this can starve sediment further along the coastline.

- **Infrastructure**: located along the UK coastline there are roads, railways, chemical plants and shipping ports. This has led to large cities and industrial areas developing, which has led to coastal management techniques being used to protect high-value land.

- **Agriculture**: rising sea levels and coastal erosion are leading to the loss of farmland. Farmland has a low economic value, so often is not protected by coastal management techniques.

DO IT!

Formation of a spit

1 Using Figure 14 and the information provided, create a flow diagram explaining the formation of a spit.

2 What is the difference between a spit and a bar?

Case study

The Dorset coast

- Much of the coastline is a World Heritage Site.
- 25 per cent of the coastline has been developed.

Natural and human impacts in Swanage Bay

- Landslides and rockfalls occur on unstable cliffs at Durston Bay. The cliffs contain internationally important fossil beds.
- Approximately 50 per cent of Swanage Bay is built up. Swanage is a residential area with an important tourist resort centred around its wide sandy beach.
- Sea defences have been built at Swanage, including a sea wall and groynes.
- North of Swanage Bay to Ballard point there are scenic limestone cliffs that are part of the World Heritage coast and contain a range of natural habitats.

DO IT!

Create a table to show how human activities can impact the coast directly and indirectly.

Challenges that coastal landscapes create and how they are managed

Rising sea levels

- Sea levels along the English Channel have risen by approximately 12 cm in the past 100 years.
- Warmer temperatures have caused thermal expansion (seawater to expand) and ice sheets and glaciers to melt.
- This could increase coastal erosion. The position of wave cut notches and platforms may change.
- Soft rock, such as clay, may erode at a faster rate.

Storms and storm surges

- **Storm surge** is a large-scale increase in sea level due to a storm. Low air pressures allow the sea level to rise, and gale force winds blow the water towards the coastline.
- Storm surges can last from hours to days and can span hundreds of kilometres, causing large amounts of damage.
- In December 2013, a North Sea storm and very high tides created a large storm surge.
- Due to early warnings and coastal defences, major damage and deaths were avoided.

DO IT!

Create a mind map on the issues for coastal landscapes caused by climate change and its impacts on people.

Coastal management

Integrated Coastal Zone Management (ICZM) is a sustainable way of managing the coast by looking at the whole coastal area and the interests of all its users. There are several possible plan policies.

1. Do nothing – no investment in defences against flooding.

2. Hold the line – maintain the existing shoreline by building defences.

3. Managed realignment – allow the shoreline to change naturally but manage and direct the process.

4. Advance the line – build new defences on the seaward side.

Planners use a cost-benefit analysis to compare economic, social and environmental costs to choose the best form of coastal protection.

There are three different types of coastal management:

1. **Hard engineering**: the use of human-made structures to protect the coastline.

2. **Soft engineering**: methods that work with natural processes to protect the coastline.

3. **Managed retreat**: the controlled retreat of the coastline.

DO IT!

Create a poster showing the economic, social and environmental reasons why we should protect the coastline.

Hard engineering

Sea walls

A sea wall is a concrete wall built at the base of a cliff or along sea fronts in towns. Many sea walls have a curved face or slope away from the sea, to reflect the power of the waves back out to sea.

Advantages of sea walls	Disadvantages of sea walls
• effective at reflecting the power of the sea • can last for many years if well maintained • used as a walkway or promenade • don't affect the movement of sediment	• can be visually unappealing • very expensive • can restrict access to the beach

Table 1 Advantages and disadvantages of sea walls

Rock armour

Rock armour is piles of large boulders arranged at the base of a cliff to reduce the power of waves.

Advantages of rock armour	Disadvantages of rock armour
• relatively cheap • structure is easy to build and maintain • lasts a long time if well maintained	• rocks used are taken from other coastlines or abroad • does not fit in with the local geology • visually unappealing

Table 2 Advantages and disadvantages of rock armour

Gabions

Gabions are wire cages filled with rocks and placed to support a cliff and to take the power of the waves.

Advantages of gabions	Disadvantages of gabions
• cheap to make and easy to construct • can improve the drainage of a cliff • over time vegetation will grow, helping them to blend into the coastline	• in the short term they look very unattractive • cages only last for 5–10 years before rusting

Table 3 Advantages and disadvantages of gabions

Groynes

Groynes are wood or rock structures built out to sea from the coastline. They trap sediment moved by longshore drift, making the beach larger. A wider beach will reduce the power of the waves.

Advantages of groynes	Disadvantages of groynes
• create a wider beach, which is good for tourists • not too expensive • can last for a long time if well maintained	• interrupt longshore drift, which starves beaches further down the coastline of sediment • can be unattractive

Table 4 Advantages and disadvantages of groynes

Numerical skills

Hard engineering

A local council wants to protect 2 km of coastline using a hard engineering technique. Which of the following would be the most cost effective?

- Sea wall: £5000 per metre
- Rock armour: £1000 per metre
- Groynes: £5000 each (placed every 200 metres)
- Gabions: £110 per metre

DO IT!

Rank the four types of hard engineering from the most to the least effective. Explain your order.

Soft engineering

Beach nourishment

Beach nourishment involves the addition of sand or shingle to a beach to make it wider.

Advantages of beach nourishment	Disadvantages of beach nourishment
• quite cheap and easy to maintain • blends in with the beach that is already there • good for tourists	• will need constant maintenance as sediment is removed through longshore drift • sediment has to be sourced • sediment has to be transported to the beach

Table 5 Advantages and disadvantages of beach nourishment

Reprofiling

Reprofiling involves the reshaping of the beach, as the beach level is often lowered in the winter by destructive waves.

Advantages of reprofiling	Disadvantages of reprofiling
• blends in with the beach, keeping a natural look	• major reprofiling works can be expensive • a steep beach may be unattractive to tourists

Table 6 Advantages and disadvantages of reprofiling

Dune regeneration

Sand dunes are natural buffers, created when waves deposit sand along the coastline, but they can be easily destroyed during storms. During dune regeneration, marram grass is planted to help stabilise the dunes and fences are put up to stop people trampling across the dunes and causing erosion.

Advantages of dune regeneration	Disadvantages of dune regeneration
• small impact on the natural environment • can control the public's access to natural ecosystems	• can be unattractive • need to be regularly maintained, especially after storms

Table 7 Advantages and disadvantages of dune regeneration

NAILIT!

Make sure that you understand the difference between hard and soft engineering techniques and why they may be used in different areas along the UK coastline.

DOIT!

Explain why you think hard or soft engineering is more effective at managing the UK coastline.

STRETCHIT!

Research which areas of coastline would be suitable for managed retreat. Name some examples.

Managed retreat

Managed retreat is the policy of allowing an area of low-value land to be naturally eroded or flooded.

Advantages of managed retreat	Disadvantages of managed retreat
• takes pressure off the land further down the coastline • cheaper than continuing to maintain hard engineering defences • good for the environment, as it encourages natural habitats to develop	• people may have to be relocated, which affects communities and can be expensive in the short term • large areas of agricultural land can be lost

Table 8 Advantages and disadvantages of managed retreat

DOIT!

Create a poster showing the advantages and disadvantages of managed retreat.

CHECKIT!

1 State the four types of coastal transport.

2 Describe the difference between constructive and destructive waves.

3 Explain the link between weathering and mass movement.

4 Using a diagram, explain the process of longshore drift.

5 Name two coastal landforms created by erosion.

6 Describe how sand dunes change over time.

7 Explain how the process of deposition creates a spit.

8 Using a diagram, explain the formation of a stack.

9 State the three types of coastal management.

10 Describe the costs and benefits of two types of hard engineering.

11 Explain what type of coastline would be best for the use of managed retreat.

12 Examine the potential conflict between using different types of coastal management along the coastline.

4.3 River processes

OUTCOMES

By the end of my revision I will be able to:

- Describe how the shape of river valleys changes as rivers flow downstream.

- Explain how distinctive fluvial landforms result from different physical processes.

- Explain how river landscapes are influenced by human and physical processes.

- Suggest different management strategies that can be used to protect river landscapes from the effects of flooding.

Changes in rivers and valleys

A **drainage basin** (or catchment area) is the area of land drained by a river and its tributaries (Figure 15).

A river is divided into three sections: the **upper**, **middle** and **lower courses**. Each course has a distinct valley shape, river velocity (speed) and bedload (sediment transported by the river) (see Figure 16 and Table 9).

Figure 15 Drainage basin

Figure 16 Long profile of a river

Upper course	Middle course	Lower course
• steep gradient	• gentle gradient	• very gentle gradient
• shallow depth	• deeper	• very deep
• narrow, steep-sided channel	• flatter channel with steep sides	• flat channel with gently sloping sides
• quite fast velocity	• fast velocity	• very fast velocity
• steep V-shaped valley	• U-shaped valley	• wide, flat valley
• waterfalls and interlocking spurs	• meanders and floodplains	• meanders, ox-bow lakes, floodplains and levées

Table 9 Changes of a river from source to mouth

DO IT!

Using Figure 16, draw a sketch of the long profile of a river. Annotate it to show the different features of each course.

Fluvial processes

Rivers carry out three main processes as they move downstream:

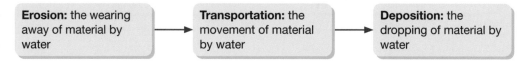

Erosion: the wearing away of material by water → **Transportation:** the movement of material by water → **Deposition:** the dropping of material by water

Erosion

The ability of a river to wear away the land depends on its velocity (how fast it is travelling). Erosion can be **vertical** (downwards) or **lateral** (sideways).

There are four different types of erosion:

1. **Hydraulic action:** this is the force of the water hitting the river bank and river bed.

2. **Abrasion:** the load that is carried by the river scrapes along the bank and bed and wears them away.

3. **Attrition:** the stones carried by the river hit each other and break up into smaller pieces.

4. **Solution:** material is dissolved when the water travels over rocks, that make the water acidic.

Transportation

A river transports, or carries, the load in four different ways:

1. **Traction:** large particles roll along the river bed.

2. **Saltation:** smaller particles bounce along the river bed.

3. **Suspension:** smaller sediment floats in the water.

4. **Solution:** the dissolved material is carried in solution.

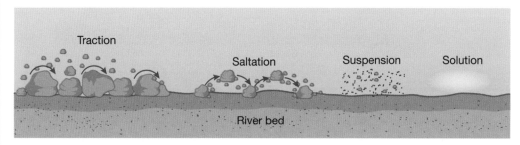

Figure 17 Types of transportation

Deposition

Deposition occurs when a river loses velocity and slows down. This is because it loses the energy to carry material.

- Large rocks get deposited in the upper course of the river, as they are too heavy to be carried very far.

- Smaller particles held in suspension are deposited when a river slows down (for example, on a river bend where there is greater friction).

- Most deposition takes place at the mouth of the river where the river loses energy when it meets the sea.

DO IT!

1 Describe three processes of erosion.

2 Describe three processes of transportation.

3 Explain why velocity is so important in erosion, transportation and deposition.

Fluvial landforms

Rivers have distinct landforms as they move down the long profile towards the sea.

Interlocking spurs

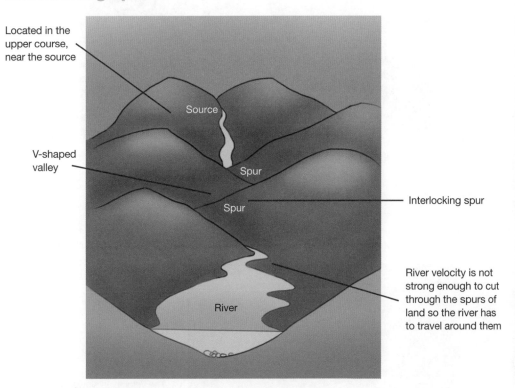

Figure 18 Interlocking spurs

Labels on figure:
- Located in the upper course, near the source
- V-shaped valley
- Source
- Spur
- Spur
- Interlocking spur
- River
- River velocity is not strong enough to cut through the spurs of land so the river has to travel around them

Waterfalls

Waterfalls occur where the river flows over two different rock types. The softer rock is less resistant and more easily eroded than the harder rock.

This slow gradual retreat of the waterfall creates a gorge which is a steep-sided valley (see Figure 20).

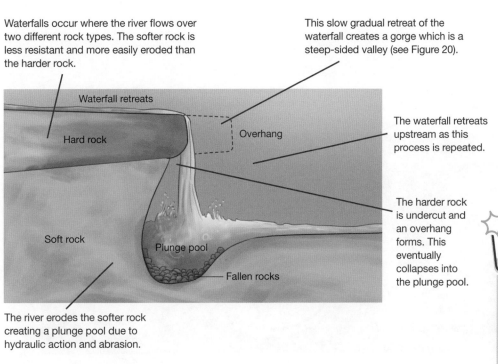

Labels on figure:
- Waterfall retreats
- Hard rock
- Overhang
- The waterfall retreats upstream as this process is repeated.
- Soft rock
- Plunge pool
- Fallen rocks
- The harder rock is undercut and an overhang forms. This eventually collapses into the plunge pool.

The river erodes the softer rock creating a plunge pool due to hydraulic action and abrasion.

Figure 19 Waterfall formation

SNAP IT!

Snap an image of Figure 19. Use it to help you remember how a waterfall is formed.

DO IT!

DO IT!

Write a paragraph to explain how a waterfall is formed. Use all the following words:

- overhang
- retreat
- erosion
- gorge
- less-resistant rock
- plunge pool
- undercutting.

DO IT!

1 Write a paragraph to explain how a meander is formed. Describe the changes over time.

2 Draw a sequence of diagrams to show how a meander can lead to the formation of an ox-bow lake.

STRETCH IT!

Draw your own cross-section through a meander. Annotate it to show the main features of a meander. You should include the river cliff, slip-off slope, areas of erosion and deposition and the thalweg.

Figure 20 Gorge

Meanders

The **thalweg** is the fastest line of velocity in a river. It swings from the outside of one bend to the outside of the next bend.

This process of erosion on the outside of a bend and deposition on the inside of a bend causes the river to move across the valley floor.

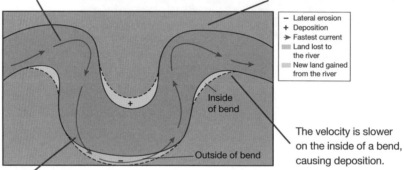

- Lateral erosion
- + Deposition
- → Fastest current
- Land lost to the river
- New land gained from the river

Inside of bend

The velocity is slower on the inside of a bend, causing deposition.

Outside of bend

The velocity is stronger on the outside of a bend causing erosion.

Figure 21 Meander

Ox-bow lakes

The neck of a meander is gradually eroded and narrows.

During a period of flood, the neck of the meander is broken through and the river takes the course of least resistance to form a new straight channel.

Over time, the meanders start to move towards each other.

The meander is then cut off by deposition. This leaves behind an ox-bow lake.

ox-bow

Figure 22 Ox-bow lake

Floodplains and levées

A floodplain is a wide, flat area of land either side of a river.

Floodplains are formed:

- When a meander migrates from side to side causing the valley sides to erode and become wider, creating a wide, flat valley floor.

- During a period of flood when silt is deposited on to the floodplain and builds up layers of fertile land.

Figure 23 Floodplain

A levée is the raised river bed created by sediment from the river during a flood. Material is deposited at the sides of the river and builds up over time.

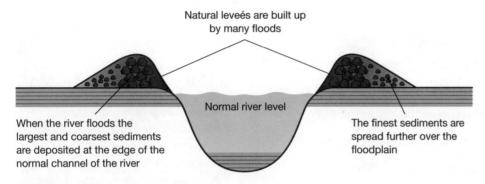

Figure 24 Levée

Flood risk and management

Factors that increase the risk of flooding

Flooding occurs when there is an increase in the volume of water and it overflows onto the land surrounding the river. A number of human and physical factors can increase the risk of flooding (Table 10).

Physical factors	Human factors
Precipitation: a sudden heavy downpour can lead to flash floods, or long periods of steady rainfall can lead to flooding.	**Urbanisation**: creates impermeable surfaces, such as roads, and drains and sewers speed up the movement of water to the river.
Saturated soil: waterlogged ground will not allow the water to soak in.	**Deforestation**: the removal of trees means less interception of rainfall, so water gets to the river channels more quickly.
Geology: impermeable rock that does not allow water to soak in allows faster surface run-off to the river.	
Steep slopes: water will run off a steep slope in a mountainous area much more quickly.	**Agriculture**: water travels more quickly along ploughed furrows and fields that are left unplanted.

Table 10 Human and physical factors that can increase the risk of flooding

Hydrographs

Hydrographs show the amount or volume of water in a river (discharge) following a storm.

A number of factors affect the shape of a hydrograph. A 'flashy' hydrograph has a short lag time and a high peak. This occurs in an area where there is:

- a small drainage basin
- impermeable rock
- urbanisation

- steep relief
- saturated soil
- heavy rainfall.

A low, flat hydrograph shows a long lag time and a low peak. This occurs in an area where there is:

- a large drainage basin
- permeable rock
- forest

- gentle relief
- dry soil
- light rainfall.

STRETCH IT!

For each type of hydrograph, explain why these factors affect its shape:

- size of drainage basin
- land use
- rock type
- soil type
- amount of rainfall
- relief.

Graphical skills

Look at the hydrograph in Figure 25.

1 When was the peak rainfall?

2 When was the peak discharge?

3 Calculate the lag time.

NAIL IT!

Make sure you can describe the human and physical factors that can increase the risk of flooding. Explain how this can be demonstrated using a hydrograph.

Figure 25 Flood hydrograph

Case study

The River Severn: how human and physical processes interact to cause flooding

The River Severn is the UK's largest river. Historically, it was a trade route and settlements grew along it, including Shrewsbury, Bewdley and Gloucester.

The UK floods of 2007

- The summer of 2007 had very heavy rainfall that caused flooding in June and July.
- In England and Wales rainfall was double the average for June and July.
- Worcestershire saw four times its average rainfall.
- In one event, 140 mm of rain fell in a few hours.
- Rainfall was caused by a series of depressions moving across the UK.
- May to July was the wettest period since records began in 1766.
- Rainfall fell on saturated soil that resulted in increased surface run-off.
- In urban areas, impermeable surfaces resulted in immediate run-off.
- Flash flooding overwhelmed drainage systems in some cities.
- Tewkesbury lies at the confluence of the Rivers Severn and Avon, and was badly hit by floods.

Managing floods

Flooding in the UK is increasing due to the following reasons:

- an increasing population
- changes to land use, for example urban development
- changes in weather patterns as a result of climate change.

Hard engineering

Hard engineering is the use of human-made structures to prevent or control flooding. These can be very expensive to install, but are often used to protect areas of high value, such as housing estates. Hard engineering schemes have a number of costs and benefits (Table 11 on page 90).

Soft engineering

Soft engineering is when natural river processes are managed to reduce flood risk. Soft engineering projects may include:

- **Afforestation** – the planting of trees to increase interception and absorption of rainwater.
- **Wetlands and flood storage** – areas of land are allowed to deliberately flood and become flood storage areas.
- **Floodplain zoning** – areas of land on the floodplain are divided up to allow certain types of land use. Land nearer the river is used for low-cost uses, such as parkland. High-cost uses, such as housing or industry, are kept further away from the river so they are protected from flooding.
- **River restoration** – returning a river to its natural state and allowing its natural features to slow down water flow, such as meanders and wetlands.

DO IT!

Categorise the causes of flooding into human and physical.

DO IT!

1 Describe the costs and benefits of two hard engineering flood management schemes.

2 Describe the costs and benefits of two soft engineering flood management schemes.

STRETCH IT!

Suggest why some people might prefer soft engineering schemes to hard engineering schemes.

	Benefits	**Costs**
Dams and reservoirs	• regulate flow of water • store water • allow for slow release of rainfall • multi-functional (hydroelectric power (HEP), recreation, irrigation)	• very expensive • flood large areas of land permanently • people moved from their homes
Channel straightening	• speeds up the flow of water • protects the vulnerable area next to the channel	• increases flood risk downstream • silt can build up in concrete channels • concrete channels are unattractive and unnatural
Embankments	• raised river banks allow the river to hold more water during a flood • can be sustainable if dredged material is used • protect towns and cities from flooding	• high concrete walls can look unattractive
Flood relief channels	• new river channel bypasses the urban area • redirects the river away from a town during periods of heavy rain	• expensive

Table 11 The costs and benefits of hard engineering flood management schemes

CHECK IT!

1 State the three fluvial processes that occur in a river.

2 Describe three processes of erosion.

3 Describe three processes of transportation.

4 Explain how and why material is deposited.

5 Describe how a waterfall is formed.

6 Give three facts about how meanders are formed.

7 Explain how floodplains are formed.

8 Explain how levées are formed.

9 Give two human and two physical factors that increase the risk of flooding.

10 a Explain the difference between hard and soft engineering.

b Give an example of each.

11 Explain how human and physical processes interacted to produce flooding around the River Severn in 2007.

1 Name three types of mass movement.

2 Name two coastal landforms created by deposition.

3 Describe the process of freeze-thaw weathering.

4 Describe two processes of fluvial erosion.

5 Describe the difference between hard and soft engineering.

6 Describe the differences in the effects on a shingle beach of constructive and destructive waves.

7 Describe how groynes reduce the effects of longshore drift.

8 Describe how a river changes from source to mouth.

9 Explain why stacks are more likely to form in sedimentary rocks such as chalk, than in igneous rocks such as granite.

10 Explain how a waterfall is formed.

11 Explain the human and physical factors that increase the risk of a flood.

5 The UK's evolving human landscape

5.1 Changing people and places

THE EXAMINATION!

- This section is tested in Paper 2 Section B.
- You must know Changing people and places and Accessible rural areas, and have completed one case study of how a major UK city is changing.

OUTCOMES

By the end of my revision I will be able to:

- Explain the key elements of the human landscape in the UK, including differences between urban and rural areas.
- Explain how population changes and globalisation are affecting the UK.

Comparing areas in the UK

Population density (see Figure 1): the urban core has a high population density with over 200 people per km² compared to low rural population density of 1–100 people per km².

Age structure (see Figure 2): urban core areas have a larger number of young adults, whereas rural populations tend to be older.

Economic activities: there is a large range of tertiary jobs in urban areas, including retail, offices, corporate headquarters, public and leisure services. In rural areas, there are jobs in primary industries such as farming, fishing and forestry and tertiary jobs in tourism.

Settlements: in urban core areas there are large settlements, with cities, towns and some conurbations. In rural areas there are smaller market towns and villages, plus isolated farmhouses.

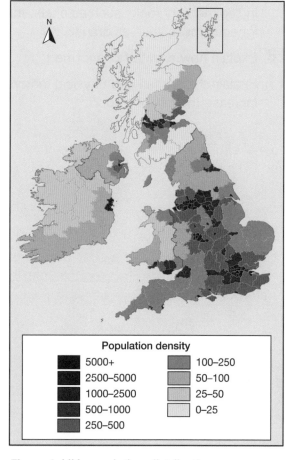

Population density

5000+	100–250
2500–5000	50–100
1000–2500	25–50
500–1000	0–25
250–500	

Figure 1 UK population distribution

DO IT!

1 Using Figure 1, describe the population distribution in the UK.

2 Using Figure 2, compare the population pyramids for London and Cornwall.

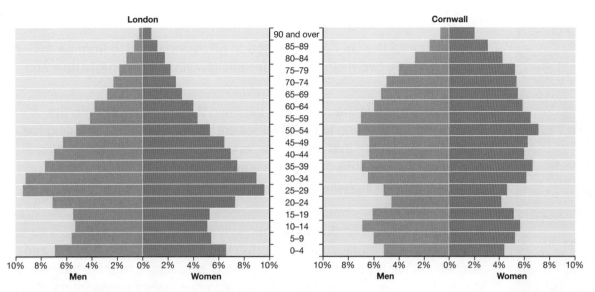

Figure 2 Population structures of London and Cornwall

Regional disparities

The rural periphery is the area furthest away from the urban core. The features of the rural periphery are:

- **Lower population density**: you get fewer people living on more dispersed settlements the further you get from the urban core.

- **Older populations**: young people move out of rural areas in search of work in the urban core and older people move in to rural areas for retirement.

- **Lower incomes**: many of the jobs are in farming or tourism and have much lower incomes.

- **Higher transport costs**: people have little access to public transport (which tends to cost more) and so they have to rely on cars and travel longer distances to shops and services.

Reducing the disparities

To make rural peripheral areas more attractive to investors, the government and EU have used incentives to attract business.

1 **Enterprise zones**: the government gives incentives to businesses such as help with start-up costs and tax incentives. However, these tend to be given to peripheral urban areas rather than peripheral areas where they are most needed.

2 **Regional development grants**: small funding grants are given to help new start-up companies with advice and support.

3 **EU grants**: funding is given by the EU to areas that have a GDP that is less than 75 per cent of the country average (for example, Cornwall). As the UK exits the EU, it is assumed that EU grants will cease.

4 **Improvements to transport**: investment is made to help make some rural areas more accessible (for example, new road and rail links in Scotland).

DO IT!

1 Give three ways in which the rural periphery is disadvantaged compared to the urban core.

2 Explain how the government has helped areas of the UK like Cornwall attract investment.

The UK's changing population

The population of the UK had increased to 65 million by 2015 from 54 million in 1965. There are two main reasons for this growth: net immigration and rising birth rate.

- **Net immigration** is the difference between those who move into the country and those who leave. Over recent years, the number arriving has been almost double that of those who leave. International immigration has increased because of free movement around EU member states, and globalisation has increased the demand for workers in the knowledge economy.

- **Birth rates** have risen due to women in their twenties having babies earlier (due to a lack of employment opportunities following the recession), and women in their thirties and forties having babies later (because they have delayed for careers). The birth rate has also risen due to immigrants of child-bearing age having larger families.

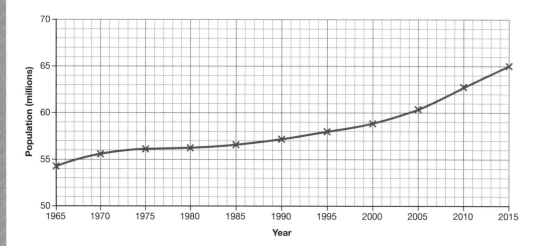

Figure 3 Data for the UK population

Impacts of immigration in the UK

Positive impacts	Negative impacts
• Increased multiculturalism and cultural awareness	• Increases population density in urban areas
• Immigrants fill gaps in the job market	• Increases pressure on services such as schools and health services
• Balances out the UK's ageing population	• Some believe immigrants take the jobs of British-born workers
• Immigrants pay taxes to the UK government	

Table 1 Impacts of immigration in the UK

DO IT!

1 Draw a line graph to show the changes in population.

2 Describe the growth in UK population.

3 Explain two reasons for the changes in population.

DO IT!

Explain how immigration has had a range of positive and negative impacts on the UK.

The UK's changing economy

The economic structure of the UK has changed over the last 50 years, with varying differences across the country.

Example

An area of economic decline: North-East England

North-East England used to be dominated by primary and secondary industries, with coal mining, ship building and the iron and steel industries employing large numbers of people. From 1950 to 1990, 127 coal mines were closed as the coal seams were exhausted. Also, competition from cheaper manufactured goods and ships from abroad meant a decline in secondary employment from 40 to 10 per cent. Most employment in the area is now in the chemical industry, car manufacturing and tourism. The public sector (government) accounts for 22 per cent of employment – the largest share of employment roles in the region.

Example

An area of economic growth: South-East England

The growth areas of the economy are in the knowledge economy in London (in areas like law and finance), and in engineering and electronics along the M4 corridor. This means the South-East has had very low levels of unemployment at around 6 per cent. Businesses actively choose to locate in the regions in and around London. This is because the area is accessible with good transport links, including a network of motorways and railways and four airports. The area has highly skilled and university-educated graduates to work in the hi-tech and finance industries. London is the centre of political and government decision making. The government has also encouraged hi-tech firms to locate along the M4 corridor and in other places around the South-East.

DO IT!

Give three comparative sentences that describe the differences between the economic activity in North-East and South-East England.

Impacts of globalisation

Globalisation is the term used to describe increased connectivity, communication and trade between countries. Globalisation depends on three key elements:

- **Networks** – trade blocs that link countries together.
- **Flows** – of goods, services, people and raw materials between countries.
- **Global players** – the organisations and people that have the most influence on the global economy.

Globalisation has been possible for a number of reasons.

- **Free trade**: trade without tariffs or taxes on imports. For example, as part of the EU, the UK was able to trade freely around Europe.

DO**IT!**

Draw a mind map that shows the reasons for globalisation.

- **Foreign direct investment (FDI)**: the flows of capital (money) from one country to another. For example, UK companies can invest in many other countries with few or no restrictions. Other countries can also invest in the UK without restrictions. This has helped the UK economy grow, especially the financial and technology sectors.

- **Transnational companies (TNCs)**: large companies that operate in more than one country. They are powerful players in the global economy and involve a range of industries, from cars to electronics to food. TNCs have set up UK branches, providing jobs and supporting the UK economy.

- **Privatisation**: the change of ownership from being run by the public sector (the government) to the private sector (owned by shareholders or private individuals). Many UK industries have been privatised, such as electricity, water and the postal service.

Figure 4 Flows of investment into the UK, showing projects and jobs created in the UK from different regions of the world

CHECK**IT!**

1 Describe the differences between 'urban core' and 'rural periphery'.

2 Explain two ways in which the UK government has attempted to reduce regional differences in the UK.

3 State two reasons why the birth rate in the UK has increased in recent years.

4 Explain why the secondary sector has declined in the UK.

5 Explain what is meant by the term 'knowledge economy' and why it has grown in the UK.

6 Assess the importance of globalisation to the changes to the UK economy.

5.2 Case study of a major UK city

OUTCOMES

By the end of my revision I will be able to:

- Describe how a major city in the UK is changing.
- Explain how employment, services and the movement of people affect the city.
- Analyse how the changing city creates challenges and opportunities, and how different strategies can be used to improve life in the city.

You may have studied any UK major city, such as London or Birmingham.

Your case study should include:

- Facts about location, site and situation.
- The structure of the city.
- The population of the city, including migration into and out of the city.
- The inequalities between different parts of the city.
- The challenges facing cities in terms of decline and growth.
- Regeneration and rebranding of areas of the city.
- How the city can be made more sustainable.
- The relationship between the city and rural areas.

Case study

London: A changing city

London's site and situation

Site: London's site was chosen for the River Thames where it was still shallow enough to cross, allowing a way to travel and trade. The river also acted as a supply of water. The land was flat for building and fertile for growing crops. The eastern area was deep enough to become a port for ships.

NAILIT!

Site and situation

Make sure you understand the difference between site and situation. **Site** is the geographical location. A city's **situation** includes the reasons a place develops and its location relative to the surrounding area.

DO IT!

Give three benefits of London's connectivity with other places.

Situation: London was closer to Europe than the country's other major cities, and, as it had a port, it was able to trade easily. London's location in the international time zones means it is central – Asia is 5–7 hours ahead and the USA 5–8 hours behind – which is beneficial in terms of the financial markets. As the capital city of the UK, London has increased prominence globally compared to other cities in the UK.

London is important for its connectivity with other places around the country and the rest of the world.

- Heathrow airport is one of the biggest and busiest airports in the world and is a major hub for world travellers. The Eurostar train service connects to other major cities in Europe.

- London is a central point for many motorways: most major motorways lead out from the M25 orbital motorway surrounding London. Many major railway lines travel out from London, with fast services to most other major cities within the UK.

Figure 5 London's connectivity

SNAP IT!

Snap an image of the map in Figure 5. Use an online mapping or travel service to calculate the distance and times taken to travel from London to other major UK cities.

London's structure

Figure 6 London's structure

Figure 7 CBD, inner city and suburbs

As you travel through a city, you will see there is a structure and a particular arrangement of buildings from the centre radiating outwards. Each zone of the city has a distinct land use, ranging from retail and offices in the Central Business District (CBD), to industrial and terraced housing in the inner city and to more spacious residential zones in the suburbs. The land is more expensive in the CBD, which is why there is a higher density of taller buildings.

	CBD	Inner city	Suburbs
Age of buildings	Oldest part of the city	Some old terraced housing and factories from late 19th century Some new modern buildings	Newer buildings: many late 20th century
Density of buildings	Highest density of the city	High density	Lower density
Land value	Most expensive	Middle value	Lowest value
Land use	Offices, retail, commercial, financial, government and leisure and entertainment	Residential: mix of terraced housing, converted industrial buildings, apartment blocks Some industrial buildings	Residential with bigger detached and semi-detached houses Some out-of-town shopping centres or industrial parks
Environmental quality	Crowded and polluted due to traffic congestion Large urban parks	Some polluted and derelict areas Some newly regenerated areas and parks where the environment is cleaner	Houses have gardens and there may be less traffic congestion, so the air quality is better

Table 2 Features of London's CBD, inner city and suburbs

Give two characteristics of each of:

1 the CBD

2 the inner city

3 the suburbs

Figure 8 Aerial photo of a city

SNAPIT!

Snap an image of Figure 8 and use it to remind yourself of the different features and land uses of the city.

Migration in London

Migration is causing London's population to grow faster than at any other time. Between 2000 and 2013, 1.9 million people settled in London from abroad.

There are two different types of migration that are causing this growth:

- **internal migration**: young people between 21–35 years old who are recent graduates, moving from other parts of the country in search of better job opportunities and the London lifestyle.

- **international immigration** from two groups:

  - **Skilled workers** who come to London to take up well-paid jobs in the knowledge economy or skilled jobs in professions where there are shortages of UK-born workers. These migrants are usually White, qualified professionals from the EU, Australia and USA.

  - **Unskilled workers** who work in jobs that are unattractive to UK workers (for example, because they have unsociable hours): for example, bin collectors, childcare workers, construction workers and restaurant or hotel staff. Many of these workers come from the EU, India and Pakistan.

Migration and ethnic communities

Immigrants tend to cluster in similar areas within London, usually in areas in the inner city where rents may be cheaper. They also cluster in order to continue with cultural traditions and customs and access specialist services and shops, such as places of worship. They are also able to work together as a community against any discrimination.

Different boroughs have different experiences of migrants within their communities.

- Newham is a low-income borough and has a high rate of ethnic diversity, with 39 per cent of the population from an Asian background and 26 per cent from a Black ethnic background. Houses are mostly rented. There are high rates of poverty and there is increased pressure on local services, especially schools and social services.

- Richmond is a high-income borough, with higher than average incomes. As a result, home ownership is high, as is the cost of housing. Here, 85 per cent of the population is White with only 7 per cent being from an Asian background.

DO IT!

Using Figure 9, describe the pattern of ethnic group distribution across London.

Give three problems that ethnic group distribution can bring.

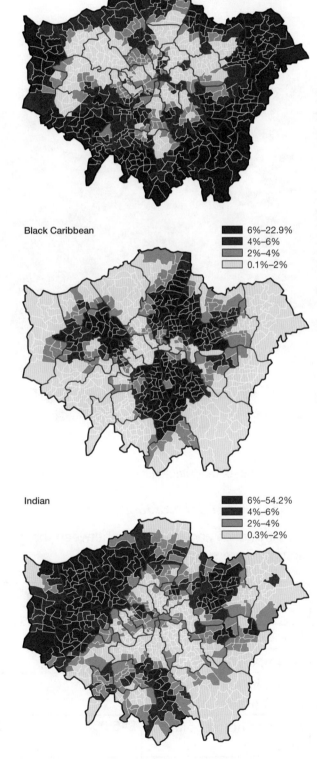

White British

- 75%–94.8%
- 60%–75%
- 50%–60%
- 8.7%–50%

Black Caribbean

- 6%–22.9%
- 4%–6%
- 2%–4%
- 0.1%–2%

Indian

- 6%–54.2%
- 4%–6%
- 2%–4%
- 0.3%–2%

Figure 9 Map showing ethnic clustering in London

Describe the pattern of multiple deprivation in London.

London's inequalities

Deprivation is a lack of wealth and services, with low standards of living caused by low incomes, poor health and low educational qualifications.

Over two million people in London are classed as living in poverty: this is nearly 30 per cent of the total population of London! This is because of the huge disparities in income between the richest and poorest people in London.

Key

Area decile

1 (Most deprived)
2
3
4
5
6
7
8
9
10 (Least deprived)

0   5   10 km

Figure 10 Index of Multiple Deprivation in London

Comparing London boroughs

Key similarities and differences between the boroughs of Newham and Richmond are summarised in Table 3.

How do the following show the level of deprivation of places?

- Income
- Education
- Health

	Richmond upon Thames	Newham
Life expectancy	83 years	77 years
Unemployment	3.8%	8.5%
% pupils achieving 5A*–C grades at GCSE	70%	57%
Average household income	£46 000	£28 000

Table 3 Similarities and differences between Newham and Richmond

In deprived areas of London, low income levels mean there are more disadvantaged children on free school meals. In wealthier areas, more people are likely to go to university and get better paid and skilled jobs. More people in low income areas have long-term health problems, due to lifestyle choices, smoking and drinking alcohol, poor diet and poor living conditions.

Areas facing decline

Parts of London have faced decline for three reasons: de-industrialisation, suburbanisation and decentralisation (Table 4).

Reason	What happened?	Example(s)
De-industrialisation	Industries closed down as there was a decline in manufacturing or heavy industry. The closures caused high unemployment and communities of people to move out of the area to find work, resulting in depopulation.	The London Docklands area in East London (the port closed due to container ships being too big to navigate up the Thames).
Suburbanisation	People moved out of the inner city to the outer suburbs causing further depopulation. In the suburbs the houses were bigger, with gardens and more open space. This was made possible due to improvements in transport to allow people to travel back into the city for work.	People left the inner-city areas of London, such as Camden and Hammersmith, for suburbs like Twickenham and Bromley or beyond to the home counties in towns such as Guildford and Reading. This was due to the development of the underground and electric trains.
Decentralisation	Business and retail moved out of the city centre to places where they had more space. Out-of-town shopping centres and business parks were built in the urban–rural fringe where they could attract customers and employees who could get there easily by car or public transport.	The Bluewater shopping centre in Kent near the M25. Stockley Park business park near the M25 and M4. Heathrow airport.

Table 4 Reasons for decline

DO IT!

Explain why transport and accessibility led to:

- Suburbanisation
- Decentralisation

Figure 11 The Bluewater shopping centre

DO IT!

1 Look at Figure 11. Give three reasons why this location was chosen for Bluewater shopping centre.

2 Explain the impact out-of-town shopping centres could have on the city centre shops.

Regeneration of the city

Re-urbanisation is the regrowth of a city as people move back into the city. This has happened in London for a number of reasons (Figure 12).

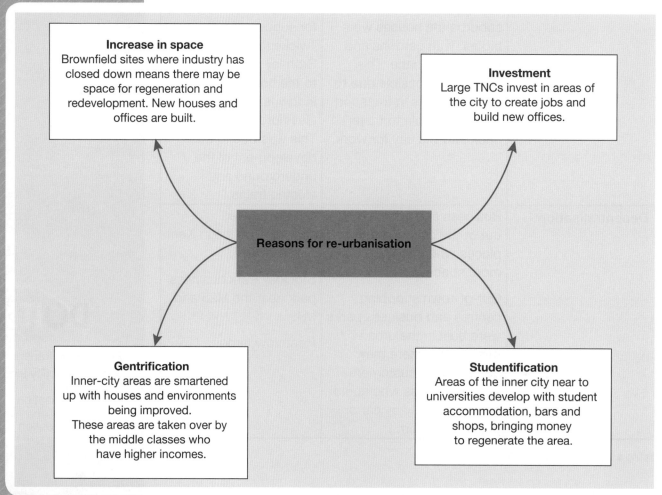

Increase in space
Brownfield sites where industry has closed down means there may be space for regeneration and redevelopment. New houses and offices are built.

Investment
Large TNCs invest in areas of the city to create jobs and build new offices.

Reasons for re-urbanisation

Gentrification
Inner-city areas are smartened up with houses and environments being improved.
These areas are taken over by the middle classes who have higher incomes.

Studentification
Areas of the inner city near to universities develop with student accommodation, bars and shops, bringing money to regenerate the area.

Figure 12 Reasons for re-urbanisation

The London Olympic Park regeneration

The Queen Elizabeth Olympic Park in East London is an example of a regeneration project, where an old industrial area is redeveloped and improved. It is also a good example of how a place can be rebranded – where the image of a place is changed.

Figure 13 Before and after pictures of the Olympic Park

The site for the Olympic Park was chosen as it was an area that had suffered from de-industrialisation and depopulation for many years. The environment was poor and pollution levels were high; buildings had been left derelict and the land was toxic with chemicals.

The area improvements include:

- Leisure facilities from the Olympic games: the swimming pool, velodrome and stadium are all used by local people.

- The environment by the river, which was cleaned and is now an area of park land and a nature reserve.

- New offices, housing and tourist facilities that replaced the old derelict buildings.

- Transport facilties including extensions to the Jubilee Line (London underground) and bus routes; Stratford railway station became an international terminal for the Eurostar.

- Westfield shopping centre built in nearby Stratford to make it a destination for shopping.

These changes have attracted young people back into inner city London because the area now has an image as a desirable place to live. However, the Olympic development has also had some negative impacts.

- The new housing is too expensive for the original residents, who have had to move out of the area.

- The jobs in the shopping centre and leisure industry are low-paid and lower-skilled, so people find it hard to afford to live there.

- Costs of living in London are high and continually increasing.

NAILIT!

Make sure that you understand what **sustainable** means: meeting the needs of people now and in the future, without damaging the environment.

Sustainable cities

Cities face a number of problems and challenges that can affect the environment and people's quality of life. City governments have tried to come up with solutions that are sustainable.

Problem	Sustainable solutions in London	Measures of success or failure
Transport Pollution and congestion from increased numbers of vehicles on the road.	• Congestion charge, where drivers have to pay to enter central London from Monday to Friday. • Hybrid buses that are cleaner and more fuel-efficient. • Over 4000 electric charging points for electric cars.	• A 6% increase in the numbers of bus passengers. • Electricity generation still produces some carbon dioxide. • Not many people have an electric car.
Housing High demand for houses leading to increased prices, so little affordable housing.	• Some housing developments that have up to 50% designated as affordable housing. • The 'First Steps' scheme designed to help low-income workers buy a proportion of a property.	• Many properties still too expensive and beyond the budgets of many low-income workers.
Employment	• Businesses offering more flexible working hours to avoid rush hour congestion. • People encouraged to work from home, taking advantage of e-mail and internet technology.	• Numbers of home workers increased from 4.3% to 8.6%. • Only possible in certain types of business and not many companies have agreed to flexible working time.
Energy High levels of air pollution in cities due to the number of houses, buildings and cars so need to reduce energy consumption.	• All new housing developments built with energy-efficiency in mind. • 'BedZed' properties in Sutton use 80% less energy for heating and 50% less water; all homes have insulation and car sharing and cycling are encouraged. • Solar panels on roofs generate electricity for individual houses.	• Not enough schemes like this to make a difference. • Solar panels still expensive, even with subsidies.

Green spaces	• More green spaces and parks needed to provide areas for recreation and improve quality of life.	• More green space being used up to meet housing shortages, building on farmland and green belt land.
Waste Large city with a high population density means a lot of waste and rubbish to be disposed of.	• Plans to reduce the amount of waste produced. • Recycling bins all over the city. • Household recycling schemes set up by local councils.	• Recycling targets still quite low. • Effectiveness relies on people sorting and recycling their own waste. • Some schemes are complicated, with different coloured bins making people unsure what can be recycled.

Table 5 Problems of sustainability and solutions in London

NAIL**IT!**

You may be asked to 'evaluate' the success of something, such as the success of strategies to make urban living more sustainable.

To do this you need to be able to offer a range of strategies, describe how they work and say if they have been successful or not. For the highest grades, think 'how far...' they have been successful. You must add a conclusion that is clearly on one side or the other, stating whether you think it has been a success or not.

CHECK**IT!**

1 State three reasons why London's site and situation are so beneficial.

2 Describe two features of each of the CBD, inner city and suburbs.

3 Explain why ethnic communities cluster together in certain areas of a city.

4 State two reasons for the differences in levels of deprivation across a city you have studied.

5 Assess the need for regeneration of an area of a city you have studied.

6 Explain two strategies for making cities more sustainable.

DOIT!

State three possible sustainable solutions.

For each one, give an advantage and a disadvantage.

5.3 Accessible rural areas

OUTCOMES

By the end of my revision I will be able to:

- Explain the relationship between cities and rural areas.
- Describe challenges facing rural areas and discuss solutions.

Relationship between rural and urban areas

Rural areas have also experienced economic and social changes, especially if they are accessible to London.

 Example

Exeter

Exeter is an example of a city that is growing economically, despite being located 170 miles from London. This is due to an increase in the number of 'footloose' industries, especially in IT. Footloose industries are not tied to any particular location, so can locate anywhere there is a suitably educated workforce.

Exeter has the advantages of:

- Cheaper rents compared to London.
- An airport with daily flights to London and other cities across the UK and Europe.
- Regular, fast train services every day to London.
- Road access to the rest of the UK via the M5 motorway.

Although it has benefits, economic growth also brings a number of challenges to rural areas, particularly because it means an increase in the number of people moving there. The attractive scenery and cleaner air makes rural locations popular places both for families and for retired people. The challenges population growth brings include:

- An increased demand for housing, which causes house prices to rise and may include a need to build on greenfield sites.
- A lack of affordable housing for people on lower incomes.
- Increased pressure on services such as education and health care.
- Increased pressure on roads and rail services, both for the local population and for extra visitors, during peak times for tourism.

DO IT!

Draw a quick sketch map showing the location of Exeter.

Annotate it to show the advantages of the location and explain how each advantage has helped boost the economy of Exeter.

You could repeat this task for a rural area that you have studied.

Rural challenges

Rural areas that are a long way from urban centres face a number of challenges, especially with employment, housing and access to services.

 Case study

Cornwall

Cornwall is the most south-westerly county in England and is very popular as a tourist destination. However, life in Cornwall can be difficult.

Employment

Traditional sources of primary employment in Cornwall have declined.

- **Farming**: due to supermarkets cutting the price for milk, many dairy farmers have sold their business to larger companies and there are now 60 per cent fewer dairy farms in Cornwall.

- **Fishing**: EU fishing quotas and overfishing have meant a shortage of fish stocks, causing many fishermen in Cornwall to struggle to make a living.

- **China clay quarrying**: due to competition from cheaper china clay from abroad, many quarries have closed and jobs have been lost.

Most jobs in Cornwall are now in tourism. However, these jobs are low-paid and seasonal. Wages in Cornwall are the lowest in the country (about £320 per week compared to a UK average of £400 per week).

It is hard to attract new businesses to Cornwall for two main reasons:

1 **Accessibility** – Cornwall has no motorways and one main railway line. This means it takes a long time to get to Cornwall and even longer to travel across the whole county.

2 **Lack of large settlements** – there are no big towns in Cornwall, meaning no large population centres with potential employees. Many young people leave Cornwall in search of jobs elsewhere, to find more opportunities.

Figure 14 Map of Cornwall (roads and main towns)

Access to services

Cornwall is one of the most deprived counties in the UK in terms of access to services.

Health

Few villages now have their own doctors' surgeries, despite there being many elderly residents. There is only one major hospital in the county, in Truro, which is a long way from most people, so it can take a long time to reach hospital in an emergency.

Education

Many teenagers have to travel a long way to school by bus. Getting to sixth form college is even more difficult, with many students having to travel up to 30 miles on expensive bus services.

Public transport

Only 70 per cent of villages have a bus service and these may only run a couple of times per day. This makes it difficult for people without access to cars. Narrow country lanes make bus travel slow and difficult.

Solutions to rural challenges

In rural areas, solutions have had to be developed that can improve employment opportunities. In Cornwall they have tried to boost tourism by developing new attractions.

The Eden Project

Figure 15 The Eden Project

The Eden Project opened in 2001 in an old disused china clay quarry just outside St Austell. The aim was to create an all-weather, indoor and outdoor tourist attraction that was also environmentally sustainable.

Inside the two domes, or biomes, are tropical rainforest and Mediterranean plant displays. As well as plants, there are also cafés, a large shop selling local products, a zip wire ride and summer music concerts.

The Eden Project has been able to employ 700 people, many in all-year roles. There has also been a 'knock-on' effect, generating other jobs in the local area to provide accommodation, pubs and other attractions for tourists. Overall, the Eden Project is estimated to have made £1 billion for the local economy, as 13 million people visited in its first 10 years.

However, there are traffic problems in the local area because people still mostly travel to the Eden project by car, rather than using cycle paths or public transport. Also, visitor numbers are falling and there don't seem to be many repeat visits: once people have been, they don't usually visit again.

Farm diversification

As farmers' incomes have fallen, they have had to find new ways to generate income. They have done this through farm diversification.

1 **Tourist accommodation**
   Many farmers have converted old barns into tourist accommodation, making attractive holiday cottages in a farm environment. Others have used fields as campsites, building toilet and shower blocks and sometimes swimming pools and children's playgrounds. However, converting barns can remove potential nest sites for some species of birds.

2 **Farm shops**
   Some farmers sell produce directly from the farm, such as meat, vegetables, milk and eggs. They also sell locally produced food and crafts, which helps the suppliers in the local area. Some farm shops have benefited from EU funding: for example, Lobbs Farm received £200 000 to set up their shop. This shop now employs twelve people and has an annual turnover of £700 000.

DO IT!

1 Explain why employment levels and wages are low in Cornwall.

2 Give two reasons why there is poor access to services in rural areas.

DO IT!

For each solution to rural challenges described in the text, draw up a list of advantages and disadvantages of each scheme.

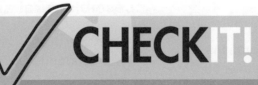
CHECK IT!

1 Explain how economic change has affected rural areas.

2 Describe two similarities and two differences between the effects of economic change on urban and rural areas.

3 Assess the need for diversification to improve the quality of life in rural areas.

The UK's evolving human landscape

Changing people and places

1 Define the term 'population density'.

2 Describe the distribution of the population in the UK.

3 Explain why the population density varies across the UK.

4 Give three problems in the rural periphery.

5 Explain two government solutions to encourage development in the rural periphery.

6 Explain two reasons for the recent growth in the UK population.

7 Define the term 'de-industrialisation'.

8 Describe how the economy of the North-East of England has changed.

9 Explain why the South-East of England has experienced economic growth.

10 Compare the economies of two contrasting regions of the UK.

11 Define the term 'globalisation'.

12 Explain how transnational corporations (TNCs) and Foreign Direct Investment (FDI) have affected the UK economy.

Case study of a major UK city

1 Describe the site and situation of a major UK city that you have studied.

2 Explain why connectivity is important in the development and growth of cities.

3 Give two features for each of the Central Business District, the inner city and the suburbs.

4 Give two reasons why people want to migrate to a major UK city you have studied.

5 Describe the impacts of international migration on a city.

6 Explain what the Index of Multiple Deprivation is.

7 Compare two areas of a city you have studied in terms of income, education, health and housing.

8 Define the following terms: suburbanisation, decentralisation and re-urbanisation.

Accessible rural areas

1 Compare the site and situation for Exeter and London.

2 Describe the challenges economic growth brings to rural areas.

3 Compare the access to services available in London with those of Cornwall.

4 Explain the meaning of 'diversification', using examples from a rural area of the UK.

6 Geographical investigations

OUTCOMES

By the end of my revision I will be able to:

- Recall the two fieldwork enquiry questions that I investigated during my GCSE Geography course.
- Understand the process of geographical enquiry.
- Select, measure and record fieldwork data.
- Use a wide range of geographical skills to process and present fieldwork data.
- Draw conclusions from fieldwork data.
- Understand how to answer questions using different command words.

Introduction

You will have carried out two geographical enquiries during your GCSE Geography course that will have included the collection of primary data as part of a fieldwork exercise. The two enquiries will have been based on the physical and human geography elements that you have studied. They will have involved you investigating a geographical question, for which you will have collected a range of fieldwork data and secondary data to help you answer the question.

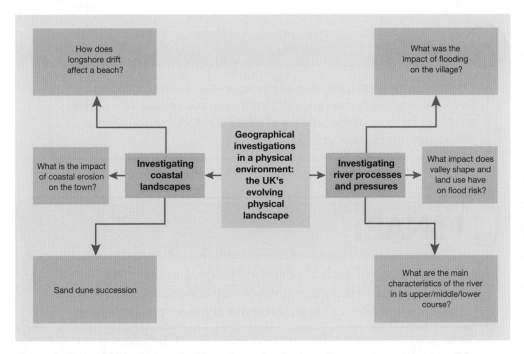

Figure 1 Geographical investigations in a physical environment – some possible areas of enquiry

THE EXAMINATION!

- This section is tested in Paper 2 Section C1 (Fieldwork in a physical environment) and C2 (Fieldwork in a human environment).

NAIL IT!

Geographical investigation

Remember that this is the process of finding the answer to a geographical question or hypothesis.

DO IT!

Look at Figure 1. Identify the geographical investigation that you carried out in a physical environment, and which topic it relates to: either 'Investigating coastal landscapes' or 'Investigating river processes and pressures'. You must recall the title of your investigation in the examination.

STRETCHIT!

Complete a mind map showing all the ways in which you collected fieldwork data in a physical environment to help you answer your enquiry question. Try to recall the process of data collection that you went through and record how you did it.

DOIT!

Look at Figure 2. Identify the geographical investigation that you carried out in a human environment, and which topic it relates to. Make sure that you know the title of your geographical investigation as you must recall this in the examination.

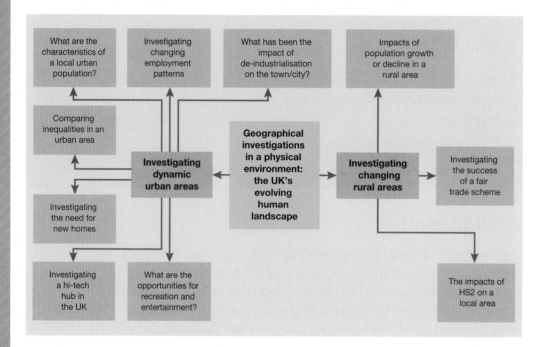

Figure 2 Geographical investigations in a human environment – some possible areas of enquiry

STRETCHIT!

Complete a mind map showing all the ways in which you collected fieldwork data in a human environment to help you answer your enquiry question. Try to recall the process of data collection that you went through and record how you did it.

SNAPIT!

Snap an image of each of your mind maps. Discuss these with a friend, describing the ways in which you collected your fieldwork data in both a physical environment and a human environment.

How to revise for Paper 2 Section C

Revision and preparation for the fieldwork questions in Section C of Paper 2 will be different from that needed for Sections A and B. You will be expected to answer two questions: one question in Section C1 Fieldwork in a physical environment (either 'Investigating coastal landscapes' or 'Investigating river processes and pressures') and one question in Section C2 Fieldwork in a human environment (either 'Investigating dynamic urban areas' or 'Investigating changing rural areas'). Each question has two parts:

- questions on the use of fieldwork materials from an unfamiliar context

- questions on the geographical investigation that you carried out.

In the fieldwork section of the examination you will need to know the **techniques** that can be used to collect geographical data through fieldwork and the **methods** that can be used to present geographical data. You will also be expected to interpret and explain maps, diagrams and geographical data. Your main revision of knowledge and understanding for Paper 2 will be completed when you revise the topics within 'The UK's evolving physical landscape' and 'The UK's evolving human landscape'.

What you need to concentrate on is:

- your ability to answer the style of questions that appear in section C focusing on geographical investigations

- becoming familiar with the process of geographical investigation

- making sure that you can explain and interpret a range of geographical data to reach conclusions.

The Edexcel GCSE Geography Exam Practice Book that accompanies this Revision Guide provides a set of questions based on the geographical investigations section, to help you become familiar with the revision process.

DO IT!

Look back at the two geographical investigations that you completed during your GCSE geography course. Make sure that you include time in your revision schedule to focus on these and practise your geographical skills.

The process of investigation

There are six strands of geographical investigation that you can be asked about in the examination. The questions could relate to either of the geographical investigations that you carried out, or to data from unfamiliar investigations included in the question paper. It is important that you understand each of the six strands clearly so that you know which aspect of the fieldwork you are being tested on. Here are the six strands.

1 Questions investigated through fieldwork

This is the selection of a suitable geographical question that you can set out to answer. You will need to know the titles of the two geographical investigations that you carried out, in both a physical environment and a human environment, as you need to write these out as part of the examination. You also need to be able to justify **why** it is a suitable investigation and **how** each question relates to an area of geography that you have studied as part of the GCSE course. Finally, it is important that you are aware of the potential **risks** of carrying out fieldwork activities and how these risks might be reduced – perhaps in the form of a simple risk assessment.

2 Measuring and recording data

There are two types of data that can be used in your geographical investigation: primary data and secondary data.

- Primary data is where you physically collect the data yourself – for example, measuring the width of a river, or counting the number of pedestrians on a street. You are expected to have carried out both **quantitative** (numerical) and **qualitative** (subjective) primary data collection.

- Secondary data is where somebody else has collected the data – this could be using data from a website or reading an article in a newspaper.

You need to be able to show that you understand how you could collect appropriate physical and human data. You also need to be able to describe and justify the actual process of how the data is collected and the sampling methods that you may have used.

3 Processing and presenting fieldwork data

For this part of the geographical investigation, you need to be aware that there is a wide range of cartographical and graphical methods that you can use to present your data, including maps, line charts, bar charts, pie charts, pictograms, histograms with equal class intervals, divided bar charts, scattergraphs and so on. You will need to be able to draw and complete maps and graphs from data provided in the examination, and be able to write about selecting appropriate data presentation methods.

4 Describing, analysing and explaining fieldwork data

A key part of your geographical investigations will be making sense of your data. This is the process of summarising the data that you have collected, then carrying out an analysis of the data, followed by some explanations of the results of the fieldwork data. You may have also carried out some statistical analysis of the data that you collected (for example, using the median or mean, or by calculating quartiles and the inter-quartile range).

5 Reaching conclusions

This is the part of the geographical investigation that is often most overlooked. It involves referring back to the original enquiry question that was set and producing a brief summary of the results of your data analysis to in order answer that question. This can often be in the form of a short paragraph that gives a concisely written response to the investigation question.

NAILIT!

Look back through the two geographical investigations you carried out. Make sure that you understand the data presentation methods you used in both. Make sure that you know why you used those methods of data presentation and that you could explain this in the examination.

NAILIT!

For both of the geographical investigations that you have worked on, make sure that you have an analysis of the results of the data that you collected and that you know what it means. It really helps to have produced a range of maps and graphs that you can refer back to in the examination. Next, draft a written conclusion to both of your investigations, so that you know the answers to the questions that are being investigated.

6 Reflecting critically

Finally, you will need to be aware of the strengths and weaknesses of your investigations and how they could be improved. There are four aspects of this section that you need to be able to evaluate:

- any problems that you may have had collecting your data
- the limitations of the data that you collected
- suggestions of any other data that you could have collected
- how reliable your conclusions were.

Your fieldwork

Work through both of the geographical investigations that you carried out and create a table to record the work you did for each of the six strands of geographical investigation. Remember that you will need to do this for **both** of your geographical investigations: one in a physical environment and one in a human environment.

The Paper 2 examination

You need to know what the examination paper will look like, so that you can be well prepared (also see the Edexcel GCSE Geography Exam Practice Book).

- Fieldwork appears as Sections C1 and C2 in Paper 2. Each section is worth 18 marks, giving a total of 36 marks plus marks for spelling, punctuation and grammar.

- The time allowed for the whole Paper 2 examination is 1 hour 30 minutes – that's 90 minutes – and there are 94 marks available (including spelling, punctuation and grammar). That means you should work to a timescale of one minute for one mark. For example, an eight-mark question should take you about eight minutes to complete.

- You must answer the questions that relate to the human physical geographical investigations you carried out (either 'Investigating coastal landscapes' or 'Investigating river processes and pressures', and either 'Investigating dynamic urban areas' or 'Investigating changing rural areas'). There will be questions that relate to fieldwork in general, as well as about the geographical investigations that you carried out.

- The types of question vary. There will be:
  - one to two mark skills questions, such as *plot*, *complete* or *calculate* on Figures provided in the examination paper
  - short-answer questions that may ask you to *describe*, *suggest* or *explain* (two to four marks)
  - one longer answer question (eight marks) that will usually ask you to make some form of assessment or judgement.

- You should have a full range of stationery ready for this examination, including a sharp pencil, a ruler and a calculator.

NAILIT!

Data response questions

You should be aware that you will need to respond to fieldwork data that is provided in the examination paper. You need to be familiar with a range of data presentation techniques and be able to both describe and explain what the data shows.

• Section A of Paper 2 covers 'The UK's evolving physical landscape' and Section B covers 'The UK's evolving human landscape', both of which are covered in previous sections of this Revision Guide.

Academic skills required

You need to be able to do the following.

- Use a range of geographical fieldwork techniques to investigate questions and issues in relation to geographical investigations.

- Use a wide range of geographical skills, such as:

  - cartographic (interpreting maps)

  - graphical (interpreting and drawing graphs)

  - numerical (e.g. using percentages)

  - statistical (e.g. calculating means)

  - qualitative data (using people's opinions)

  - quantitative data (using numerical data as facts).

- Use a well-developed academic writing style that shows an ability to interpret, analyse and evaluate information, communicate findings, justify and provide conclusions in relation to geographical investigations.

- Recognise command words and write answers that do what they say.

Raising the standard of your answers

- Follow the command word – answer the question in the way that is asked!

- Complete the fieldwork data questions as accurately as possible. Make sure that you have the right equipment to be able to do this in the exam. You may be required to do calculations as well.

- Respond to the data provided when asked. This might mean that you need to describe any patterns in the data, explain what they mean, or even suggest alternative ways of presenting the data.

- In the longer questions with more marks, you will need to answer based on the two geographical investigations that you carried out. You could be asked questions about any of the six strands of geographical investigations. For these questions, you will always be asked to state the title of your geographical investigation. You **must** use evidence from your geographical investigations and your own understanding throughout your answers.

Example eight-mark question and answers:

You have carried out your own fieldwork investigating the impact of coastal management on coastal processes and communities.

Assess the success and reliability of your data collection methods for your geographical investigation.

Give the title of your geographical investigation.   [8 marks]

STRETCH IT!

You need to be able to draw conclusions from the data that you collected for your geographical investigations. You need to be able to relate it to the question you originally set and produce a written statement that summarises your findings.

DO IT!

Without looking at the two possible student answers on the next page, write your own answer on one of your geographical investigations. In the examination you will have about 18 lines to write your response, plus two lines to write the title of the investigation, so use this to judge the length of your answer. Try to write your answer in eight minutes. Compare your answer with the two provided and make a note of what you could have done to improve it.

Student answer A

Title of geographical investigation: How does a beach change?
Throughout my fieldwork, I got some very accurate results and there was a lot of evidence to explain my results in my conclusion. The problem I had getting the results was that they were all similar to each other. This made it hard to get an average overall. If I repeated the work, I would manage my time better and not rush collecting my data on the beach. I would go back again for another day. The strength is that I collected the data accurately using the ranging poles. I could ensure that the data is more reliable if I repeated my tests more than once to make sure that they were accurate.

Feedback

Student answer A above shows a vague recollection of collecting data on a beach and some understanding of the fact that the data may have been reliable. Unfortunately, the title is too vague, there is very little reference back to the question and little explanation of the success of the investigation. It highlights the fact that you need to know all the six strands of your geographical investigation; if you don't, it is very difficult to answer these questions well.

Student answer B

Title of geographical investigation: To what extent does the beach profile at Barton-on-Sea change from west to east?
The beach profile was measured from shore to sea at ten sites 100 metres apart using ranging poles and a clinometer, and the size of the sediment was measured along the east-west transect. Overall, my data collection was relatively successful as the results allowed me to conclude that the beach profile does change along the transect because the beach becomes much steeper as you move westwards. The data collection that I carried out could have been more reliable and I would improve it in several ways. Firstly, I could have taken more accurate measurements. This would involve making sure that the ranging poles that were used to measure the beach profile were placed in the ground at the same depth each time. To do this I could use a ruler and make sure that it was the same for both ranging poles – this would have increased the accuracy and

the reliability. Secondly, due to lack of time I only took one set of readings and it would have been useful to take more readings so that I could find the average to make it more reliable. Thirdly, I should have made sure that the measurements of the sediment sizes were recorded more accurately.

Finally, I could have carried out a pilot study to identify any problems that there may have been in collecting the data and I could have researched a greater range of secondary sources to help understand the reasons why the beach profile changes.

Feedback

Student answer B focuses on the two key elements of the question: the **success** and the **reliability** of the data collection methods. Firstly, it is evident that this student knows the title of the investigation question they set out to answer. There is then a clear reference to the fact that the data collection was successful because it was possible to answer the investigation question. This is followed by a comment on the reliability of the data and how the data collection could have been improved. This answer would gain the better mark in the examination.

CHECKIT!

The exam

1 Which exam paper and section is the geographical investigations questions found in?

2 a How many minutes per mark are available in this examination?

 b Are there skills questions in this examination?

 c Name the things that you need to remember about the final examination based on your geographical investigations.

The enquiry process

1 Describe and justify the locations of your geographical investigations.

2 State the six strands of investigations that you could be examined on.

3 Explain how your geographical investigations relate to the topics you have been taught.

Academic skills required

1 Explain the method of calculating the interquartile range.

2 Describe how you would complete an isoline map.

3 Explain how you would justify data presentation methods.

Exam command words

1 Explain what is meant by the following command words:

 a *suggest*   c *explain*

 b *calculate*   d *assess*.

7 People and the biosphere

7.1 Biomes

OUTCOMES

By the end of my revision I will be able to:

- Explain the distribution and characteristics of biomes, including the examples of tropical rainforests, deserts and tundra.
- Explain ecosystems and how they are affected by local factors.

THE EXAMINATION!

- This section is tested in Paper 3 Sections A and D.
- You must know biomes, the factors influencing them and interactions within them.
- You must know that the biosphere provides resources and services, but is exploited by humans.

Distribution and characteristics of major biomes

There is a pattern of biomes (large-scale global ecosystems) largely based on distance from the equator (latitude) (see Figure 1). This pattern is modified by mountain ranges and by distance from the sea. Tropical to Mediterranean ecosystem patterns are clearest in Africa, where there is nearly a mirror image north and south of the equator. The mid-latitude to polar ecosystem pattern is clearest in the northern hemisphere because there is more land.

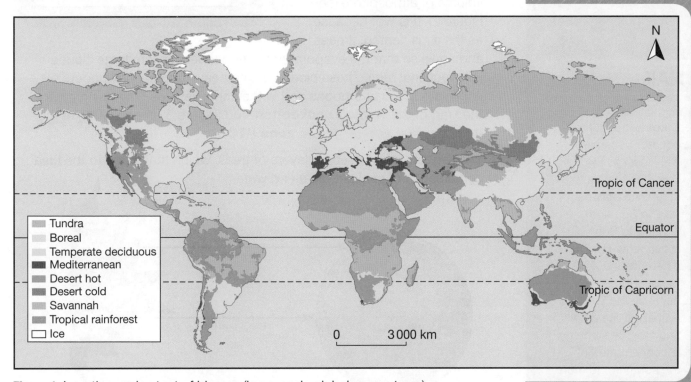

Figure 1 Location and extent of biomes (large-scale global ecosystems)

NAILIT!

Make sure that you know the difference between location and distribution. **Location** is the precise position on the Earth's surface of a geographical feature, such as a tropical rainforest, often using latitude and longitude, or place names. **Distribution** is the amount and spatial arrangement (or spread) of a geographical feature in a region or different parts of the world.

NAILIT!

Remember that it is **not** hotter at the equator because it is closer to the Sun. The distance difference between pole to Sun and equator to Sun is very tiny. The difference in temperature is because the Earth is shaped like a ball: and the Sun's energy is concentrated at the equator and more spread out at the poles (see Figure 2).

STRETCHIT!

Mountains are cooler and wetter than other areas, so ecosystems change with altitude. Warm ocean currents, such as the Gulf Stream, keep land areas warmer and wetter; cold currents keep areas drier as there is less evaporation.

Tropical rainforests

1. Tropical rainforests are located mostly between the tropic lines either side of the equator: the Tropic of Cancer in the northern hemisphere and the Tropic of Capricorn in the southern hemisphere. The largest concentrations are in South America (e.g. Brazil), West and Central Africa (e.g. Democratic Republic of Congo) and South-East Asia (e.g. Indonesia).

2. These areas are very hot and wet for most of the year, although some have a dry season. Average temperatures are between 25 and 30 °C and precipitation is between 2000 and 3000 mm a year. It is very hot because the Sun's energy is concentrated on a small surface area and in a small volume of atmosphere (see Figure 2). It is wet because, as the air is heated, it rises and cools so that the evaporated water condenses into large clouds (convectional rain). These clouds create heavy tropical downpours, especially in the afternoons and in the cool evenings. The rising air is the start of the Hadley convection cell (Figure 3 on page 122) at the intertropical convergence zone (ITCZ).

SNAPIT!

Snap an image of Figure 1 and use it to remind yourself of where the major biomes of the world are located. Think about **why** they are in these locations.

3. The vegetation is based on layers of trees, which thrive due to the ideal combination of sunlight, heat and water.

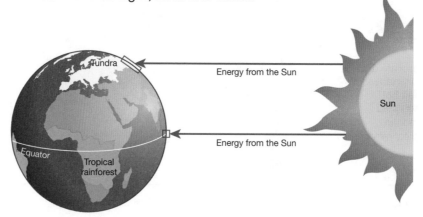

Figure 2 Differences in the concentration of energy from the Sun

Hot deserts

① Hot deserts are found either side of the Tropic of Cancer and Tropic of Capricorn where it is hot and dry (over 30 °C, with less than 250 mm rainfall a year – see Figures 2 and 3). At night, temperatures drop dramatically as there are no clouds to trap the heat of the day. This creates a large diurnal temperature range.

② Hot deserts are found where air sinks on a large scale as part of the global atmospheric circulation, such as the Sahara and Kalahari deserts in Africa. This occurs where the air in the Hadley convection cell moves from high altitude to ground level. This air is dry because most of its moisture was left behind near the equator (Figure 3). As the air sinks, it warms and any moisture left is in the form of water vapour, so there are few clouds. The air is also stable and without turbulence, because any humid air that exists is not lifted up to cool.

③ There are few plants because of the lack of moisture and poor soil – only ones that have adapted, often by storing water – and animals usually only come out at night.

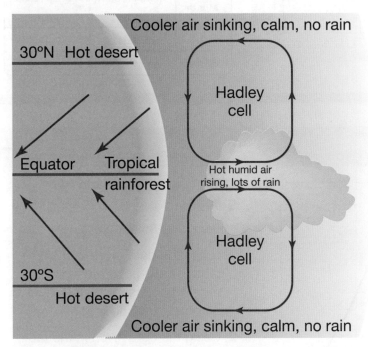

Figure 3 Links between the Hadley convection cell and tropical rainforest and hot desert ecosystem locations

Create a mnemonic to help you remember what happens in the Hadley convection cell and how it produces the location of tropical rainforests and hot deserts.

NAILIT!

Make sure that you understand that the lower layer of the Earth's atmosphere has very large convection cells. When air rises, unstable conditions are created that lead to rain. When air sinks, stable conditions are created and it is dry.

Graphical skills

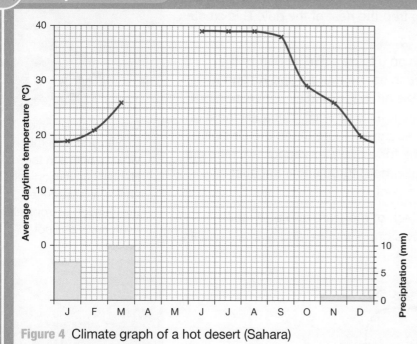

Figure 4 Climate graph of a hot desert (Sahara)

Climate graph (line and bar graph)

Make a copy of Figure 4.

1 Using the data given in the table below, accurately plot the missing points for temperature to complete the line graph.

2 Using the data given in the table below, accurately plot the missing bars for rainfall to complete the bar graph.

Month	Temperature (°C)	Precipitation (mm)
April	32	7
May	36	1

Graphical skills

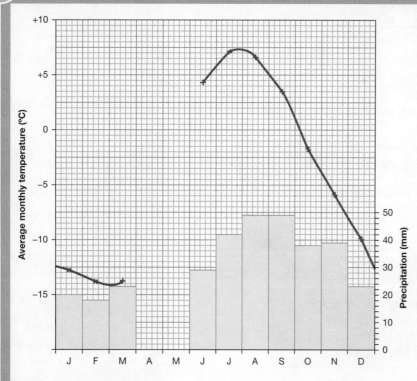

Figure 5 Climate graph for a tundra ecosystem (Greenland)

Climate graph (line and bar graph)

Make a copy of Figure 5.

1 Using the data given in the table below, accurately plot the missing points for temperature to complete the line graph.

2 Using the data given in the table below, accurately plot the missing bars for rainfall to complete the bar graph.

Month	Temperature (°C)	Precipitation (mm)
April	–7	28
May	0.2	19

Tundra

1 Tundra biomes are found in zones in and around the polar regions. There is only a small amount of tundra in the southern hemisphere because there is limited land at the correct latitude. However, there are large areas in the northern hemisphere – especially Alaska (USA), northern Canada and northern Russia along the shores of the Arctic Ocean.

2 Temperatures are below 0 °C for most of the year and peak at about 10 °C in the short summer. Precipitation is below 250 mm because evaporation rates are low and the air is stable because it is sinking. It is so cold here because the Sun's energy is spread out over a larger surface area and larger volume of atmosphere, due to the Earth being shaped like a ball (see Figure 2). Also, north of 66.5° the Sun never rises during the middle of winter.

3 There are few plants because it is so cold. Any plants grow low to the ground to avoid bitterly cold winds, and animals have adapted to the cold conditions, often with thick fur.

- **Large-scale biomes** such as tropical rainforests, hot deserts or tundra (see Figure 1). Biomes are influenced by global factors such as climate: rainfall, temperature, hours of sunshine and seasons over thousands of years.

- **Areas within biomes** are influenced by local factors such as altitude, rock type, soil characteristics and amount of water (drainage).

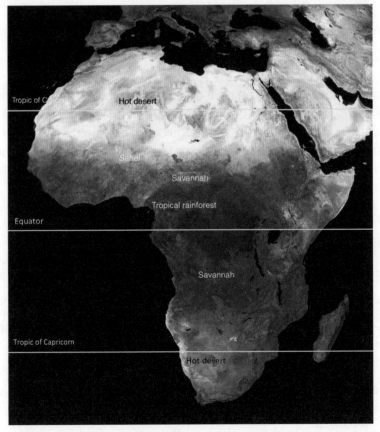

Figure 6 Composite satellite image of the continent of Africa showing biome locations through colour

DO IT!

Look at Figure 6. Close your eyes and remember the image, concentrating on the colours and the equator and tropic lines. Describe the pattern of biomes to a friend, or close your book and try drawing the pattern of biomes from memory.

Local factors

Altitude

The height of the land above sea level affects climate conditions. It is cooler, windier and usually wetter at higher altitudes. In mountainous areas, steeper slopes mean that soils are thinner. These differences create clear vegetation zones, from low altitude where growing conditions are easier, to high altitude where growing conditions are more difficult.

Rock type

Hard rocks like granite erode and weather at a slower rate, producing thinner soils. Soft rocks like clays erode and weather at a faster rate, producing deeper soils. Vegetation will usually grow better in deeper soils. Some rocks are impermeable and do not let rainwater pass through them, so water stays on or near the surface. Other rocks are permeable and allow rainwater to pass through them, so the ground may be dry and the water stored underground. Plants and animals need water for life.

Soils

Soils are a mixture of minerals from rocks, decayed vegetation (humus) and air spaces that may contain water. Plants usually grow best in soils rich in minerals and humus, with just the right amount of water. Loams are the best soils for plants, as they contain roughly equal proportions of sand, clay and silt particles: sand grains provide spaces for air and water, clay provides minerals and silt is light (which is easier for roots to penetrate). Too much sand leads to dry soils lacking minerals; too much clay and soil becomes waterlogged; and too much silt means soil can be eroded easily.

Drainage

Impermeable rocks or clay soils often cause rainwater to stay on the ground surface, sometimes causing waterlogging. However, in drier climates rivers may flow over the ground, creating areas alongside where plants can grow. Permeable rocks or sandy soils allow rainwater to move down deep into the soil or rock, and the surface becomes dry, so fewer plants grow.

Interactions within ecosystems

The parts of an ecosystem can be divided into abiotic and biotic:

- **Abiotic** means the non-living parts of an ecosystem, such as soil and water.
- **Biotic** means the living parts of an ecosystem, such as plants and animals.

The living and non-living parts of an ecosystem interact (or interrelate) through several systems, such as the nutrient cycle and water cycle. The living parts interact within a food web (made up of many interlinked food chains).

Links within an ecosystem are often in both directions. Here is one example.

- Leaves from a tree fall to the ground, decompose and add nutrients to the soil (forming humus); the tree then absorbs these nutrients (dissolved in water) through its roots.

NAILIT!

Decomposed vegetation in the soil is known as humus. This is an important source of nutrients for plants and helps to bind soil together by holding moisture.

- Plants and animals may cause biological or biochemical weathering, breaking rock or dissolving it to help create soils in which plants or creatures can live.
- Plants absorb carbon dioxide from the atmosphere and put oxygen back (photosynthesis); oxygen is used by animals, which then put carbon dioxide back into the atmosphere (respiration).

Food web and food chain

Food is the way in which energy is passed from one level of an ecosystem to the next. These levels are called trophic levels (see Figures 7 and 8).

- A **food chain** is where living things are placed in a line of what eats what (see Figure 7).
- A **food web** is where many food chains link together within an ecosystem, with certain living things being the food for several creatures (Figure 8) or one creature eating lots of things.

NAILIT!

Make sure that you can describe and explain the interactions within an ecosystem using the correct terms, such as: food chain, food web, biotic, abiotic, producer, primary and secondary consumers, photosynthesis and respiration.

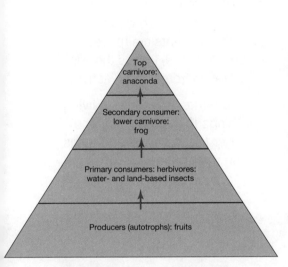

Figure 7 A tropical rainforest food chain

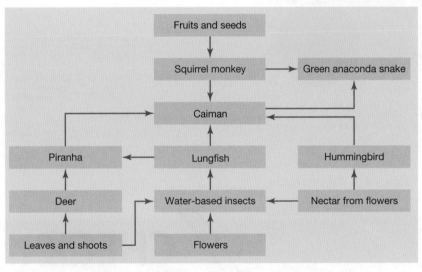

Figure 8 Part of a tropical rainforest food web

SNAP IT!

Take an image of Figure 8 and compete with a friend to see who can spot the most food chains. Think about what would happen to other parts of the ecosystem if the caiman became extinct.

DO IT!

With a friend, each create four multiple-choice questions that test understanding of the terms associated with food webs. Test your friend. Ask them to test you with their questions.

Producers, consumers and decomposers

1. Primary producers are sometimes known as autotrophs – these are plants that automatically convert sunlight, water and minerals through the process of photosynthesis into energy and starches so that they can grow.

2. Plants are the basis for all the other levels of creatures in an ecosystem, as they are the food (leaves, nectar, seeds, fruits, nuts) for consumers.

③ Consumers are either herbivores/primary consumers (creatures that eat plants), carnivores/secondary consumers (creatures that eat other creatures) or omnivores (creatures that eat both plants and animals).

④ When producers or consumers die, they accumulate on or in the ground. Here decomposers (such as bacteria or fungi) break them down into basic minerals, which become nutrients within an ecosystem.

Nutrient cycle

- Mineral nutrients accumulate in soil, dissolve in rainwater and are absorbed by plants through their roots. Some important minerals are carbon, nitrogen and phosphorus.

- Nutrients help plants to grow, and the minerals are then passed on to consumers through the food web. The cycle is completed when leaves fall to the ground to become litter, which decomposes, or waste products from animals are added to the soil along with their bodies when they die. In this way, nutrients are moved around (Figure 9) unless there is interference from human activity.

- Nutrients are stored in living things (biomass), soil and litter (dead leaves and twigs on the ground).

Add dissolved nutrients in rain

Fall of leaves, twigs, branches and trees

BIOMASS

Deforestation or harvesting by people removes nutrients from the system

LITTER

Uptake of nutrients by plants through their roots

Rain runs off ground and carries nutrients away

Decomposition (decay) of litter releases nutrients

SOIL

Bedrock is broken down by weathering into nutrients

Water washes nutrients deeper into the soil (leaching)

Figure 9 A nutrient cycle

CHECK IT!

1 Give the location of the tundra biome.

2 Describe the climate of the hot desert biome.

3 Name one South-East Asian country with a tropical rainforest biome.

4 Explain how climate has created the tropical rainforest biome.

5 For each local factor affecting biomes, describe the best conditions for plant growth.

6 Explain the role of the Hadley convection cell in influencing the location of hot deserts and tropical rainforests.

7 Explain why the tropical rainforest biome has a larger amount of living things than hot desert and tundra biomes.

8 Give an example of a biotic factor.

9 Describe two differences between a food chain and a food web.

10 Explain how plants help to balance the gases in the atmosphere.

11 Describe how nutrients are cycled through an ecosystem.

7.2 Biosphere resources and regulation

129

OUTCOMES

By the end of my revision I will be able to:

- Describe how people depend on the biosphere and how resources are being used up.
- Analyse how biosphere resources are affected by population growth, economic development and increasing wealth.

People have always depended on the biosphere for resources such as food, medicine, building materials and fuel, and for regulating services such as balancing gases in the atmosphere, keeping soils healthy and controlling movement of water. However, over time, people have taken more and more things from the biosphere (such as water, energy and minerals). Taking resources from the biosphere has often changed or damaged it.

Examples of biosphere resources include:

- Hunting of animals and gathering of fruits for food.
- Development of grasses into arable crops, such as wheat and rice for food.
- Wood for fuel and timber for building.
- Cotton for clothing.
- Biofuel crops, such as ethanol from sugar cane and *Miscanthus* grass for burning.
- Plants to create medicines, such as the periwinkle to treat leukaemia and poppies for painkillers.

Examples of biosphere services include:

- Balancing the amount of carbon dioxide and oxygen in the atmosphere. This supports plant and animal life and regulates the average temperature of the Earth – for example, by storing carbon dioxide in plants (notably trees) or the oxygen/carbon dioxide exchange in photosynthesis.
- Nutrient cycling. This keeps soils healthy by moving nutrients from dead plant litter to the soil with the help of decomposers (e.g. worms and bacteria) – see Figure 9.
- The interception and absorption of rain by trees and other vegetation. This is an important part of the hydrological cycle, which slows down the movement of fresh water back to the sea.

DO IT!

Copy and annotate Figure 10.

1 Show where there have been significant changes in the number of days taken in a year to use up the resources provided by the Earth.

2 Give the main reasons for the decline in the number of days taken.

NAIL IT!

A **biosphere resource** is something that can be used by people in their lives, at home or at work – for example, using fertile soils to grow food to eat. A **biosphere service** is something that enables people to live on the planet – for example, providing the right amount of oxygen in the air for people to breathe.

Exploitation of the biosphere

The world's population continues to increase very rapidly, more countries have industrialised and the average wealth of individuals has gone up. These factors increase the amount of resources taken from the biosphere, which disrupts the natural systems that keep everything balanced. In 2017, the Global Footprint Network estimated that the natural resources for the year had been used up by 2nd August (known as 'Earth Overshoot Day') – see Figure 10.

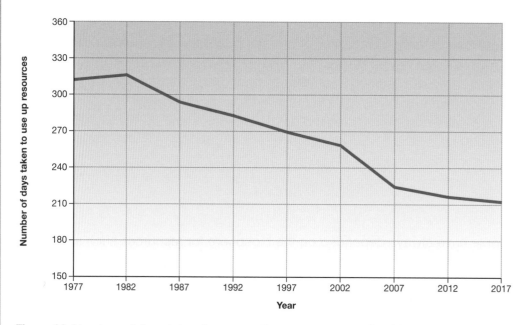

Figure 10 Number of days taken to use up the resources provided by the Earth in one year (based on 2017 data)

Trends

- **Economic development**: Emerging countries such as India, China, Mexico, Indonesia and Brazil have developed businesses and industries that have increased their energy use and consumption of other resources. Many use hydro-electric power, but this often means that large areas of natural vegetation are lost due to flooding behind a big dam. For all countries, one of the cheapest ways of getting metals or coal is open-cast mining, but this strips away all vegetation and soil layers.

- **Population growth**: A larger population leads to more biosphere resources being consumed. World population is predicted to continue growing (perhaps at a slower rate). As the population of countries has increased there has also been a demand for more living space. Much of this is around cities, so land has been cleared to build housing. Around cities of developing and emerging countries there is also removal of vegetation for firewood and clearance for farms (food supply).

- **Increased wealth**: When people have more money, they can buy and consume more biosphere products. Much of this is indirect: for example, in developing and emerging countries, plantations of a single export crop (such as palm oil) have replaced natural forests. Palm oil is used in many products from ice cream to shampoo. Another example is the demand for meat. This is one reason why fields of soya have replaced tropical rainforest, as the soya is used to feed cattle around the world.

STRETCH IT!

Humanitarian crisis in Yemen (2017)

Internal divisions, along with external military intervention and blockade, greatly reduced the resources available for people in Yemen (a developing country located in the Middle East). The civil war destroyed health, water and sanitation infrastructure, and disrupted farming. Without external food supplies, famine and malnutrition followed. In October 2016, a cholera epidemic started and by August 2017 over 2000 people were dying from the disease each month. By November 2017, 3.23 per cent of the population were infected. NGOs such as Médecins Sans Frontières helped treat the cholera with the latest medical technology and 22 cholera treatment centres.

DO IT!

Working with a friend, challenge each other to explain how one out of (a) increased wealth (b) population growth or (c) economic development leads to the use of more resources and brings forward 'Earth Overshoot Day'.

Population and resource theories

The maximum number of people that the Earth can support (carrying capacity) is uncertain. There are two theories that look at the link between population and resources. These theories help us to investigate questions such as how much food the biosphere can provide.

Malthusian theory

Malthus predicted that population growth would be faster than the growth in resource supply (Figure 11). At some point there would be a population 'crash', especially among poorer people, until a balance between resources and numbers of people was reached. The population reduction would be a result of natural factors (such as spread of disease) and human factors (such as fighting over living space and resources).

Evidence to support this theory includes worldwide epidemics (AIDS, strains of flu, Ebola virus), famines, droughts and lack of clean fresh water, civil and regional wars, and an increasing number of refugees and internally displaced people.

Boserupian theory

Boserup predicted that, as population growth takes place, the pressure of resources forces people to invent new ways of using or creating resources, increasing the carrying capacity of the Earth (Figure 11) and allowing population increase to continue. Solutions may include improvements to food production, better infrastructure (e.g. water supply systems) and more efficient use of resources.

Evidence to support this theory includes the fact there has not yet been a worldwide collapse in population. In fact, world population more than doubled between 1967 and 2017, from 3.5 billion to 7.5 billion. There have been improvements to farming around the world, including special seeds (high-yielding varieties), machinery and artificial fertilisers. Other improvements include more efficient use of energy and the recent development of 'green technologies' (e.g. the development of hybrid and electric cars), which are reducing negative impacts on the biosphere.

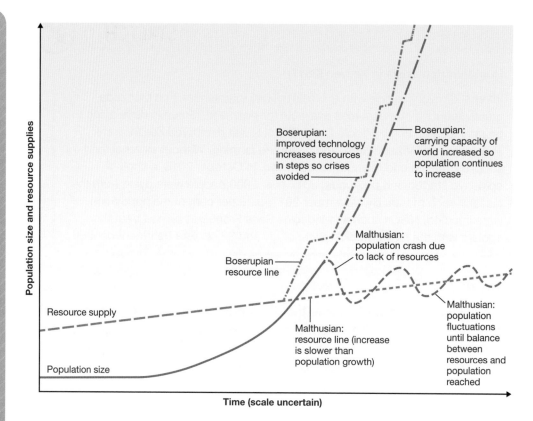

Figure 11 Graph showing the link between population and resources as predicted by Malthus and Boserup

Snap an image of Figure 11 and use it to identify the differences between the ideas of Malthus and Boserup. Think about which theory you believe to be correct. Is it possible for both of them to be correct?

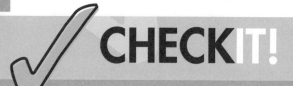

1 Identify two resources provided by the biosphere.

2 Describe one service provided by the biosphere.

3 Explain why world population growth has increased the use of biosphere resources.

4 Identify one way in which humans may directly damage the biosphere.

5 Give the definition of carrying capacity.

6 Describe the relationship between population and resource growth as suggested by the Malthusian theory.

7 Explain why Boserup believed that the carrying capacity of the world could be increased.

People and the biosphere

Biomes

1 Describe the location of the hot desert biome.

2 State two main characteristics of the tropical rainforest biome.

3 Give two examples of small-scale local factors affecting a biome.

4 a Give two reasons why contrasting biomes have developed in different parts of the world.

   b Explain the role of the Hadley convection cell in influencing the location of hot deserts and tropical rainforests.

Local factors

1 a Describe how photosynthesis helps to regulate the atmosphere.

   b Explain how nutrients are cycled within a biome.

   c Explain the role of decomposers in a nutrient cycle.

2 Explain the difference between a food chain and a food web.

Biosphere resources and regulation

1 a Give the definition of a biosphere service.

   b State two resources that people are able to get from the biosphere.

2 Explain why an increasing amount of biosphere resources have been used over the last 50 years.

3 Describe two ways in which people may change the balance within a biome by extracting resources.

4 a Give two differences between the Malthusian and Boserupian population/resource theories.

   b Assess the evidence that may be used to support the Malthusian theory.

Advice is given in more detail on how to approach the 'Making geographical decisions' questions on these topics in Chapter 10.

8 Forests under threat

8.1 Tropical rainforests

THEEXAMINATION!

- This section is tested in Paper 3 Sections B and D.

- You must know tropical rainforests and taiga biomes.

- You must know that within these biomes there are interdependence, adaptation, threats and management challenges.

OUTCOMES

By the end of my revision I will be able to:

- Explain the key features and location of the tropical rainforest biome.

- Analyse threats to the tropical rainforest biome and how to reduce them.

Introduction

A natural ecosystem develops a balance between all of its parts (**biotic** and **abiotic**) over a long period of time. In this way, biomes remain stable (change very little) unless there is a significant event to cause change. Change can be:

- **change caused by human activity**: this includes the removal of natural vegetation and the alteration of soils to create farmland (Figure 1), as well as climate change caused by emissions of greenhouse gases over the last 200 years

- **change caused by physical conditions**: parts of biomes may face extreme weather conditions (such as drought or strong storms) and diseases or pests (such as bark beetles killing pine and spruce trees in the Rocky Mountain National Park, USA).

Figure 1 Deforestation in Brazil: an aerial view of a large soy field eating into the tropical rainforest

Characteristics of tropical rainforests

Physical characteristics

1. Tropical rainforests have a clear structure with different layers of vegetation. The tallest isolated trees, like the kapok, that grow over 50 m tall, are known as emergent trees. Below are at least two levels of trees forming canopies from their dense green leaves, with those in the main canopy about 35 m tall. Below is a shrub layer with young trees where enough sunlight gets through the canopy (Figure 2). There is little vegetation at ground level as it is dark, so there is less food for animals. Most year-round food is found in the canopy layers so creatures such as spider monkeys have adapted to living high in the trees. Ground-level vegetation is only dense where there is sunlight, such as along riverbanks.

DOIT!

Make your own sketch of Figure 1. Label all the differences between the forest and deforested areas that you can identify.

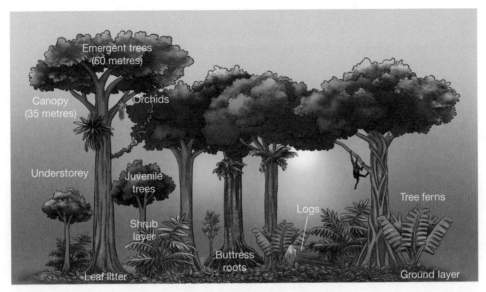

Figure 2 The structure of the Australian tropical rainforest

NAILIT!

Make sure that you understand the influence of heat and water in the tropical rainforest on the growth of plants, especially trees, and on nutrient cycling.

(2) The growing season for plants is 12 months, as it is always hot and wet – ideal growing conditions. With such a wealth of food it is not surprising that the tropical rainforest is the most biodiverse ecosystem on the planet. It is home to about 50 per cent of all species, with many found only in a small area.

(3) The hot, wet conditions also speed up nutrient cycling. The largest store of nutrients is in the large trees (biomass). The litter from these decomposes quickly in the top soil layer. The shallow roots of the plants absorb them quickly before they are washed away.

(4) Soils lack nutrients because nutrients are recycled quickly back into plants or washed deep into the soil by heavy tropical rain.

DOIT!

Create a podcast to explain why the tropical rainforest has the greatest biodiversity of all the biomes on Earth.

Interdependence

- As with all ecosystems, each part of a tropical rainforest is linked with and depends on other parts. For example, trees provide food and a place for creatures to live; in return, these creatures spread the seeds of the trees to new growing places. There is a complex food web (Figure 3).

- The nutrient (or mineral) flow in a tropical rainforest is fast because it is so hot and wet, so chemical reactions are faster. Leaves and branches that fall on to the ground decompose quickly and the nutrients enter the top layer (horizon) of the soil; the roots of the trees are shallow and spread out so that they can quickly absorb the minerals, before they are washed deep into the soil by the heavy tropical rain (a process called leaching) (Figure 4).

SNAPIT!

Snap an image of Figure 2. Use it to remind yourself of the four different levels within the rainforest and what each layer is like. Can you explain the natural processes happening in the main canopy layer and at ground level?

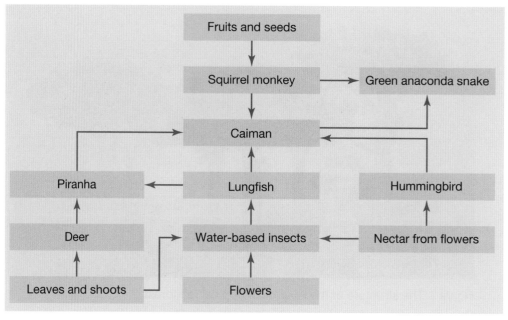

Figure 3 Part of a tropical rainforest food web

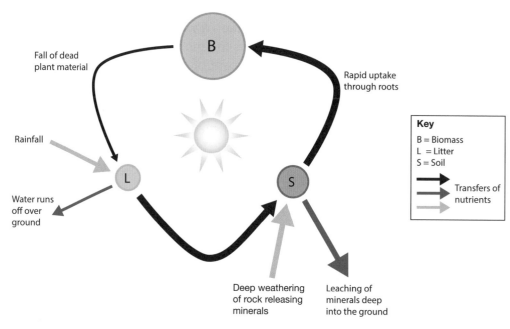

Figure 4 Nutrient cycling in a tropical rainforest

Look at Figure 4. Plan an answer to a question that asks you to describe the stages in a tropical rainforest nutrient cycle.

- The soils are not very fertile. They lack nutrients because of leaching. Most of the nutrients in the tropical rainforest ecosystem are stored in the vegetation (for example, trees 50–60 m tall). If the trees are removed, the nutrient cycle is interrupted and problems occur as fewer nutrients are left within the ecosystem.

- Trees transpire moisture through their leaves, which then evaporates into the air. This is called evapotranspiration and creates high humidity. When the air temperature cools in the evenings, night condensation takes place forming large clouds, which then cause rainfall. Without this transpiration, the tropical rainforest areas would be drier.

- People have lived in the forest for thousands of years, using the resources that the forest provides. These native (indigenous) people developed a balance with the natural systems. However, modern people have the motive and ability to damage the tropical rainforest on a much larger scale.

Adaptations of plants and animals

Plants have adapted by:

- growing tall to reach the sunlight

- having large leaves that pivot on their stalks to capture and follow sunlight

- having waxy leaves with drip tips, so that the heavy rainfall runs off the tree quickly and mosses and other small plants can't grow on them

- having buttress roots that give stability at the base of the tallest trees

- having shallow root systems to obtain nutrients from the top layer of soil before they are washed away (leaching).

Animal life has adapted in a number of ways.

- Monkeys and similar mammals can climb and swing between trees to find food.

- Gliding snakes can flatten themselves into a ribbon to glide between trees, and have backward-pointing scales to be able to climb trees.

- Flying squirrels have skin between their legs and arms and bodies so that they can jump and glide between trees.

- Insects and small animals have developed camouflage to be harder for predators to spot.

- Frogs lay their tadpoles in pools of water trapped in flowers in the canopy layer.

Biodiversity issues

The tropical rainforest is the most biodiverse ecosystem on Earth. This is partly because it has been relatively unaffected by past changes to global climatic cycles, so living things have had lots of time to evolve. Each small area is home to different living things, so the destruction of even a small area can cause the extinction of plants and animals, losing biodiversity. It is likely that many living things have become extinct without scientists even finding them.

Loss of biodiversity may cause issues such as:

- Extinction of species endangering others in the food web.

- Loss of genetic material from which to find medicines or new food resources.

- An unbalanced ecosystem making the rainforest less resistant to change, especially sudden changes.

NAILIT!

Make sure that you understand the term 'biodiversity'. This means the number and variety of living organisms (species) within a given area. It may also be used to refer to the variations between biomes, ecosystems and species.

NAILIT!

Make sure that you understand that adaptations are designed to increase the chances of survival of plants and animals. For example, why do the trees grow so tall or why do some squirrels glide from one tree to another?

DOIT!

Plan an answer to a question that asks you about the problems created for an ecosystem and people by a loss of biodiversity.

Remember that the question is asking about problems created in an ecosystem **and** problems that affect people.

Reasons and causes of deforestation

Commercial farming

This is on a large scale in many tropical rainforest areas, with clearance for growing soya to feed cattle, to create grazing land for cattle, or to create plantations for export crops (such as palm oil) or biofuels (such as sugar cane). The main reason behind this is to make money for farming businesses (agribusiness) and the government (export taxes or tariffs) as there is a demand for these products from developed countries.

Subsistence farming

Indigenous people have lived in harmony with the forest for thousands of years. However, recently people, many from overcrowded cities, have moved into the forest and cleared patches to make fields to grow their own food and get wood for fuel. The problem is that the soils are not fertile, so more forest is cut down and burned. The reason behind this is poverty: the people have few alternative ways of getting food. Population growth means that large numbers of people can be involved.

Commercial logging

Hardwood trees (such as mahogany) are a valuable resource and are cut down, as are many other trees around them to provide access for the logging machinery and transport. The main reason for this is the demand for hardwoods for furniture in developed countries, which makes money for logging companies and the governments of developing or emerging countries.

Mining

Tropical rainforests cover very large areas of land on three continents. In the soils and rocks under these areas there are a lot of valuable resources, such as gold and oil. Metals and minerals are often extracted using open-cast techniques, which means removing all the vegetation to get at the soils and rocks underneath. Roads, railways and whole settlements are built to house and transport workers and machinery, which also means clearing the forest. The reasons behind this include:

- providing raw materials for the industries of developing and emerging countries

- making money for mining companies and the governments of developing and emerging countries (partly to help pay off international debts)

- meeting demand for products from developed countries.

Hydro-electric power

Developing and emerging countries cannot afford expensive fuels to create electricity, so they often build dams and large reservoirs on major rivers. The construction activity and associated roads, settlements and power transmission routes create deforestation, and the reservoirs flood large areas of forest. The electricity is needed to help power businesses and industries and to supply people's homes.

NAILIT!

Remember that the **reasons** for deforestation are not the same as the **ways** in which deforestation may occur. A reason for deforestation is to make money, while a way is logging trees and selling the timber.

Threats from climate change

Some human activities are direct threats to the forest, such as logging and farming, but there are also indirect threats from climate change, many of which are still uncertain.

- Trees could grow faster (due to more carbon dioxide (CO_2) in atmosphere) but also tree death rates could increase, creating a less stable ecosystem.

- Drier conditions in some areas, such as the south and east of the Amazon rainforest, could increase tree deaths and forest fires. As trees die there is less evapotranspiration, which increases the risk of local drought.

- Stronger storm activity could blow down more trees, especially the tallest ones.

- Drier conditions could lead to a biome shift from forest to tropical grasslands (savannah).

- Species extinction could take place due to increased temperatures and/or drier conditions. Many animals have adapted to local habitats, and forest fragmentation (continuous forest being broken up due to humans cutting down trees and clearing land) means that migration is difficult.

- The Amazon tropical rainforest could reach a 'tipping point', where a series of small changes lead to a major change, due to drought and fire.

Impacts of deforestation

Cutting down the tropical rainforest may have serious consequences at all scales, from local to global (Figure 5):

- Locally, the soil may be exposed by deforestation, enabling the rain to wash it away (erosion) and leaving nothing for natural plants or farmers' crops with to grow in.

- Regionally, the climate may become drier. With fewer trees, the rate of evapotranspiration is reduced, so the air is less humid and rainfall decreases, making it even more difficult for plants to grow.

- Nationally, a country may gain money from selling resources obtained from tropical rainforest areas, but eventually these may be used up, leaving fewer ways of making money.

- Globally, the rate of absorption of carbon dioxide is reduced as there are fewer trees to use the gas during photosynthesis. This means that more carbon dioxide stays in the atmosphere, contributing to global warming.

Rates of deforestation

1. Humans have always cut down the tropical rainforest. Indigenous tribes made their homes from timber and cleared small patches of land to grow crops, for example. However, this had little long-term impact and was sustainable.

2. Modern humans with technology, such as large machinery, have cut down much larger amounts of forest. There are pressures from growing populations who need somewhere to live and farm, and there are pressures for making money so that a country can develop. Large companies can make money and people can move out of poverty.

DO IT!

Study the following data giving the original size of the Amazon tropical rainforest and its size now.

Original area of Amazon tropical rainforest: 4 100 000 km^2

Area of Amazon tropical rainforest in 2015: 3 300 000 km^2

Calculate:

a the area of the forest that has been lost (in km^2)

b the percentage of the forest now remaining.

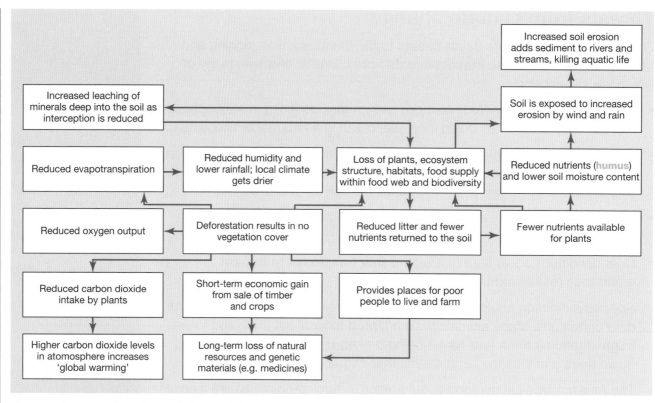

Figure 5 Impact of tropical rainforest deforestation

3 Deforestation rates have varied over time (Figure 6) depending on economic influences, such as demand for palm oil, soya, beef, open-cast mining of metals and supplies of hydro-electric power (HEP). However, if current rates continue, the tropical rainforest could be all gone within 100 years.

DO IT!

Study Figure 6. Describe the pattern of forest loss in the Amazon region of Brazil.

☐ Deforested area
▨ Breeding area with herds larger than 100 000 heads of cattle
▨ Fields under crop (soy, maize, sugar cane, rice, beans, cassava, coffee, orange, cacao)

Figure 6 Deforestation in the Amazon tropical rainforest, Brazil

Example

A tropical rainforest: Malaysia

Malaysia is in South-East Asia and 67 per cent of the country was originally covered with tropical rainforest. However, it has the fastest rate of deforestation in the world.

Causes of deforestation

- There is logging to get tropical woods for export, which brings money into Malaysia.
- Hydro-electric power (HEP) stations have been built with dams and reservoirs. These provide electricity for businesses and industries in Malaysia.
- Mining of tin and drilling for oil and gas take place in the rainforest so that Malaysia can sell products and improve energy security.
- Plantations of palm oil have been created to produce an export product to bring money into Malaysia.
- Population growth has encouraged settlements and farming in the forest, providing people with a place to live and make a living.
- Roads have been cut through the forest so that companies can get to the logging areas, mines, energy projects and new settlements.
- Forest fires caused by 'slash and burn' methods of clearing the forest for farming have spread and caused considerable damage.

Impacts (negative and positive) of deforestation

- Biodiversity is reduced and wildlife such as orang-utans are threatened by loss of habitat.
- Soils are exposed to erosion once the forest structure is destroyed.
- The extent of climate change is increased as the forest's ability to absorb carbon dioxide is reduced.
- Transpiration is reduced, so local areas become drier.
- Jobs are created by the primary and secondary industries based on forest products, and tertiary jobs are linked to exporting the products.
- Malaysia earns money from timber, metal and energy exports, which can help develop the country.
- Water and air pollution result from the forest activities.
- Soils may be degraded so much that the land cannot be used for anything.
- An unsightly rainforest reduces ecotourist numbers.

Sustainable management

Ways of decreasing deforestation rely on organisations, people and governments working together. This is not easy to achieve.

Value of tropical rainforests

People

- For indigenous people, the tropical rainforests are their home, providing resources for shelter, food and medicines.

DO IT!

1 Create a revision card that has four bullet points showing the causes of deforestation in Malaysia, or the tropical rainforest you have studied.

2 Create a revision card that has four bullet points showing the impacts of deforestation in Malaysia, or the rainforest you have studied.

NAIL IT!

Remember that the tropical rainforest is in South America, West and Central Africa and South-East Asia. Within these world regions the tropical rainforest overlaps several countries. For example, the Amazon rainforest is mostly in Brazil, but it is also found in Bolivia, Peru and Colombia. In South-East Asia, tropical rainforests are found in Indonesia, Malaysia and northern Australia.

NAILIT!

Carbon is found in several forms. The Earth's natural systems move carbon between the biosphere, atmosphere, oceans and rocks, as well as storing it in these places for a long or short time.

- For people with economic motives, tropical rainforest offers a timber resource, agroforestry crops, other foods, medicines, scientific, aesthetic and ecotourism value.

- The tropical rainforest also helps to balance the amounts of oxygen and carbon dioxide in the atmosphere, providing the oxygen that people need to breathe and storing carbon.

Natural environment

- The tropical rainforest ecosystem has an influence on local climate, and scientists think that it may have an important influence on global climate too.

- It is the oldest biome and has the greatest biodiversity by far, with complex food webs and unique examples of evolution on Earth.

- It acts as a store of carbon within the carbon cycle, balancing the gases in the atmosphere.

Sustainability strategies

Sustainable farming

- Agroforestry involves using native trees of different types to maintain some of the forest structure and habitats, sometimes also using canopy trees to provide shade for cash crops.

- Growing crops that produce a crop every year (such as mango and rubber) reduces the need to clear new areas of forest.

Sustainable forestry

- Selective logging involves choosing carefully where to extract timber and the type of timber to extract. For example, mahogany has been a popular wood in developed countries because of its colour, but these trees grow on their own and to get to them a lot of other trees are cut down. An approach using other, more numerous types of tree instead would reduce needless deforestation.

- As well as selective logging, the deforested area could be immediately replanted with the same trees as those removed, which would maintain the forest area and biodiversity.

DOIT!

Study all the information on sustainable strategies for using the tropical rainforest. Decide which you think is the best approach. Write down three reasons why you think this.

SNAPIT!

Find an image of tree replanting in a tropical rainforest and Snap it! Use this to remind you of the steps necessary to persuade people to carry out replanting of tropical rainforests.

Figure 7 Tree replanting

Conservation and education

- Conservation means looking after the forest so that it is not damaged. It does not necessarily mean preventing human use of the forest, but it does involve protection, such as national parks or wildlife reserves where human activities are restricted by law. It can also include 'buffer zones' where carefully monitored human activity takes place to ensure that any deforestation is under control.

- People in all countries can be educated about the value of the tropical rainforest and also about farming and logging methods that cause minimal damage without affecting their income or access to resources.

- The Convention on International Trade in Endangered Species (CITES) is designed to stop trading in animals and plants. The convention has been signed by 183 countries, so international monitoring and punishments are possible. However, illegal trade is still increasing as it is profitable for the criminals, and it is difficult to check that each country is doing their best to protect species.

Ecotourism and international agreements

- Ecotourism is popular because people wish to see undisturbed natural areas. Local people living in tropical rainforests can gain jobs and income by being guides, offering accommodation or selling local craft products. Local people can make more money from visitors than they could by destroying the rainforest.

- Protected wilderness areas and national parks give some legal protection to forests and limit human interference, with people monitoring and patrolling areas (for example, Jau National Park in Brazil). However, often these are huge and difficult to manage (Jau covers an area larger than the country of Wales!).

- All countries are linked, especially economically. Some developed countries may influence the developing countries that have tropical rainforest by helping with monitoring deforestation, or through directly funding international organisations or programmes. For example, reducing emissions from deforestation and degradation (REDD) provides financial incentives to protect natural forests and uses international expertise. However, it does not provide a clear definition of a forest and does not tackle the reasons for deforestation.

Debt reduction

Many developing countries, such as Brazil, borrowed money in the past to help build expensive schemes to aid development of the country. However, these countries were often unable to pay back the money and are now in debt. One type of international agreement is a 'debt-for-nature swap' or debt reduction, where some of the money owed is written off in return for establishing tropical rainforest protection areas (such as national parks).

NAILIT!

A lending organisation, such as the World Bank, will negotiate with the government of a country that owes it money to agree to write-off some of the debt, as long as the country promises to legally protect a specified size of natural area. This benefits the country (reduced debt) and the world (saves biodiversity). But it is difficult to monitor the protection of the natural area from outside the country.

DOIT!

With a friend, test each other in turn to describe an advantage or disadvantage of each global action to manage tropical rainforests sustainably.

Recover degraded land
Where pressures from people have been high, replant variety of trees to restore biodiversity and reduce soil erosion.

Stop forest destruction
Modern machinery used to clear large areas of forest. Burning of forest adds to damage. Biodiversity lost.

Use forest sustainably
Indigenous people living in harmony with nature. Forest structure maintained.

Maintain forest peatland
Prevent encroachment into wetland habitats. Make nature reserve.

Figure 8 A REDD sponsored project

DOIT!

Using Figure 8, draw a simple flow diagram to show the steps needed to reduce deforestation using REDD principles.

CHECKIT!

1 Name the tallest layer of trees in the tropical rainforest structure.

2 Explain how a tropical rainforest affects the local climate.

3 a Describe three ways in which tropical rainforest plants have adapted to their environment.

  b Explain three ways in which tropical rainforest animals have adapted to their environment.

4 Explain why the soils in the tropical rainforest biome usually lack nutrients.

5 Explain why the food web in a tropical rainforest is complicated.

6 Give one reason why a country may wish to cut down its tropical rainforests.

7 a Name and locate an area of tropical rainforest that you have studied.

  b Give three ways in which this tropical rainforest has been deforested.

  c Explain three impacts of the deforestation in this tropical rainforest.

8 Describe the possible changes to the tropical rainforest biome caused by climate change.

9 Explain why the rate of deforestation in an area of tropical rainforest may vary over time.

10 Give two reasons why tropical rainforests are considered to be valuable.

11 a Explain why some people think that replanting trees is the best sustainable strategy for tropical rainforests.

  b Explain why some people think that the education of people is the best way of achieving sustainable management of tropical rainforests.

12 Suggest the advantages and disadvantages of using the REDD sustainable strategy.

8.2 The taiga biome

OUTCOMES

By the end of my revision I will be able to:

- Explain the key features of the taiga biome and where it is located.
- Analyse the threats to the taiga biome and how they may be reduced.

Characteristics of taiga (boreal) environments

Physical characteristics

- Taiga consists of coniferous forests largely made up of pine and spruce trees in a sub-arctic environment. Taiga is found in Scandinavia, Canada (boreal) and northern Russia.

- Temperatures in winter may drop below −40 °C. There is very little precipitation, with a maximum around 70 mm in warmer summer months when temperatures may reach +16 °C.

- The very cold winters and short summers make it difficult for plants and animals to live on land. There is also a lack of sunlight in winter. However, in the brief summer, temperatures allow wildlife to be more active.

- In places, the ground is frozen solid for a large part of the year (sporadic permafrost) and only thaws out in the short summer. This helps to create lots of lakes.

- The cold climate limits plant growth, and nutrient cycling is slow. There is also little animal life, so biodiversity is low.

Graphical skills

Climate graph (line and bar graph)

Make a copy of Figure 9.

1 Using the data given below, accurately plot the missing points for temperature to complete the line graph.

2 Using the data given below, accurately plot the missing bars for rainfall to complete the bar graph.

Month	Temperature (°C)	Precipitation (mm)
April	3.7	21
May	11.3	40

NAILIT!

The very cold temperatures have a major influence on what these sub-arctic areas are like. Even though there is only a little snow each year, it is so cold that the snow does not melt and covers everything for about seven months. Winds can also add a strong wind-chill factor, which makes the air temperature feel even colder.

NAILIT!

In a cold environment, the number of plants and animals is very low compared with other large-scale biomes. Biodiversity is low and food webs are less complex.

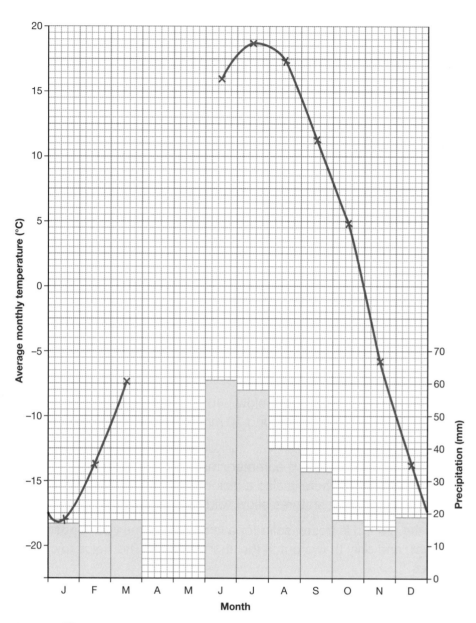

Figure 9 Climate graph for a taiga biome (Canada)

Interdependence

As in all ecosystems, the different parts are linked together and depend on each other, especially in a food web with lots of evergreen trees and insects in the summer (Figure 10). Some animals and birds migrate to find food or a warmer climate, others may hibernate (such as the brown bear).

Nutrient cycling is very slow due to cold temperatures and low annual precipitation, so most nutrients are stored in the litter (such as pine needles) because it only decomposes very slowly. This makes transfers to the soil and biomass take a long time (Figure 11). The litter from pine and spruce trees is also acidic and only plants that can tolerate this can grow.

Indigenous people, such as the Inuit, have adapted to the cold climatic conditions and natural patterns. As it is not possible to grow crops, they depend on the hunting of animals such as caribou, seals and fish for food, tools, clothing and shelter.

SNAP IT!

Snap an image of Figure 10. Use it to learn three interdependencies within the taiga biome.

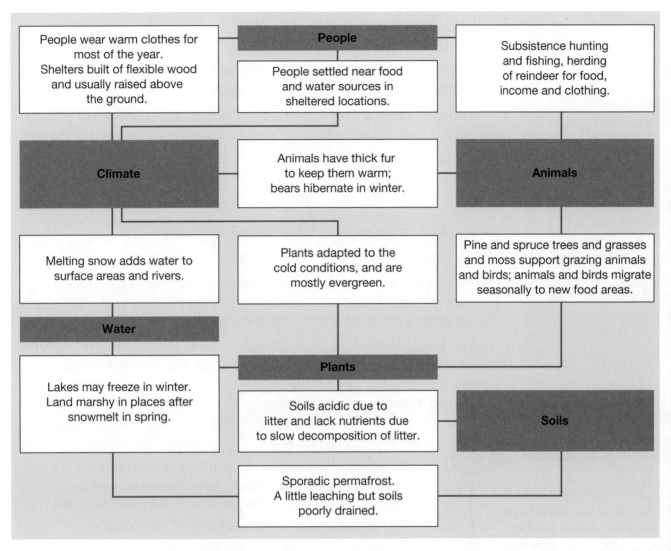

Figure 10 Links between climate, water, soils, plants, animals and people in a taiga biome

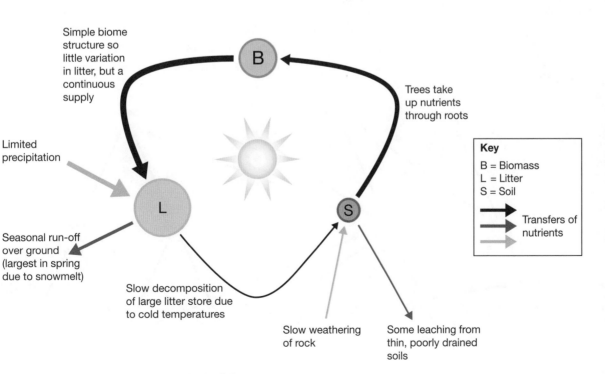

Figure 11 Nutrient cycling in a tropical rainforest

Adaptations of plants and animals

Adaptations of plants

- Coniferous trees keep most of their needle leaves all year; summers are so short that there is not enough time to regrow them each spring.

- The needle leaves are hard, with a small surface area and a waxy coating to protect them from the freezing winter conditions and retain water.

- Trees have a conical shape with branches angled down; they can withstand strong winds and shed snow quickly before it breaks branches off.

Adaptations of animals

- Many bird species migrate, flying south for the winter.

- Bears hibernate during the winter months in a warm den.

- White camouflage is used by grazing animals (herbivores such as the snowshoe hare) so that they cannot easily be spotted against snow and ice by secondary consumers (e.g. timber wolves).

- Caribou have wide hooves to help them move over waterlogged ground and two layers of fur to keep them warm. Bears are omnivorous, (for example, eating fish and berries) so they can change their food sources according to the seasonal food supply.

Biodiversity issues

- Sub-arctic food webs are simpler and less productive than others and are fragile due to the difficulty of surviving in the very cold climate. This means that a small change in conditions may cause a large loss of biodiversity.

- The lack of biodiversity makes the taiga biome fragile; if a small part is damaged, the whole food web (Figure 12) can be affected. Cold temperatures mean that plant growth is very slow.

- Nutrient cycling is slower due to the lack of warmth and moisture, so any damage to soils or removal of vegetation makes it difficult for the taiga (boreal) biome to recover.

NAIL IT!

As food supplies change through the seasons some animals (such as caribou) migrate to find food, while others hibernate in winter after putting on as much weight as possible in the short summer (such as bears).

STRETCH IT!

Know some names of plants and animals to add detail to your answers: plants such as white spruce, soapberry and caribou moss; animals such as moose, snowshoe hare and woodland caribou. Can you link some of these in a food chain?

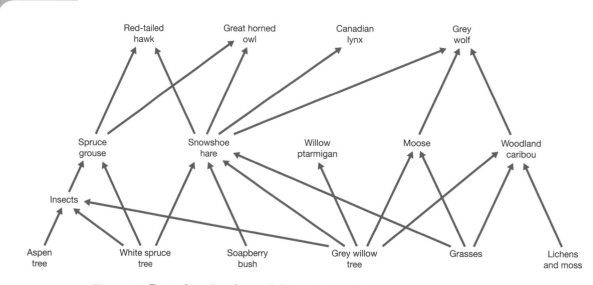

Figure 12 Part of a taiga (boreal) food web in Canada

Threats to the taiga biome

Value of taiga areas

There are few places left on Earth that have not been used by people, and even these are likely to have been affected by climate change brought about by emissions of greenhouse gases. Therefore, the taiga (boreal) biome, which has been affected less by people, is worth protecting.

- Some areas in northern Canada and Russia are almost wilderness areas where humans do not dominate the landscape. In these areas, natural processes and systems take place with less interference and therefore can be considered wild.

- Remote wildscapes allow comparisons with areas that have been changed, reminding people of the importance of the beauty of nature and the cultures of indigenous peoples.

Threats to taiga areas

- Pine trees of the boreal forest are cut down to provide valuable softwood (for building and paper). There is little vegetation under these trees, and the litter (which is the biggest store of nutrients) is greatly reduced. A barren landscape can result.

- There are valuable minerals, such as oil, underneath the taiga biome area and damage to soils, lakes and the sporadic permafrost can be caused by large-scale mining operations. Oil remains in the ecosystem for a long time due to the cold that prevents it being broken down.

- Acid rain is caused by burning fossil fuels in power stations and industry. Winds carry pollution (sulfuric acid) into boreal forest areas. Here, the pollution seeps into the ground and lakes, killing trees by attacking their roots and killing life in lakes and rivers. Soils in these areas are already acidic due to the leaf litter from the trees, so the environment quickly becomes too acidic for wildlife.

- HEP dams built across rivers prevent fish (such as salmon) migrating to spawning areas, and create reservoirs that flood habitats of birds, caribou and wolves. Forty per cent of Canada's HEP electricity is from places in its boreal forest.

- Natural threats also exist, such as wildfires and pests and diseases, which can kill many trees when they have become weakened.

Threats from climate change

- Earlier leaf growth and fruiting of the boreal forest in Europe due to spring temperatures arriving earlier each year.

- Pine and spruce trees move to higher altitudes and further north with warmer temperatures.

- Change to breeding areas, and population size, of sub-arctic birds due to reduced snow cover and changes in location of shrubs.

- Increase in number of wildfires in sub-arctic coniferous forests in North America due to warmer conditions and more lightning storms.

- Increase in number of pests, such as the bark beetle attacking pine and spruce trees in the boreal biome.

DO IT!

Draw a revision diagram summarising the reasons why a taiga biome is fragile and vulnerable to change.

STRETCH IT!

Wilderness areas are disappearing. For example, 3.4 million km² has been lost in the last 25 years. About 20 per cent of the world's land area is still classified as wilderness – that's 30 million km². So at the rate of disappearance over the last decade it could all be gone within 200 years.

Managing the taiga biome

There are very few international agreements covering management of taiga (boreal) forests. Most management is at the national level.

Use of technology

- Oil extraction in Alaska needs to be done with great care. In particular, the oil, which is warm, has to be transported by pipeline from northern Alaska to its southern coast through the taiga (boreal) zone. This has been made possible by raising the pipeline up on stilts and adding radiators to take the heat from the oil away into the air, which stops the warm oil melting the permafrost. It has also been raised up in caribou migration areas to allow them to pass underneath.

- The expansion of information and communications technology gives indigenous communities access to education and health care and allows them to preserve their culture in a knowledge network. Internet companies have located in sub-arctic environments to save costs on cooling the computer equipment.

- Sustainable forestry involves planning by large timber companies to use their machinery to efficiently remove and then replant the pine and spruce trees that they harvest.

Role of governments (national and international)

- Governments have control over their territory. This means they can set aside areas just for nature – such as the Wrangell-St Elias National Park in Alaska, USA – or only issue a limited number of oil exploration licences. In this way, they can balance the need to make money and find resources to support the country's development with the need to protect nature from serious damage.

- National governments should follow all international treaties, protocols and laws; for example, the UN Convention on Biological Diversity (2010).

- UNESCO has designated over 200 natural World Heritage Sites around the world (such as the Virgin Komi Forests (1995) in Russia) to offer international recognition and protection for significant natural areas, protecting the ecosystems and scenery. This encourages monitoring of forest health, wildlife populations, ecological disturbances and invasive species.

- Climate change agreements, such as Paris 2015, aim to reduce greenhouse gas emissions. This may limit the amount of melting ice and permafrost, and alterations to ecosystems.

NAILIT!

The UN Convention of Biological Diversity (2010) required countries to reduce losses of biodiversity and undisturbed primary forest, and to increase the amount of protected areas. In 2017, only about 2.8 per cent of the world's taiga (boreal) forest was protected.

Example

A boreal national park: Wrangell-St Elias, Alaska, USA

Alaska is one of the USA states and has a large area of the boreal (taiga) biome. In 1980 a law was passed called the Alaska National Interest Land Conservation Act (ANILCA), which not only protects the natural ecosystems by having permits to control sport hunting in the national parks, but also helps Alaskan natives (e.g. Athabascans) continue their subsistence way of life by protecting the fish, animals and plants they rely on.

Wrangell-St Elias NP is the USA's largest national park, covering over 53 000 km^2 in south-eastern Alaska. It is managed by the US National Park Service, whose rangers monitor and patrol the park. It was established to achieve a number of aims, including:

- to keep ecosystem diversity
- to protect subsistence resources
- to monitor climate change and find solutions.

In 1979, Wrangell-St Elias NP also became part of a large World Heritage Site, which brought international recognition and protection. Apart from the subsistence of the Athabascans and controlled hunting, the main activity within the park is tourism (mostly hiking and wildlife viewing) and facilities are provided for them (visitor centres and a campground). Around and within the national park areas are owned privately and by local governments, so as well as threats from climate change, the national park is also under pressure from active mining and other developments.

Role of conservation groups

- Greenpeace has campaigned against tar sands and logging in the taiga (boreal) forest areas. It wants urgent action to prevent further losses of this forest in their 2017 report *Eye on the Taiga*.

- In Canada, the Canadian Boreal Initiative (conservation coordination group) and the Boreal Songbird Initiative (conservation non-governmental organisation, NGO) have called for greater protection of boreal forests, held meetings and published information.

DO IT!

Make a table listing the different people, organisations or businesses that are linked to taiga (boreal) forests in the first column and a second column that states their main view of using and managing this forest. Create a mnemonic to help you remember these groups.

Graphical skills

1 Using the data in Table 1, draw a pie chart using a suitable software package (such as Excel) or draw proportional circles over each country on a digital world outline map.

2 What pattern of forest loss do you notice from your completed graph or map?

Country	% loss of taiga (boreal) forest
Russia	7.2
USA (Alaska)	5.9
Canada	4.5
Norway	1.0
Sweden	0.8
Finland	0.2

Data source: Greenpeace

Table 1 Loss of intact forest landscapes between 2000–2013

 # CHECKIT!

1 a Give one characteristic of the taiga (boreal) environment.

  b Give one characteristic of the taiga climate.

2 a Describe two ways in which plants have adapted to the taiga climate.

  b Explain two ways in which animals have adapted to the taiga climate.

3 Describe how two named parts of a taiga (boreal) biome are linked.

4 Explain why a taiga (boreal) biome can be considered fragile.

5 Name one reason why the taiga forests can be considered to be valuable.

6 Describe how logging is a threat to biodiversity in taiga forests.

7 State two ways in which climate change may cause changes to the taiga biome.

8 Explain the role of conservation groups in helping to protect taiga forests.

9 Suggest whether governments **or** logging and mining companies have the most important role in protecting taiga forests. Explain your choice.

Forests under threat

Tropical rainforests

1   a Describe the structure of a tropical rainforest.

   b Explain why there is little vegetation at the ground level in a tropical rainforest.

2   How long is the growing season in a tropical rainforest?

3   Explain why the soils in a tropical rainforest lack nutrients.

4   Explain how tropical rainforest trees affect the local climate within the ecosystem.

5   a Where do most creatures live in the tropical rainforest structure?

   b Give one reason why most creatures live in this part of the structure.

6   Explain why there is a very wide range of adaptations of plants and animals to the environmental conditions in a tropical rainforest.

7   Outline one issue caused by a loss of biodiversity in a tropical rainforest.

8   a State one likely local impact of cutting down part of a tropical rainforest.

   b State one likely global impact of cutting down the tropical rainforest.

9   Compare the impact of indigenous people and people with strong economic motives on the tropical rainforest.

10 Explain two ways in which climate change may threaten tropical rainforests.

11 a Explain four causes of deforestation within the tropical rainforest.

   b Describe the impact on the natural environment of the deforestation in the tropical rainforest.

   c Describe the impact on people where deforestation is taking place.

12 a Why do so many people think that it is important to protect the tropical rainforest global ecosystem?

   b Choose one sustainable strategy for looking after the tropical rainforest and explain how this strategy would help.

Taiga (boreal) biome

1   Name an area of the world with taiga (boreal) forests.

2   a Describe two features of a taiga ecosystem.

   b Describe two features of a taiga climate.

3   a State two natural links within a taiga ecosystem.

   b Explain one link between nature and people in a taiga ecosystem.

4   a Explain why biodiversity in a taiga ecosystem is much lower than in most other global ecosystems.

   b Give one reason why taiga ecosystems are vulnerable to change.

5   a Explain three causes of forest loss in the taiga biome.

   b Compare the impact of indigenous people and logging companies on the taiga forest.

6   Explain why global agreements to limit climate change are important to the biodiversity of the taiga biome.

7   a Suggest why it is proving difficult to manage taiga forest areas on a global scale.

   b Choose one strategy for conserving a taiga forest area and explain how it would help.

8   Explain why there are conflicting views about how to manage taiga forests.

Advice is given in more detail on how to approach the 'Making geographical decisions' questions on these topics in Chapter 10.

9 Consuming energy resources

9.1 Energy resources

THE EXAMINATION!

- This section is tested in Paper 3 Sections C and D.
- You must know energy types, their extraction and use.
- You must know the benefits and costs of using oil and renewable energy sources.

OUTCOMES

By the end of my revision I will be able to:

- Describe the need for energy resources and the types of energy resource we use.
- Explain issues in energy access, supply and consumption.
- Analyse the production and use of energy and the changes in energy needs around the world.

Types of energy and environmental impacts

Energy is fundamental to human development. The overall development of countries and the quality of life for people depend on energy resources being readily available. A resource is something that can be used by people.

For people and industries to progress beyond a basic level, a source of energy is needed. Within their daily lives, people need energy – for example, for cooking, heating and light. Industries and businesses need to have enough energy to operate on a larger, more efficient scale. There is a range of energy resources available, from non-renewables such as oil to renewables such as hydro-electric power.

Types of energy

Energy resources can be placed into three categories:

- **Non-renewable**: finite resources, which will run out because it takes millions of years for them to form. Examples include oil, natural gas and coal, which are formed by geological processes and so are sometimes known as fossil fuels.
- **Renewable**: resources that will always exist because of short-term natural processes and so can be reused. Examples include wind, solar and hydro-electric power.
- **Recyclable**: resources that can be reused if the source is made sustainable or after reprocessing. For example, biofuels can be replanted so that there is a future supply, or used uranium from nuclear power stations can be put through a process where it can be reused.

DO IT!

Summarise why energy is considered to be an essential resource.

154

The **energy mix** of a country or world region is the proportion of each of these energy types being used. This depends on the types of energy resource available and has implications for environmental impacts.

Environmental impacts

- Where fossil fuels are being used, the production of carbon dioxide (CO_2) is much higher. This is a major gas causing the enhanced greenhouse effect (climate change) because it traps heat within the atmosphere. Locally, other products of burning fossil fuels, such as sulfur gases, may cause air pollution, especially in urban areas, or lead to acid rain that kills wildlife by making soils and lakes too acidic.

- Mining of coal and uranium may damage the landscape and ecosystems in the area, especially if it is open-cast mining, where vegetation, soils and surface rock layers are removed.

- Drilling for oil and then transporting it carries the risk of spills, which can poison soils and water areas, killing plants and animals in that environment.

- The uranium used in nuclear power stations is radioactive, and some of the waste products remain radioactive for a long time. Radioactive products have the potential to seriously damage large areas if there are accidents during their use, transport or reprocessing.

- The demand for biofuels may cause the removal of natural vegetation to create fields of a biofuel crop; deforestation for wood may damage the structure of a forest and allow soil erosion.

- Placing solar panels or wind turbines in scenic areas may spoil the landscape, and wind turbines have been known to kill flying birds.

- Hydro-electric power often requires a large dam and reservoir, which change the landscape and flood a large area (Figure 1), drowning natural vegetation, changing river processes and sometimes causing small earthquakes.

Figure 1 Tarbela Dam on the Indus River

Global inequalities in supply and consumption

Access to energy resources

There is an uneven distribution of energy sources around the world.

- **Fossil fuels** are located where **geological processes** formed and moved them millions of years ago, so oil is concentrated in certain regions, such as the Middle East.

- **Geothermal energy** can be obtained where there is **magma** close to the ground surface, so this is concentrated in a few countries, such as Iceland (Figure 2).

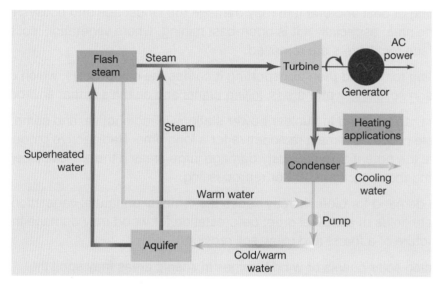

Figure 2 Geothermal power system

- Where there are steep-sided valleys and plentiful rainfall, countries can build dams and store water in reservoirs to create **hydro-electric power (HEP)** (e.g. Three Gorges Dam, China). Large rivers can be used with a system called 'run of the river', which just uses the natural flow levels of a river (e.g. Santo Antonio, Brazil).

- **Solar energy** can be used where there are clearer skies to receive long hours of, or intense, sunlight (e.g. Germany).

- **Wind energy** requires open areas exposed to fairly strong consistent winds (e.g. Denmark).

- **Biomass**, mainly wood, is a source of energy for many poor people who neither have access to, nor can afford, other energy resources.

These supplies are affected by the level of technology of a country. For example, the energy resource cannot be used unless the country can extract the fossil fuel from the ground or build wind turbines. Some resources are in remote **locations**, making them difficult to extract, and remote rural areas in developing countries do not have an electricity supply.

Consumption is influenced by a number of factors.

- The demand for energy has been increasing over time. More and more countries (e.g. China) are emerging economically and their industries and businesses use more energy. Also people have become wealthier, which has increased the household use of energy, especially transport.

NAILIT!

The top four energy producers are China, the USA, Russia and Indonesia. This is because they have their own energy resources, along with lots of people and industries demanding energy.

DOIT!

Discuss with a friend how each energy supply and consumption factor will affect the future. Perhaps allocate + and – points to each to see if supply or consumption wins the battle. Will there be a balance in the future?

- Fossil fuels (oil, coal, natural gas) are still the major source of energy around the world, but supplies are finite and will run out.

- Since 1990, the world's energy consumption has increased by over 60 per cent. Developed countries use seven times more energy than emerging countries and 14 times more than developing countries.

- Top consumers of energy per person are Canada, the USA, Iceland, Norway, Sweden, Finland, Russia, Saudi Arabia, Bahrain, the United Arab Emirates, Australia and New Zealand. Countries using the least are in sub-Saharan Africa and South Asia.

- Sub-Saharan Africa depends mostly on biomass, with about 700 million people cooking on open fires.

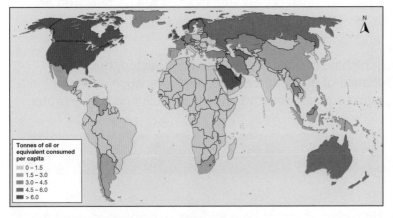

Figure 3 World consumption of energy, 2014

SNAPIT!

Snap an image of Figure 3 and use it to remind you of the world energy consumption pattern. Think about why there are differences in energy consumption around the world.

Opportunities and challenges in a developed country: the UK

During the UK industrial revolution, coal was the most important energy source. Since the 1950s, we have been in the 'oil age'– although not much oil is used in the production of electricity. Energy demand had been increasing until recently, but greater efficiency of use, higher costs and conservation strategies have stabilised energy use in the UK.

The UK's primary energy mix is diversifying because:

- Oil is due to run out in the second half of this century.

- Natural gas supplies have to be transported long distances by pipeline.

- There is concern over climate change as all the fossil fuels release carbon dioxide into the atmosphere.

- Renewable energy technologies have been developed.

Fossil fuels still dominate the UK energy mix, but the use of renewable energy sources, such as bioenergy and wind, is increasing.

Reduced domestic supply

1 Coal reserves in the UK have decreased. The only coal left is more difficult to obtain or would cause great environmental damage, making it more expensive than imported coal.

2 The UK has natural gas reserves in the southern part of the North Sea, but these have largely been used up (37 per cent left), and supplies have been imported since 2004.

(3) Oil was obtained from under the central and northern parts of the North Sea, but these reserves are now significantly depleted (42 per cent left). Some new oilfields are still being opened (e.g. east of the Shetland Islands), but extraction peaked in 1999, and production is now only a third of peak production (see Figure 4).

(4) UK and EU regulations regarding carbon dioxide emissions are forcing coal-fired power stations to close or convert to other fuels (e.g. biomass).

(5) Nuclear power stations are reaching the end of their productive stage and radioactivity is still worrying, especially after disasters such as at Fukushima, Japan, in 2011.

(6) There has been a large investment in wind energy, especially offshore wind farms, and fields of solar panels (renewables are up over 400 per cent since 2000). However, these only generate a small amount of the UK's electricity and funding is still uncertain.

(7) Fracking for gas in shale rocks has also been suggested, but this is controversial because of environmental side-effects, such as minor earthquakes, ground subsidence and chemicals polluting groundwater.

Numerical skills

Proportion, magnitude and ratio

Study Table 1, showing data on how the UK's production of primary fuels has changed recently.

(1) Complete the table by calculating the index figures for natural gas and coal. The base year is 1990, so this is given an index of 100. For example, to calculate the natural gas index for 2000:

$$108.4 \times 100 \div 45.5.$$

(2) Use the index figures for oil, natural gas and coal to create a graph to show the changes.

(3) Bioenergy and waste as an energy source has increased a lot, making it difficult to plot on a graph with the other primary fuels. Use single log graph paper to create a line graph to show all four primary fuels. Use the log axis for the production index.

(4) Using your graph (or graphs) and the data in Table 1, describe what has happened to the UK's primary fuel production since 1990.

Primary fuel	1990	Index	2000	Index	2010	Index	2014	Index
Oil	100.1	100	138.3	138.2	69.0	68.9	43.7	43.7
Natural gas	45.5	100	108.4		57.2		36.6	
Coal	56.4	100	19.6		11.4		7.3	
Bioenergy and waste	0.7	100	2.3	328.6	5.9	842.9	7.9	1128.6

Table 1 UK production of primary fuels 1990 to 2014 (million tonnes of oil equivalent)

STRETCHIT!

The UK's last deep coal mine closed in 2015. In 2014, 86 per cent of the UK's coal supplies were imported, mostly from Russia; 45 per cent of the UK's natural gas was imported, mostly from Norway; and 42 per cent of the UK's oil was imported from Norway and member countries of the Organisation of the Petroleum Exporting Countries (OPEC).

Also in 2014, approximately 14 per cent of the UK's energy was from low-carbon sources, of which 50 per cent was from nuclear (but declining) and 30 per cent was from bioenergy (increasing). The energy sector still accounted for most of the UK's greenhouse gas emissions, but total emissions were falling – down 36 per cent in 2014 compared with 1990 and down 25 per cent since 2005, showing a faster rate of decline over time.

Figure 4 North Sea oil and gas fields

Economic and environmental issues

1. Non-renewable fossil fuels (oil, coal, natural gas) produce carbon dioxide when burned; this greenhouse gas contributes to climate change. As supplies dwindle, the costs for consumers will increase. There are high costs involved with exploiting the more difficult to get at reserves and the environmental damage from fracking and opencast mining is extensive.

2. Nuclear power is controversial. Some people see it as a non-polluting source of energy, while others are worried about accidents and the high costs involved in disposing of radioactive waste and decommissioning power stations at the end of their productive life.

3. Wind energy is a renewable energy resource with low long-term financial costs and no carbon dioxide emissions once operating. However, wind farms are considered unsightly by some people due to their large size, and their construction can disrupt natural environments, such as the seabed. There are jobs linked to research and development (R&D) of this future resource.

 DOIT!

Create five multiple-choice questions on how the UK's energy supply has changed. Use these to test a friend.

NAILIT!

Make sure that you can give advantages and disadvantages of using the UK's main energy sources such as nuclear and wind energy, as well as the possible widespread use of fracking.

 DOIT!

List three economic issues arising from energy use in the UK.

Areas of surplus and deficit

An **energy gap** exists in parts of the world where energy supplies are not enough to meet energy demands. This situation exists due to energy supplies being too low and/or human consumption too high. The country with the largest energy gap is India.

DOIT!

Look at Figure 5, showing which areas of the world have high and low levels of energy access and security.

Write a list of areas that have enough energy supplies and another list of those that do not have enough energy. (Use names of continents, world regions, countries, or parts of countries.)

Do the areas in each list have anything in common that influences the amount of energy they have?

NAIL**IT!**

Make sure that you know and can use key terms associated with energy.

- **Energy consumption** is the amount of energy consumed by a country or area, usually given as an amount per person.
- **Energy supply** is the amount of energy produced by a country or area, usually given as an amount per person.
- **Energy security** exists where a country or area produces enough energy to meet its needs.
- **Energy insecurity** exists where a country or area does not have enough energy to meet its needs.
- **Energy gap** is the difference between the amount of energy available and the amount of energy needed or consumed.

Global patterns of energy supply and consumption

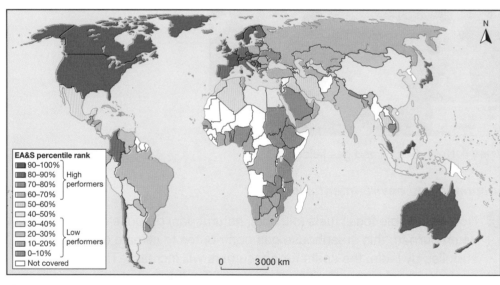

Figure 5 World energy access and security (EA&S)

Reasons for increasing energy consumption

Global energy consumption tripled between 1965 and 2015, and is expected to double again by 2040. There are a number of reasons for this.

- **Economic development**: as emerging countries catch up with developed countries, there is a lot more industry and business in the world, an intensification of farming and greater use of transport. **Globalisation** has also expanded trading and economic links. All of these activities use energy in greater quantities.

- **Increasing population**: the more people there are, the more energy gets used, especially as people become wealthier and can afford to use more electricity and transport. They also buy more consumer products, which means more industrial activity takes place (see Figure 6).

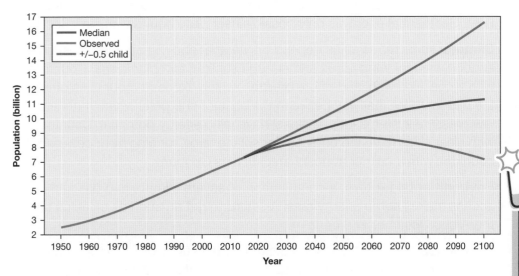

Figure 6 World population growth and predictions

- **Technology use**: the availability and range of technology in people's homes and within countries has increased greatly since 1965. These technologies often use electricity and require national electricity grids and fuels for power stations. Car ownership has also increased rapidly in developed and emerging countries, so the demand for oil has increased. There is a reliance on non-renewables such as oil in developed countries (e.g. USA), but in developing countries poorer people depend on traditional biomass fuels (e.g. Democratic Republic of Congo).

DO IT!

Draw a flow diagram to show how changes to the economy, population and technology have led to an increase in energy use.

SNAP IT!

Snap an image of Figure 7. Study this and think about the reasons behind the pattern. For example, why are some countries much higher consumers of energy than others? Why are some countries much lower consumers of energy than others?

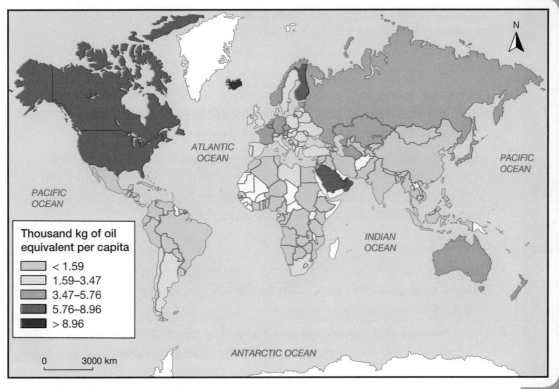

Figure 7 World energy consumption per capita (per person) in 2014

Factors affecting energy supply

Physical factors

- **Geology**: fossil fuels and uranium were formed by geological processes and are only found in certain places, such as the large oil reserves in the Middle East. Geothermal energy is only possible near plate boundaries, as in Iceland.

- **Climate**: some renewables depend on weather and climate factors, such as enough wind for wind farms and enough sunlight for solar farms. Countries with a coastline with land-shore breezes, which exposed mountains or in the mid-latitudes (halfway between the equator and pole) where there are low pressure systems (depressions) have wind energy potential. Countries with clear skies have the potential for solar energy, ranging from deserts to countries with a calmer atmosphere, such as Germany.

- **Environmental factors**: a combination of severe climate and difficult access makes some energy reserves hard to get at, such as oil fields under the Arctic Ocean or in Siberia.

- **Landscape factors**: mountainous areas often suit hydro-electric and wind power because there are higher amounts of rainfall and stronger winds. Shallow sea areas have proved suitable for offshore wind farms.

Costs of exploitation and production

- The value of an energy source is linked to demand and the amount of it: if it is in demand or is running out, the value goes up, making it worthwhile for companies to look for more of that resource. This has happened with oil because there is a strong dependence on it at the moment.

- The cost of converting a primary energy source to electricity is another consideration, as are the high costs of refining oil into petrol and diesel.

- The level of development in a country affects its ability to explore and develop its own energy resources, due to costs and the level of technology required.

Technology

- Changes in technology change the type of resource required. For example, steam engines needed coal, while motor vehicles need oil. Many electrical appliances and gadgets today require more electricity.

- Extraction technologies have also changed, with the ability to drill for oil and natural gas in deeper oceans or to carry out fracking. Wind and solar technologies continue to improve, so renewables are now a genuine alternative to fossil fuels in electricity production.

Political factors

- Countries will try to be self-sufficient in energy production and develop policies to support this aim, such as the UK giving permits for fracking and investing in wind farms.

- Countries may also depend on being friendly with other countries, so that they can trade for their energy resource and use political alliances to secure them.

- In some countries, corruption or civil unrest may disrupt energy supplies.

DO IT!

Summarise the factors affecting the availability of energy supplies in 50 words. Think about whether the physical or human factors are more important.

- Environmental laws and aims are being set internationally, which requires countries to meet sustainable and environmental targets in energy use and production.

STRETCH IT!

Government energy policies

The governments of Germany and Japan have changed their minds about using nuclear energy. This follows the disaster at Fukushima in 2011, which made them realise that radioactivity is potentially very dangerous. The UK government had promoted solar and wind energy with subsidies, but then withdrew them, stating that these industries needed to be competitive in the energy market, and that renewable energy costs were being passed on to consumers. The 2008 recession also put pressure on government budgets.

Net importer of energy	Million tonnes oil equivalent	Net exporter of energy	Million tonnes oil equivalent
China	508	Russia	571
Japan	422	Saudi Arabia	406
India	290	Australia	235
USA	258	Indonesia	232
South Korea	233	Canada	185
Germany	197	Qatar	174
Italy	115	Norway	167
France	114	Kuwait	131

Table 2 Highest net importers and net exporters of energy, 2014

 Graphical skills

Imports and exports of energy

Using the data in Table 2 and a blank outline map of the world, draw bars over the relevant countries on the map using a scale (perhaps 1 cm = 100 million tonnes oil equivalent) to show net energy imports (yellow) and net energy exports (green). Make sure that you give a title, key and scale for the bars.

Does the pattern match Figure 7 on page 161?

A useful way of analysing global energy consumption is to consider not only the **total** amount of energy used by a country, but also how much is used **per capita (per person)** and what the main primary energy sources are.

Selected country	Development level (World Bank 2017)	Location	Energy consumption per capita (2014) kg of oil equivalent per year	Main primary energy sources
Iceland	Developed	NW Europe	17 916	Geothermal
Canada	Developed	N America	7874	Oil, natural gas
UAE	Developed	Middle East	7769	Natural gas
Indonesia	Developing	SE Asia	5122	Oil, coal, natural gas, biomass
New Zealand	Developed	Oceania	4560	Oil, natural gas, geothermal
Japan	Developed	East Asia	3471	Oil, natural gas, coal
UK	Developed	W Europe	2777	Natural gas, oil
China	Emerging	East Asia	2237	Coal, oil
Greece	Developed	SE Europe	2124	Oil, natural gas, lignite (soft coal)
Chile	Developed	S America	2050	Biofuels, HEP
Brazil	Emerging	S America	1485	Oil, biofuels, HEP
Bolivia	Developing	S America	789	Natural gas, HEP
Nigeria	Developing	W Africa	763	Biomass, oil
India	Developing	S Asia	637	Coal, biomass, oil
Kenya	Developing	E Africa	513	Biomass, oil, HEP, geothermal

Source: data from the World Bank (2014, 2017)

Table 3 Energy consumption per capita compared with development and primary energy sources for selected countries

Table 3 shows that developed countries tend to use more energy per capita (per person) than developing countries, but that there is a dependence on fossil fuels. African countries use a low amount of energy per person, but poorer people depend on biomass (e.g. wood, dried dung) for cooking and heating. Iceland uses a lot of energy per person, but has energy security because a lot of renewable energy is available from geothermal sources. Many countries of all types still depend on fossil fuels, which could create problems for them in future when the fuels start to run out or get too expensive to import (e.g. Japan).

DO IT!

Study Table 3.

1 Which of the selected countries may face the most energy problems in future? Explain why.

2 Which countries may face the fewest energy problems in the future? Explain why.

CHECK IT!

1 Name one reason why people need energy resources.

2 Give a definition of a non-renewable energy resource.

3 Explain one way in which hydro-electric power (HEP) may damage the environment.

4 Explain how geological processes have determined the access countries have to fossil fuels.

5 State two reasons why people believe that it will be difficult to meet the future energy needs of the world.

6 Explain the role of government regulations in determining the future energy mix of the UK.

7 Identify **one** advantage and **one** disadvantage of producing nuclear energy.

8 Explain why energy consumption around the world is increasing.

9 Suggest why Japan may face energy insecurity in the future despite its declining population.

9.2 Oil

OUTCOMES

By the end of my revision I will be able to:

- Describe the countries that provide oil and their access to resources.
- Explain the importance of oil to all countries and its effect on global politics.
- Analyse the benefits and costs of oil as a resource.

Introduction

Oil is a finite resource and is only found in certain places around the world, so there is a lot of trade in oil and a lot of searching for new oil reserves or types of reserve. It is moved from source points to demand locations by tanker and pipeline. A lot of money is involved and large companies (transnational corporations, TNCs) have grown (e.g. Exxon-Mobil and BP). Relations between countries can become strained because of oil, and wars have even been fought over it. The largest inter-governmental organisation linked to oil is OPEC (Organisation of the Petroleum Exporting Countries), which is strongly influenced by Saudi Arabia because they have the world's largest conventional crude oil reserves.

DO IT!

Study Table 4. Create a podcast that explains which top ten countries may be benefitting the most from recent oil patterns and which ones should be worried in the longer term.

(Hint: Compare the reserves, production and consumption.)

Oil reserves (*= includes tar sands)		Oil production		Oil consumption	
Country	**% of world**	**Country**	**% of world**	**Country**	**% of world**
Venezuela	17.6*	Saudi Arabia	13.4	USA	19.5
Saudi Arabia	15.6	USA	13.4	China	13.1
Canada	10.0*	Russia	12.2	India	4.8
Iran	9.3	Iran	5.0	Japan	4.2
Iraq	9.0	Iraq	4.8	Saudi Arabia	3.8
Russia	6.4	Canada	4.8	Russia	3.4
Kuwait	5.9	UAE	4.4	Brazil	3.1
UAE	5.7	China	4.3	South Korea	2.8
Libya	2.8	Kuwait	3.4	Germany	2.6
USA	2.8	Brazil	2.8	Canada	2.3

Table 4 Oil data for top ten countries in each category, 2016
Source: data from BP Statistical Review 2017

Graphical skills

World oil reserves by world region

Using the data in Table 5, create a doughnut-shaped pie graph to show the distribution of oil reserves by world region. Study your graph and a world political map and think about how this distribution may affect the development of countries in different parts of the world.

World region	Middle East	South and Central America	North America	Eurasia	Africa	Asia Pacific	Europe
% of total	47.7	19.2	13.3	8.7	7.5	2.8	0.8

Table 5 Oil reserves by world region, 2016
Source: data from BP Statistical Review 2017

STRETCH IT!

Using information from Tables 2, 3 and 4 and your own knowledge, suggest why geopolitical issues are likely to arise due to the patterns of oil reserves.

Geopolitics and oil

Oil supplies and prices are affected by world and regional, political and economic situations. Over time these appear to be creating a greater range in oil price fluctuations (Figure 8).

- The Middle East has the world's largest oil reserves, so any tension or conflict in this region affects oil prices. There have been several wars and countries from outside the region have got involved (e.g. UK, USA, Russia) to try to secure oil supplies. Prices usually go up during these events.

- Within OPEC there are occasional disagreements on production targets and pricing. This affects world supplies and brings higher or lower oil prices for the rest of the world.

- Political decisions can affect demand, such as China's decision to industrialise rapidly, which increased their demand for oil imports and forced world prices up.

- Political decisions can affect supplies, such as Canada's decision to exploit the non-conventional oil source in their oil sands, which added more oil to world production and so decreased the oil price.

- Those countries with oil and those with a willingness to supply it may create alliances (e.g. Canada supplying the USA). Russian oil is in demand in East Asia (e.g. Japan and China), but these countries are wary both of the dependence that this may create and the fact that Russia has stopped supplies to countries at times of political disagreement.

- Economic recessions reduce demand for oil because countries try to use less energy and become more efficient. Consumers buy fewer goods, which reduces the oil price.

Figure 8 Crude oil prices from 1940 to 2017 alongside major world events (US dollars per barrel based on 2016 currency value)

Impact of energy insecurity with oil

Exploration of difficult and environmentally sensitive areas

If a country is short of energy (or money for development), it may be encouraged to extract oil and gas resources from any possible source. This may lead to the clearance of natural ecosystems (such as boreal forests in Canada or tropical rainforest in Brazil) or oil and gas exploration in cold environments (such as the Alaskan tundra, the Arctic Ocean or deep water in the Gulf of Mexico).

Economic and environmental costs

All types of business will be affected if there is not enough oil. The economy of a country will decline and power cuts may become a regular occurrence – in Brazil, for example. This may lead to:

- people facing higher energy bills and being without electricity in their homes at times; industries not being able to operate at full capacity

- a reduction in pollution, but it may encourage risky exploration and developments, such as fracking (oil and gas) or drilling for oil in deeper water, which increases the risk of oil spills

- a pressure to grow biofuels for oils, which reduces the area available for food crops or increases destruction of natural environments.

Example

Conventional fossil fuel extraction: Amazonia natural gas

In Peru, the Camisea project was started in 2004 to extract natural gas reserves estimated to be 385 billion m³. These reserves are expected to last until 2034. The project was financed by foreign sources and the operations are also mostly foreign-owned. Pipelines take the natural gas to a processing plant near Cuzco; from there, pipelines take the gas to Lima, the capital, and to the port of Pisco, where the gas is prepared for export – mostly to Mexico.

Exports began in 2008. A pipeline to take the gas to southern cities and copper mining areas of Peru is under construction. The natural gas reserves will supply 95 per cent of Peru's needs. Exploration of the area for more reserves continues. However, the area has been described as a 'fragile biodiversity hotspot' and is the home of indigenous tribes, such as the Nanti. In 2014, lawsuits were filed to stop expansion into the national park and indigenous areas of the Kugapakori-Nahua-Nanti Reserv. In 2016, presidential election debates often focused on the benefits and problems of the Camisea gas resource.

Advantages

- Peru has a cheap source of fuel, with consumers saving US$13.7 billion in electricity costs between 2004 and 2014.

- The companies producing, transporting and selling the gas have paid about US$8 billion to the national and regional governments in taxes and royalties since extraction started.

- The gas reserves are contributing 0.08 per cent to Peru's gross domestic product (GDP) growth each year, and are predicted to add between US$23 billion and US$34 billion to Peru's economy before the reserves run out.

- The country has energy security, with natural gas supplies and gas-powered electricity-generating stations offering controllable production.

Disadvantages

- Tropical rainforest has been cleared for the gas operations and pipeline construction (Figure 9), including areas set aside as parks and reserves.

- Indigenous tribes have been disrupted, losing their home areas and being infected with illnesses from the outsiders.

- Camisea natural gas is a finite resource and will run out.

- The exploration, production and distribution of the natural gas is very expensive – beyond the means of the country – so money had to be borrowed and foreign companies were brought in.

Figure 9 Damage to the tropical rainforest by natural gas pipeline construction in Peru

Photographic interpretation skills

Make a labelled sketch of Figure 9 to show all the changes caused to the natural environment by the pipeline construction.

Example

Unconventional fossil fuel extraction: Alberta oil sands

Under the boreal forest in the Province of Alberta in Canada there is a very large deposit of oil sands (bitumen – a heavy oil) covering over 140 000 km^2 (Figure 10). The oil-coated sands are found near the surface and over 75 m underground in a sparsely populated area. Those near the surface, mainly near the Athabasca River, are extracted by open-pit mining; the deeper deposits are extracted by pumping steam into wells, which separates oil from sand grains, allowing it to be pumped to the surface.

Figure 10 Canadian oil sands exploitation

The oil sands have become Canada's most important oil resource, with reserves estimated to be about 177 billion barrels, predicted to last nearly 190 years. By the end of 2016, 11.4 billion barrels had been produced from this unconventional oil field. By mid-2017, the average monthly production was 1.24 million barrels a day; this is predicted to double by 2030. Production has increased as the oil price increased after 2000, because extracting this oil is more expensive than with conventional crude oil.

These reserves have provided Canada with a stable source of energy that it can export, mainly to the USA through pipelines. Revenue has contributed hugely to Alberta and Canada, improving quality of life and the economy.

There are major environmental concerns because the open-pit mining leaves massive scars in the landscape (Figure 10), clears large areas of boreal forest (Figure 11) and dumps contaminated water and sand in ponds. Poisonous chemicals may leak into the Athabasca River and into groundwater, harming wildlife. A lot of natural gas is used as an energy source to heat the water for extraction processes, which releases double the 'greenhouse' gases emitted by conventional oil production. The impacts on human health are uncertain and may not be known for decades.

Mining companies have to restore open-pit areas by draining and filling in ponds and planting grasses.

DO IT!

Produce a revision card summarising the advantages and disadvantages of an example of a location where conventional fossil fuel extraction is taking place.

DO IT!

Look at Figure 11 and read the case study.

1 Describe the changes that have taken place in the featured area between 2000 and 2016.

2 Explain the likely impacts that have taken place on the natural environment in this area.

Figure 11 Comparison of Athabascan oil sands mining in September 2000 and July 2016

DO IT!

Create a revision diagram showing how energy insecurity with oil can affect many geographical aspects of a country.

Industrial output

Industries may have to reduce production if there are oil shortages. This may lead to:

- businesses making less money, causing unemployment
- price increases or an increased dependence on imported products
- changes in the trade balance, with more imports than exports.

Potential conflict

If oil supplies are insecure, there may be conflict, such as:

- between consumers, because of higher prices
- between businesses, industries and the government within a country
- between economically competing countries if one is keeping oil costs lower than they should be, creating an unfair advantage
- over areas with key energy sources, such as the Middle East; new oil reserves, such as the Arctic Ocean; or important routes for the transfer of oil, such as the Black Sea area.

CHECK IT!

1 Explain why oil is a finite energy resource.

2 Describe the distribution of oil reserves around the world.

3 Name an oil trans-national corporation.

4 Explain why global oil consumption is increasing.

5 Europe only has 0.8 per cent of the world's oil reserves. Explain how this could be a problem for European countries.

6 a Explain why oil can be the cause of armed international conflicts.

   b Suggest the likely impact on the world oil price of tensions and conflicts in the Middle East.

7 Describe the environmental costs of extracting an unconventional oil resource in a developed country such as Canada.

9.3 Strategies to reduce energy demand

OUTCOMES

By the end of my revision I will be able to:

- Describe how energy demand can be reduced and supply can be increased.
- Describe how energy supply and use may change in the future.

Sustainable energy use

Sustainable energy use means reducing pollution, using renewable options and improving energy efficiency.

Conservation

Conservation involves reducing our use of energy (for example, by walking or cycling and by making devices more efficient).

Home design

All buildings, especially people's homes, can be designed to conserve energy by:

- insulating roofs and walls
- double- or triple-glazing windows with thermal glass
- using energy efficient appliances (A+++ rating)
- fitting solar panels, micro-wind turbines and ground-source heat pumps
- changing lifestyle habits to include switching off appliances when not in use, using electronic gadgets less frequently and turning down central heating thermostats (and wearing more clothing instead).

Workplace practices

Business premises can do similar things to 'home design', but can also:

- use lights that switch off automatically when not in use
- encourage workers to cycle or car share to work
- avoid heating unused spaces, such as storerooms and corridors
- use more natural lighting via windows instead of electric lighting
- use heating and air conditioning only when necessary.

Sustainable transport

Walking and cycling are suitable for shorter journeys as no energy is used. Also, cities have bicycle-hire schemes and congestion and emissions charging zones. However, for some people, and for longer journeys, this may not be possible, so alternatives include using public transport or using small energy-efficient cars, car sharing and using cars that run on ethanol, a biofuel.

DO IT!

Decide what you think is the best way of making energy use more sustainable in the future. Write down at least two reasons to back up your argument for the one that you think is the best.

Reduce demand

With increased wealth and availability of personal transport and technology, energy use has increased. In order to reduce demand:

- people need to change their attitude towards energy use, making an effort to use less (Figure 12)
- governments need to pass laws to make manufacturers produce more energy-efficient products and use energy-efficient technologies during manufacture
- governments can charge different amounts of road tax depending on how eco-friendly a vehicle is.

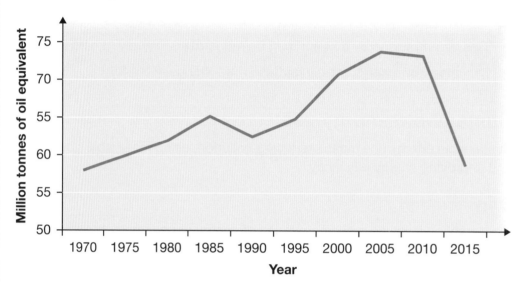

Figure 12 Domestic energy use in the UK, 1970–2015

Efficient technology

- Cars have become more efficient, with improvements in engine technology and weight reductions. Hybrid engines have reduced the amount of petrol or diesel burned during use, and electric cars may be a further step forward (depending on how the electricity they use is created).
- Combined heat and power can increase power station efficiency by over 30 per cent.
- Household appliances are now more efficient at using energy.

Non-renewables

- **Fossil fuels:** conventional power stations can be made more efficient by reusing the heat created during the generation of electricity. This combined heat and power system reduces the amount of fossil fuel used and can produce up to 50 per cent more energy. Conventional power stations can burn biomass as well as coal and natural gas, making electricity generation cheaper and slightly more eco-friendly. Using natural gas rather than coal or oil is better as it produces lower quantities of greenhouse gases. Capturing carbon dioxide emissions and storing them underground makes power stations more environmentally friendly for the future.
- **Nuclear:** used nuclear fuel (uranium rods) can be reprocessed so that uranium can be retrieved to use again. However, some developed countries have decided that the potential danger from radiation is too great a risk.

Strategies to increase energy supplies

Overview of strategies

Renewables

The aims of developing renewable energy resources include reducing the carbon footprint, achieving better energy security and diversifying the energy mix. Table 6 summarises the positive and negative aspects of different renewable resources.

Resource type	Positives	Negatives
Biofuels	• Renewable if new vegetation is continually planted • Affordable for poorer people • Can be used in large and small power stations	• Releases carbon dioxide into atmosphere • Can lead to deforestation • Reduces land area for food crops
Geothermal	• Cheap energy source • No carbon dioxide emissions • Can generate electricity, heat homes and provide hot water	• Limited to certain locations where magma is close to the surface • Needs expensive and complex technology • Only the electricity produced can be transported long distances
Hydro	• Produces very cheap electricity • Flexible power generation to meet demand • Creates a reservoir for water supply	• Very expensive to build • Can destroy a large natural area • Can displace many people from their homes
Hydrogen	• Only waste by-product is water • Fuel cells using hydrogen are more efficient than an internal combustion engine • Hydrogen can be produced from a variety of sources	• Not found separately so another energy resource must be used to create the hydrogen gas • Hydrogen is an energy carrier or way of storing energy rather than an energy source • Hydrogen gas can catch fire easily
Solar	• Low maintenance required once installed • No noise pollution • No carbon dioxide emissions during electricity production	• Very large solar farms may be required, using up farmland • Metals and materials used in manufacture can harm environment • Some consider them a visual pollutant
Tidal	• Countries with a coastline of estuaries and bays can use this source • No carbon dioxide emissions • Electricity generated twice every day	• Only a few locations have a large enough tidal range • The tidal barrage interferes with nature • The construction may be large and unsightly
Wave	• Countries with coastline and long fetches can use this technology • Can use the motion of small waves • No carbon dioxide emissions	• Technology not yet proven to be reliable • Power supplies dependent on wave conditions which vary a lot • Cannot be used by landlocked countries
Wind	• Free energy source, so cheap electricity • Multiple wind turbines create flexibility to generate different amounts of energy • Can use inexpensive micro-turbines for individual farms or homes	• Wind turbines can be very large and obtrusive • Extra costs involved if located offshore • Reportedly endangers wildlife

Table 6 Positive and negative aspects of renewable sources of energy

DO IT!

Put the eight renewable sources of energy listed in Table 6 into rank order according to how successful they would be at increasing future energy supplies.

Give three reasons for your top and bottom choices.

Example

A local renewable energy scheme: Chambamontera, Peru

Sustainable energy supplies

In the Andes Mountains of Peru there are steep slopes, poor road networks and isolated farming communities. It is too costly to provide grid electricity, and even if it were available, poor people would not be able to afford it. Instead, they use fuelwood for cooking and heating and kerosene lamps for light. There is plentiful rain, with rivers flowing in the valleys, so a sustainable energy option is micro-hydro-electric power. Micro-hydro is suitable for small rivers, does not inflict significant damage on the natural environment and is a renewable source of energy. It works by diverting water at an intake weir through constructed channels on the mountainside to a storage tank. The water runs through a pipe down a slope and through a turbine, which is turned to generate electricity. The water then returns to the river. As there is no dam, there is no flooding and costs are very low.

The poor people still need financial and planning help, and this has been provided by the NGO Practical Action. One community to benefit has been Chambamontera, which has about 60 families. A micro-hydro scheme was started in 2008, costing US$45 000 and generating 15 kW of electricity. Most of the funding was from international aid but 6 per cent came from the village families. Chambamontera micro-hydro is an example of a bottom-up scheme, where the local community decided what they needed and now run the scheme.

Benefits

- Cheap renewable electricity is created (US$0.14 per kW).
- Energy is provided for homes and small businesses – including household businesses.
- There is little damage to the environment as there is no reservoir.
- Deforestation is reduced as fuelwood is not needed and side-effects such as soil erosion are reduced.
- Kerosene (a fossil fuel) use is reduced, so the health of people in their homes has improved.
- Energy is provided for the school (computers and internet) and health centre (refrigeration).

Problems

- Poor people still have to pay for the electricity and any initial loans that they had arranged.
- The scheme has a 25-year lifespan, so eventually will need new investment (equipment and maintenance).
- There is some visual pollution on the sides of the valley and some alteration to the flow of the river.

DO IT!

Create a revision card summarising four key points about an example of a local sustainable energy supply that you have studied. Make sure that you concentrate on the energy aspects.

Energy futures

There is a range of views about the development and use of energy resources in the future. These range from not changing anything and keeping the current energy mix ('business as usual') to achieving a totally sustainable energy mix (based on renewables and recyclables). Reasons behind these contrasting views include:

- Opportunity to sell an energy resource for a business to make as much money as possible for a business, or for a country to help its development and future economic security.

- Having access to an easily available and reliable energy resource with technology that is proven and available now.

- Having access to cheap, efficient energy resources and technologies to keep costs down in order to improve quality of life and enable businesses and industries to make more profit.

- Having enough energy resources to meet the demands of a growing, wealthier population and the businesses and industries that need electricity and fuels for transport.

- Improving efficiency of energy resource use so that existing resources last longer and there is time for the development of new sources of energy.

- Concerns about safety of energy technologies, including the potential hazards to people and the natural environment.

- Concerns about short-term and long-term damage to the natural environment caused by energy use, such as local water and air pollution and enhanced global warming from carbon dioxide (CO_2) emissions.

- Greater awareness, through education, of the need to consider carbon and ecological footprints created by human use of energy resources.

Attitudes have started to change (from the top of this list to the bottom) as the severity of climate change is realised, air pollution in cities has increased, and globalisation has enabled people to become more aware of the damage created at the primary fuel extraction sites.

NAIL IT!

Most schemes involving resources can be divided into two groups: top-down and bottom-up. Top-down schemes are large, expensive and use a high level of technology, and are decided by a national government and international corporations or governments, such as the natural gas exploitation at Camisea in Peru. Bottom-up schemes are usually small, less expensive, use intermediate technology, and are decided by local communities with the help of NGOs, such as the micro-hydro at Chambamontera in Peru.

DO IT!

1 Create five cards with the following headers:

- Consumer in a developed country

- Large oil company (trans-national corporation, TNC)

- UK government

- Climate scientists working for the UN

- Greenpeace environmental group

2 Read the eight reasons for contrasting views, and match each one with one or more of the groups. On each card, write the reasons that you think go with that group.

3 Ask a friend to check your matching. Discuss any that they think are wrongly matched.

STRETCH IT!

Read the eight reasons for contrasting views and match them to the these groups:

- Government of Saudi Arabia

- Government of India

- Consumer in an emerging country

- Rural resident in Alberta, Canada

- High-tech TNC located in Silicon Valley, California

Explain your thinking.

Footprints

Carbon footprint

The carbon footprint considers the lifestyle of individuals and how their activities and choices emit carbon dioxide (CO_2) into the atmosphere. Common categories include:

- **Home** – House type, levels of insulation, energy sources and consumption, thermostat settings, energy efficiency of appliances, number of gadgets, length of time in shower and number of trees and shrubs in garden.

- **Food** – Distance that foods have travelled (food miles), the amount of meat eaten, packaging of foods and amount of food waste.

- **Travel** – Numbers of cars (including their fuel type and consumption), travel distances and times, use of public transport or alternative transport such as walking and cycling, and number and distance of flights.

- **Products and services** – Number of electrical items used, amount of clothing and cosmetics bought, recycling habits and use of facilities, recreational activities and number of contracts for TV, internet and phone.

- **Work** – Size of heated or air-conditioned space, energy sources and consumption, sources of food and drink, business and commuting trips, and waste and recycling policies and facilities.

Ecological footprint

The Global Footprint Network compares the things that people need from nature each year (such as oil crops and fuel wood) – including the ability of natural processes to absorb pollution (such as carbon) and wastes – with the actual amount that the planet provides (biocapacity) in a year (Figure 13). The world as a whole has had a negative balance since 1970.

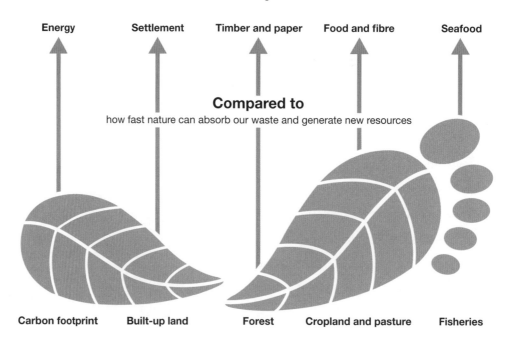

The ecological footprint
measures how fast
we consume and generate waste

Energy   Settlement   Timber and paper   Food and fibre   Seafood

Compared to
how fast nature can absorb our waste and generate new resources

Carbon footprint   Built-up land   Forest   Cropland and pasture   Fisheries

Figure 13 Diagram showing the parts of the ecological footprint calculation

DO IT!

Create a labelled picture diagram that shows all of the things that your household could do better to reduce their carbon footprint.

Country	Biocapacity per capita (gha)	Ecological footprint per capita (gha)	Deficit (−) or reserve (+)
Australia	15.7	8.8	+ 6.9
Brazil	8.8	3.0	+ 5.8
Canada	16.2	8.8	+ 7.4
China	0.9	3.6	
India	0.4	1.1	− −0.7
Indonesia	1.2	1.4	− 0.2
Peru	3.9	2.3	+ 1.6
Russia	6.9	5.7	
Saudi Arabia	0.5	5.6	+ 5.1
USA	3.8	8.6	

Table 7 Ecological footprint for selected countries (2013 data from GFN's 2017 report; gha = global hectares)

STRETCHIT!

Study Table 7. Consider the types of country shown (developed, emerging, developing) and their world locations. What ecological footprint patterns do you notice? Why do these patterns exist?

DOIT!

Look at the data in Table 7. Calculate the deficit or reserve of:

1 USA: the biggest oil consumer

2 China: the biggest importer of energy

3 Russia: the biggest exporter of energy.

 CHECKIT!

1 Identify two ways in which a home can be made more energy-efficient.

2 Give one way in which a government can encourage businesses to use less energy.

3 a Give a definition of 'energy security'.

  b Explain why developing renewable energy resources is important to achieving energy security in a country.

4 Describe the main features of biofuels.

5 a Explain the positives and negatives of wind energy.

  b Explain why using HEP to increase energy supplies can be controversial.

6 Choose a local renewable energy scheme. Give one benefit and one problem of the scheme.

7 a Give one reason why climate scientists want to greatly reduce the use of fossil fuels.

  b Explain why some people and organisations in developed countries do not want to change the energy mix.

8 Suggest the reasons why the USA has a large ecological deficit.

Energy resources management

1 Explain how energy resources help to improve the lives of people.

2 Explain why biofuels are classed as a recyclable resource.

3 Identify two ways in which extracting a fossil fuel resource can damage the environment.

4 Suggest the landscape and climatic conditions needed for a country to develop hydro-electric power (HEP).

5 Explain the conditions necessary for solar energy.

6 Explain why world demand for energy has increased over time.

7 a Give one reason why the UK's use of its energy mix is changing.

  b Explain why the UK's use of its fossil fuel resources is in decline.

  c Explain why environmental concerns have arisen in the UK from plans to develop non-fossil fuel resources.

8 Explain why energy supplies are unevenly distributed around the world.

9 Give a definition of 'energy insecurity'.

10 Suggest why China was the world's largest importer of energy in 2014.

11 Explain why Iceland (very high) and Kenya (very low) had such contrasting energy consumptions per capita in 2014.

Oil

1 Explain what OPEC is.

2 Explain why Saudi Arabia has the largest conventional crude oil reserves in the world.

3 Explain why the USA consumed more oil than any other country in 2016.

4 Explain why the oil consumption in many African countries is very low.

5 Name a country or world region that faces energy insecurity.

6 Suggest the likely impact on the world price of oil of a global economic recession.

7 China has industrialised rapidly in the last 20 years. Explain why this change has increased the world oil price.

8 Give one environmental problem arising from oil exploration in an environmentally sensitive area, such as the Alaskan tundra.

9 a Give two features of a conventional fossil fuel extraction scheme that you have studied.

  b Explain the advantages and disadvantages of extracting a conventional fossil fuel from an area of tropical rainforest in a developing country, such as Peru.

10 Explain the environmental costs of developing an unconventional fossil fuel resource in an environmentally sensitive area, such as the oil sands in the boreal forests of Canada.

Strategies to reduce energy demand

1 Describe one way in which travel habits can be changed to reduce energy use.

2 Explain how workplaces can be made more energy-efficient.

3 Describe one way in which technology can help reduce energy consumption.

4 a Give a definition of 'energy mix'.

   b Give a definition of 'carbon footprint'.

5 a Explain two disadvantages of using hydrogen as an energy source.

   b Compare the costs and benefits of solar power and biofuels as future energy sources.

6 Suggest why small-scale local energy schemes are more suitable for developing countries than large-scale energy schemes.

7 Give one reason why the governments of Japan, Germany and France have decided to reduce the proportion of energy produced by nuclear power.

8 a Give one reason why Exxon-Mobil, the world's largest oil company, wants to explore the Arctic Ocean region for more oil reserves.

   b Explain why some people and organisations in developed countries want to change the energy mix to use mostly renewables.

9 Explain how a carbon footprint calculation can help a household or business to reduce the rate of climate change.

Advice is given in more detail on how to approach the 'Making geographical decisions' questions on these topics in Chapter 10.

10 People and environment issues: Making geographical decisions

THE EXAMINATION!

- This section is tested in Paper 3 Sections A to D.
- A resource booklet is provided in the exam.

DO IT!

Energy issues

Look at Figure 1. Make a list of all the issues you can spot.

OUTCOMES

By the end of my revision I will be able to:

- Explain the processes and interactions between people and the environment.
- Analyse related issues at a variety of scales.

Introduction

Geographical topics are examined separately in Papers 1 and 2 for the first two exams, but in the real world everything is interlinked, so the 'Making geographical decisions' question paper tests your ability to see the wider picture. Complicated situations arise in real life, where the processes in and links between human and physical geography result in problems that require decisions to be made to solve or reduce them.

- **Climate change**: as temperatures get warmer, there will be more tropical storms. Areas where it is wetter may become flooded and other areas could be drier, with an increased risk of **drought**.

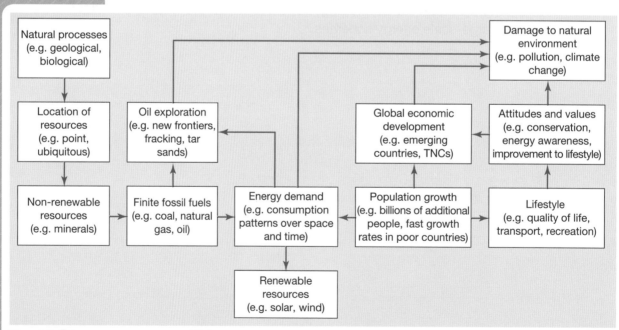

Figure 1 Resource management links

STRETCH IT!

Study Figure 1, especially the links between the boxes. On a copy of Figure 1, add other boxes and arrows to show all other geographical links.

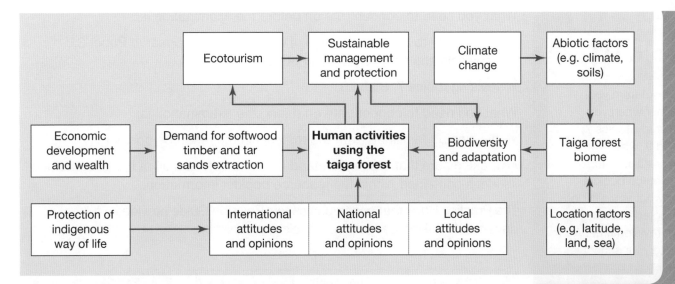

Figure 2 Taiga (boreal) forest environment management links

 STRETCHIT!

Study Figure 2. Think about the attitudes and opinions of stakeholders at the international, national and local levels. Suggest the difficulties that are created by contrasting attitudes and opinions in the decision-making processes that manage taiga forest environment areas.

SNAPIT!

Snap an image of Figure 2. Compete with a friend to see who can spot the most issues that may arise in a taiga forest environment. You can add to this from your own learning.

How to revise for 'Making geographical decisions'

Revision and preparation for Paper 3 'Making geographical decisions' will be a little different from Papers 1 and 2. Paper 3 is based on Topics 7, 8 and 9, although knowledge and understanding may be needed from the other topics you have studied during your course.

In the 'Making geographical decisions' examination, you will be given a real issue to consider, which will be outlined in a resource booklet provided in the examination. Your main knowledge and understanding revision for Paper 3 will be completed when you revise the topics within People and environment issues, which include Topic 7 'People and the biosphere', Topic 8 'Forests under threat' and Topic 9 'Consuming energy resources'.

 DOIT!

Look at Figure 2. Think about the variety of attitudes and opinions that may exist in the management of taiga forest environments. Note down the reasons why people, governments or organisations (the stakeholders) have contrasting attitudes and opinions regarding the situations in the taiga forest environments.

DO IT!

Find out from your teacher when you will study Topics 7, 8 and 9, when you will practise using a resource booklet and what you will be expected to do in your own revision time. Add this to your schedule.

NAIL IT!

Make sure that you can describe and explain interactions and links within any geographical topic, such as those shown in Figures 1, 2 and 3, using the correct terms. This should help you secure a high spelling and grammar mark for longer answers.

DO IT!

With a friend, research geographical issues that have been in the news (from anywhere in the world) over the last two years. Create a table of two columns: 'Issue and location' and 'How issue was or can be managed'.

What you need to concentrate on before the examination is:

- your ability to answer the style of questions that appear in Paper 3, especially the decision-making question

- revising topics 7, 8 and 9.

What you need to concentrate on during the examination is:

- developing familiarity with the material in the resource booklet

- making sure that you understand the links between all of the geographical ideas contained within the resource booklet information.

The Practice Book that accompanies this Revision Guide provides a fully developed 'Making geographical decisions' question.

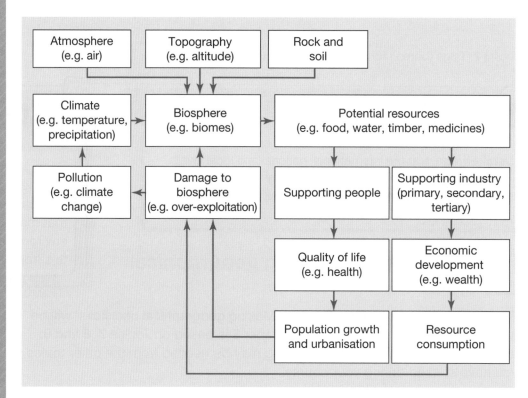

Figure 3 People and the biosphere interactions

Possible issues

There is a range of possible geographical issues covered by Topics 7, 8 and 9. It would be a good idea for you to link these to real-world issues that arise between one and two years before your actual examination. Possible issues include the following.

1 Managing the reduction of carbon dioxide (CO_2) emissions, such as actions by individuals, families, organisations, businesses and governments.

2 Managing changes to natural environments, such as controlling deforestation and protecting wilderness areas.

3 Managing urban environments, such as air and noise pollution, traffic congestion, green spaces and use of brownfield or greenfield sites.

4 Managing environmental impacts of industrial activity, such as degradation of environment, derelict land and air and water pollution.

⑤ Managing the energy security of a country and achieving energy sustainability in the future.

⑥ Managing the various impacts of population growth on human and natural environments.

The resource booklet

You need to know what the resource booklet will look like so that there are no surprises (also see the Edexcel GCSE Geography B Exam Practice Book):

- There will be about eight or nine pages in the resource booklet with about ten figures, including information in a wide range of formats, including: text, diagrams, maps, graphs, tables and photographs.

- The information will be divided into four sections: (A) Topic 7 'People and the biosphere', (B) Topic 8 'Forests under threat', (C) Topic 9 'Consuming energy resources' and (D) 'Making geographical decisions'.

- Some figures may be included in the examination paper (for example, where you have to complete a map or graph). You must consider and use the information from these in the examination, as well as the ones given to you in the resource booklet.

- Make sure that you become familiar with **all** of the figures in the resource booklet before trying to answer any questions in the examination. Note in particular where pieces of information support each other or contradict each other. Allocate time for reading the resource booklet in the examination.

- You are not allowed to take any notes into the examination.

The Paper 3 examination

It is important to know what the question paper will look like so that you are well prepared (also see the Edexcel GCSE Geography B Exam Practice Book):

- Paper 3 'People and environment issues: Making geographical decisions' will have 64 marks.

- The time allowed for the whole examination is 90 minutes and there are 64 marks available (including four marks for SPaG), so you should work to a timescale of one minute for one mark **after** time for reading the resources booklet. For example, a four-mark question should take you four minutes to complete. Leave at least twelve minutes for the final question in Section D.

- There is no choice of questions; you must answer all of those set. It is best to do the questions in this examination in the order they are set, as they are linked, leading your thinking towards the final longer question.

- The types of question vary from one-mark skills questions (such as, *plot, complete* or *calculate* on figures provided in the exam paper) to multiple-choice (one mark) and medium-length answer questions that ask you to *explain* (four marks). There is also one long-answer *decision-making* question (16 marks), which includes an allocation of four SPaG marks.

- You must have a full range of stationery ready for this exam, including a calculator.

DO IT!

Draw a flow diagram (perhaps similar to Figures 1, 2 or 3) to show the issues associated with:

1 either extracting resources from the biosphere or balancing population growth and resource demand;

2 either the threats to tropical rainforests from climate change or creating and maintaining protected areas in the taiga (boreal) forest.

NAIL IT!

You should appreciate that there are several steps involved in a decision-making process. One of these is the ability to use geographical evidence and give geographical reasons for the decision or choice of option(s).

NAILIT!

Decision-making involves the use of evidence from the resource booklet and your studies to determine how significant something is, such as a view or opinion. When making an assessment, you need to all of the factors involved and then sort them to identify the most important.

Academic skills required

- Use a wide range of geographical skills, such as:
  - cartographic (map interpretation)
  - graphical (graph interpretation and drawing)
  - numerical (e.g. using percentages)
  - statistical (e.g. calculating means)
  - qualitative data (using people's opinions)
  - quantitative data (using data facts).
- Use a well-developed academic writing style that shows an ability to use evidence, appraise advantages and disadvantages, evaluate, justify and provide conclusions.
- Recognise command words, such as *describe* or *compare*, and write answers that do what the command word says.
- Appreciate the opinions, attitudes and values of the people affected or involved with an issue (often called stakeholders).
- Identify and understand the links between the economic (money), social (people) and natural environments within geographical situations and issues.
- **Synoptic thinking:** make sure that you try to develop an ability to identify and understand the links between all of the different physical and human geography topics studied. Part of understanding an issue is to see how different geographical processes interlink to cause something to happen.
- **Decision making:** make sure that you are able to make geographical decisions. This means evaluating (looking for good and bad points from) a range of possible options and choosing the best one based on the evidence available.

Raising the standard of your answers

- Follow the command word – answer the question in the way intended!
- Use evidence from the resource booklet to back up every point that you make. For example, evidence can be in the form of generalisations, quoting a short piece of text, quoting a fact or figure, getting information from a graph or map, or making reference to what a photo shows.
- In any longer answer questions, you should take evidence from specified resources and any others that are relevant. You may also need to show your own understanding of a topic.
- Use correct geographical terminology as much as possible.
- In the final 16-mark question, where you are asked to make a decision on which of three options is the best solution, you must remember that there is no correct answer. State your choice clearly in the space provided. Give the advantages of your choice with clear evidence quoted from the resources, but also recognise that your choice may still have some problems; again, make sure that you use evidence from the relevant resources. You should also state the disadvantages of the other options, with the evidence from the resources. You **must** use evidence from the resource booklet and your own understanding throughout your answer.

STRETCHIT!

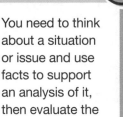

You need to think about a situation or issue and use facts to support an analysis of it, then evaluate the situation or issue before making a judgement about the situation or issue.

Example eight-mark question and answers

Study Figure 4, which shows views and facts about the development of unconventional oil resources in Canada's boreal forest zone.

Assess the reasons why some individuals and groups are not in favour of developing unconventional oil resources.

Use Figure 4 and your own understanding to support your answer. **[8 marks]**

NAILIT!

Make sure that you understand this term and can use the ideas in the examination. **Sustainability** involves making sure that bad impacts are reduced or eliminated and good impacts are increased. This includes trying to make sure that, in the future, people and the natural environment do not experience a decline in the quality of life and, if possible, have a better quality of life.

Athabascan Indians have lived in the boreal climatic zone for thousands of years and over this period of time adapted to live in harmony with the natural environment, with much of their culture based on this lifestyle. An example is their belief in animal spirits, which is linked to animal behaviours and the success of hunting. They see that all parts of the environment are closely linked together and that alterations to one part may affect other parts. However, there are growing threats to both the Athabascan Indians and the boreal environment, many of which are linked to the extraction of oil sands (sometimes known as tar sands). This involves extracting water from rivers, the disposal of wastes, accommodation for thousands of workers, removal of forests and open-pit mining. For example, the Athabascan River flows through oil sands mining areas and then through settlements such as Fort McKay, leading to contamination of water supplies and poisoning of fish. There have been some health issues, such as skin rashes. Also, the carbon dioxide emissions from extracting oil from sands amounted to 8.5 per cent of Canada's total in 2015.

The responsibility for management has been delegated by the Canadian government to the Province of Alberta, which has favoured economic projects. The money ($1.48 billion in 2016/17) from the oil sands greatly benefits Alberta and Canada, creating jobs (136 000 direct jobs) and tax revenue that is used to support health and social programmes and infrastructure projects, including carbon capture and storage schemes costing $1.24 billion over 15 years. According to Natural Resources Canada, even though oil sands extraction has increased, it only occupies a small area compared to the total area of boreal forest, with the total area of oil sands operations only occupying 1.4% of Canada's forested area. The Canadian Forest Service is working with oil companies to find ways of reducing negative impacts on the forest ecosystem and reclaim the land disturbed by oil sands activities.

According to Greenpeace the boreal (taiga) forest has about half of the world's undisturbed primary forest. They are concerned that the 2010 UN Convention on Biological Diversity, which includes a target of reducing the loss of this type of forest by 50%, is not being met by governments. According to the World Bank, Canada's forested area reduced from 3.48 million km² in 1990 to 3.47 million km² in 2015.

NAILIT!

The examination is very likely to involve the need to understand and appreciate the views and opinions of other individuals, groups or organisations. Make sure that you are able to put your own views and opinions aside, so that you can understand why these stakeholders see an issue in a certain way, and understand why conflicts arise.

Figure 4 Views on oil sands extraction in the boreal forest of Canada

Student answer A

Athabascan Indians live in the area where oil sands are being developed so they do not like it. There are growing threats to both the Athabascan Indians and the boreal environment as the river flows through where they live and they get skin rashes. The oil sands extraction leaves great scars in the landscape where large machines have dug out the sands and taken them to the factory. The Indians are worried that taking out the oil upsets the balance found in the boreal biome. Greenpeace are also concerned because forests are being lost such as Canada's forested area reduced from 3.48 million km^2 in 1990 to 3.47 million km^2 in 2015.
However the government are in favour of developing the oil sands as it brings in a lot of money which they can use to make things better for people living in Canada.

Feedback

Student answer A shows a clear understanding of two views against developing the oil sands, and some data from Figure 4 is used. There is also some use of knowledge and understanding from their studies. However, there is some close copying of text, which limits the student's expansion of the answer to include the relative significance of factors or points. The last sentence is not relevant to the question and so does not add anything that can be credited.

Student answer B

The development of unconventional oil resources, such as oil sands, is not supported by many people and groups. On a global scale, environmental groups, citizens and governments are concerned about CO_2 emissions from burning fossil fuels which are causing climate change. According to Figure 1, the extraction of oil from the sands in Canada is producing a significant percentage of Canada's total CO_2 emissions. In Alberta, Canada, oil sands are mined at the surface, which removes boreal forest leaving large scars in the landscape, so is responsible for some of the small loss of Canada's total forest between 1990 and 2015 of 0.01 million km^2. This has a negative impact on the boreal ecosystem, threatening species that live in the forest.

DO IT!

Without looking at the two possible student answers shown, write your own eight-mark answer to the exam question. In the exam you will have about 20 lines on which to write your response, so use this to judge the length of your answer. Try to write your answer in eight minutes after reading Figure 4 for four minutes. After you have written your answer, compare it with the two provided and make a note of what you could have done to improve your answer.

Also, pollutants from the mining operations can enter rivers, such as the Athabascan River, poisoning wildlife (e.g. fish) and even people - as shown by the skin rashes experienced by people living in Fort McKay. The Athabascan Indians are therefore against the development of oil sands as it directly affects them and their culture, which involves living in harmony with nature. Other indigenous peoples hold similar views, - for example, those affected by extraction of natural gas from the Amazonia area of Peru. Greenpeace opposes the development of unconventional oil resources because of the losses of primary forest and biodiversity; they say that countries, such as Canada, should do more to protect forests and abide by the 2010 UN Convention on Biological Diversity.

Feedback

In Student answer B, the student recognises the need to consider the global reasons for not developing unconventional oil resources, uses the full range of views available, and includes the application of linked knowledge and understanding from Figure 4 along with, in a couple of places, their own understanding of biomes and resources. The sentence structures do convey the relative importance of factors mentioned, but could have identified more clearly which was the most important (perhaps in a short conclusion). This answer would gain higher marks in the examination.

CHECKIT!

The examination

1 In which examination paper and section is the decision-making question?

2 a Approximately how many minutes per mark are available in this examination?

   b What skills questions are there?

   c State what you need to remember about the final question in the 'Making geographical decisions' examination.

The resource booklet

1 Describe the types of resource that could be present in the resource booklet.

2 Give the sections that the resources will be divided into.

3 Explain why you need to have an understanding of geographical ideas beyond the resource booklet.

Academic skills required

1 Give the method of calculating a mean.

2 What is an interquartile range?

3 Describe how you would identify a pattern in a choropleth map.

Command words

1 Explain the command word *assess*.

2 Explain the command word *plot*.

3 Explain how you would justify a decision.

Glossary

abiotic   the non-living part of an ecosystem, such as soil

abrasion   the wearing away of cliffs by sediment thrown by breaking waves

accessibility   how easy it is to get to and from a place

adult literacy rate   the number of adults in a country who can read and write (usually expressed as a percentage)

afforestation   planting of trees on a large scale

agribusiness   a large farm or group of farms organised and managed efficiently to make as much profit as possible

aid   the giving of money, expertise or technology by one country to another to help development

aquifer   a layer of rock that contains groundwater

attrition   erosion caused by rocks transported by waves that bump into each other and break into smaller pieces

autotroph   a plant that uses sunlight, nutrients and water to grow (sometimes called producers)

beach nourishment   the addition of sand or shingle to a beach to make it wider

biodiversity   the number and variety of species found within an ecosystem

biomass   the weight of living matter (all the plants and animals) in a given area; organic matter used as fuel in a power station

biome   a large-scale global ecosystem, such as a tropical rainforest (see large-scale global ecosystem)

biotic   the living part of an ecosystem, such as plants

birth rate   the number of live births in a year within a population of an area (usually expressed out of one thousand people)

canopy   a layer of trees within a forest ecosystem

carbon footprint   the amount of carbon dioxide produced by a person, household or business

carrying capacity   the maximum number of people that the Earth can support

central business district (CBD)   area found at or near the centre of a city, where financial offices, government offices, company headquarters, retail outlets and entertainment centres are found

chawl   older tenement building with poor or no facilities, in which the poorest people may end up living in a rapidly growing city

climate   the long-term patterns of average precipitation and temperature, including hot and cold seasons or wet and dry seasons, for an area

climate change   a significant change in the expected long-term patterns of average precipitation and temperature for an area; this may be a natural change or due to human activities

colonial expansion   the historical takeover of overseas territories by a powerful country, usually for economic benefit

commercial farming   the growing of crops or rearing of livestock to make money

composite (strato) volcano   type of volcano with steep sides and composed of layers of different materials, explosive due to lava with a high gas pressure. Usually found at destructive plate boundaries

conservative plate margin   region where two tectonic plates slide past each other horizontally

constructive waves   waves that build up beaches by pushing sand and pebbles further up the beach

consumer   a person, or group of people, who buys or uses things; or in an ecosystem, a creature that eats plants or other creatures

convergent plate margin   region in which two tectonic plates are moving towards each other, resulting either in subduction or folding and uplifting

corrasion   acids contained in sea water will dissolve some types of rock such as chalk or limestone

Corruption Perceptions Index   measures the quality of the government of a country and fairness of decision-making

counter-urbanisation   movement of people out of city centres towards the countryside due to improvements in technology and transport permitting home working

cycle of poverty   a situation where poor people become stuck in poverty with no way of changing their conditions

cyclones   tropical storms that occur in South-East Asia

death rate   the number of people who die in a year within a population of an area (usually expressed out of one thousand people)

debt reduction   also known as 'debt-for-nature swap', occurs when there is an agreement between a country that owes a huge amount of money internationally and a lender such as the World Bank, where some of the debt is wiped away in return for legal protection of part of an ecosystem

decomposer   a living organism, such as fungi or beetles, that helps the breakdown of dead living matter

deforestation   the cutting down of trees on a large scale

de-industrialisation   a stage in economic development where manufacturing industries decline and close down, while service industries grow

Demographic Transition Model (DTM)   a graph representing changes in the population of a country or region, by tracking birth and death rates and population size over a long period of time

depopulation   a decline in the number of people in an area, especially due to movements away (emigration)

desertification   the change in a semi-arid area to a desert because of a change in natural processes or damaging human activities

destructive waves   waves that erode beaches with a strong backwash that removes beach material

developed country   a country with very high human development, in which, for example, average wealth is high, education and health are well supported and tertiary and quaternary sector businesses are mature. Example: United Kingdom

developing country   a country with low human development, in which, for example, average wealth is low, education and health may not be well supported and primary sector businesses dominate. Example: Afghanistan

discharge   the volume of water flowing in a river

diurnal temperature range   the daily change in temperature between day and night

divergent plate margin   region in which two tectonic plates are moving apart each other, resulting in volcanoes, earthquakes or the formation of ridges

diversification   a process where a business that cannot sustain its main income expands into other areas of business to keep it viable. For example, farmers with falling income may set up tourist accommodation or farm produce shops

drainage basin   an area of land drained by a river and its tributaries

drought   a situation where the fresh water supplies are well below the amount needed to support the population of an area

dune regeneration   the planting of marram grass to stabilise natural sand dunes and prevent erosion

ecological footprint   the amount of resources used from the Earth to support a population

economic development   the creation of industries and businesses in a country or region in order to make money

ecotourist   a person who goes on holidays to appreciate and look after nature; a type of holiday that causes little or no damage to the natural environment

emergent tree   a very tall tree that is above the canopy layer

emerging country   a country with medium or high human development, in which, for example, average wealth is moderate, education and health are becoming better supported and secondary sector businesses dominate, with some tertiary sector activity. Example: Brazil

energy gap   the difference between the amount of energy available for a country and the amount of energy needed

energy mix   the variety of sources of energy production of a country

enhanced greenhouse effect   the warming of the atmosphere caused by human activities, extra to the warming caused by natural processes

environmental sustainability   the long-term balance of natural systems

erosion   wearing away or removal of material by a moving force such as water

evapotranspiration   the process where plants give off water through their leaves and then this water is evaporated from the leaf surface into the atmosphere

famine   a situation where there is not enough food for the population of a place

fetch   the distance over which a wave can travel uninterrupted

finite resource   resource that is only available in a limited amount that will run out over time

floodplain   flat area of land forming the valley floor either side of the river channel

food chain   a simple sequence of links between living things within an ecosystem, where one living thing eats another

food web   a complex series of links between living things within an ecosystem where energy is transferred through food

Foreign direct investment (FDI)   when businesses from one country invest money in the businesses and industry of another country

formal economy/employment   businesses and industries that offer regular wages and contracts, with a set place of work or work routines, which follow laws and pay taxes

fossil fuel   an energy source that was created by geological processes, such as oil

Frank's dependency theory   economic theory that says some countries will become richer by exploiting other countries, creating a rich core developed region and a poorer developing region

freeze-thaw weathering   when water seeps into cracks in rocks, freezes and expands, eventually breaking the rock apart

gabion   wire cage filled with rocks built at the base of a cliff or along sea fronts in towns, to protect the coast from erosion

geological process   a process linked to the formation of rocks, either sedimentary, igneous or metamorphic

geothermal energy   a source of heat from very hot magma underground that can be used to turn water into steam and create cheap electricity or provide heating to homes and settlements

glacier   a slowly moving mass or river of ice formed by the accumulation and compaction of snow on mountains or near the poles

global atmospheric circulation   the large-scale pattern of movement of air in the atmosphere, such as convection cells and trade winds

globalisation   the linking of people and countries all over the world by various processes such as communications, trade, migration, money and culture

greenhouse effect   the trapping of heat within the atmosphere by denser gases, such as carbon dioxide

greenhouse gas   one of the denser gasses responsible for trapping heat in the atmosphere, such as methane or carbon dioxide

gross domestic product (GDP)   all of the money made within a country divided by the total population to find a mean of how much money each person makes in a year

gross national income (GNI)   all of the money made within a country and from overseas investments, minus debts, divided by the total population to find a mean of how much money each person makes in a year

growing season   the number of months in a year when the average temperature is high enough for plants to grow

groyne   wood or rock structures built out to sea from the coastline, to trap sediment produced by longshore drift

Hadley convection cell   one of the main large-scale movements of air in the atmosphere, found either side of the equator all around the planet

hard engineering   the building of entirely artificial structures using various materials such as rock, concrete and steel to reduce, disrupt or stop the impact of river or coastal erosion

hard rock coasts   coastline formed largely from rocks resistant to erosion, such as igneous granite

hotspot   region of volcanoes away from plate margins, caused by magma rising through the mantle and a weakness in the Earth's crust

Human Development Index (HDI)   a measure of how developed a country is using social and economic indicators

human rights   people have the right to experience life without persecution from others, this is supported through the United Nations

humanitarian crisis   a situation where the lives of many people are threatened by a natural or man-made hazard

hurricane   a tropical storm located in the Atlantic (in the Pacific they are known as typhoons)

hydraulic action   the force of the river against the banks causing air to be trapped in cracks and crevices. The pressure weakens the banks and gradually wears it away

hydro-electric power (HEP) a source of electricity created by water flowing through turbines

hygiene the absence of germs through cleanliness and understanding of how to reduce illness

hyper-urbanisation a situation where a city expands rapidly due to an extended period of people migration into the city

igneous rocks rocks formed from volcanic activity

impermeable rock rock that does not let water pass through

indigenous native to an area

infant mortality the number of deaths of children under the age of one year, usually expressed out of one thousand live births

industrial period of time when business is dominated by manufacturing industry, and tertiary industry develops

informal economy/employment the part of the economy that is not official, often involving no fixed place of work or regular income with no taxes paid and no welfare plan

infrastructure the structures and things that are needed to support businesses, industries or people, such as transport networks, power and water supplies

inner city area of a city found around the central business district, with a mix of property types such as old industrial buildings, older terraced housing and newer high-rise apartments

intermediate technology a level of machinery and equipment that is above a simple level (hand tools) but below the complicated level (high-tech), usually more affordable and easier to understand

international aid help given by a country or international organisation to a poorer country or one in need of assistance

international migration movement of people between countries

intertropical convergence zone (ITCZ) the linear area where the two Hadley cells meet near the equator; it moves according to the season, for example, in the northern hemisphere summer it is north of the equator but in winter it is south of the equator

land use describes what the land in cities is used for

latitude the distance, north or south, from the equator (based on an angle)

leaching the loss of water-soluble plant nutrients from the soil

levée raised bank found on either side of a river, formed naturally by regular flooding, or man-made as a flood defence

life expectancy the average number of years from birth that a person living in a place can be expected to live

location place where something is found in relation to other important places or features

longitude the distance east or west from the Greenwich meridian line (based on an angle)

longshore drift transport of sediment along a stretch of coastline caused by waves approaching the beach at an angle

magma molten rock below the Earth's surface

megacity any city that is home to over ten million people

managed retreat controlled retreat of the coastline, allowing flooding to occur over low-lying land

metamorphic rocks rocks formed from existing rocks that are changed when subjected to extreme heat or pressure

microfinance loan the lending of a small amount of money to poor people so that they can make significant improvements to their lives and work in times of hardship

migration the permanent movement of people from one place to another for at least one year

million city any city that is home to over one million people

nationalised describes businesses owned and run by the government, rather than shareholders or private individuals

natural hazard a natural event (for example, an earthquake, volcanic eruption, tropical storm, flood) that has the potential to cause damage, destruction and death

natural increase the increase in the population size of an area due to the birth rate being higher than the death rate

natural resource a product from natural systems, such as ecosystems or geological processes, that is of use to people

national migration movement of people within a country

non-government organisation (NGO) an organisation that is not run by a government, but independent such as a charity

nutrient a mineral that can be used by a living organism to help it grow and develop

nutrient cycle   the way in which minerals are stored and moved around within an ecosystem

organic   derived from living organisms

permafrost   the ground that is frozen all year except for a thin upper layer in summer

permeable rock   rock that lets water pass through

photosynthesis   the process plants use to grow by using sunlight, carbon dioxide and water

polar region   an area of the Earth near either the North or the South Pole

post-industrial   a period of time when the number of secondary industries has declined to be replaced by tertiary businesses

precipitation   all types of water falling from the air, such as rain, snow, sleet, or hail

pre-industrial   a period of time when most employment is to be found in farming, fishing and mining, before manufacturing and other industries have developed

primary effect   direct effect on people or the environment caused by a tectonic hazard such as a volcanic eruption or earthquake. Examples include collapsed buildings and deaths due to lava or falling objects

primary producer   a plant that is at the base of a food web or trophic levels, which is able to use sunlight to grow (using the process of photosynthesis)

primate city   any world city that is at least twice as big as the next largest city in the same country

private sector   describes businesses owned by shareholders or private individuals, rather than the government

privatisation   where nationalised businesses and industries are 'sold off' by a government to be run separately without government interference

public sector   describes businesses owned and run by the government, rather than shareholders or private individuals

pull factor   any reason why people are attracted to a place

push factor   any reason why people want to leave a place

quality of life   a way of considering the well-being of people by looking at a wide range of factors linked to health, housing, employment, clean water, food supply, education and political freedom, for example

quaternary sector   industries providing information services, such as computing, ICT, consultancy (business advice) and research and development

recession   an economic situation where businesses and industries find it difficult to sell things and so everyone is poorer; on a world scale this has happened about every 50 years

refugee   a person fleeing from one country to another to escape the threat of death

regeneration   investment of money, infrastructure or business in a place to help it recover from a decline

relief   the height of land

remittance   an amount of money sent home to families by migrants working in another country

renewable energy   a source of power that is not using fossil fuels but instead uses something that will not run out, such as wind or sunlight

reprofiling   the reshaping of a beach to restore it, for example after winter storms

research and development   the way in which businesses and industries stay ahead of their rivals by investigating new ideas and products

resource   (see *natural resource*)

rock armour   piles of large boulders arranged at the base of cliffs to protect the coast from erosion

Rostow's modernisation theory   economic theory that says all countries go through similar stages of economic development, but at different times

rotational slip   occurs when saturated soil and weak rocks move along a curved surface

rural–urban fringe   the zone around a large settlement which has a mixture of urban and rural land uses and a mixture or rural and urban processes

rural–urban migration   the movement of people from rural areas into towns and cities, with a permanent change of residence

savannah   tropical grassland

sea wall   a concrete wall built at the base of a cliff or along sea fronts in towns, to protect the coast from erosion

secondary effect   indirect effect on people or the environment caused by a tectonic hazard such as a volcanic eruption or earthquake. Examples include avalanches and landslides triggered on nearby mountains

sedimentary rocks   rocks formed by small particles eroded and deposited in layers and compressed over millions of years

service   in a biosphere, a process that maintains the biosphere. For example, photosynthesis and carbon dioxide storage in plants helps to maintain the amounts of carbon dioxide and oxygen in the atmosphere

service sector also known as the tertiary sector, is the collection of businesses based on providing a service for people or other businesses, such as banking and insurance

shield volcano type of volcano with gently sloping sides and composed of layers of solidified lava, with frequent, gentle eruptions of basaltic lava. Usually found at constructive plate boundaries or hot spots

shrub layer a low level of vegetation in a biome, below the canopy layer but above the ground layer

site geographical location (of a city)

situation the reasons a place (often, a city) develops and its location relates to the surrounding area

soft engineering involves the use of the natural environment surrounding a river, using schemes that work with the sea or river's natural processes.

soft rock coasts coastline formed largely from rocks that are less resistant to erosion, such as clay

solar energy ways of collecting and using the power of the Sun, for example, through solar panels to create electricity

spending on education and health the quality of life of a population often depends on their health and being able to read and write, so governments invest money in these services

sporadic permafrost describes conditions for an area of land that is frozen solid for most of the year and only thaws out in a short summer period

strato volcano see **composite (strato) volcano**

storm surge situation in which a high tide is higher than normal due to lower pressure brought on by a cyclone. This may cause extensive flooding

subsistence farming growing of food and rearing of animals just to feed a family. Sometimes surpluses may be sold

suburb area of a city found toward its edges, with lower density housing, some areas of retail outlets and entertainment centres and green, open spaces

sustainable ensuring that a situation or process can continue into the foreseeable future without damaging the natural environment

sustainable development for a city, meeting the needs of the present without compromising the ability of future generations to meet their own needs

taiga (boreal) biome region consisting mainly of coniferous forests in a sub-arctic environment

tariff money collected by a government as a tax on importing or exporting goods or services

thalweg the line of fastest flow along the course of a river

trading the selling or exchange of goods and services, usually between countries

transnational corporation (TNC) a large international business that has factories or offices in several countries around the world

transpiration the process of plants giving off water through their leaves

trophic level the arrangement of 'feeding groups' within any ecosystem, from plants at the base to top carnivores at the peak

tsunami extreme water wave caused by earthquakes, volcanic eruptions, erosion or falling meteors

tundra a cold semi-arid environment with very cold temperatures for most of the year and only a sparse vegetation of lichens, grasses and small shrubs

typhoon the name given to a tropical storm cyclone in the Pacific (in the Atlantic they are known as hurricanes)

urban sprawl the spread of urban land uses and influences into a rural area surrounding a city or large town

urbanisation the rise in the percentage of people living in an urban area compared to rural areas

water cycle the ways in which water is stored and moved on the planet

'Western' culture a way of living; applied to countries whose population is historically largely based on European immigration, such as the USA, Australia or Europe itself. The model is that of freedom, wealth and the ability of any person to be successful

wilderness an area of the Earth that has not been altered by human activity, or has only experienced minimum human interference

wind energy ways of collecting and using the movement of the air, for example, by windmills or modern turbines in wind farms to create energy

world city any one of the world's most important cities, having a disproportionate role in global current affairs

Check It! Answers

1 Hazardous Earth

1.1 The world's climate system (p. 14)

1 Areas of low pressure are found where the air is rising; winds on the ground move towards areas of low pressure. Areas of high pressure are found where the air is sinking; winds on the ground move outwards from areas of high pressure.

2 Three causes of natural climate change; any three from:
   - Changes in the Earth's orbit. These include eccentricity, which is the change in the elliptical paths of the Earth around the Sun; precession, which is the natural wobble of the Earth; and tilt, which is the change in the Earth's tilt between 21.5 and 24.5 degrees.
   - Solar output, which is the cyclical change in solar energy linked to sunspots.
   - Volcanic activity.
   - Asteroid collisions.

3 Volcanic ash can block out sunlight, reducing temperatures; sulfur dioxide emitted during a volcanic eruption mixes with water vapour and forms sulfuric acid, which reflects the Sun's radiation, reducing temperatures.

4 Ice cores contain layers of ice formed from fallen snow. Each layer represents a year of snowfall. Air bubbles are trapped in this ice; these contain the mixture of chemicals in the air from the time the snow fell. Measuring the amount of carbon dioxide in the air bubbles enables climatologists to reconstruct past global temperatures.

   Each ring in a tree trunk represents the tree's growth for a single year. Growth is faster and greater in warmer, wetter conditions (meaning the rings are further apart), and slower in cooler, drier conditions (meaning the rings are closer together). Living trees represent recent climate conditions; fossilised tree remains represent more ancient climate conditions.

5 The greenhouse effect is the way that gases in the atmosphere trap heat from the Sun. Like the glass in a greenhouse, they let heat in, but prevent most of it from escaping.

6 The greenhouse effect is natural, whereas the enhanced greenhouse effect is caused by humans. Added pollution, including carbon dioxide and other greenhouse gases, has meant more heat is trapped in the atmosphere and has caused temperatures to rise.

7 Any two from:
   - Burning fossil fuels, which releases carbon dioxide into the atmosphere. Higher concentrations of carbon dioxide trap more of the energy from the Sun, causing average global temperatures to rise. Increases in population and increases in people's wealth over time cause more fossil fuels to be burned, increasing the temperature further.
   - Farming/agriculture, especially cattle and rice farming, causes more methane to be released into the atmosphere. Methane is a greenhouse gas, so higher concentrations of methane in the atmosphere traps more of the energy from the Sun, causing average global temperatures to rise.
   - Deforestation/cutting down trees means there are fewer trees to take in carbon dioxide (which is required for photosynthesis). Trees are also natural stores of carbon dioxide, which is released to the atmosphere if the wood from the trees is burned.

8 There may be more flooding in some parts of the world due to heavy rainfall. This could affect parts of the UK, e.g. Somerset. Low-lying coastlines are more at risk of coastal flooding due to sea-level rise e.g. Bangladesh, and there may be more extreme weather events such as droughts in sub Saharan Africa, e.g. South Sudan and heatwaves in places like the UK.

9 Predictions of future climate change (including average global temperatures) are uncertain because:
   - Modelling climate is very complicated, with many variables to analyse, so predictions are made that include an explanation of the uncertainties they involve.
   - The future growth of the human population (which affects climate through farming, pollution from industry and transport, etc.) is hard to predict.
   - Humans are changing the amount of fossil fuels burned, especially by changing to hybrid or electric vehicles, but the policies of governments in different countries change (often in unpredictable ways) due to political opinions and economic concerns. This uncertainty carries over into problems for trying to estimate how much carbon dioxide humans will produce from their activities in future.
   - In many countries, people are starting to change their lifestyles to reduce pollution, e.g. by recycling waste, using public transport and making their homes more energy efficient. Human behaviour is very difficult to predict.

1.2 Extreme weather events (p. 19)

1 Tropical cyclones develop in the tropics, over areas of ocean and away from the equator.

2 Tropical cyclones do not form on the equator because the Coriolis force is too weak.

3 Air is heated above warm tropical oceans, causing the air to rise rapidly. The upwards movement draws up water vapour from the ocean surface. As the air rises it cools, causing the water vapour to condense, forming large clouds that create thunderstorms. The condensing water vapour releases heat energy, which accelerates the process of evaporation and drawing ever more water vapour up from the ocean. Several thunderstorms join to form a giant spinning cyclone. As the cyclone moves across the ocean, it gains energy and strength.

4 A primary effect is one that is caused directly by the cyclone, e.g. injuries caused by flying debris picked up and blown at high speed by the cylone winds. A secondary effect is caused by a primary effect, e.g. if the cyclone causes a storm surge that leads to the flooding of a town or city, there may be injuries or deaths due to the flooding.

5 Using Cyclone Alia as the example, immediate responses were to send out teams of workers, the police and the military to help evacuate affected people; find missing people; provide immediate supplies of food and water; clear roads and restore power to assist with the emergency effort. Long-term responses included developing early warning systems; building coastal embankments to protect against storm surges; building storm shelters to protect people that have evacuated their homes; rebuilding damaged roads, houses and facilities.

6 Management strategies to reduce the effect of tropical cyclones have positives and negatives. Positives of monitoring storms using satellites: people can be informed of up-to-date information and be given early warning when the storm changes in strength or increases in speed. This data can be used to predict the path of the tropical cyclone, which allows governments to warn citizens and evacuate people, if necessary, to reduce death toll and injury levels. Strengthening windows and building cyclone shelters helps to protect the people who may be affected by the tropical cyclone and so to reduce the number of people injured or killed. Finally, planning enables people to be educated on what to do in the event of a tropical cyclone.

   There are negatives to some of these methods, for example, when predicting a cyclone, the information may be incorrect, as the path of a cyclone can be unpredictable. It is more difficult to warn people in developing countries as communications are not as good with less advanced technology and less access to mobile phones and televisions. People in developing countries are less likely to be able to afford storm protection and so there is a higher chance of buildings collapsing or being damaged.

1.3 Tectonic hazards (p. 29)

1 Earthquakes mostly occur near plate margins, which in turn are found mainly on or close to the coast of countries.

2 Any two differences from:
   - Oceanic crust is more dense than continental crust.
   - Oceanic crust tends to be made up of basalt, continental crust tends to be made up of granite.
   - Oceanic crust is thinner than continental crust.
   - Oceanic crust is formed at divergent plate margins, continental crust is formed by volcanic activity caused at convergent plate margins.

3 Earthquakes and volcanoes happen at plate margins because this is where two or more plates meet due to convection currents and/or slab pull and ridge push. Tensions and pressure build up and their release results in an earthquake at conservative plate margins. At destructive plate margins, melting rock and the rise of magma produces volcanoes.

4 Constructive, destructive and conservative.

5 Where two continental plates of low density meet folding and uplift occur.

   Neither of the two plates is subducted because the continental rocks are relatively light. This causes the formation of fold mountains, e.g. the Himalayas.

6 At a convergent plate margin, two plates move towards each other. When an oceanic and a continental plate meet, the denser oceanic plate is subducted (pushed downwards) beneath the lighter continental plate, creating deep ocean trenches and fold mountains. The released pressure can cause strong earthquakes and can cause magma to rise, resulting in explosive volcanic eruptions. When two continental plates meet, fold mountains are formed and earthquakes may occur, but there is no volcanic activity.

7 Primary effects: these happen *directly* as a result of an earthquake or volcano. Secondary effects: these occur *indirectly* as a result of an earthquake or volcano. They can happen hours, days or weeks later, e.g. fires and the spread of disease.

8 The primary effects of the L'Aquila earthquake were that 308 people died and 1500 people were injured. Furthermore, 10 000–15 000 buildings collapsed or were severely damaged, including the hospital, churches and medieval buildings. This left 67 500 people homeless and cost US$16 billion. The secondary effects were landslides, which affected transport, and a drop in the number of people going to L'Aquila university following the earthquake.

9 There is evidence to support this being true. This is shown in the Nepal earthquake where 9000 people died and 20 000 people were injured compared to the L'Aquila earthquake in Italy where 308 people died and 1500 people were injured. Furthermore, following the Nepalese earthquake nearly 3 million people were left homeless compared to 67 500 people in the L'Aquila earthquake. This shows the extent to which people are affected more in developing countries after an earthquake.

   However, there are often more economic effects in a developed country, for example, the L'Aquila earthquake cost US$16 billion whereas the Nepal earthquake cost US$5 billion. In conclusion, the social effects are often more devastating after an earthquake in a developing country but the economic effects can be higher in a developed country.

10 The benefits of living near a volcano are: potential geothermal power source, volcanoes produce fertile and nutrient-rich soil for farming, volcanoes can provide jobs via the tourist industry and also mining jobs.

11 There are a number of ways of making buildings earthquake proof, e.g. deep foundations to prevent collapse of a building, strong double-glazed windows to prevent glass shattering down, a strong steel frame which means the building is more flexible, cross bracing to stop floors from collapsing and a damper in the roofs that acts like a pendulum, which reduces sway.

2 Development dynamics

2.1 Development and inequalities (p. 40)

1 Inequality means that there is a large difference between countries and/or sections of a population within a country in terms of quality of life or wealth.

2 One economic measure, such as GNI, which is a measure of all the profit made by a country's businesses (inside and outside the country); GNI per capita or GDP per capita.

   One social measure, such as life expectancy, which reflects the living conditions and level of health care in a place. (Other examples: literacy rate; infant mortality rate; access to safe water.)

   One political measure, such as the Corruption Perceptions Index, which shows how fair decision-making at government level is.

3 Any two possibilities such as: developing countries have lower education levels than emerging countries; developing countries have worse levels of health care than emerging countries; developing countries have higher infant mortality rates than emerging countries; people in developing countries are poorer than those in emerging countries; developing countries are in Stage 1 or Stage 2 of the demographic transition model while emerging countries are in Stage 3; developing countries have fewer doctors per 1000 people than emerging countries; developing countries have higher disease rates (e.g. tuberculosis) than emerging countries.

4 a In a developing country, the birth rate is very high and may increase if better living conditions reduce infant deaths. The death rate declines very quickly from very high to quite low.

   b In developing countries, economic development increases because of improvements in health care and living conditions, which create a better and larger workforce. Education gives people more skills to be able to work better on farms (more food) or factories (more money). This is a transition from a developing country to an emerging country.

5 Overpopulation is where there are too many people for the resources available, so people lack food, water, energy and jobs, creating a lower quality of life. Underpopulation creates a similar problem, with too few people to work and develop the resources available, so people again are unable to improve their quality of life. Both overpopulation and underpopulation hold back development.

6 Two physical causes, such as: climate may or may not favour development depending on suitability to type of development; resources are not evenly spread, those areas with resources develop while those without do not; locations may or may not favour trade, for example, those by the sea may be able to develop ports; the presence or absence

of natural hazards also affects development, with those subject to natural hazards being held back.

   Two human causes, such as: the presence or absence of a trading network with other countries, those with such a network will develop more; the ability to attract foreign direct investment (FDI) can determine the level of development; external influences may determine the level of development, such as through a colony linked to an empire country, or the amount of aid received.

7 The cycle of poverty describes a situation where countries remain poor because the processes and situation within the country all continue the poverty. An example is a government lacking money to invest in infrastructure, so businesses and industries cannot improve and so cannot pay taxes to the government.

8 People face health problems because there is a lack of investment in health care or water and sanitation systems. People are therefore more exposed to disease and then the expensive medicines and care required are not available.

9 There is no correct answer to this question. Either push or pull factors or a combination of both may be more important, depending on local situations. Jobs and money are the key factors; a lack of jobs and poverty are push factors, job opportunities and wealth are pull factors.

10 a The modernisation theory (by Rostow).

   b Weaknesses of the dependency theory include its inability to explain why some very poor countries have developed, or why there are many positive links between rich and poor countries.

2.2 Development strategies (p. 44)

1 A top-down approach is government-led while a bottom-up approach is local community led; top-down consists of large expensive schemes while bottom-up consists of small affordable projects.

2 The multiplier effect is the process where money spent results in a larger effect on the economy, as the money is spent again and again. It is also where one improvement directly causes another improvement. There is a positive 'knock-on' effect.

3 a TNCs may bring benefits to developing countries such as: employing local people, so providing wages and skills; providing factories and helping linked local businesses and industries develop; introducing new technologies to the country.

   b TNCs may bring problems to developing countries such as: exploiting the workforce by only paying low wages; taking profits out of the country and not paying taxes; putting too much pressure on the government.

4 a Aid may help a country develop by reducing a weakness, allowing a multiplier effect to start, e.g. educating people so that they have the skills to do their jobs better or providing finance for major projects, such as hydro-electric power schemes that provide cheap electricity and perhaps better water supplies.

   b Fairtrade targets poorer people, e.g. farmers, to give them a reasonable income from which they can improve their lives, whereas debt relief targets a whole country or the government to reduce a massive financial burden, so that money can be invested in things to help develop the country.

   c Both microfinance loans and intermediate technology can help poorer people, so they are similar because they both avoid dependency on external aid. Small loans can be used to improve farming, send children to school or improve housing. Intermediate technology also makes small improvements to farming and perhaps to water and energy supplies.

2.3 Rapid economic development and change (p. 51)

1 a 'Economic change' means the changes that have taken place in the industrial structure (primary, secondary, tertiary, quaternary), the types of industry and business, the types of employment and the wealth of the country.

   b 'Environmental change' means the changes to the natural environment, such as to ecosystems, rivers, the landscape and air quality.

2 Answers will vary according to case study. In this Revision Guide, the example is India.

   a The advantages that India has include: a large young adult workforce that includes scientifically and technically qualified people; an English speaking population; ports on the coast for access to trading by sea; a key position between East Asia and the Middle East and Europe.

   b Cultural characteristics include: strong links with Indian migrants around the world; Hindi and English official languages; main religion Hindu (80%) but many others as well; caste system.

   c The socio-political challenges that exist include: religious divide; caste divide; 20% of population live in poverty, especially in rural areas, despite the emerging economy of country; conflicts with neighbouring countries (e.g. Pakistan); rapid population growth (to over 1.3 billion people) with future ageing population issue and current young adult population and gender imbalance (too many males).

   d Political and economic globalisation have strongly influenced India because it is a member of the Commonwealth, G20 group and UN; USA TNCs invest in India; India now taking the lead in South Asia through aid and economic/political influence; Indian TNCs in Europe and North America; fully involved in the world trading network (1.3% of world goods exports, 3.3% of world service exports). So India is strongly linked into global systems, especially trading to try and become wealthier and more developed, and helping developing countries through the New Development Bank.

3   The quality of life in India has slowly improved according to some measures of development. For example, life expectancy has increased and mortality rates are lower, more people have access to clean water and the number of children in secondary schools has doubled. HDI has increased slowly but not as fast as other countries due to regional disparities, especially in rural areas. Economic development has also caused some problems, such as pollution in urban areas and rivers.

3 Challenges of an urbanising world

3.1 Trends in urbanisation (p. 57)

1   Urbanisation is an increase in the proportion or percentage of people who live in urban areas.

2   The populations of developing and emerging countries are generally higher than developed countries in the first place. There are high birth rates and high levels of rural–urban migration because job opportunities are concentrated on secondary, tertiary and quaternary industries that often require cities in which to operate/flourish. All these factors combine to make megacities more likely.

3   London is an important world city because (any two or three reasons from the following): English is the main language spoken; the UK has strong trading links with many countries across the world, partly for historical or political reasons (UK had industrial revolution earlier than many other countries; UK is linked with many former colonies through e.g. the Commonwealth); London has well-developed transport links with the rest of the world; world's oldest parliamentary democracy seen as a model for many other countries; useful location in terms of time zones (a few hours ahead of most US cities and a few hours behind Asian and Middle Eastern cities); well-developed leading city within Europe.

4   Any sensible job suggestions, including: formal – legal profession, financial services (banker etc.), police, doctor, nurse, factory worker, etc.; informal – shoe shiner, street seller, child minder, domestic cleaner, bar tender, etc.

5   Developed: no primary industry; some secondary; mostly tertiary including tourism, education, finance, etc.; growing quaternary industry such as IT, media and culture; jobs mostly formal.

Emerging: little primary industry; some secondary; much tertiary; some quaternary; jobs a mix of formal and informal.

Developing: little primary industry; growing secondary; much tertiary; no quaternary; many informal jobs but increasing number of formal jobs.

6   Pre-industrial: jobs mostly in primary industry, such as farming, fishing and mining; small but very slowly developing secondary industry, and an even smaller tertiary industry with no quaternary industry. Example: Eritraea.

Industrial: primary industry in steep decline; rapidly developing secondary industry (the dominant type of employment) due to development of industrial manufacturing methods; rapidly developing tertiary industry due to increased expectations and higher disposable income of majority of people; little or no quaternary industry. Example: Jamaica.

Post-industrial: little primary industry; declining secondary industry; developing tertiary industry (the dominant type of employment); rapidly developing quaternary industry. Example: Australia.

3.2 Changing cities over time (p. 66)

1   Any two from: immigration; developing port and harbour; site; location; strong pull factors (employment opportunities, favourable government, developing transport and technology).

2   Decline of the biggest employment base (the car industry), due to cheaper/better quality imported cars and the use of technology e.g. robots on the assembly line.

3   Old, deserted buildings renovated and turned into residential properties; new office buildings built for tertiary and quaternary industries; new retail and entertainment centres; a cleaner environment; higher proportions of younger and formally employed people living and working in the area.

4   Diagram that shows the key urban zones, including (from centre to outside): Central Business District at heart, labelled with offices and shops (or similar); inner city, with apartments and high-density housing; suburbs, with medium-density housing and some industrial; rural-urban fringe, with low-density housing; some corridors of industry and new developments. Other labels dependent on the case study selected.

5   The population of Mumbai has grown very rapidly, increasing from about 8 million in 1970 to 21 million in 2011. This is also called hyper-urbanisation. The majority of the population (about 12 million in 2011) are housed in slums.

6   India is an emerging economy enjoying substantial growth; much of this economic growth is driven by secondary and tertiary industry, which tends to be more easily developed within cities. The growth in job opportunities and wealth in Mumbai, linked to improved transport, education and healthcare facilities, acts as a significant pull factor, drawing in people from rural areas and from overseas. The majority of migrants to Mumbai are in their 20s and 30s, meaning that there has been an increase in the birth rate that exceeds the death rate.

7   Any three push factors from: poor farmland and uneven climate conditions making farming difficult, with low wages; poor access to services including education and healthcare; fewer jobs in farming due to mechanisation; high levels of poverty.

Any three pull factors from: economic growth producing many job opportunities across a range of high- and low-skilled work; improved education and healthcare; higher wages, even in the low-skilled jobs; more opportunities for people to better themselves.

8   Rapid population growth has required rapid growth in support services such as education, transport and healthcare, along with an expansion of leisure and entertainment facilities. All these areas of growth in services provide many job opportunities.

4 The UK's evolving physical landscape

4.1 UK physical landscapes (p. 70)

1   The north and west of the UK are mountainous whereas the south and east are flatter and lower with more fertile soils. This suggests that harder and less permeable rocks are present to the north and west, as they are less easily weathered and eroded, whereas softer, permeable rocks are found to the south and east.

2   The River Thames flows from the source at Thames Head in an eastern direction and ends after 346 km in the North Sea near Southend-on-Sea. The River Thames passes through the city of Oxford and continues to travel south-east near the city of Reading, before meandering through Henley-on-Thames, Marlow and Windsor. The Thames flows through Greater London and Central London. The river passes the Thames Barrier and ends via the Thames Estuary in the North Sea.

3   Tough resistant rock such as granite and slate form some of the UK's most dramatic mountain ranges e.g. Arran, Scotland. Chalk forms distinctive hills in the South Downs and Wiltshire. London is a good example of a clay landscape.

4.2 Coastal landscapes (p. 82)

1   Solution, suspension, saltation and traction.

2   Constructive waves are low in height and surge up the beach with a strong swash and weak backwash. They carry and deposit large amounts of material and make beaches more extensive. Destructive waves are high and steep waves with a strong backwash and weaker swash, which means that they remove sediment and can cause the destruction of beaches.

3   Weathering is the weakening or decay of rocks in situ, on or close to the ground surface. This weakening of the rock can lead to mass movement, which is the downward movement of material under the influence of gravity. This can be by sliding or slumping, etc.

4   Diagram that shows clearly: direction of prevailing wind; tendency for swash (wave inbound to shore) to follow the prevailing wind direction; backwash (wave outbound from shore) tending to move away perpendicular to shoreline; direction of longshore drift that results; some attempt in the diagram to show how material accumulates in the direction of the swash, moving along the coastline.

5   Possibilities include: an arch, a wave cut platform, a stack, a wave cut notch, a sea cave, a headland, and so on.

6   Sand dunes begin as embryo dunes that form around deposited obstacles such as pieces of wood or rocks. Over time, these develop and become stabilised by vegetation, such as Marram grass, to form foredunes and tall yellow dunes. In time, the vegetation will decompose and add organic matter to make the sand more fertile. This allows a range of plants to colonise the back dunes. Wind can form depressions in the sand called dune slacks, in which ponds may form.

7   Spits are formed where the coastline changes direction and bends sharply. Longshore drift occurs on the side of the coastline facing/that is more perpendicular to the prevailing wind; meaning the swash carries materials including sand and other sediment along this coastline until the sharp change in direction, at which point the waves detach from the shore and carry the sediment out to sea. Over time, this sediment builds up, parallel to the side of the coastline facing the prevailing wind. Eventually enough sediment gathers for a spit of land to form, which continues over time to increase the size of the spit.

8   Diagram showing the stages of formation of a stack, including: headland with line of weakness; crack enlarged by hydraulic action and abrasion; crack further enlarged to form a cave; headland with caves 'back to back' and getting closer; arch formed as the two caves join; weathering weakening the land above the arch; land collapses to leave behind a stack.

9 Hard engineering, soft engineering and managed retreat.

10 Two possible types of hard engineering are groynes and rock armour. Groynes: benefits – can create a wider beach due to trapping sediment, they are not too expensive and help deflect the energy of the waves. Costs: groynes are not too expensive to build, but they interrupt the process of longshore drift, which starves beaches further down the coast, leading to increased rates of erosion, e.g. on the Holderness coastline. Rock armour: benefits – rock armour is relatively cheap and easy to maintain and it absorbs the energy of the wave, which protects the cliffs. Costs: the rocks need to be sourced from another part of the country or abroad, and they often don't fit in with the local geology.

11 Managed retreat is a deliberate policy allowing the sea to flood or erode an area of relatively low-value land. This happens in areas where it would cost more to protect the land than it would were it to be left to erode e.g. farmland.

12 Managed retreat encourages the flooding and erosion of land, which is the opposite of hard engineering designed to halt flooding and erosion, and of soft engineering designed to maintain or grow the existing coastline. Having two different types of coastline management next to each other on a coastline may cause erosion in certain areas to accelerate. For example, an area of concrete seawall next to an area of low-lying land designed for managed retreat might deflect the wave energy onto the managed retreat area and speed up the land retreat. Eventually this may affect land behind the sea wall and cause that land to flood and retreat as well. Having soft engineering next to managed retreat might also produce problems: the materials being deposited on the soft engineering beach are likely to accumulate in the soft engineering area, thus speeding up the procees of erosion.

4.3 River processes (p. 90)

1 The three fluvial processes are: erosion, transportation and deposition.

2 Any three of the four different types of erosion described: hydraulic action, abrasion, attrition and solution. Described: hydraulic action – the force of the moving water in a river hitting the river bank and river bed. Abrasion – the load carried by the river scrapes along the bank and bed and wears them away. Attrition – the stones carried by a river hit each other and break up into smaller pieces. Solution – the material carried by a river dissolves when the water travels over rocks, making the water acidic.

3 Any three of the four different types of transportation described: traction, saltation, suspension, solution. Described: traction – large particles roll along a river bed. Saltation – smaller particles bounce along the river bed. Suspension – smaller sediment floats in the water. Solution – dissolved material is carried in solution.

4 Material is deposited when a river loses velocity and slows down, as it no longer has the energy to erode or transport sediment.

5 A waterfall is formed when a river flows over two different rock types, eroding a softer rock layer under the harder rock. This creates a plunge pool due to hydraulic action and abrasion. The harder rock is undercut and an overhang is formed, which eventually will collapse into the plunge pool as it is unsupported. The waterfall retreats upstream as this process is repeated.

6 Three facts about meander formation: the thalweg is the fastest line of velocity in a river, flowing on the outer side of bends; erosion occurs on the outside of the bend of a river where the flow is faster; deposition occurs on the inside of the bed where the river flow is slower; meanders move downstream over time due to erosion; a meander neck can be cut off to form an ox-bow lake.

7 Floodplains are formed when a meander moves from side to side causing the valley sides to become wider apart, creating a flat valley floor.

8 Levées are formed when sediment from the river is deposited on a floodplain during times of flood and builds up to form raised banks at the sides of the river.

9 Two human factors that increase the risk of flooding are urbanisation creating impermeable surfaces, which increases run off, and deforestation, which means that there are fewer trees and therefore less interception of rainfall. Two physical factors that increase the risk of flooding are steep relief that increases the speed with which water reaches the rivers, and heavy precipitation, where flash floods increase the volume of water in a river.

10 a Hard engineering is the use of human-made structures to prevent and control flooding, usually expensive to install and used to protect areas of high value. Soft engineering is when natural processes are used to manage river processes and floods.

   b An example of hard engineering is the building of embankments to raise the height of the river banks so they can hold more water during floods. An example of soft engineering is afforestation, where trees are planted to increase the interception and absorption of water.

11 Physical processes: climate change leading to more extreme weather events; very heavy rainfall in June and July (up to four times the usual average); rain fell on soil already saturated; two rivers close to each other (the Severn and the Avon) were both affected. Human processes: settlements (towns, cities) built alongside the rivers for purposes of trade; increasing populations with housebuilding near to rivers; drainage systems built to deal with usual monthly averages of rainfall not extreme weather; towns/cities had extensive areas of impermeable surfaces.

Combination of heavy rainfall and impermeable surfaces plus insufficient drainage led to water collecting in town/city centres. Building near to rivers combined with having two rivers surrounded by saturated soil to cause significant flooding. Possibly, human contribution to climate change made such extreme weather events more likely.

5 The UK's evolving human landscape

5.1 Changing people and places (p. 96)

1 Population density: urban core has over 200 people per square km; rural periphery has between 1 and 100 people per square km. Economic activities: urban core has mostly tertiary jobs; rural periphery largely primary jobs with some tertiary jobs (tourism). Settlements: urban core has large settlements (cities, towns, conurbations); rural periphery has much smaller settlements (towns, villages, some isolated farmhouses).

2 Any two from: enterprise zones set up in peripheral areas, with government financial support to encourage new and existing businesses to have their offices in more rural areas; regional development grants offering start-up funding and support for businesses; EU grants to assist economic development in areas that have a GDP less than 75% of the national average; improvements to transport to make areas more accessible.

3 Any two from: women in their twenties have had babies earlier (due to a lack of employment opportunities caused by the recession), and women in their thirties and forties have had babies later (because they have delayed to focus on their careers); immigrant families have tended to have more children.

4 Competition from cheaper goods manufactured in other countries; tertiary industry has grown, drawing people from the secondary industry to more attractive jobs.

5 'Knowledge economy' is a term that describes quaternary industry including IT/programming, online service companies, electronics design and development, data-driven industries, all of which require high-skilled employees and rely on ready access to information (knowledge).

6 Trade without taxes or tariffs has been possible for the UK within the EU, plus the EU has negotiated favourable trade deals with many countries or blocs outside the EU. Foreign direct investment has been growing, in which UK-based companies invest in companies or facilities outside the UK, and vice versa, largely without restrictions. Transnational companies have established UK branches, partly because of English being the main language, and partly because of the ease of trading within the EU.

5.2 Case study of a major UK city (p. 107)

1 Any three from: London's site is on a major river, near the coast, so is easily accessible. London is closer to the European mainland than the UK's other major cities. Time zone, being a few hours ahead of the USA and a few hours behind East Asia, mean that the business days overlap, with London able to coordinate the business. Heathrow is one of the world's biggest and busiest airports. London has road and rail links to all the other major cities in the UK, some of which offer fast services.

2 For each area, any two from:
   CBD: highest density of buildings; oldest part of the city; most expensive land; used for offices, government, retail, leisure, entertainment, financial and commercial; crowded and polluted but with large urban parks. Inner city: high density; mix of old and modern buildings; middle land values; mix of residential and industrial buildings; some polluted and derelict areas, but some recently regenerated areas and parks. Suburbs: lower density; newer buildings; lower land values; residential with larger houses, some shopping centres and industrial parks; houses have gardens, and pollution due to traffic is less.

3 To access cheaper rents; to share cultural traditions and customs; to access specialist shops and services including places of worship; to reduce the likelihood of discrimination.

4 Answers will vary depending on the case study. Using London as an example, any two from: much lower average earnings for some jobs, leading to disadvantages for children in their education; higher incidence of smoking, drinking alcohol, poor diet and living conditions, leading to greater long-term health problems; higher levels of unemployment leading to less disposable income and hence fewer service industry jobs.

5 Answers will vary depending on the city studied. Answers should include a statement of features of the area, relating those features to factors such as average income levels, availability of transport and service industries; an analysis of the area's features and opportunities compared to the rest of the city; and a conclusion stating how great the need for regeneration might be, based on the evidence provided.

6 Many strategies are possible, but possibilities include: making transport less polluting and more fuel-efficient; introducing laws to compel housing developers to make a percentage of their properties more affordable;

employers offering more flexible working hours or the ability to work from home, to reduce congestion in the city; ensuring all new buildings maximise energy efficiency; enhancing the amount and quality of green spaces within the city; reducing waste and recycling more.

5.3 Accessible rural areas (p. 111)

1 Many tertiary and quaternary industries are concentrated in large cities, leading to a flow of people and income out of rural areas and into cities. This has benefited some rural towns and cities, but also reduced the wealth of the most rural areas. Increased workforce flexibility, thanks to improvements in technology and transport, means some workers have moved out of cities and into rural areas, which has affected: the availability and cost of housing (prices have increased); a lack of affordable housing; increased pressures on services such as education and health care; increased pressure generally on transport services.

2 Any two similarities from: improved technology; improved transport; increased pressure on housing and house prices (upwards). Any two differences from: different rates of improvement of technology and transport between rural and urban areas (e.g. high-speed broadband connections are generally rolled out faster in cities than in rural areas); different levels of transport facilities (cities very well served, rural areas less well served); different perceptions of the level of and need for immigration.

3 Diversification can be argued for or against. On the one hand, diversification may help to keep a smaller business running, by providing alternative sources of income that compensate for the reduction of profit on traditional activities (e.g. farmers offering holiday accommodation or setting up retail facilities to sell farm produce). On the other hand, to remain competitive in the original market, it may be more effective for individual farms to form cooperative organisations or be merged with other farms, to increase economies of scale.

6 Geographical investigations (p. 120)

The exam

1 Paper 2, Section C.

2 a Approximately one minute per mark.

b Yes.

c Will need to answer one question from Section C1 'Fieldwork in a physical environment' (either 'Investigating coastal landscapes' or 'Investigating river processes and pressures') and one questions from Section C2 'Fieldwork in a human environment (either 'Investigating dynamic urban areas' or 'Investigating changing rural areas'. Each question will contain two parts: one part focuses on the use of fieldwork materials from an unfamiliar context, the other part focuses on the geographical investigation carried out as part of the fieldwork.

The enquiry process

1 Answers will depend on the student's selection of locations for the investigations.

2 Questions investigated through fieldwork; measuring and recording data; processing and presenting fieldwork data; describing, analysing and explaining fieldwork data; reaching conclusions; reflecting critically.

3 Answers will depend on the student's selection of locations for the investigations.

Academic skills required

1 Put the data into order from smallest value to largest value. If there are n data values, the lower quartile is given by the $(n + 1)/4$ th value, and the upper quartile is given by the $3(n + 1)/4$ th value. The interquartile range = upper quartile – lower quartile. This can also be done by using a single-axis scattergraph with the data set plotted on it.

2 Connect all data points with the same value using a continuous line.

3 Method chosen and justified will depend on the investigation and the types of data collected. For example, measuring rainfall totals by month produces a set of discrete values over the course of a year. Often, a bar chart will be the most appropriate way to show this type of data. Another example would be using the annual level of foreign direct investment to show the trend. In this case a scatter plot or continuous line graph would best represent this data.

Exam command words

1 a 'Suggest: There is more than one possible answer; present the one (or more) that you are asked for.

b Calculate: Use the data given to determine a value as an answer. Make sure to include any working and state the correct units.

c Explain: give reasons for something happening.

d Assess: make an informed judgment.

7 People and the biosphere

7.1 Biomes (p. 128)

1 The tundra biome is found in zones around the polar regions, mainly in the northern hemisphere including in Alaska (USA), northern Canada and northern Russia.

2 The hot desert biome is very dry (less than 250 mm of rain a year), has high daytime temperatures (over 30 °C), and low night-time temperatures.

3 Indonesia (other examples include Malaysia, Laos, Thailand, Myanmar, Cambodia, Papua New Guinea and the Philippines).

4 Near the equator the temperature is very hot due to the concentration of the Sun's energy, and very wet due to high evaporation rates and condensation caused by the rising air where Hadley cells meet. This climate creates ideal growing conditions for plants which need warmth and moisture.

5 Altitude: Lower altitudes are better because they are more sheltered, warmer and not too wet. Rock type: Softer rocks are better because they weather more quickly, producing deeper soils and a rock with medium permeability is best so that some water is retained. Soils: Loam soils are best because they drain well, have nutrients and are light enough for plant roots to grow through. Drainage: The ground must not be too impermeable or permeable so that waterlogging is avoided but there is enough water in the ground for plants.

6 The Hadley cell has rising humid air near the equator (at the ITCZ). This causes condensation and a large annual precipitation, which supports a large amount of plant growth in the tropical rainforest. The air in the Hadley cell descends away from the equator at about 30°N and 30°S.

As the air descends, it warms and moisture is evaporated. This creates stable conditions with clear skies and a lack of precipitation. This makes it very difficult for plants to grow in the hot dry conditions of deserts.

7 Biomass is greater in the tropical rainforest because there are ideal growing conditions for plants which then support complex food web. While hot deserts have suitable temperatures but lack moisture for growth, so there are fewer plants and animals, and tundra areas are too cold and also dry so plants are small and have a simpler food web.

8 Biotic factors are living things, such as plants and animals.

9 A food chain is a simple linear sequence, e.g. grass → zebra → lion. A food web has a complex pattern of interlocking food chains. In a food web it is likely that there are several key living things that either eat several things or are the food source of several things.

10 Plants absorb carbon dioxide and give off oxygen during the process of photosynthesis, this helps to balance these two gases in the air.

11 Nutrients, such as nitrogen, accumulate in the soil from weathered rock and decomposed litter (humus). These are then absorbed by the roots of plants to help them grow. Parts of a plant may be eaten by herbivores and the nutrients are passed on to them. When plants become dormant they drop their leaves, and animals may leave their waste products on the ground. Decomposers then release the nutrients from these materials into the soil.

7.2 Biosphere resources and regulation (p. 132)

1 Resources include: food such as animals, fruits, arable crops; wood for fuel and timber; cotton for clothing; biofuel crops; medicines.

2 One service, such as: controlling and balancing the hydrological cycle. This is achieved by plants, especially trees, intercepting and absorbing rainfall, so slowing the movement of rain into the soil, ground and rivers. This helps water to be stored in the ground and prevents rivers from having 'flash' floods.

3 With more people in the world, more biosphere resources are needed to support them. Consumption has increased as there are more 'mouths to feed', but also more living space is needed, which causes the loss of natural areas and greater conversion of natural areas into farmland.

4 Damage may be caused by: logging of trees, destroying habitats for animals, clearing natural vegetation for farmland or housing, mining resources by open-cast methods, flooding areas behind dams, and pollution and contamination of areas.

5 Carrying capacity is the maximum number of people that an area, country or world can support.

6 Malthus said that population grows much faster than resources, therefore there will be a crisis when there are not enough resources for the population.

7 Boserup was optimistic that the carrying capacity of the world would be increased because when people are put under pressure of a resource crisis they will respond by inventing ways of making resources last longer or find new resources to use, so allowing the world to support more people.

8 Forests under threat

8.1 Tropical rainforests (p. 144)

1 The emergent layer (about 50 metres tall).

2 Tropical rainforests affect the local climate through the transpiration of moisture into the air. This condenses in the cool of the evening, leading to heavy rain. If deforestation has taken place, areas often become much drier.

3 a Adaptations of plants include: growing tall to get access to sunlight; tall trees have buttress roots to help them balance;

shallow root systems to get nutrients before they are washed away; leaves that pivot around to follow the Sun; waxy leaves to shed water and prevent moss build-up.

b Adaptations of animals: ability to climb trees because most food is found in the canopy layer (35 m above ground level); ability to glide between trees to move around the canopy to find more food; camouflage so that predators find it more difficult to see them; frogs laying eggs in pools of water in flowers and plants in the canopy layer.

4 In the hot, wet conditions, chemical reactions and the actions of decomposers are fast, so nutrients from the litter are quickly broken down and absorbed by the extensive shallow roots of trees, so they do not stay in the soil for long. Most nutrients in this ecosystem are stored in the biomass. The heavy tropical rain causes leaching in the soil, which is where nutrients are washed down very deep into the soil away from the surface layer.

5 Complex food web is the result of biodiversity that has developed over an extremely long time period in ideal growing conditions, which has provided plenty of producers on which the higher trophic levels can feed.

6 Any one of: to make money from forest resources, perhaps from exports, to help develop the country; to use rainforest resources to support industries and create jobs within the country; to provide living space for poorer people in the country; to build infrastructure such as dams for hydro-electric power so that there is cheap electricity for people and businesses.

7 a Location may vary, in this revision guide it is Malaysia in South-East Asia.

b Ways of deforesting include: logging; flooding by reservoirs; mining activities; establishing plantations; building homes or establishing smallholdings with 'slash and burn'; building roads.

c Negative impacts include: reduction in biodiversity as tree and plant species and the habitats for animals are lost; removal of vegetation exposes soils to wind and rain erosion, and degradation can be so bad that the land can never be used again for growing plants; transpiration by trees is reduced when they are removed leading to a drier local climate. Positive impacts include: creating jobs in forestry, mining or exporting businesses; earning money for the country to help it develop from selling products from tropical rainforest areas.

8 Climate change may cause: faster tree growth but increased tree deaths; drier climatic conditions locally with increased risk of wildfires and drought; more trees blown down by stronger storms; change from tropical forest to tropical grassland; extinction of species as they cannot adapt to the quick changes in conditions and habitat.

9 The rate of deforestation may vary over time due to: (i) changing demand for rainforest products such as soya and beef; (ii) changes to the rate of population growth; (iii) changes to government policy on schemes and developments; (iv) pressure to reduce deforestation from conservation organisations or international protocols; (v) pressure to pay off international debts.

10 Reasons include: provision of important medicines which provide cures for human ailments; providing oxygen and absorbing CO_2 on a global scale; providing resources such as timber and food; supporting an indigenous way of life and culture; influence on global climate; scientifically important as the oldest and most biodiverse biome.

11 a Replanting trees may be best because this method replaces any forest that has been destroyed, and, given time, the same structure and habitats will be provided for wildlife. It would also help restore the area of forest, protecting soils and the climatic conditions.

b Educating people may be the best because if people understand the process and links within the tropical rainforests, they may change their attitudes and actions. For example, they may not buy mahogany furniture or palm oil products, and some may be able to apply pressure on governments or companies to stop damaging activities or to help with conservation.

12 Advantages of REDD include: allows indigenous people to continue to use the forest in a sustainable way; recovers degraded land so that it can regenerate; stops the destruction of forest and maintains natural areas. Disadvantages of REDD include: requires considerable financial support; relies on international expertise; does not provide a clear definition of forest; does not tackle the reasons behind deforestation.

8.2 Taiga (boreal) biome (p.152)

1 a Characteristics of environment include: coniferous forests (pine and spruce trees); frozen ground (sporadic permafrost); lots of lakes; slow nutrient cycling.

b Characteristics of climate include: very cold winters (−40 °C); Little precipitation (wetter in summer); long winters and short summers.

2 a Plant adaptations include: evergreen trees because summers are too short to grow new leaves; waxy needle leaves to retain moisture and protect from cold; conical tree shape with downward-sloping branches to withstand winds and let snow fall off easily.

b Animal adaptations include: seasonal migration of birds and animals, moving to warmer areas during winter months and returning to the taiga in the summer when it is warmer and food is available; animals not able to move may hibernate during the cold winter months when there is no food available (e.g. bears); some animals change the colour of their fur or feathers to match the seasons, especially becoming white in winter, in order to escape detection by predators; animals have layers of fur to keep them warm in the cold temperatures.

3 Any two (see Figure 10, page 147): such as people and animals – native peoples practice subsistence hunting and fishing to obtain food, clothing and tools, and in Lappland reindeer are herded to provide these items and some income of money.

4 The taiga biome is fragile because of the harsh climatic conditions which means that it is a struggle for plants and animals that live there to survive, therefore anything that may alter the balance can cause damage quickly. The lack of biodiversity means that if a small part of the ecosystem is damaged there can be widespread changes.

5 Reasons include: being able to monitor change shows how climate change and other human influences may affect nature; supports indigenous peoples and culture; a biome that has experienced less impact than others, including wilderness areas.

6 Logging is a threat because the boreal forest has a simple structure and if the trees are removed there is little vegetation left and the litter store of nutrients can be quickly depleted. Wildlife dependent on trees lose their habitats and source of food, and without nutrients plants and other wildlife will not return.

7 Two ways from: Earlier leaf growth and fruiting as temperatures get warmer earlier in spring; gradual movement of trees to a higher altitude over decades; sub-Arctic birds breeding and feeding areas may change due to reduced snow cover and earlier melting; more forest wildfires due to drier warmer climate; increase in number of pests, trees and other plants (e.g. bark beetle).

8 Conservation groups can help because they bring the public's attention to the damage being done to the taiga biome, including the publishing of detailed reports, holding meetings and co-ordinating pressure on governments and businesses to protect and stop damaging the taiga.

9 No correct answer. Governments have the ability to pass laws to protect areas, establish national parks or reserves, and limit the number of commercial permits for logging and mining activities; but they may be interested in making money for the country in order to improve quality of life for the whole population. Logging and mining companies are the ones active in the taiga area and they can plan their activities to be sustainable, for example logging companies can use the latest machinery to efficiently remove trees and then replace the trees that they have harvested; however, these companies may be motivated most by profit rather than conserving nature.

9 Consuming energy resources

9.1 Energy resources (p. 164)

1 Reasons include: development of countries by providing power for businesses and industries; providing power for people to use in their homes to help improve the quality of their lives and for basic needs such as cooking and heating.

2 A non-renewable resource is finite, which means that at some point it will run out e.g. oil.

3 HEP may cause damage by flooding a large area of land upstream of a dam, this also changes the flow of rivers and may cause small earthquakes.

4 Geological processes have helped determine which countries have access to fossil fuels because the conditions for their formation over millions of years only existed in some places and not everywhere. So some countries have oil, natural gas and coal and others have none.

5 Reasons include: the world's population continues to expand, so there are more people that need energy supplies; as more and more countries become developed there will be more industries and businesses demanding energy supplies; as countries develop people will become wealthier and able to afford energy supplies, so consumption will increase. In all these cases there may not be enough energy supply to meet the demand.

6 UK government regulations will determine the future energy mix because of following international treaties on reducing CO_2 emissions, so there will be investment in renewables and a reduction in the use of fossil fuels; as fossil fuels run out the government grants permits to extract gas from shale rocks (fracking).

7 Nuclear energy advantages include: no CO_2 emissions produced; recyclable energy resource so will last a long time; relatively cheap electricity produced. Nuclear energy disadvantages include: harmful radioactivity produced during accidents and by waste materials (need secure long-term storage); high costs of waste disposal and decommissioning of nuclear power stations.

8 Energy consumption is increasing because of a much larger population, so there are more people to use energy; countries are developing and have more transport, businesses and industries using energy (e.g. China); people are generally becoming wealthier and can afford to use technologies that need energy, such as vehicles and appliances in homes.

9 Japan may face energy insecurity in the future because it does not have many energy resources of its own and relies on imported fuels, especially non-renewable fossil fuels. It has also had problems with its nuclear energy programme after the tsunami in 2011 caused a major nuclear accident at Fukushima. Japan's economy relies on exporting manufactured goods such as electronics and so its industries in the future will continue to need lots of energy.

9.2 Oil (p. 170)

1 Oil is a finite resource because it is a fossil fuel and took millions of years to form.

2 Oil reserves are found at certain points around the world, such as the Middle East (48% of total) (e.g. Saudi Arabia), Gulf of Mexico (USA, Venezuela), northern North America (Alaska (USA) and Canada), and Russia.

3 Exxon-Mobil is the largest oil TNC.

4 Oil consumption is increasing because most world technology is still based on this energy resource (e.g. transport), and as populations, industrialisation and trade increase so does the use of oil.

5 Europe's low oil reserves could be a problem for European countries as they will depend on imports, and if prices increase so will the costs for people, businesses and industries. This will make it more expensive to live and reduce the profits of companies. It may also create an economic recession.

6 a Oil is a very valuable resource and essential to developed and emerging countries. Access and control of oil supplies is therefore important, this encourages countries to strongly protect their supplies – such as the USA getting involved in armed conflicts in the Middle East.

   b Tensions and conflicts in the Middle East are likely to cause uncertainty about oil supplies. This will increase the value of oil and push up prices.

7 Environmental costs of unconventional oil resources include: open-pit mining scars the landscape; large areas of boreal forest are removed; water contaminated with chemicals is stored in surface ponds; chemicals may leak into the groundwater and rivers; greenhouse gases are released from burning natural gas used to heat water used in the extraction process.

9.3 Strategies to reduce energy demand (p. 177)

1 Two ways include: insulation of roofs and walls; double glazing of windows using thermal glass; using energy efficient appliances; using renewable energy such as solar panels; changing lifestyle to use less energy

2 Ways include: taxes or charges on energy use; laws to make businesses use more energy efficient methods and produce energy efficient goods; support the use of vehicles using hybrid or electric technologies; convert power stations from coal to biomass; campaigns to educate people on energy conservation.

3 a Energy security means that a country or area has enough energy to meet its needs.

   b Renewable energy resource development is important because conventional non-renewable resources, especially oil, are running out. Replacements need to be found to produce the energy to fill the gap left by the non-renewables.

4 Biofuels are produced from plants and are grown as a crop, either in the form of oils or woody material.

5 a Positives explained, such as: it is a cheap energy source once the machinery is in place, because the wind is free; wind farms with many turbines can create energy for thousands of homes; it is a flexible energy source because micro-turbines can be used for individual homes or farms in remoter locations. Negatives explained, such as: wind turbines are often very large and so are considered unsightly and spoil views; wind farms may be costly if they are located offshore in the sea; wind turbines have moving blades which endanger birds, and when they are placed offshore, disturb the seabed.

   b Using hydro-electric power to create energy is controversial, because a large area of land is flooded to create a reservoir behind a dam, and people may have to move from their homes and fertile farmland may be lost. The dam may be unsightly and there is a lot of change to the landscape. They are also very expensive, which may make them unsuitable for a developing or emerging country.

6 Students may choose any example. Answer here assumes the Chambamontera scheme in Peru is chosen.

   Benefits include: cheap electricity for local people and businesses; local environment not damaged; clean energy source provided, which improves people's health; school and health centre benefit from electricity.

Problems include: there is a cost for the electricity which poor people may not be able to afford; after 25 years new investment will be needed; some parts of the scheme are unsightly.

7 a The main reason is that fossil fuels produce CO_2 which is the main greenhouse gas causing climate change, so reducing the use of coal, oil and natural gas would dramatically cut CO_2 emissions. This would make it easier to manage the changes brought by a warmer climate.

   b Some do not want a change to the energy mix because technology and infrastructure is based on the use of conventional fuels, any change would be expensive because new machinery, vehicles and infrastructure would need to be developed. Or they would want access to easily available and reliable energy resources, which are the ones that have been proven up to this point in time. Or instead of changing the mix just make the use of current energy sources more efficient, making them last longer and giving time for the full development of alternative energy sources.

8 The USA has a large ecological deficit because it has a low biocapacity per person and a high ecological footprint per person; these are the result of a developed country with a wealthy population and lots of industries, and a high use of aeroplanes and road vehicles for transport. Also there is a large-scale exploitation of resources within the country, such as oil extraction.

10 People and environment issues: Making geographical decisions (p. 187)

The examination

1 Paper 3 Section D.

2 a One minute per mark after allowing time to read the resource booklet.

   b There is a wide range of possible skills questions in this examination, these will have command words such as plot, complete or calculate. You must be able to interpret maps, graphs, use numbers and statistics, and extract information from figures, as well as complete maps and graphs, annotate images, and carry out calculations using a calculator.

   c For the final question you must remember: state your choice of the options clearly; give the advantages of your option choice; recognise the weaknesses or problems associated with your option choice; state some disadvantages of the other options; throughout your answer use evidence from the resource booklet (or your studies) to support the advantages or disadvantages you include. Leave at least 12 minutes to complete this question. This longer answer will also assess your SPaG.

The resource booklet

1 A wide range of resources could be included within the resources booklet, including all types of map, graph, diagrams, tables of data, extracts of text, and photographs.

2 The resources will be divided into the themes of topics 7, 8 and 9, namely people and the biosphere (Section A), forest under threat (Section B) and consuming energy resources (Section C).

3 An understanding of geographical ideas is needed beyond the resource booklet because marks in some of the longer answers will be linked to your ability to recall what you have studied during the course, and in particular in topics 7, 8 and 9. Figures 1, 2 and 3 show some of the ideas that you may need to recall. This is an important part of showing your ability to think synoptically in geography, that is the ability to understand links between all the human and physical geography topics that you have studied during the GCSE course.

Academic skills required

1 A mean is calculated by finding the sum (total) of a set of data and dividing it by the number of pieces of data in the set.

2 Put the data into order from smallest value to largest value. If there are n data values, the lower quartile is given by the $(n + 1)/4$ th value, and the upper quartile is given by the $3(n + 1)/4$ th value. The interquartile range = upper quartile – lower quartile. This can also be done by using a single-axis scattergraph with the data set plotted on it.

3 A pattern on a choropleth map can be identified by using the shading or colour categories shown in the key to the map. Describe the distribution of the higher categories and then the distribution of the lower categories. Descriptive words such as clustered, scattered or random may be useful, along with use of compass directions or names of places.

Command words

1 The command word 'assess' means that you should show the significance of something, with evidence to support your assessment. You must consider all the possible factors and say which are the most important.

2 The command word 'plot' means to complete a graph (or map) by adding the point, line or bar accurately according to the data given.

3 Justifying a decision involves giving your reasons for a choice backed up by evidence. All options must be considered so that the reasons for the decision are clear. Evidence must be taken from a range of resources and knowledge and understanding from your geographical studies.

Review It! Answers

1 Hazardous Earth (p. 30)

1   Global atmospheric circulation is the pattern across the Earth of the movement of air. Areas of high pressure and dry conditions are found where the air sinks towards the ground. Areas of low pressure and wetter conditions are found where the air rises. Winds on the ground transfer heat and moisture, moving outwards from areas of high pressure and towards areas of low pressure, giving rise to global circulation of air and different climate zones around the Earth.

2   Any two reasons from: changes to the Earth's orbit around the Sun (including eccentricity, precession and tilt), changes to the energy output of the Sun (including solar cycles and sunspots), changes to the amount of volcanic activity, and collisions with asteroids.

3   The effects of a tropical storm can be reduced by: monitoring the weather through satellites to provide early warnings and protection through reinforcing windows or building houses on stilts to protect against flooding from storm surges.

4   Earthquakes and volcanoes mainly occur along plate margins.

5   Developing countries can prepare for tropical cyclones in a number of ways:
   - Improving weather forecasting and providing access to radio or TV broadcasts to citizens.
   - Developing weather satellites to improve weather forecasting and storm tracking.
   - Installing early warning systems to protect and evacuate coastal communities.
   - Publicising methods of preparation for cyclones, via village meetings, posters and demonstrations.
   - Developing storm surge defences including coastal embankments and coastal shelters for people.

6   Tropical cyclones are formed through the following processes; first, the air is heated above the warm tropical oceans, causing air to rise rapidly. This upward movement of the air draws up water vapour from the ocean's surface. The evaporated air cools as it rises, which causes it to condense to form large thunderstorm clouds. As the air condenses it releases heat, which powers the storm and causes more and more water to be drawn up from the ocean. Several thunderstorms can join together to form a giant spinning cyclone. It will officially be classified as a storm when winds reach 63 km/h. As the cyclone moves across the ocean it develops in strength and then when the cyclone hits land it loses its momentum as friction with the land causes it to slow down and weaken.

7   Tropical cyclones develop where there are areas of extreme low pressure above warm tropical oceans. Countries in the tropics and on coastlines are most vulnerable, because of their location. Areas of low-lying land near the coast are most vulnerable to storm surges and strong winds. Poorer countries are less well equipped to protect against and respond to the effects of tropical cyclones.

8   When two plates meet, the denser oceanic plate is subducted beneath the less dense continental plate. As the oceanic plate moves downwards it melts and this creates magma, which is less fluid than at a constructive margin. The magma can break through to the surface to form a steep-sided composite volcano. Eruptions are often very violent and explosive.

9   There are cyclical changes in solar energy outputs linked to sunspots. A sunspot is a dark patch on the surface of the Sun. The number of sunspots increases from a minimum to a maximum over a period of 11 years. The more sunspots there are, the more heat that is given off from the Sun, which can lead to higher temperatures on Earth.

10 Carbon dioxide accounts for approximately 60% of enhanced greenhouse emissions and concentrations have increased by 30% since 1840. Concentrations have increased due to the burning of fossil fuels in industry and power stations. Higher concentrations of carbon dioxide are also caused by transport, such as car exhausts, and deforestation reduces the amount of carbon dioxide taken out of the atmosphere by photosynthesis.

11 There were a range of primary and secondary effects of the 2015 earthquakes in Nepal. A primary effect was the amount of people that were killed and injured in the earthquakes. In total 9000 people died and 22 000 people were injured. These levels were high as the earthquake happened in a developing country, which meant that buildings were not constructed to strict codes and so a large number of buildings were destroyed. Secondary effects included avalanches caused by the earthquake, including one on Mount Everest where 21 people were killed and one in the Langtang region which resulted in 250 people missing.

Communication links were disrupted with landslides blocking roads. Overall, the earthquake had an extremely big impact on Nepal and cost US$5 billion in damage.

12 Global climate and weather are huge and complicated systems, making it very difficult to predict with great certainty how much the climate will change and as it does change, what effects this will have. It is also uncertain:
   - how many countries will reduce their carbon dioxide emissions (some may increase those emissions for e.g. political reasons)
   - how quickly fossil fuel use will be reduced
   - how quickly the world population will increase
   - how quickly and to what extent people will change their lifestyles in response to climate fears.

13 There is evidence to support or to reject this statement. Comparisons and conclusions are difficult, due to the different magnitudes, timings and depths of different earthquakes. A developed country will have a more developed infrastructure than an emerging or developing country. Infrastructure is expensive to replace. The L'Aquila earthquake in Italy in 2009, for example, cost US$16 billion but the earthquakes in Nepal in 2015 cost US$10 billion, although the earthquakes in Nepal were of a higher magnitude. More developed countries may have made adaptions to buildings, or they may be built to better building laws, resulting in fewer deaths and injuries. In the Nepal earthquakes, 9000 people died and 20 000 people were injured, compared to the 6.3 magnitude earthquake in L'Aquila in Italy, where 308 people died and 1500 people were injured. However, the number of deaths may also be related to the level of development of a country, as developed countries usually receive aid very quickly after an earthquake but it may take days for remote areas in developing countries to receive aid due to damage to the communications infrastructure. The economic effects in a developed country will be higher but the social effects are generally more devastating in a developing country.

2 Development dynamics (p. 52)

Development and inequality

1   For example: level of education (e.g. literacy rate), level of health care (e.g. life expectancy, people per doctor), happiness index; political freedom, gender equality; average incomes, access to safe water.

2   a and b Some examples are given in Tables 1 (page 33) and 2 (page 37), also see Figure 1 on page 31.

   c Developing countries and are at different stages of development. Developing countries have yet to generate enough money that can be spent on making improvements to living conditions or building businesses and industries to perhaps start a multiplier effect. Developed countries have already been through the growth stage and have wealth to invest in improving people's lives and to help businesses grow.

3   a GNI measures the economic development of a country, based on wealth created by businesses and industries inside and outside the country. It is expressed as an average (US$) per person.

   b Infant mortality data can be used to show development by comparing countries; low infant mortality usually means that the living conditions and health care system are of a higher standard than in those countries with a high rate of infant mortality.

   c HDI is a strong measure of development as it uses both social and economic data, and so covers a wider range of development than other single indicators. The data has been collected by the UN for over 25 years, making it a reliable and trustworthy measure. Weaknesses include the lack of data on the condition of the natural environment and human rights.

4   a In an emerging country: death rate continues to decline, but more slowly, with signs of levelling off. Birth rate declines rapidly from a high level to get nearer to the death rate level.

   b The birth rate is linked to development changes, such as advances in health care and birth control and the changing role of women. Many women obtain regular jobs and choose to have fewer children and, with more machinery, not as many children are needed to work.

5   a A cooler and wetter climate is more suitable for farming, providing enough food for people, sustains fewer diseases and is a more suitable working environment. Places that are too hot, too cold or too dry create difficulties for people.

b Countries without resources are at a disadvantage in a trading situation, as are countries that are unable to balance their imports and exports. Some trade is unfair: rich countries are more powerful and make more money from trade by selling more valuable manufactured goods or modern services, while poor countries may lose money when trading by only selling low-value raw materials or cheap manufactured products.

c Social factors may cause inequalities between countries because education and health levels are different. If people lack education then they cannot develop the skills needed to do jobs better and if their health is poor they do not have the strength to work effectively.

6 a Any one country or world region could be chosen, such as India (emerging), which has 22% of its population living on less than US$1.90 a day, or countries such as South Africa (emerging) 16.6%, Haiti (developing) 54% and Madagascar (developing) 82%.

b Developing countries are too poor to be able to provide a health care system, modern medicines, safe clean water or basic sanitation to all areas. Core urban areas often have better levels of health care, because money is spent in these areas.

c A cycle of poverty keeps people poor because it is very difficult to break any of the negative factors (e.g. the country lacks money to develop infrastructure), and therefore the parts of the cycle keep influencing each other in a downward spiral. For example, if there are no industries making and selling things then there are no better paid jobs and people stay poor.

7 a A refugee is a person who is forced to leave their country because of the strong possibility of death from a natural or human disaster (e.g. drought or war).

b The push factors out of a developing country include: few better paid jobs, poor health care, lack of schools, disease, and poverty. Pull factors from a developed country include: job opportunities, good health care, better education, security and wealth.

8 Modernisation theory is based on stages, which are linked in a sequence, with countries at different stages but with the positive outcome of all able to reach the 'top' stage. Dependency theory is based on a process, with flows of goods, raw materials, people and wealth and power, which places countries in the core or the periphery with the negative outcome that some are kept in poverty.

Development strategies

1 A 'bottom-up' development scheme consists of decision-making at a local level, involving the people directly. It is usually low-cost and uses appropriate technologies and is often supported by the expertise (and money) of NGOs.

2 a Remittances are amounts of money sent to families in home countries by migrants.

b Infrastructure means the systems, such as roads, power supplies, water supply and sewerage/sanitation networks, etc. These provide the essential framework for industry in an area.

c Improvements to infrastructure can help industries and businesses establish themselves, employ people and make money. If safe water supplies are available, people are healthier and able to work better. Better education systems help people to have more skills to use in better paid jobs.

d The parts of the multiplier effect cycle are all positive and therefore have the effect of improving the next part. Each part supports the next throughout the cycle, ensuring that there is continuous improvement.

3 a An NGO is an organisation independent of any government, usually a charity, which raises money through donations and has its own aims, such as Oxfam or Save the Children.

b NGOs usually support smaller development projects and aim to provide what local communities need (a bottom-up approach). Often these use intermediate/appropriate technology; sometimes projects are in the form of emergency aid when there has been a disaster.

c International aid may not always reduce the development gap, for example when there is not enough given to make a big difference, or there is corruption in the country or community that the aid is given to, so that it doesn't reach the poor people who need it.

4 Any two from: the level of technology can be understood by people; it is cheaper; it uses less expensive energy; it is easier to repair; it reduces dependency on outside help.

5 Fairtrade may be better as it makes sure that farmers or the people producing goods receive a reasonable price directly. They receive more money than if big companies or governments had been involved.

6 a Two debt-reducing schemes are: 'debt-for-nature' swaps which wipe out some of the debt, and the HIPC initiative (1996), which arranges deferred payments for countries in financial difficulties.

b Microfinance loans are provided directly to poor people so that they can use the money to improve their lives. Loans to a country are usually used for big schemes, which often do not directly help poor people in a developing country.

Rapid economic development and change

1 a Environmental change means the changes that have taken place to the natural environment, usually in the form of damage (such as deforestation and pollution), and usually as a result of rapid industrialisation and absence of enforced regulations.

b Economic change is linked to money, wealth, business and industry. Socio-cultural change is linked to people and their lives, such as quality of life.

2 Answers will vary according to case study. Here the example is India.

a Two advantages such as: strong links to rest of world through emigrants, who also send back remittances; English speaking population makes it easier to carry out international business; successful TNCs; large young adult workforce.

b Two obstacles such as: corruption in government and business; caste system which creates discrimination; conflict with neighbouring countries; uneven distribution of wealth; poverty and inequality; undeveloped infrastructure; future ageing population issue; gender imbalance; overuse of water; rapid urbanisation rates and slum conditions.

3 Answers will vary according to case study. Here the example is India.

a One political change, such as: independence from the UK in 1947; recent national elections have been democratic and more inclusive of castes; government encourages foreign trade.

b One economic change, such as: now an economic leader in Asia (ranked 7th in world according to GDP in 2016, and expected to reach 3rd); GDP per capita increased from $385 in 1990 to $1616 in 2015; decline in importance of agricultural sector and increase in manufacturing and services; promotion of exports by government.

c One environmental change, such as: serious air pollution in cities; overuse of water from rivers and ground; deforestation; desertification; high carbon dioxide (CO_2) emissions.

d One socio-cultural change, such as: the development of Indian cinema, known as Bollywood; slow improvement in quality of life since 1990 – life expectancy longer, lower mortality rate, more children in school; growing 'middle-class'; very high birth rates; slum conditions in urban areas.

e India has experienced both positive and negative changes. Changes include: the improvement in HDI, but its position in the world rank order has decreased. There has been an increase in life expectancy and school attendance. Considerable wealth has been earned from exports such as pearls, precious stones and metals, but the wealth gap between poorest and richest people has increased. Better health care and living conditions has increased population size, which provides a young workforce but also strains resources such as water and will create an ageing population issue in the future. There are democratic elections, but unrest between caste groups continues to cause problems. There are environmental issues as a result of development, with deforestation for farmland and living space leading to soil erosion and increased risk of flooding, and with pollution from industries, especially in urban areas. Trade has increased in goods and services but India has a large trade deficit ($118 billion in 2015/16).

4 Answers will vary according to case study. Here the example is India.

a India's industrial structure has changed from being based on agriculture (until mid-1970s) to one based on manufacturing (up to 2008) and services (since 2000). (See Figure 12 page 48). Manufacturing in India involves products such as medicines, vehicles, machinery, fuels and precious stones and pearls.

b India used to receive significant amounts of FDI, such as from the UK through the Department for International Development (DFID). DFID supported a variety of development schemes which helped India to become an emerging economic country. NGOs, such as Practical Action, also help with projects aimed at poorer people in India, such as health education, clean water and housing. However, as India has grown in wealth it is now a giver of aid rather than a receiver, especially to poorer neighbouring countries. This may mean that some poorer people in India will not now receive the help that they need.

c India is a Commonwealth country and UN member, with political links around the world. It is a member of the South Asian Association for Regional Cooperation. It has a key position between East Asia and the Middle East and EU. It trades a lot with wealthy countries such as USA, UK, China, UAE and Singapore. It has developed major ports to make this trade easier. Indian TNCs (e.g. Tata Steel) are operating in other countries such as Netherlands, Belgium, Ireland and Canada.

d Quality of life has not increased rapidly as there has been corruption in business and within some levels of government; environmental damage has made the living conditions of some people (e.g. Shudras) worse; there has been rapid population growth (the total population is now over 1.3 billion people), which has meant that there are more people to provide jobs, resources and services for; there is a rich–poor divide within the country, with a number of billionaires nationally but also many people living in squalor in urban slums as wealth and opportunities have not spread to everyone; the caste system still exists and disadvantages those in 'lower' castes such as cleaners (Dalits) and there is still gender inequality (only 12% of MPs are women); there are very large numbers of children and young adults to provide with services such as education; in rural areas services and amenities are lacking, especially clean water, and urbanisation rates are so fast that local governments cannot afford or keep up with providing infrastructure and services.

3 Challenges of an urbanising world: Review it! (p. 67)

Trends in urbanisation

1 Megacity: city with a population of more than 10 million people. Primate city: city that is at least twice as big as the next largest city in their country.

2 **a** Cities in developed countries are undergoing a process of growth due to re-urbanisation, in which abandoned industrial areas are redeveloped. This is attracting younger people back into city living, and also bringing in immigrant workers to work in the service sector.

   b Cities in developing countries are mostly experiencing rapid growth, due to the rapidly growing economies.

3 People migrate from rural areas to the city due to both push and pull factors. The push factors are: drought, which affects crop yields; sustainable farming not making people enough money and a lack of job opportunities or education services. Pull factors in the developing world, e.g. to Rio de Janeiro, are: the chance of a better quality of life, with better job prospects in factories and better access to education, health care and housing.

4 The formal economy employs workers receiving a regular wage, paying taxes and enjoying employment rights. Examples include manufacturing, company headquarters and financial services. The informal economy involves workers who work largely for themselves, pay little or no taxes and have no employment rights. Examples include street sellers and shoe shiners.

5 **a** Developed world cities have economies that usually involve no primary industry (e.g. mining, agriculture or fishing), some secondary industry (e.g. factories), a large amount of tertiary industry (service-based sectors such as finance, tourism and education) and a developing quaternary industry (e.g. IT, media and culture). Jobs are mostly formal in nature.

   b Developing world cities have economies that usually involve little primary industry, a growing secondary industry, a growing amount of tertiary industry and little or no quaternary industry. Jobs are mostly informal in nature.

Changing cities over time

1 The Central Business District is found in the centre of a city, and contains financial and government offices, retail outlets and entertainment centres. Land use is very high density with tall buildings and very high prices. Transport facilities are very good.

2 Counter-urbanisation occurs when people move out of the city into more rural areas and commuter towns, due to the opportunities presented by improved transport and technology, and rising inner-city property prices.

3 Suburbanisation occurs when a city becomes too noisy, crowded and polluted. These push factors in turn lead to excessively high property prices, high crime rates and poor health. Improved transport links mean people can move to the outer edges of cities to find quieter, cheaper, safer and healthier places to live.

4 A city centre might have experienced decline due to a number of factors:
   - De-industrialisation and the movement of manufacturing facilities to the outskirts of the city, or to other cities, or even abroad.
   - Rapidly increasing property prices causing local residents to move away from the city centre.
   - Major national or international economic events, such as the 2008 crash and subsequent recession, causing the shrinkage or closure of many businesses.
   - The pull factor of improved environment, better leisure facilities and cheaper housing being developed on the outskirts of cities.

5 Answers will depend on the city a student has studied. An example might be London.
   - Founded due to its beneficial site (on a major river with helpful physical geography) and situation (close to continental Europe with good access to the sea).
   - Growth due to urbanisation as a result of the industrial revolution (including the development of manufacturing processes, factories and transport links), with many people moving into the city from the countryside.
   - Expansion into surrounding areas due to surburbanisation, facilitated by improved transport links and the desire of people to move away from the crowded, polluted and noisy city centre.
   - De-industrialisation due to decline of manufacturing industries and growth of service industries, with comparatively high unemployment, leading to many people moving out of the city.

   - Counter-urbanisation as people working in financial and service industries based in the city centre, could afford to move to larger houses in a more appealing environment around the edges of the city.
   - Re-urbanisation of former industrial areas such as London's Docklands, where transnational corporation headquarters have been built and new residential apartment blocks developed.

Megacity in a developing country: Mumbai

1 Mumbai's site is on a series of low-lying islands with a deep-water harbour, which makes development easier and helps with transport links and the import and export of goods. Its situation includes a 10 km waterfront that has enabled manufacturing industries to develop, with major export opportunities via sea links to the markets of the Middle East and Europe. Mumbai also has a strong set of overland links, mainly by rail, to the rest of India and Asia in general. As part of one of the fastest growing countries of the world (by population), Mumbai has access to many workers in most sectors.

2 The population of Mumbai has grown very rapidly, causing problems for people who seek to live in the city. Most people cannot afford the property near the city centre, so housing has developed rapidly on land around the city, as well as temporary squatter dwellings.

3 Squatter settlements have little or no access to utilities such as water, sewage facilities, electricity or gas. This makes everyday life difficult and can be hazardous, due to the accumulation of waste and the easy spread of disease. The settlements are crowded and accommodation is temporary and not very well built, making them unsafe and meaning a major event such as monsoon rains can damage or destroy people's homes.

4 Many people moving to or living in Mumbai already have limited or no qualifications, and only temporary accommodation. They seek work in very low-paid roles and do not have the qualifications or experience for many formal roles. There are many opportunities in informal employment, such as service jobs in the city, unregulated manufacturing jobs, which people take on simply to earn enough money to live by.

5 Answers will vary according to the environmental problems chosen. Two examples are as follows. Many people live in areas that have little or no sanitation, meaning that waste builds up close to housing, leading to pollution, widespread scavenging animals such as rats and the potential for disease to develop and spread rapidly. The rapid growth of the population means that transport systems cannot cope, leading to overcrowding, safety hazards and air pollution.

Sustainable development

1 Top-down development involves a large-scale, centrally organised plan, typically funded by central government. It requires major changes to city features and facilities, including the development of substantial transport links, rapid building of large numbers of homes and the relocation of large numbers of people.

   Bottom-up development involves a series of small-scale, locally organised projects, each developed to meet a specific need. It is typically funded by local organisations or charities. It involves small numbers of people and relies on the initiative of local people to publicise and run.

2 Any three advantages from: well-funded, centrally coordinated with high visibility, involves a number of organisations, has government support, can make a significant impact in the medium- and long-term.

   Any three disadvantages from: not well understood at a local level, may not involve local residents or businesses, may not be well managed to suit the local people's needs, can be resented due to e.g. the need to relocate many people, requires consistent and significant funding to be successful.

3 Any three advantages from: well understood at a local level, enjoys local residents' support, focused on a particular need or development, can achieve its aims in a relatively short time, low cost.

   Any three disadvantages from: may not be understood by central government or large businesses, only achieves benefits for a small area or number of people, cannot solve major issues such as the need for accommodation or improved transport links.

4 Students' assessments should include specific examples from the cases they have studied, with suitable justifications and reasoning. Both top-down and bottom-up development can be successful, there is no single 'correct' choice.

4 The UK's evolving physical landscape (p.91)

1 The three types of mass movement are rock fall, landslide and mudflow.

2 A spit and a bar.

3 Freeze-thaw weathering occurs when water flows into cracks within rocks. In cold spells, the water freezes and expands, making the cracks wider. As temperatures rise, the ice melts and the cracks may lead to pieces of rock becoming detached. This sequence repeats each time temperatures fall below freezing.

4 Hydraulic action, where the force of the water hits the river bank and bed. Abrasion, where load carried by the river scrapes along the river bed and bank and wears it away.

5 Hard engineering uses artificial structures such as sea walls and groynes to reduce erosional processes to help protect the coastline. Soft engineering involves replacing or extending beaches by adding sand or shingle, or by reshaping the existing beach after longshore drift has changed its shape, or by regenerating sand dunes.

6 Destructive waves have a strong backwash that removes pebbles and can result in the gradual destruction of the beach. Constructive waves have a stronger swash up a beach and a weak backwash, meaning that material is deposited on the beach and can help build the beach up.

7 Longshore drift is the movement of sediment along a beach. If waves approach at an angle, sediment will be moved up the beach diagonally and be transported back at right angles to the sea. This will move sediment along the beach in a 'zigzag' pattern. Groynes are fences placed at right-angles to the shoreline, meaning that the material moved by longshore drift collects against each groyne rather than being moved all the way along the beach.

8 At the source in the upper course, the river is shallow and has a steep-sided channel, the valley is V-shaped and there is a steep gradient. Waterfalls and interlocking spurs are found here. In the middle course, the valley is U-shaped and the channel is wider and deeper. Meanders and floodplains occur in this section. In the lower course, the gradient is gentler and the valley is very wide and flat. The river is much wider and deeper with a very fast velocity. Here you will find meanders, ox-bow lakes, floodplains and levées, leading eventually to the river mouth.

9 The formation of stacks occurs over a long period of time. Stacks form because of erosion of rock by waves, starting at points of weakness, then forming a cave, then an arch and finally a stack as the rock above the arch collapses. This is much more likely to occur in softer, sedimentary rocks because the erosion is more pronounced and more rapid. Igneous rocks are usually too hard for significant erosion to occur.

10 Waterfalls occur where a river flows over two different rock types. The softer rock is more easily eroded than the harder rock. With the layer of softer rock beneath the harder rock, the river erodes the softer rock faster, eventually cutting back under the layer of harder rock because of hydraulic action and abrasion. This starts to form a hollow in the softer rock, and the water falls over the harder rock onto the softer rock with increasing force, the longer the fall. A plunge pool is formed beneath the waterfall.

11 Physical factors: sudden heavy falls of rain or prolonged periods of lighter rain, causing water to build up in streams and rivers until they overflow; waterlogged ground around the river, meaning that new water arriving has to stay on top of the waterlogged ground; impermeable rocks cause faster run-off of water into rivers; where water drains from land into rivers down steep slopes, there is a higher risk of the river flooding.

Human factors: urbanisation creates many areas of impermeable surfaces (roads, concreted areas, large buildings) meaning water may collect on the ground in cities and towns, or may run off faster into the nearest river, causing the river to overflow further down its course; deforestation (the removal of mature trees), particularly on slopes early in the river's course, causes there to be fewer plant roots able to take up some water, meaning that water flows down to the river more quickly after heavy rainfall; fields that are left as bare soil cause rapid drainage of water across the surface of the field, as it travels along ploughed furrows and is not absorbed by plant roots..

5 The UK's evolving human landscape (p. 112)

Changing people and places

1 Population density = number of people living in an area / size of area.

2 The urban core has a high population density (over 200 people per square kilometre), with urban areas concentrated in South-East England (London), central England (Birmingham/West Midlands), parts of Northern England (Manchester, Leeds, Liverpool, Newcastle), parts of Scotland (Glasgow and Edinburgh) and Northern Ireland (Belfast). Rural areas have a low population density of between 1 and 100 people per square kilometre, with rural areas found in much of South-West England, Wales, East Anglia, Northern England, much of Scotland and parts of Northern Ireland.

3 Major cities have developed in favourable sites and situations, such as near the coast and/or on major rivers, and where industrial and other economic activities are best concentrated. Many rural areas are inaccessible and it is difficult or very costly to provide facilities such as utilities and technology such as broadband. The population has naturally migrated to the most successful cities.

4 Any three from: ageing population increasing the burden on local services such as healthcare (younger people tend to move to urban areas to take advantage of better work opportunities); lower incomes due to majority of jobs being in lower-paid industries such as farming or tourism; higher transport costs due to less public transport and a

reliance on cars; less access to, and higher costs of, utilities such as electricity and gas, and technology such as broadband.

5 Any two from: the UK government has established enterprise zones to assist businesses with start-up costs and tax incentives; the UK government offers some rural development grants to help businesses with advice and support; the EU funds areas that have a GDP of less than 75% of the national average; the UK and local governments have invested in improving transport links.

6 Net immigration has increased: partly because of free movement within the EU and partly because more qualified workers have been needed in industries and services such as the knowledge economy and healthcare. Birth rates have risen due to: women in their 20s having babies earlier on average (a result of lack of employment opportunities as a consequence of the recession); women in their 30s and 40s having babies later on average (as a result of focusing on their careers before starting a family); and a tendency for immigrants to have larger families than the UK average.

7 A reduction in secondary industry (manufacturing and other heavy industry) causing unemployment and the movement of people away from city centres in order to find work.

8 There has been a trend away from primary and secondary industry and into tertiary industry, as a result of the closure of uneconomic or uncompetitive businesses and facilities such as steel foundries, coal mines, oil refineries and shipbuilding yards, and the growth of service industries such as tourism, leisure and the knowledge economy.

9 The South-East of England is accessible with good transport links including motorways and four major airports. The local population has a high proportion of highly skilled and university-educated graduates. London is the centre of political and government decision-making, and is a financial centre of global importance. All these factors have led to businesses specialising in the knowledge economy (IT, law, finance, engineering and electronics) establishing headquarters in the South-East and providing many new employment opportunities. This has led to significant economic growth and a rapid recovery from the recession.

10 Any valid comparison of two UK regions. Example: North-East England has had a declining economy due to the major industries and employers being in primary and secondary industries such as mining, steelmaking, production of cars and oil refining. Competition from cheaper overseas suppliers and a change in the UK economy in favour of service industries and the knowledge economy has led to many businesses in the North-East closing down or shrinking. South-East England has had a large and growing economy due to the major businesses and industries being focused on the tertiary and quaternary sectors, such as law, finance, IT, engineering, electronics, tourism and other service industries. These sectors are the major areas of growth in the world economy.

11 Globalisation describes increased connectivity, communication and trade between countries.

12 Foreign direct investment works in two ways. UK-based companies can invest in many other countries with few or no restrictions, meaning that, for example, technology companies can site their headquarters and service operations in the UK, but invest in other countries for manufacturing where costs are lower. Other countries can also invest in the UK with few or no restrictions, meaning that many overseas transnational corporations establish branches in the UK, and some major industries (such as Japanese car makers) have established production lines in the UK so as to gain access to EU markets.

Case study of a major UK city

1 Answers depend on the city a student has investigated. Using London as the example: London's site is near the coast and close to mainland Europe, as well as on one of the UK's major rivers, the Thames. The land is relatively flat and the city has expanded into many surrounding areas. London's situation is closer to mainland Europe than other major UK cities, and it has a port and three major airports enabling it to trade easily with other nations. It is located in a time zone a few hours behind East Asia and a few hours ahead of the United States, meaning that working days overlap conveniently with the major economies of the world. In addition, good transport links (road, rail) enable London to link with most of the rest of the UK.

2 Connectivity enables people to travel between cities, making trade easier and enabling businesses to expand into new markets. It also enables a city that may lack certain resources (such as skilled people, or rare materials such as certain metals, minerals and oil) to access those resources and use them with the city's own resources to build a larger range of products or offer a wider range of services. Connectivity is now also technological, making use of services such as broadband internet, video telephony and cloud computing to empower businesses and people located within cities to communicate around the world. Good technological capability enables a city to benefit from the growth globally of tertiary and quaternary industries such as finance, law, IT, engineering and services such as tourism and education.

3 For each region of a city, any two from the following: CBD – high density of buildings; most expensive land; land used for offices, company

headquarters, commercial, financial, government and leisure; often a poor quality of environment due to overcrowding and pollution from transport. Inner city – high density of buildings but not as dense as the CBD; middle value land; mix of commercial and high-value residential properties; better environment with parks and regenerated areas but still polluted by transport. Suburbs – lower density of buildings; land used largely for residential properties, mostly houses rather than apartments/flats, and some shopping centres and parks; a better environment with less transport pollution and houses mostly have gardens.

4 Answers depend on the city a student has investigated. Using London as the example, any two from: growing economy in tertiary and quaternary industries means good availability of well-paid jobs; being a primate city means excellent access to most other countries via transport and technological connectivity; established local immigrants from many countries enhance the appeal to other citizens of their countries; world-class entertainment and leisure facilities.

5 International migration has benefits: it enhances the provision of services such as healthcare and support for tourism; there is a high availability of skilled workers to develop tertiary and quaternary industries; it enhances the breadth of cultural diversity, e.g. by opening restaurants specialising in different international cuisines. There are also drawbacks: it increases pressure on local services such as healthcare, transport and education; it may lead to immigrants of particular nationalities or cultures clustering together rather than integrating with existing local populations; it can cause greater deprivation if house prices are pushed upwards and more people have to live in poverty by e.g. performing low-earning service jobs.

6 The Index of Multiple Deprivation measures the level of deprivation in different areas of a city, by comparing relative wealth of residents, their average income, their quality of health and access to healthcare, their educational qualifications and access to education, and their life expectancy.

7 Answers depend on the city a student has investigated. Using London as the example, Richmond has a high average income of £46 000 per year, good educational availability and performance with 70% of students achieving 5 A* to C grades at GCSE, good average health with a life expectancy of 83 years, and high quality (but expensive) housing. In Newham, average income is much lower on £28 000, educational achievement is reduced at 57% of students achieving 5 A* to C grades at GCSE, less good average health with a life expectancy of 77 years, and much lower quality housing at a lower, but still expensive, average price.

8 Suburbanisation: improvements in transport and access to connective technology enables people to move out of the inner city into the suburbs, from where they can commute to work or work from home.

Decentralisation: businesses, factories and retail outlets move to out-of-town sites where they have more space at cheaper rates, and can attract workers and customers with an improved environment, better transport access and larger facilities.

Re-urbanisation: the regrowth of more central city areas as abandoned old factory and other sites are converted to attractive residential properties, with a cleaned-up environment and improved transport facilities.

Accessible rural areas

1 **London:** site is near the coast and close to mainland Europe, as well as on one of the UK's major rivers, the Thames. The land is relatively flat and the city has expanded into many surrounding areas. London's situation is closer to mainland Europe than other major UK cities, and it has a port and three major airports enabling it to trade easily with other nations. Good transport links (road, rail) enable London to link with most of the rest of the UK. Rents and property prices are very high.

Exeter: site is near the coast but further from mainland Europe, on a smaller river (the Exe). The land is relatively flat but the city is surrounded by rural areas and is close to two National Parks. It has an airport but with many fewer flights from fewer destinations. It has good transport links (road, rail) but these mostly link directly to London, Bristol and Birmingham, which have much better links. Rents and property prices are much lower than in London.

2 Economic growth in rural areas brings a number of challenges, including: limited accessibility, with poor or low-volume transport access mainly by road, and a high dependence on distant cities for air transport; limited access to technological developments (e.g. broadband internet access is low speed or non-existent); increased demand for housing with limited opportunities for new developments; increased pressure on limited services such as healthcare and education; lack of access to highly qualified potential workers.

3 London: excellent transport (road, rail and air); good and readily available healthcare, with many local hospitals; excellent technological access such as high-speed broadband; excellent leisure and tourism facilities.

Cornwall: limited transport (road with some rail); good healthcare but limited availability and often at some distance away; poor technological access with little or no high-speed broadband; attractive local scenery and a number of tourist sites, but difficult to access and increasing numbers of tourists cause travel and accommodation problems.

4 Diversification is where a business adds different types of service or product provision compared to its original, core business. For example, a farm's core business is agriculture, providing either crops, cattle for milk and meat, or other animals for meat – or a combination of all of these. A farm can diversify into retail (selling farm or craft products), leisure (providing tourist facilities and accommodation) or other services, such as conference facilities for businesses.

7 People and the biosphere (p. 133)

Biomes

1 Hot desert biomes are located on the tropic lines, Cancer and Capricorn. They are found in the south-western USA, northern Africa and central Asia in the northern hemisphere, and western South America, southern Africa and Australia in the southern hemisphere.

2 Very hot climate (between 25 and 30 °C). Very humid climate (between 2000 and 3000 mm of precipitation). Other characteristics could include: Three main layers to structure, emergent (50 metres tall), main canopy (35 m) and sub-canopy; complex food web; rapid nutrient cycling; most nutrients in the biomass; soils very poor in nutrients.

3 Any two from: altitude, rock type, soils or drainage.

4 a Climate is a major influence on the development of biomes, with the amount of heat and moisture determining which plants can grow. Seasonal changes are more pronounced with distance from the equator, with less heat energy from the Sun per unit area available close to the poles, and this affects the adaptations of plants.

b The Hadley cells meet at the equator with hot humid air rising to cause heavy rainfall. This rainfall supports the growth of large trees and a complex forest structure – the tropical rainforest. At about 30° north and south of the equator the Hadley cell circulation descends, by this time the air has lost most of its moisture and so there is very little rainfall – creating hot desert conditions.

Local factors

1 a Photosynthesis is the process used by plants to use sunlight and carbon dioxide from the atmosphere with water to grow, a by-product of this is the release of oxygen into the atmosphere. Therefore, photosynthesis helps to balance the amount of carbon dioxide and oxygen in the atmosphere.

b Nutrients move between biomass, litter and soil with the shedding of leaves by plants, decomposition of this litter to create humus and then plants reabsorbing nutrients through their roots.

c Decomposers such as fungi and bacteria are important because they break down dead plant and animal matter into basic minerals, which can then be reused within the nutrient cycle.

2 A food chain is a simple sequence of links between living things, with each step in the chain occurring between two living things. A food web is a complex series of links between a number of living things within a biome, and consists of several food chains combined together.

Biosphere resources and regulation

1 a A biosphere service is where nature is maintaining the correct balance within essential natural systems that support life, including human life, such as the hydrological cycle.

b Any two from: food (animal- and plant-based); wood for fuel or building; cotton for clothing; biofuel crops; medicines.

2 More biosphere resources are being used over time because (a) the human population of the world has grown, so there are more people needing resources or the space occupied by forests; (b) there are more industries making things and many of the raw materials used come from the biosphere, (c) people have become wealthier and are able to buy more goods which have been made from biosphere resources (e.g. palm oil).

3 Any two from: open-cast mining, which strips away the living vegetation layer and soils; flooding large areas behind a HEP dam, which destroys large areas of vegetation; wood being used for fuel by poorer people in developing countries, which may lead to deforestation; increasing demand for meat to eat, which causes replacement of forests with soya crops for cattle feed; demand for palm oil in consumer products in developed countries has simplified forest structures.

4 a Any two from: Malthus says that population growth will be faster than resource growth while Boserup says that resource growth will keep up with population growth; Malthus says that there will be a major population 'crash' while Boserup says that this will be avoided; Malthus says that a balance between population numbers and resources will be reached through natural and human factors reducing the population, while Boserup says that a balance will be reached through the use of technology and improved efficiency.

b Evidence that suggests that Malthus is correct includes worldwide epidemics (e.g. flu pandemics), famines in eastern Africa, wars in the Middle East, children dying in developing countries because they cannot get access to fresh clean water, refugee movements from Africa to Europe or Central America to the USA. This evidence collectively suggests that the Earth's carrying capacity has been reached. However, the numbers of deaths are a very small percentage of the world total population, although they may be very significant locally.

8 Forests under threat (p. 153)

Tropical rainforests

1   **a** The structure has three main layers: emergent (50 m tall), main canopy (35 m) and sub-canopy. The shrub and ground layers are not significant.

   b The canopy layer, which consists of evergreen trees, blocks sunlight from reaching the ground layer. Without sunlight the vegetation cannot photosynthesise and grow.

2   All year or 12 months (as the temperature is always above the minimum needed for growth and there is plenty of rain).

3   Tropical rainforest soils lack nutrients because the heat and moisture cause rapid decomposition, and because the shallow roots of plants absorb the nutrients quickly before they are washed deep into the soil structure by heavy rain (process of leaching).

4   The trees transpire moisture into the atmosphere during the day. In the evening, when the air temperature cools, this moisture condenses to form clouds from which heavy rain falls. This cycle keeps the local climate wetter.

5   **a** Most creatures live in the canopy layer.

   b This is where most of the food is (fruits, nuts, nectar). The ground level is dark and plants do not grow well, so there is little food at this level.

6   There is a wide range of adaptations as this is a very old ecosystem, relatively unaffected by world climate cycles, and so creatures have had a long time to evolve. Ideal growing conditions (hot, wet, sunlight) have enabled plants and animals to adapt to a balance with the elements and also with each other.

7   Any one from: extinction of species; disruption of food chains and webs; loss of genetic material that could have been useful to people; the ecosystem becomes more fragile and less resistant to change (e.g. in climate).

8   **a** Any one from: the soil is exposed to erosion; possible local flooding; natural vegetation unable to regrow; loss of local biodiversity.

   b Any one from: the absorption of carbon dioxide is greatly reduced, so it is not stored and more remains in the atmosphere, increasing the 'greenhouse effect'; loss of global diversity; loss of potential health products/cures.

9   Indigenous populations have a smaller impact than those with strong economic motives. Tribes make their homes from timber and clear small patches of land for crops, using only what they need to survive and affecting only a small area. Those with economic motives have access to machinery which can destroy large areas quickly. This is particularly significant with open-cast mining, which strips away large areas of forest, or reservoirs that flood large areas. The World Bank and large companies invest in developing countries to build dams for the generation of electricity.

10 Climate change is an indirect threat to tropical rainforests. Threats include: drier conditions increasing tree deaths and forest fires and causing instability in the forest ecosystem; stronger storms, which can blow down the emergent trees and change the forest structure; complete change from forest to grassland ecosystem due to prolonged lack of rainfall; extinction of species due to higher temperatures, lower rainfall and the disappearance of local habitats.

11 **a** Four causes of deforestation: logging of tropical hardwoods to export, bringing money into the country; cheap electricity needed for businesses and industries so hydro-electric power stations with dams have been constructed; mining of tin and extraction of oil and gas to provide resources for the country and export income; palm oil plantations to create an export product and income; population growth means that living space is needed for poorer people, who can use the area.

   b Impacts: reduction of biodiversity; wildlife endangered by loss of habitats; soils exposed to erosion; transpiration reduced; absorption of carbon dioxide reduced.

   c Impacts on people: jobs created in mining, farming, energy, logging; export earnings from selling rainforest related products abroad; water and air pollution increased by human activities in rainforest; soils degraded to a point where they will no longer produce crops; climate change caused by upsetting the carbon dioxide and oxygen balance in atmosphere; more extreme climate events – floods, droughts.

12 **a** The rainforests can provide medicines to help improve health, and they provide important food and timber resources, which could be managed sustainably. The loss of biodiversity could disturb natural balances, cause losses of invaluable natural products and cause species to become extinct. The rainforest is believed to help balance the composition of gases in the Earth's atmosphere, which may be important to reducing climate change.

   b Any sustainable strategy, such as international agreements: most countries are linked through globalisation processes, and communications tools such as the internet can help educate and persuade all of those in emerging or developing countries and developed countries of the need to aim for sustainability. Developed countries can provide monitoring of rainforest areas (e.g. satellite technology) so that it is known how much is being cut down and whether protected areas are being damaged, and provide funding through schemes such as REDD, which emphasises management steps, such as stopping deforestation, using forests sustainably, recovering degraded land and expanding forest cover.

Taiga (boreal) biome

1   Taiga or boreal biome is found in Scandinavia (e.g. Sweden), Canada and northern Russia.

2   **a** Any two from: coniferous forests made up of pine, fir and spruce trees; plants are small and grow close to the ground; nutrient cycling is slow; biodiversity is low; simpler food web than most other biomes; animals migrate or hibernate in winter months.

   b The climate has: very cold winters (−18 °C average in January, but can reach −40 °C); low precipitation (e.g. 350 mm a year in Saskatoon); short, warm summers (+18 °C average in July).

3   **a** Within the food web the plants (e.g. grey willow tree) provide food for herbivores (e.g. snowshoe hare), which in turn provide food for carnivores (e.g. great horned owl). Nutrient cycling is slow due to cold temperatures and little water, which slows decomposition, so transfers of nutrients between biomass, litter and soil take a long time.

   b Indigenous people hunt animals (e.g. caribou, fish) and gather plants (e.g. soapberries) because it is too cold and dry to grow crops for food.

4   **a** Biodiversity is lower because the cold conditions limit the range of plants to those specially adapted, and with fewer primary producers there is less food to support a large range of animals.

   b The taiga ecosystem is vulnerable because food webs are simpler (and less productive), which means that even a small amount of damage or change can have serious consequences; the lack of biodiversity means that if one small part of a food web is removed then large parts of the food web will also be damaged; recovery time from any damage is very slow due to the climate causing difficult growing conditions; the slow cycling of nutrients means damage to soils; vegetation removal makes it difficult for the taiga ecosystem to recover.

5   **a** Any three causes from: logging for softwood timber; deforestation to access valuable minerals like oil; acid rain damaging trees; wildfires, pests and diseases.

   b Indigenous people usually live in harmony with nature, only extracting what they need in order to live, such as collecting berries from the forest or logging trees to make buildings. However, commercial logging companies want to make money and so cut down a large amount of forest to create timber or wood for paper making.

6   Global agreements on climate change are important to biodiversity in the taiga because reducing or preventing excess warming is essential to stop rapid change that would disrupt links within the ecosystem. For example, earlier leaf growth and fruiting may not match insect and animal cycles, preventing successful breeding and disrupting food chains, and migrations may happen too late. An increase in the number of wildfires may destroy large amounts of forest from which tree species may never recover. Warmer conditions encourage pests and diseases that may kill plant species and remove the food supply for other creatures.

7   **a** It is difficult to manage the taiga on a global scale because the biome stretches across a number of countries, including Russia (which often makes different political decisions to the other countries containing taiga biome), so getting all governments to agree is very difficult.

   b Strategies for conserving the taiga biome include: designating areas as national parks, wildlife reserves or UNESCO Natural World Heritage Sites; limiting the number of resource exploration licences; ensuring that all forestry operations are sustainable; countries signing and acting upon international agreements (including climate change and biodiversity).

   Any explanation of one of these, for example National Parks: areas can be set aside for nature, with only limited human interaction such as scientific research and ecotourism. This protects areas from widespread damage or interference with natural systems and cycles. Ecosystems are preserved, while limited human activity is permitted. The Wrangell-St Elias NP in Alaska is the USA's largest National Park and was founded to retain biodiversity, protect resources used by indigenous people and monitor climate change impacts. There are many positives for conservation; however, monitoring is important as hunting and tourism is still allowed and the NP is under pressure from mining around the park.

8   There are conflicting views about how to manage taiga forests because environmentalists would like to see greater protection for all wildlife so that the biome may survive into the future, while logging

and mining companies would like access to the resources that are available to make money. Indigenous people would prefer no large-scale change, so that their way of life is not disturbed, although some income may be seen as beneficial. Governments are often torn between conserving nature but also providing jobs and making money for the country, which can be used to provide services and infrastructure to improve the lives of the population.

9 Consuming energy resources (p. 178)

Energy resources management

1. Energy resources help people to cook food, heat homes and have light. They also help businesses and industries to operate, providing jobs.

2. Biofuels are a recyclable resource because the crops that produce them can be replanted, creating a sustainable supply.

3. Fossil fuels may damage the environment by producing carbon dioxide (CO_2), which is the main greenhouse gas causing climate change; other pollutants are also released, such as sulfur gas (which is responsible for some urban air pollution and acid rain).

4. The best landscape for HEP consists of steep-sided valleys, where it is easier to build a dam and create a deep reservoir of water. The best climate for HEP is one that has plenty of rainfall to keep the reservoir full.

5. Solar energy needs areas with clear skies for sunlight to activate the photovoltaic cells. The heat of the Sun can also be used to heat water in solar panels, to provide heating and hot water.

6. World demand for energy has increased because the population has grown rapidly, meaning that more energy is used. More countries are developing economically and have businesses and industries that also use energy.

7. a Any one reason from: oil and natural gas are running out (especially from the North Sea); natural gas supplies are mostly imported and these supplies could get cut off; concern over climate change is reducing the burning of fossil fuels; renewable technologies are being developed rapidly.

    b It has declined because fossil fuels have run out or reserves are now low (e.g. only 37% of natural gas reserves remain). Also there are now strict international and national regulations on carbon dioxide emissions.

    c Nuclear energy produces radioactivity. Wind turbines may kill wildlife and spoil scenery. Biofuels use up farmland.

8. Energy supplies are unevenly distributed around the world. For example, fossil fuels form in geological processes that only occur in certain places. Geothermal energy is only available where tectonic processes bring magma close to the surface. Solar energy and wind energy are linked to suitable climatic conditions, which do not exist everywhere. The technology to use these resources is not yet available to all countries.

9. Energy insecurity is where a country does not have enough energy to meet its needs.

10. China was the world's largest importer of energy in 2014 because it had rapidly industrialised. This economic development increased the demand for energy from industries, businesses and an increasingly wealthy population. It also had the world's largest population (over 1.3 billion people), all needing energy resources.

11. Iceland and Kenya had contrasting energy consumption because of their relative levels of development and their location. Iceland is a developed country with modern industries and homes, with a plentiful supply of cheap geothermal energy due to its location on the Mid-Atlantic Ridge (a plate margin where volcanic activity takes place). Kenya is a developing country with many poor people who cannot afford to buy energy and fewer energy intensive industries and businesses. Kenya is not favourably located for readily available energy resources.

Oil

1. OPEC is the Organisation of the Petroleum Exporting Countries, which controls the amount of oil extracted and exported, and so largely controls the price of oil.

2. Saudi Arabia has the largest crude oil reserves because it is located where geological processes created them in greatest quantity.

3. The USA consumes more oil because it is one of the top economic nations in the world. Many industries and businesses use oil or oil-based products. Most road vehicles and aircraft use fuels extracted from oil, such as petrol (gasoline), diesel and aviation fuel. People are relatively wealthy and so are able to afford to use a lot of oil-based products. There is a wide range of technology available based on using oil or oil-based products.

4. Many African countries are in the developing category and have low oil consumption because people are unable to afford the technology (e.g. cars) that use oil. Businesses and industries are less well developed, so there is less demand for oil or oil-based products. Oil is an expensive energy source which some countries, and people within them, cannot afford.

5. Countries facing energy insecurity include China, Japan and India. World regions affected by energy insecurity include Sub-Saharan Africa, South Asia and East Asia.

6. The world oil price is likely to drop during an economic recession because people and businesses try to save money by using less energy.

7. China's industrialisation has increased the world oil price, because oil is in greater demand. If the amount of oil supplied is reduced or limited (as OPEC may sometimes decide), prices increase because some countries and industries are willing to pay more to get oil.

8. Oil exploration in environmentally sensitive areas may cause damage to the natural environment through oil spillages, poisoning land and water. Buildings related to oil extraction and pipelines scar the landscape. In the tundra biome, buildings and machinery must be lifted above the frozen ground (permafrost) to avoid melting and subsidence.

9. Answers will vary according to case study. Here the example is Amazonia; natural gas, Peru.

    a Two features, such as: 385 billion m^3 of natural gas reserves; financed by foreign companies; pipelines to processing plants (e.g. Cuzco); supplies 95% of Peru's needs and provides exports.

    b Advantages include: cheap source of energy, which saves Peruvian people about $1.4 billion a year; Peruvian government gains revenues from taxes, which it can use to provide services and infrastructure; energy security has been achieved in natural gas and electricity; income from energy sales.

    Disadvantages include: clearance of tropical rainforest for extraction and pipelines; tribal areas have been affected; it is a non-renewable resource; there is foreign involvement. These are disadvantages because the natural environment is damaged and may not recover; tribal people lose their land and living area and have their way of life disrupted; the natural gas supply will run out; some profits and benefits are leaving Peru and going to big foreign companies.

10. Environmental costs of unconventional fossil fuel development (e.g. Alberta oil sands) include: removal of large areas of natural forest; pollution of rivers; scars on the landscape; contamination of land and groundwater; greenhouse gas emissions.

Strategies to reduce energy demand

1. Travel habits can be changed by using vehicles powered by oil-based products (diesel and petrol) less, and by using public transport, cycling or walking.

2. Workplaces can be made more energy-efficient by not heating rooms that people do not occupy (e.g. storerooms); switching lights, heating or air conditioning off in areas housing people when they are not occupied; and encouraging workers to cycle to work or car share.

3. Technology can help reduce energy consumption by improving transport efficiency – using less energy; having combined heat and power stations; using energy-efficient household appliances.

4. a Energy mix is the range and amounts of energy sources used by a country to supply its needs.

    b A carbon footprint is the amount and sources of carbon dioxide emissions from an individual, household, business or country.

5. a Hydrogen has disadvantages such as: it has to be extracted from water, and this uses considerable energy; it is an energy carrier or store rather than a new energy source; it can catch fire.

    b Solar power needs low maintenance while biofuels must be replanted each year; solar power produces electricity without any carbon emissions but biofuels do emit some; both may take up farmland that could be used for growing food crops. (Other points may be possible.)

6. Small-scale energy schemes are more suitable because they are usually low cost, use appropriate technology, are easy to understand and repair, directly provide what local people need, and do not damage the natural environment significantly.

7. One reason is the increasing concern about the serious and long-term damaging effects on people and the environment from radiation when there is a serious accident.

8. a Exxon-Mobil wants to explore the Arctic Ocean because there are likely to be large reserves of oil and natural gas there; oil and gas are running out in the rest of the world; and they want to continue to make money in the future.

    b Change to renewables is seen as desirable because: fossil fuels will run out and new sources of energy will be needed to avoid shortages; carbon dioxide emissions are causing serious climate change issues and renewables would avoid these emissions; sustainable resources will reduce energy costs in the future, improving quality of life.

9. A carbon footprint calculation shows which activities are causing the most CO_2 emissions, showing where changes need to be made to be more efficient or ways of doing things.

Index

Hazardous Earth
Climate change

Study **Figure 1**, a photograph of a volcanic eruption.

Figure 1

(1) Describe **one** way in which volcanic eruptions can affect climate change. (2 marks, ★)

....

....

....

(2) State **two** forms of evidence to help reconstruct past climates. (2 marks, ★)

Form 1: ....

....

Form 2: ....

....

NAILIT!

State

The command word *state* is an alternative to 'give' or 'name'. You need to provide a basic response. In some cases, this may be a single word or phrase.

(3) Explain how atmospheric circulation redistributes heat energy around the Earth. (4 marks, ★★★)

....

....

....

....

....

....

(4) Explain the enhanced greenhouse effect. (4 marks, ★★★)

....

....

....

....

....

NAILIT!

A four-mark question is always point marked. This means that you need to give two points and develop each of them.

(5) Explain the natural causes of climate change. (4 marks, ★★★)

....

....

....

....

....

....

(6) Explain how human activity has contributed to climate change. (4 marks, ★★★)

....

....

....

....

....

....

....

NAILIT!

Explain

The command word *explain* is asking you to give reasons for something happening. In **Question 6**, you need to set out the human causes of climate change and show an understanding of how these activities affect the climate.

WORKIT!

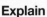

'Predictions of future global temperatures are uncertain'. Assess this statement.
(8 marks, ★★★★★)

'Assess' questions require you to make an informed judgment.

How to tackle this 'assess' question:

Step 1 Give a point to state how future global temperatures are uncertain.

Step 2 Extend your point by explaining why global temperatures are uncertain.

Step 3 Try to include an example to support your point.

Step 4 Include judgement to explain this reason why predictions of future global temperatures are uncertain.

Step 5 Repeat steps 1–4 to explain why global temperatures are uncertain. You should include three developed points.

Weather hazards

Study **Figure 2**, a world map showing the distribution of tropical cyclones.

Tracks and intensity of all tropical cyclones

| TD | TS | 1 | 2 | 3 | 4 | 5 |

Saffir-Simpson hurricane intensity scale

Figure 2

① Which **two** statements about tropical cyclones are true?

> Remember, answering multiple-choice questions should be quick. In the exam, aim to spend no more than one minute to work out your answer.

Shade **two** circles only. (2 marks, ★)

A Tropical cyclones develop over the equator. ◯

B Tropical cyclones form above warm oceans (27 °C or above). ◯

C Tropical cyclones gain energy as they hit land. ◯

D The conditions in the eye of the cyclone are calm. ◯

E Tropical cyclones only develop between August and October. ◯

② Describe **two** ways that people can prepare for a tropical cyclone. (4 marks, ★★)

Preparation 1: ....
....
....
....

Preparation 2: ....
....
....
....

> **DO IT!**
>
> **Primary and secondary effects**
>
> Make sure you understand the difference between primary and secondary effects. Memorise the primary and secondary effects of the different natural hazards, such as tropical cyclones. Learn your case studies!

③ Outline **two** effects of a tropical cyclone. (2 marks, ★)

....
....
....
....

(4) Explain the causes of tropical cyclones. (4 marks, ★★★)

....

....

....

....

....

....

....

....

NAILIT!

Make sure you learn your named examples or case studies so you can provide specific examples to support your answers.

WORKIT!

Explain the causes of tropical cyclones. (4 marks, ★★★)

With an 'explain' question, you need to make a point and then give reasons for it. Your answer should apply understanding of the causes of a tropical cyclones – you will not get more than two marks if you only state the causes.

How to tackle this 'explain' question:

Step 1 Describe one cause of a tropical cyclone (for example, warm ocean water).

Step 2 Apply understanding (for example, by explaining why warm ocean water causes the formation of a tropical cyclone).

Step 3 Repeat steps 1–2 with a second point.

(5) Using a named example, assess the impacts of a tropical cyclone. (8 marks, ★★★★★)

....

....

....

....

....

....

....

....

....

....

....

....

(6) Assess the methods used to predict tropical cyclones in a developed country.

Use a separate sheet of paper to write your answer to this question. (8 marks, ★★★★★)

Tectonic hazards

Study **Figure 3**, a world map showing the distribution of earthquakes and volcanoes.

Figure 3

(1) Describe the distribution of earthquake zones shown in **Figure 3**. (2 marks, ★)

....

....

....

....

(2) Outline **one** reason why earthquakes are found in this pattern. (2 marks, ★)

....

....

....

....

NAILIT!

Outline

The command word *outline* means that you must provide a brief account of relevant information. There is a wide range of geographical factors and processes that could be tested with this type of question, but you do not need to expand your answers.

(3) Explain why volcanoes are formed at convergent plate margins. (4 marks, ★★★)

....

....

....

....

....

....

....

....

NAILIT!

Make sure you learn the physical processes happening at each of the three types of plate margin and the landforms that are created. You could draw a flow diagram or a sequence of annotated diagrams in your revision. Include key terms and what they mean.

(4) Explain **two** ways in which people can prepare for an earthquake. (4 marks, ★★)

Way 1: ....

....

....

....

Way 2: ....

....

....

....

DOIT!

Reducing the risk of tectonic hazards

Make sure you understand how **monitoring, prediction, protection** and **planning** can all reduce the risks of tectonic hazards. Memorise how countries at different levels of development use these four management strategies.

(5) Using a named example, describe the primary and secondary effects of an earthquake or volcanic eruption. (8 marks, ★★★★)

....

....

....

....

....

....

....

....

....

....

....

....

WORKIT!

'Tectonic hazards have a greater impact in developing countries.'
Assess this statement. (8 marks, ★★★★★)

'Assess' questions require you to make an informed judgement. You need to offer both sides of an argument in your answer.

How to tackle this 'assess' question:

Step 1 Give a reason why tectonic hazards have a greater impact in developing countries.

Step 2 Extend your point by explaining it.

Step 3 Include an example to support your point (for example, the impacts of a tectonic hazard in a developing country).

Step 4 Think about how to categorise impacts in your answer (for example, social versus economic impacts).

Step 5 Repeat steps 1–3 including judgement as to why hazards can also have a great impact in developed countries (for example, economic impacts).

This is a longer written answer and not necessarily straightforward. You could make a brief plan in any spare space on the exam paper, to help you link a sequence of points in a fluent way.

NAILIT!

Spelling, punctuation and grammar (SPaG) marks

In the longer answer questions, you will be assessed on your ability to present a fluent answer using correct spelling and punctuation, good grammar (such as sentence structure) and geographical terms. Make sure that you have prepared for this. Sometimes it can make a difference of a grade!

Development dynamics
Development and inequalities

Study **Figure 1**, part of a world map showing a classification of countries using average income per person (capita).

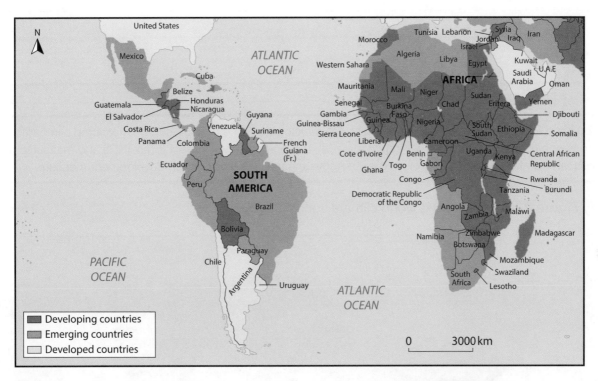

Figure 1

DO IT!

Using keys

Make sure that you always use the keys to maps carefully. For example, in **Figure 1**, in which category is Argentina? In which category is Chad? In which category are Bolivia and Zambia?

1. Using **Figure 1**, compare the classification of countries in South America with those in Africa. (2 marks, ★)

....

....

....

....

> 'Compare' in this question means look for **similarities** and **differences** in the classification categories between South America and Africa. You don't need to count the number of countries in each category. Instead, you could look for the most common categories, or missing categories.

2. **Figure 1** shows a classification of countries according to income. Suggest **one** advantage of using average income per person to measure the development of a country. (2 marks, ★★★)

....

....

....

....

(3) Explain **one** disadvantage of the Human Development Index (HDI) as a measure of a country's development. (2 marks, ★★★)

....

....

....

....

NAILIT!

You need to learn the different ways in which the development of a country can be measured – in particular, gross domestic product (GDP) per capita (person), the Human Development Index (HDI) and measures of inequality and corruption – as well as the strengths and weaknesses of each development measure.

Study **Figure 2**, a map showing world climate zones.

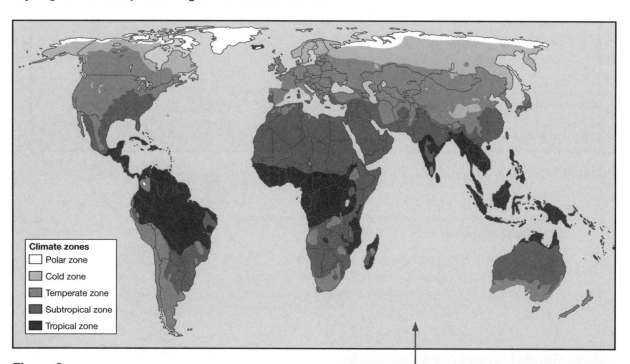

Climate zones
- ☐ Polar zone
- Cold zone
- Temperate zone
- Subtropical zone
- Tropical zone

Figure 2

Always look carefully at the figures provided. Some are there for you to extract information from. These questions usually refer to the specific figure: for example, **Question 1** says 'Using **Figure 1**'. Other figures give you clues or help, like **Figure 2** in **Question 4**.

(4) Explain how **one** aspect of physical geography and climate may cause uneven development between countries. (4 marks, ★★★)

....

....

....

....

....

....

....

Study **Figure 3**, a graph showing the share of world exports (goods) (2005 and 2014) for world regions.

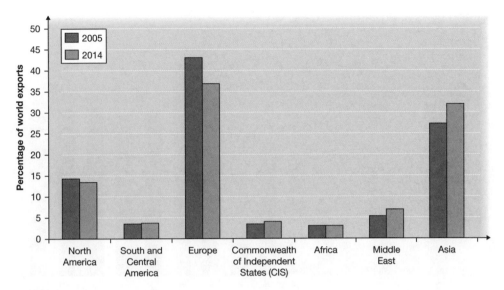

Figure 3

(5) Using **Figure 3**, state the decline in Europe's share of world exports between 2005 and 2014. (1 mark, ★)

A 2 per cent ○

B 5 per cent ○

C 7 per cent ○

D 10 per cent ○

WORKIT!

Explain how **one** aspect of economic geography may cause global inequalities. (4 marks, ★★★)

How to tackle this 'explain' question:

This 'explain' question is asking you to choose one geographical factor linked to making money (economic geography) and give reasons for it causing more development in some countries than in others (global inequalities). **Figure 3** is there to suggest one strong option – **trade** – but you could choose something else, such as a lack of FDI.

Step 1 Choose the aspect of economic geography you want to write about. If this is trade, study **Figure 3** carefully.

Step 2 State that this aspect means that some countries get richer while others stay poor.

Step 3 Apply your understanding to explain how this happens, with two or three developed sentences that identify the geographical links.

Study **Figure 4**, a graph showing the number of cases of the disease tuberculosis (per 100 000 people) in 2014 for selected countries.

Note that the graph uses a logarithmic scale.

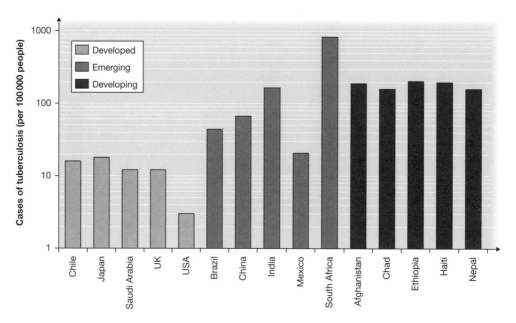

Figure 4

(6) Using **Figure 4**, calculate the difference between the number of cases of tuberculosis (per 100 000 people) in Haiti and in the USA. (2 marks, ★)

NAILIT!

A graph may have a logarithmic (log) scale on one axis (or both axes) when there is a large range in the data presented (very large numbers compared with very small numbers). **Figure 4** has a log scale on the vertical *y*-axis. Even though the horizontal lines are spaced differently from a normal graph, each line still represents a unit of measurement. Here, each line between 1 and 10 increases by 1, each line between 10 and 100 increases by 10, and each line between 100 and 1000 increases by 100. Examiners know that logarithmic graphs are tricky to interpret, so they make skills questions based on them as easy as possible.

(7) Explain why there is such a large variation in the number of cases of tuberculosis between the countries shown in **Figure 4**. (4 marks, ★★★)

....

....

....

....

....

....

....

....

(8) Suggest **two** reasons why poor health may create a cycle of poverty. (2 marks, ★★★)

Reason 1: ....

....

Reason 2: ....

....

(9) Explain how Rostow's modernisation theory accounts for the development of countries. (4 marks, ★★★)

....

....

....

....

....

....

....

DO IT!

Suggest **two** reasons why population growth in a country may have a positive impact on its development. (4 marks, ★★★)

When a question asks you for two reasons, make sure that they are different – not just the same reason written in a different way!

Study the student answer below, give it a mark out of four and suggest how it could be improved:

If a population gets bigger then there will be more workers for the businesses and industries in the country. There will be a bigger workforce that will make sure that all the jobs that need doing in the country are done. These reasons will help the country to develop more.

Development strategies

Study **Figure 5**, a graph showing outflowing Foreign Direct Investment (FDI) in $ billions by world group or region 2012–14.

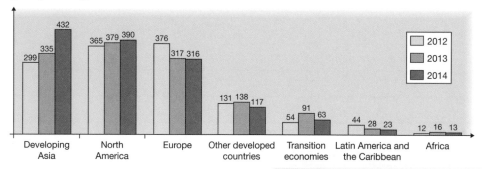

Figure 5

There may be several possible answers to a one- or two-mark question, but you only need to give one. For example, in **Question 1a**, change could be simply up or down, or a rate of change, or the size of the change. For a two-mark question, make sure you quote data or information from the Figure provided.

1. a Using **Figure 5**, compare the change in developing Asia with the change in Europe between 2012 and 2014. (2 marks, ★)

   ....

   ....

   b Calculate the difference between the amount of outflowing FDI from transition economies and the amount from Africa in 2014. (2 marks, ★)

2. Explain **one** way in which FDI can help to increase the development of a country. (2 marks, ★)

   ....

   ....

   ....

   ....

3. Suggest **one** reason why FDI is not always successful in reducing poverty within a country. (2 marks, ★★★)

   ....

   ....

   ....

   ....

NAILIT!

If you are asked for **one** reason and the question is worth **two** marks, you must provide a fully developed answer. To gain both marks, you must explore the **geographical links** in relation to the theme of the question.

④ Which of the following is the definition of fair trade? (1 mark, ★)

    A Debt-for-nature swaps to protect nature and reduce a country's debt. ○

    B Better prices and working conditions directly supporting farmers and workers. ○

    C Selling low-value raw materials and buying expensive machinery and fuels. ○

    D Developed countries giving money to developing countries to help them develop. ○

Study **Figure 6**, a graph showing the number of tourists visiting Jamaica and the income received from them.

'Calculate' in this question means work out the difference between the number of tourist arrivals in 2009 and in 2015. First follow the vertical lines for each year to where they intersect with the tourist arrivals line. Then look horizontally across to the vertical axis and work out the two values. Subtract the 2009 value from the 2015 value to calculate the difference (amount of increase). Remember to add 'millions' after the figure.

Figure 6

⑤ **a** Using **Figure 6**, calculate the increase in tourists between 2009 and 2015. (2 marks, ★)

b Using **Figure 6**, compare the trend of tourist arrivals with the trend of tourist income from 2009 to 2015. (2 marks, ★)

....

....

⑥ Suggest **one** way in which tourism may help start a multiplier effect cycle in a developing country. (2 marks, ★)

....

....

....

....

Rapid economic development and change

Study **Figure 7**, a graph showing oil production in Nigeria from the end of 2000 to the start of 2016.

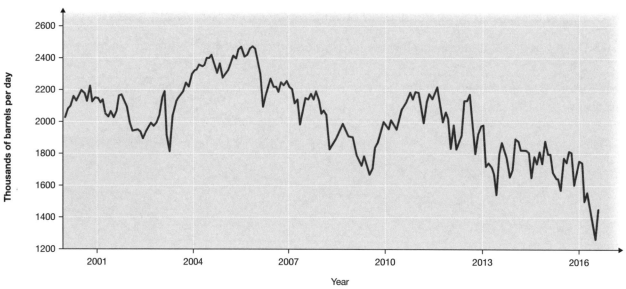

Nigeria's crude oil production

Figure 7

'Calculate' in this question means work out the difference between the amount of oil production in 2004 and the amount of oil production in 2016. First follow the vertical lines for each year to where they intersect with the production line. Then look horizontally across to the vertical axis and work out the two production values. Subtract the 2016 value from the 2004 value to calculate the difference (amount of decrease). There are two marks, so show your working.

① a Using **Figure 7**, calculate the decrease in oil production between 2004 and 2016. (2 marks, ★)

b Using **Figure 7**, compare the trend of oil production between 2004 and 2007 with the trend between 2007 and 2010. (2 marks, ★)

....

....

....

....

NAILIT!

If you are asked about 'trends', remember that there are three possibilities: a downward trend (decrease), an upward trend (increase) or no change (stays about the same). However, any of these overall trends may have wide variations within it – such as lots of 'ups' and 'downs'. There may also be no significant trend with a lot of change over time – a variable trend.

(2) For an emerging country that you have studied, describe how it is linked to other countries around the world. (2 marks, ★)

....

....

....

....

(3) For an emerging country that you have studied, describe **one** social or **one** cultural factor that is making it difficult to eliminate inequalities within the country. (2 marks, ★★★)

....

....

....

....

NAILIT!

Political, social, economic and environmental factors

Make sure that you remember examples of each of these geographical factors for the country that you have studied – identify **two** for each factor. Make sure that you use the correct one(s) in an exam question. For example, **Question 3** gives you the option of outlining **one** social factor *or* **one** cultural factor – there is a lot of overlap between these two factors, which is probably why the examiner has put them together.

(4) Explain why the industrial structure of an emerging country that you have studied has changed. (4 marks, ★★★)

....

....

....

....

....

....

....

....

NAILIT!

For this part of the specification, you must know about a **case study of an emerging country**. In the accompanying Edexcel GCSE Geography B Revision Guide, this is India. Where the question refers to 'an emerging country that you have studied', you must use your knowledge and understanding of your case study country to answer the question, including specific information and facts that you have learned.

(5) For a named emerging country, assess how far government policies and actions have caused economic growth.

Use a separate sheet of paper to write your answer to this question. (12 marks, ★★★★★)

This question needs a longer written answer and may not be straightforward. You could make a brief plan in any spare space on the exam paper, to help you link a sequence of points in a fluent way.

WORKIT!

For a named emerging country, assess how far economic growth has had a negative impact on the environment. (12 marks, ★★★★★)

How to tackle this 'assess' question:

- In this question you will need to include some **accurate description**, some **explanation** and a **judgement** on the extent to which negative impacts are the result of economic growth in your chosen and named country.

- Don't just list all the problems and issues that have affected the natural environment, or write everything you can remember about the natural environment in the emerging country you have studied. Make sure you answer the question.

Key ideas to include in your answer:

- Recall the types of economic activity found in the emerging country, especially recent ones.

- Recall specific information and facts about the rapid economic development of the emerging country, and include them to support the points you make. These should be facts about the economic activities and their locations, and examples of any negative influences, such as pollution.

- Remember that there may have been some positive impacts on the natural environment as well. If so, you should include these, so that there is a balanced assessment in your answer.

- **Economy** points may include the growth of manufacturing industries, urbanisation, expansion of sea ports, named key industries and companies, and GDP/GNI rate of increase.

- **Environmental** points may include air pollution, water pollution, pressures on land and carbon dioxide emissions.

NAILIT!

Spelling, punctuation and grammar (SPaG) marks

In the longer answer questions, you will be assessed on your ability to present a fluent answer using correct spelling and punctuation, good grammar (such as sentence structure) and geographical terms. Make sure that you have prepared for this. Sometimes it can make a difference of a grade! For example, 4 of the 12 marks in **Question 5** and the **Work it!** on this page are for SPaG.

Challenges of an urbanising world
Trends in urbanisation

Study **Figure 1**, a graph showing world population growth from 1800 to 2050 (predicted).

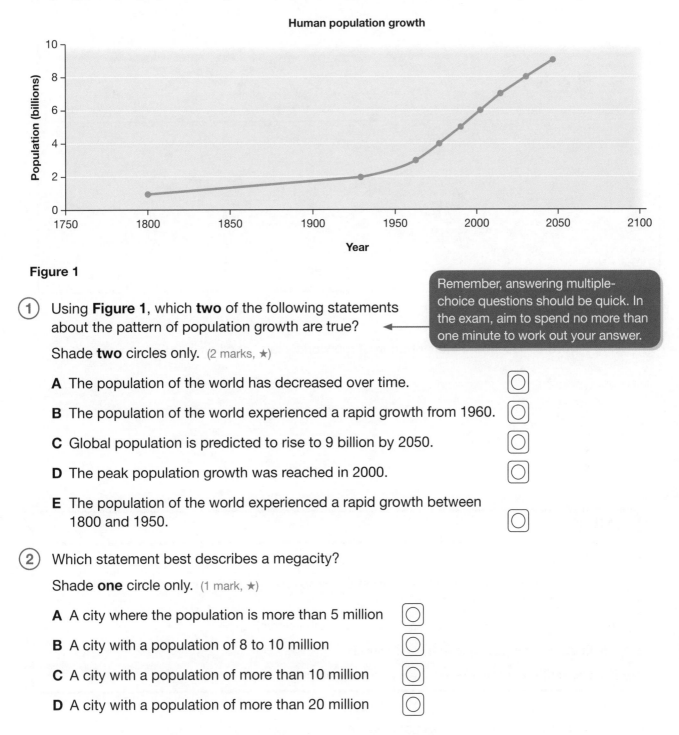

Figure 1

Remember, answering multiple-choice questions should be quick. In the exam, aim to spend no more than one minute to work out your answer.

(1) Using **Figure 1**, which **two** of the following statements about the pattern of population growth are true?

Shade **two** circles only. (2 marks, ★)

A The population of the world has decreased over time. ◯

B The population of the world experienced a rapid growth from 1960. ◯

C Global population is predicted to rise to 9 billion by 2050. ◯

D The peak population growth was reached in 2000. ◯

E The population of the world experienced a rapid growth between 1800 and 1950. ◯

(2) Which statement best describes a megacity?

Shade **one** circle only. (1 mark, ★)

A A city where the population is more than 5 million ◯

B A city with a population of 8 to 10 million ◯

C A city with a population of more than 10 million ◯

D A city with a population of more than 20 million ◯

Study **Figure 2**, a map showing the world's megacities in 2005.

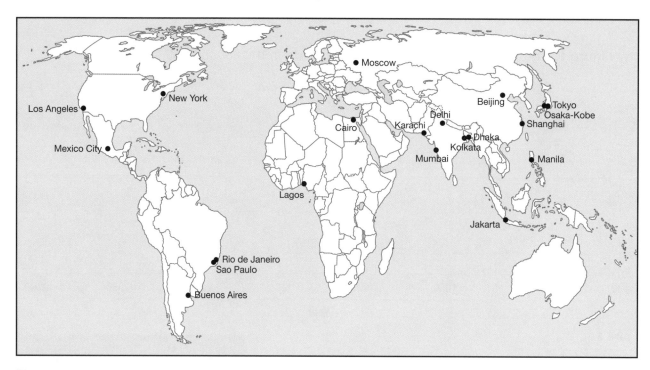

Figure 2

③ Using **Figure 2**, describe the distribution of the world's largest cities in 2005. (2 marks, ★★)

....

....

....

....

NAILIT!

Describe the distribution

The command phrase in this two-mark question is *describe the distribution*. In your answer, you need to say where the largest cities in the world are.

- Are there more in the northern hemisphere or the southern hemisphere?

- Are there more megacities in Asia or elsewhere?

- Are there any continents where there are no megacities?

④ Explain the reasons for the growth of cities in the developing world. (4 marks, ★★★)

....

....

....

....

....

....

Changing cities over time

(1) For a city you have studied, explain the advantages of its site and how the site helped the city to grow. Start your answer by naming the city. (4 marks, ★★★)

....

....

....

....

....

Study **Figure 3**, which shows a model of a developing city.

(2) Using **Figure 3**, state the land use you would expect to find in zone E.

Shade **one** box only. (1 mark, ★)

A CBD ⭕

B Heavy industry ⭕

C Squatter settlements ⭕

D Expensive housing ⭕

(3) Define the term 'informal economy'. (1 mark, ★)

....

....

(4) Explain **one** problem for people working in the informal economy. (3 marks, ★★)

....

....

....

....

....

Study **Figure 4**, which shows a rapidly growing megacity.

Figure 4

(5) Annotate the photograph in **Figure 4** to show the problems of rapid urban growth in a developing or emerging megacity. (4 marks, ★★★)

NAILIT!

When you annotate a photograph or diagram, each annotation should have a **point** and an **explanation**. For example: Open sewer, which is unhygienic and may attract rats that can spread diseases.

WORKIT!

Evaluate the success of top-down strategies to improve the quality of life in a developing or emerging megacity. (8 marks, ★★★★★)

This 'evaluate' question is asking you to say how successful the strategies were, so you need to include points both **for** and **against** the strategies chosen. You could also consider the economic, social and environmental costs and benefits.

How to tackle this 'evaluate' question:

Step 1 Give an economic, social and/or environmental benefit of the strategy.

Step 2 Extend your point by explaining the economic, social and/or environmental benefit.

Step 3 Exemplify your point by referring to a case study.

Step 4 Repeat steps 1–3 for a further two benefits.

Step 5 Repeat steps 1–4, but instead choose and explain give three costs of the strategy.

Step 6 Give a final conclusion to say if the scheme was a success overall or not.

The UK's evolving physical landscape
UK physical landscapes

Study **Figure 1**, a map of a region of the UK.

(1) Study **Figure 1**, identify area X.

Shade **one** circle. (1 mark, ★)

A An upland area made of mostly metamorphic rock. ◯

B An upland area made of mostly sedimentary rock. ◯

C A lowland area made of mostly sedimentary rock. ◯

D A lowland area made of mostly metamorphic rock. ◯

(2) Identify which **one** of the following is a sedimentary rock.

Shade **one** circle. (1 mark, ★)

A Chalk ◯

B Schist ◯

C Granite ◯

D Slate ◯

Figure 1

(3) Explain **one** way in which past glacial processes have caused the development of upland areas in North West England. (2 marks, ★)

....

....

....

(4) Outline **two** ways in which humans have modified the landscape of the UK. (2 marks, ★)

....

....

....

Coastal change and conflict

Study **Figure 2**, a photograph of Spurn Head.

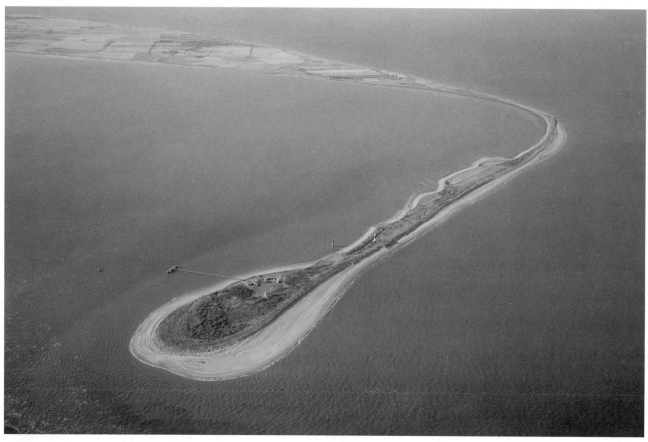

Figure 2

(1) Identify the coastal landform shown in **Figure 2**. (1 mark, ★)

....

(2) State the process that was involved in creating the landform shown in **Figure 2**. (1 mark, ★)

....

(3) Describe **one** negative impact that human activity can have on the coastal landscape. (2 marks, ★)

....

....

....

....

(4) Explain **one** example of soft engineering along the coast. (2 marks, ★)

....

....

....

....

(5) Explain the difference between constructive and destructive waves. (4 marks, ★★★)

....

....

....

....

....

....

....

....

....

....

....

....

DO IT!

Learn how coastal landforms are created by erosion or deposition. To help you remember, you could draw annotated sketches explaining the processes involved in the formation of each landform. You can also use annotated diagrams to support your answers in the exam.

(6) Explain the difference between a discordant and a concordant coastline. (4 marks, ★★★)

....

....

....

....

....

....

....

....

....

(7) Explain how sub-aerial processes are important in the formation of coastal landscapes.
(4 marks, ★★★)

....

....

....

....

....

....

....

....

(8) Explain how processes of erosion have helped to form an arch. (4 marks, ★★★)

....

....

....

....

....

....

....

(9) Explain the costs and benefits of using hard engineering to help manage a coastline.
(4 marks, ★★★)

....

....

....

....

....

....

....

(10) Assess the extent to which coastal management can be sustainable. (8 marks + 4 SPaG, ★★★★★)

....

....

....

....

....

....

....

....

....

....

....

....

....

River landscapes in the UK

Study **Figure 3**, which shows a storm hydrograph.

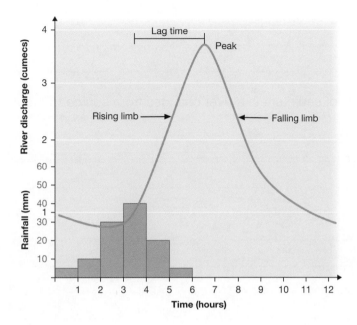

Figure 3

(1) **a** Give a definition of 'lag time' on a hydrograph. (1 mark, ★)

....

....

b Calculate the lag time using the information in **Figure 3**. (1 mark, ★)

> Don't forget that you can draw lines on graphs in the exam to help you work out answers. A ruler and sharp pencil are always useful tools for a geographer.

(2) State **two** ways the cross-section of a river changes from source to mouth.
(2 marks, ★)

....

....

....

....

(3) Explain the process of hydraulic action. (2 marks, ★)

....

....

....

....

④ Explain how climate can affect river landscapes. (2 marks, ★)

....

....

....

....

⑤ Explain how the size of sediment in a river changes from source to mouth. (4 marks, ★★★)

....

....

....

....

....

....

....

⑥ Explain **two** social impacts of river flooding. (4 marks, ★★★)

....

....

....

....

....

....

⑦ Describe **one** physical and **one** human factor that would increase the risk of river flooding.
(4 marks, ★★★)

....

....

....

....

....

....

....

Study **Figure 4**, a photograph of a river at Cuckmere Haven, East Sussex.

Figure 4

⑧ Using **Figure 4** and your own knowledge, explain how a meander is formed. (4 marks, ★★★)

....

....

....

....

....

....

....

....

NAILIT!

Make sure you learn the formation of all river landforms in four simple steps. You could show these steps as a flow diagram or a sequence of annotated diagrams in your revision. Include key terms and what they mean.

⑨ Explain **two** ways humans can alter river landscapes. (4 marks, ★★★)

....

....

....

....

....

....

....

....

(10) Assess the extent to which human actions increase the risk of river flooding.
(8 marks + 4 SPaG, ★★★★★)

....

....

....

....

....

....

....

....

....

....

....

....

....

....

....

WORKIT!

Assess the extent to which human actions increase the risk of river flooding.
(8 marks + 4 SPaG, ★★★★★)

An 'assess' question requires you to make an informed judgment. Here you need to evaluate the degree to which something (human actions) affects a natural phenomenon (river flooding).

How to tackle this 'assess' question:

Step 1 State one type of human action that can affect rivers.

Step 2 Give one way in which this human action can increase the risk of river flooding.

Step 3 Extend your point by explaining how this human action increases the risk of river flooding.

Step 4 Try to include an example to support your point.

Step 5 Repeat steps 1–4 for more types of human action. You should include three developed points.

The UK's evolving human landscape
Changing people and places

Study **Figure 1**, a map showing UK population density.

1 a Using **Figure 1**, describe the pattern of population density across the UK. (2 marks, ★★)

....

....

....

....

....

....

....

....

b State **two** reasons why the population density of the UK varies. (4 marks, ★★★)

....

....

....

....

....

....

....

....

....

....

....

Population density

- 5000 +
- 2500 - 5000
- 1000 - 2500
- 500 - 1000
- 250 - 500
- 100 - 250
- 50 - 100
- 25 - 50
- 0 - 25

Figure 1

2 The population of the UK is increasing. Explain why there has been a growth in the UK population. (4 marks, ★★★)

....

....

....

....

....

....

NAILIT!

When describing a pattern on a map, use compass directions (for example, 'in south-east England', 'north-west Scotland'). You should give any figures used in a choropleth map (for example, 'the density is over 20 per km^2').

Study **Figure 2**, a chart showing London's ethnic mix.

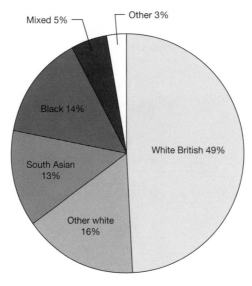

Figure 2

③ Describe London's ethnic mix as shown in **Figure 2**. (2 marks, ★)

....

....

....

....

NAILIT!

When describing a graph or chart, you should always give the general pattern at the start of your answer and then give specific data or figures.

④ State **one** advantage and **one** disadvantage of immigration to the UK. (2 marks, ★★)

....

....

....

....

....

Study **Figure 3**, which shows a picture of a closed coal mine.

Figure 3

(5) State **two** changes to the UK economy since 1980. (2 marks, ★★)

....

....

....

....

NAILIT!

Photographs can be a useful source of geographical information. Use them to find clues that will help you answer the question.

(6) Define the term 'de-industrialisation'. (1 mark, ★)

....

....

(7) Describe **two** features of the knowledge economy. (2 marks, ★★)

....

....

....

....

(8) Explain the impacts of globalisation on the UK economy. (4 marks, ★★★)

....

....

....

....

....

Dynamic UK cities

1 For a UK city that you have studied:

State the name of the city.

a Describe **one** advantage of its site. (2 marks, ★★★)

....

....

....

....

b Describe **one** advantage of its situation. (2 marks, ★★★)

....

....

....

NAILIT!

Make sure you know all of your key geographical vocabulary. Keep a glossary of key terms and use it to quiz yourself.

....

2 State **two** characteristics of the CBD of a city. (2 marks, ★★)

....

....

....

....

Study **Figure 4**, which shows a map of multiple deprivation in London.

Figure 4

(3) Describe the pattern of multiple deprivation in London. (2 marks, ★★)

....

....

....

....

(4) Define the term 'gentrification'. (1 mark, ★)

....

....

WORKIT!

Evaluate the effectiveness of an urban regeneration project you have
studied. (8 marks, ★★★★★)

This 'evaluate' question is asking you to consider how effective the project was, so you need
to include points both **for** and **against** the scheme. You could also consider the economic,
social and environmental costs and benefits.

SPaG marks give extra marks for your spelling, punctuation and grammar.

How to tackle this 'evaluate' question:

Step 1 Give an economic, social and/or environmental benefit of the scheme.

Step 2 Extend your point by **explaining** the social, economic and/or environmental benefit.

Step 3 Include an example to support your point.

Step 4 Repeat steps 1–3 for a further two benefits.

Step 5 Repeat steps 1–3, but instead choose and explain three costs of the scheme.

Step 6 Give a final conclusion that summarises whether or not the scheme has been a success.

People and the biosphere
Biomes

Study **Figure 1**, which shows the extent and location of biomes.

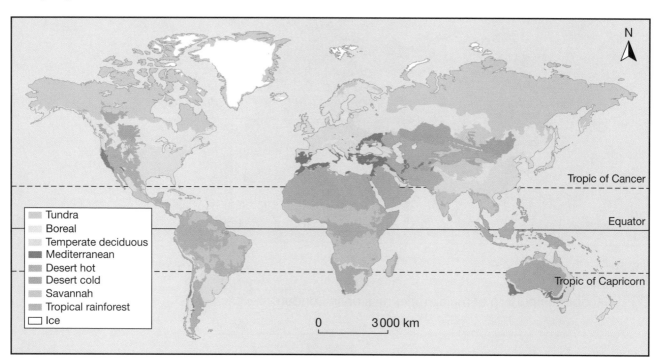

Figure 1

① Using **Figure 1**, identify the biome that is most common along the equator. (1 mark, ★)

A Hot desert ⭘

B Savannah ⭘

C Boreal ⭘

D Tropical rainforest ⭘

② Define the term 'biome'. (1 mark, ★)

....

....

③ Using **Figure 1**, describe the global distribution of the boreal biome. (2 marks, ★★)

....

....

....

....

WORKIT!

Study **Figure 2**, which shows the Hadley convection cell in the atmosphere.

Describe the weather and climate conditions found at the equatorial location of tropical rainforest shown in **Figure 2**. (2 marks, ★)

'Describe' questions only want you to give the main characteristics of something (in this case, of the weather and climate in tropical rainforest regions). You do not need to give any explanation.

Figure 2

How to tackle this 'describe' question:

Step 1 Study **Figure 2** carefully, taking note of the labels and annotations.

Step 2 Write one clear, full sentence to describe the **climate**.

Step 3 Write one clear, full sentence to describe the **weather**.

Here is an example of a good student answer.

> The climate is hot and humid all year with very little temperature range. Temperatures are usually over 25°C every day, with annual rainfall totals of around 2500 mm.

---

④ Identify which **one** of the following statements describes the climate of a boreal (taiga) biome. Shade **one** circle only. (1 mark, ★)

A Very small temperature range during a year (27 °C to 30 °C) and high precipitation (approximately 2500 mm a year). ◯

B Small temperature range during a year (20 °C to 30 °C) and very low precipitation (approximately 125 mm a year). ◯

C Large temperature range during a year (−20 °C to +14 °C) and low precipitation (approximately 500 mm a year). ◯

D Moderate temperature range during a year (5 °C to 18 °C) and moderate precipitation (approximately 1500 mm a year). ◯

NAILIT!

Always read questions carefully to make sure that you actually answer the question. For example, do not muddle 'small-scale' with 'large-scale', or 'local ecosystem' with 'biome'.

Study **Figure 3**, which shows a climate graph for a hot desert biome.

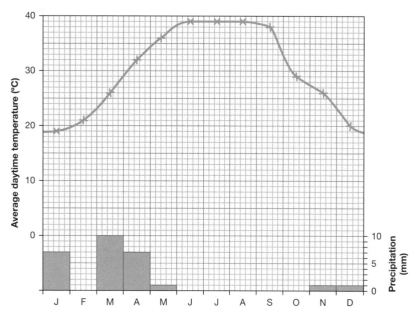

Figure 3

(5) Using **Figure 3**, which one of the following is the correct average monthly temperature for October?

Shade **one** circle only. (1 mark, ★)

A 39°C

B 32°C

C 29°C ◯

D 26°C

>
> **NAILIT!**
>
> In questions where you have to write a number as an answer, **always give the units**. For example, in Question 6, rainfall (or precipitation) is measured in millimetres (mm, so write mm after the number).

(6) Using **Figure 3**, state the average total precipitation (rainfall) for January. (1 mark, ★)

....

(7) Assess the extent to which the interactions between the biotic and abiotic parts create a balance within biomes.

Use a separate sheet of paper to write your answer to this question. (8 marks, ★★★★★)

>
> **NAILIT!**
>
> **Assess**
>
> The command word *assess* means that in your answer you must use evidence to show how significant something is. In **Question 7**, you must consider as many geographical factors as possible and identify which one (or ones) are most important. This is a harder type of question, so be prepared for it.

⑧ Explain why altitude changes the pattern of vegetation within a biome. (2 marks, ★★★)

....

....

....

....

Study **Figure 4**, which shows a nutrient cycle.

Figure 4

⑨ Using **Figure 4**, which **one** of the following statements is correct?

Shade **one** circle only. (1 mark, ★)

A Nutrients are added to the litter by run-off. ◯

B Biomass increases as leaves, twigs and branches fall to the ground. ◯

C Soil gets nutrients from the decomposition of litter. ◯

D Deforestation adds nutrients to the soil. ◯

⑩ Describe the role of water in the nutrient cycle shown in **Figure 4**. (2 marks, ★)

....

....

....

....

Study **Figure 5**, which shows a climate graph for a taiga (boreal) environment.

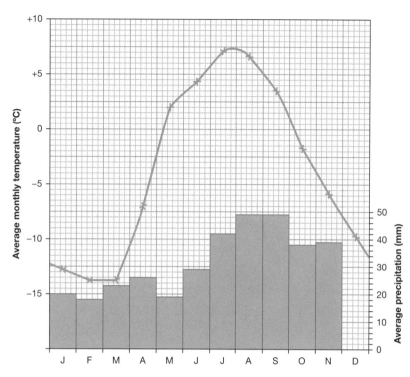

Figure 5

(11) Using **Figure 5**, which **one** of the following temperatures is the correct average monthly temperature for December?

Shade **one** circle only. (1 mark, ★)

A +7.1 °C   ◯

B −1.7 °C   ◯

C −5.9 °C   ◯

D −9.9 °C   ◯

(12) Using **Figure 5**, state the average total precipitation (rainfall) for January. (1 mark, ★)

....

Biosphere resources and regulation

(1) Define the term 'biosphere resource'. (1 mark, ★)

....

....

(2) Explain why biosphere resources are being used more now than in the past. (4 marks, ★★★)

....

....

....

....

....

....

Study **Figure 6**, a photograph of a hot desert biome.

NAILIT!

Photographs are a useful source of geographical information. Sometimes you may have to look for specific pieces of information to answer a question, and sometimes the image may be there to remind you of what you have learned (such as **Figure 6**, and **Question 3**, below).

Figure 6

(3) Using **Figure 6**, suggest why a hot desert biome is considered vulnerable. (2 marks, ★★★)

....

....

....

....

(4) Describe **two** problems for biomes that have been caused by human activities. (2 marks, ★★★)

Problem 1: ....

....

Problem 2: ....

....

Study **Figure 7**, a graph showing the number of days taken to use up the resources provided by the Earth in one year.

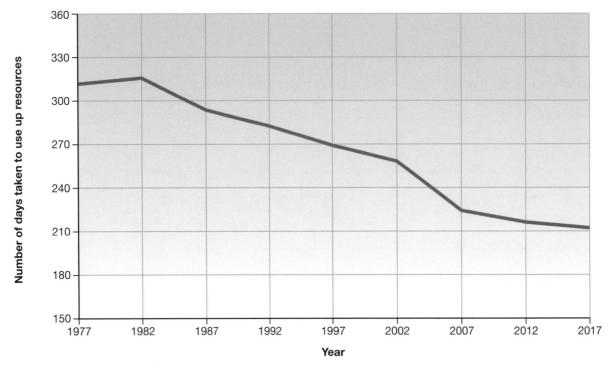

Figure 7

⑤ Calculate the decrease in the number of days taken to use up the Earth's annual resources between 1977 and 2017. (2 marks, ★)

> When you are asked to do a calculation, make sure that you show all your working out and use the correct units (for example, 'days' in **Question 5**) so that you get both marks.

 NAILIT!

Evaluate

The command word *evaluate* means that you must consider the value or success of something – its strengths and weaknesses – and reach a conclusion. You must include information and data that support your points and link to your conclusion. This is a harder type of question, so be prepared for it.

⑥ Evaluate the success of the Malthusian theory in explaining the balance between the Earth's resources and world population size. (8 marks, ★★★★★)

Use a separate sheet of paper to write your answer to this question.

WORKIT!

Evaluate the success of the Boserupian theory in explaining the balance between the Earth's resources and world population size. (8 marks, ★★★★★)

How to tackle this 'evaluate' question:

- Recall what the theory is about but do **not** just describe or define the theory as your whole answer.
- Remember, any geographical theory will have strengths and weaknesses. Try to remember as many of these as you can.
- Include information and facts (including data) that support the strengths and weaknesses that you can remember.
- Write a conclusion about its success, but remember that there is not one possible answer – the theory could be successful, unsuccessful or partly successful/unsuccessful.

Key ideas to include in your answer:

- The idea behind the theory is that as world population grows, there is pressure on resource supplies that makes people think about how to be more efficient and how to create new resources.
- Facts that support the theory include:
  - the population of the world has continued to grow, more than doubling between 1967 and 2017, without a global scale loss of life
  - there have been inventions such as hybrid and electric cars and more efficient household appliances that have made energy resources last longer
  - improvements in farming through use of machinery and other techniques have increased food supplies.
- Facts that go against the theory include:
  - there have been wars and fighting over resources, such as oil in the Middle East
  - diseases now spread quickly around the world
  - there are regular major famines in Sub-Saharan African countries
  - climate change is putting pressure on natural resources such as forests and water
  - there are a large number of refugees and displaced people around the world.
- Evaluation points include:
  - the theory has been largely correct so far but it may not be in the future due to more population pressure
  - the damage that has been done to the natural environment;
  - the Earth 'overshoot' day keeps getting earlier.

Forests under threat
Tropical rainforests

1. Which **one** of the following statements describes a physical characteristic of a tropical rainforest?
   Shade **one** circle only. (1 mark, ★)

   A Soils are very fertile with lots of nutrients. ◯

   B There are two layers of vegetation in the structure. ◯

   C The growing season is eight months a year. ◯

   D Biodiversity is high with a complex food web. ◯

Study **Figure 1**, a diagram showing a nutrient cycle in a tropical rainforest biome.

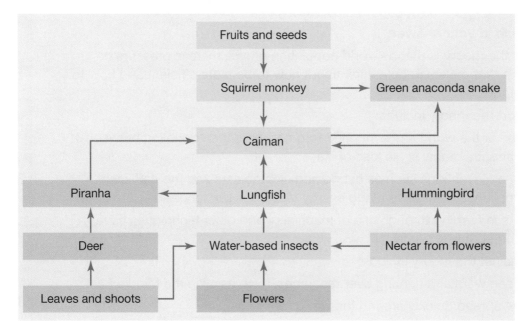

Figure 1

2. Using **Figure 1**, describe the storage of nutrients within a tropical rainforest nutrient cycle.
   (2 marks, ★)

   ....

   ....

   ....

   ....

3. Using **Figure 1**, explain the movement of nutrients within a tropical rainforest nutrient cycle.
   (2 marks, ★)

   ....

   ....

   ....

   ....

Study **Figure 2**, a photograph of tropical rainforest plants.

Figure 2

(4) Annotate **Figure 2** to show two plant adaptations to the tropical rainforest environment. (2 marks, ★)

(5) Explain why there are few plants at ground level in the tropical rainforest ecosystem. (2 marks, ★)

....

....

....

....

Study **Figure 3**, a photograph of young oil palm trees, planted after deforestation in Malaysia.

Figure 3

(6) For the tropical rainforest biome, explain **two** causes of deforestation. (4 marks, ★★★)

....

....

....

....

....

....

NAILIT!

Make sure that you know the difference between *causes* of deforestation and the *ways* in which deforestation occurs. 'Causes' refers to the underlying motives or reasons behind removing trees, rather than the methods or ways in which the trees are removed (such as by logging, road building, HEP construction, farming – although these will be mentioned within the sentences giving the reasons why these human activities are happening). Motives include overcoming poverty and making money for businesses or a country.

Study **Figure 4**, which shows indigenous territories and protected natural areas in countries with tropical rainforest in the Amazon region.

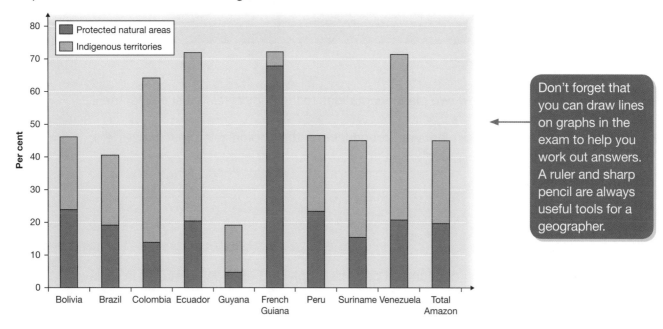

Don't forget that you can draw lines on graphs in the exam to help you work out answers. A ruler and sharp pencil are always useful tools for a geographer.

Figure 4

NAILIT!

Make sure that you know how to read and interpret compound and divided bar graphs. For example, for **Questions 7 and 8** you only need to measure the relevant shaded section and compare this with the relevant axis scale.

(7) Using **Figure 4**, name the country with the largest percentage of protected natural areas. (1 mark, ★)

....

(8) Using **Figure 4**, state the number of countries with 30 per cent or more as indigenous territories. (1 mark, ★)

....

(9) Describe **one** possible value to people of the tropical rainforest global-scale ecosystem. (2 marks, ★)

....

....

....

....

(10) Describe **one** negative impact of deforestation in an area of tropical rainforest biome. (2 marks, ★)

....

....

....

NAILIT!

Many geography questions will ask you about impacts (effects). Remember that impacts can be **positive** (good) or **negative** (bad). Always check to see if the question has specified which type of impacts you need to to consider. When you think about what the impacts are, it may help to think about three categories:

- impacts on people (social impacts)
- impacts on money, businesses and jobs (economic impacts)
- impacts on the natural environment (environmental impacts).

With a *suggest* question, the judgement you make is not right or wrong – it's what you think based on geographical ideas and information.

DOIT!

Suggest

The command word *suggest* means that there is no one correct answer. Instead, there are several possibilities to choose from, and you must present a possible case for one.

Study the following question and student answer. What mark would you give the student? How could the answer be improved?

Suggest **one** way in which replanting trees can help make tropical rainforests more sustainable. (2 marks, ★★★)

Replanting trees makes the forest bigger so that there are more plants and animals.

(11) Suggest **one** way in which educating people about conservation can help make tropical rainforests more sustainable. (2 marks, ★★★)

....

....

....

....

(12) For a tropical rainforest biome you have studied, evaluate the extent to which this ecosystem is threatened by human activities. (8 marks, ★★★★★)

Use a separate sheet of paper to write your answer to this question.

NAILIT!

Evaluate the extent

The command phrase in this eight-mark question is *evaluate the extent.* In your answer, do not just describe the threats – you must also make a judgement on how severe each threat is. You may need to compare the different human threats with each other, or compare them with natural threats.

WORKIT!

For a taiga (boreal) forest biome that you have studied, evaluate the extent to which biodiversity issues are a result of human pressures. (8 marks, ★★★★★)

How to tackle this 'evaluate' question:

- In this question, you will need to include an accurate description, some explanation and a judgement on the relative importance of human and natural pressures.
- Avoid writing lengthy definitions of biodiversity and the pressures – these can be explained in your sentences that answer the question 'evaluate'.

Key ideas to include in your answer:

- The possible changes to biodiversity such as loss of species (plants and animals), extinction of species, changes to habitats and lack of adaptation time.
- Natural pressures, which include low temperatures and wind chill (especially in winter), low precipitation (daily and per year) and short summers.
- Human pressures, including exploitation of resources such as oil, logging, increased population numbers in relatively small areas, modern lifestyle compared to traditional lifestyle, and climate change (enhanced global warming).
- Statements that link biodiversity issues to natural pressures.
- Summary sentences or a conclusion that make one of the following judgements:
  - i human pressures are more responsible for biodiversity issues and by how much, **or**
  - ii natural pressures are more responsible for biodiversity issues and by how much, **or**
  - iii human and natural pressures are equally responsible for biodiversity issues.

Taiga (boreal) forests

(1) Which **one** of the following statements describes a physical characteristic of a taiga (boreal) forest? (1 mark, ★)

   A Soils are very deep with lots of nutrients. ◯

   B Pine and spruce trees dominate the vegetation. ◯

   C The temperature is 16 °C for six months in summer. ◯

   D Biodiversity is high with a complex food web. ◯

Study **Figure 5**, a diagram showing nutrient cycling in a taiga (boreal) forest biome.

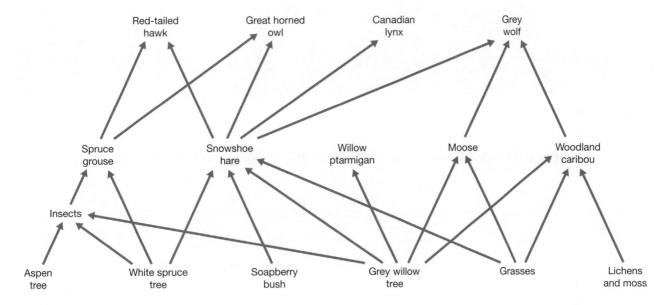

Figure 5

(2) Describe the storage of nutrients within a taiga (boreal) forest nutrient cycle. (2 marks, ★)

....

....

....

....

(3) Explain the movement of nutrients within a taiga (boreal) forest nutrient cycle. (2 marks, ★)

....

....

....

....

Study **Figure 6**, a photograph of animals in the taiga (boreal) forest in Denali National Park, Alaska, USA.

Figure 6

When annotating, make sure that you include a clear line from your words to the relevant feature in the photograph.

(4) Annotate **Figure 6** to show **two** animal adaptations to the taiga (boreal) forest environment.
(2 marks, ★)

(5) Explain why animals in the taiga (boreal) forest have different behaviours in winter and summer.
(2 marks, ★)

....

....

....

....

(6) Explain why the taiga (boreal) forest biome is considered vulnerable. (4 marks, ★★★)

....

....

....

....

....

....

....

(7) Suggest how the taiga (boreal) forest biome can be useful to people. (2 marks, ★)

....

....

....

....

Study **Figure 7**, a satellite photograph showing an area of oil sands extraction in an area of taiga (boreal) forest, Alberta, Canada.

Figure 7

NAILIT!

Satellite images

Satellite images are part of GIS (Geographical Information Systems). Sometimes satellite images have false colours, in which case a key would be provided. In true colour images you must use the colours to tell you what covers the land or what the land is being used for. For example, in **Figure 7**:

- The darkest grey areas show forests (boreal/taiga in this location).
- The slightly lighter grey areas show shorter vegetation (grasses).
- The ribbon of mid-grey down the centre is a river (muddy waters).
- The white/light grey areas show bare land with nothing growing.
- The roughly circular areas of uniform shading, surrounded by very pale 'beaches', are water areas (dark grey have less sediment; those that are light grey have more sediment).
- The fairly straight light-coloured lines are usually roads (but could be railways or pipelines).
- The fluffy white blobs with dark patches near the bottom of the photo are clouds and their shadows.

---

⑧ Using **Figure 7**, explain **two** causes of deforestation in the taiga (boreal) forest biome.
(4 marks, ★★★)

....

....

....

....

....

....

(9) Evaluate the threats to the taiga (boreal) forest biome caused by climate change. (8 marks, ★★★★★)

Use a separate sheet of paper to write your answer to this question.

NAILIT!

Evaluate the threats

The command phrase in this eight-mark question is *evaluate the threats*. In your answer, do not just describe the threats – you must also make a judgment on the severity of each threat caused by climate change. This involves comparing the different threats and rating them against each other. To do well in this answer, try to recall at least three threats.

(10) Assess the success of the different ways of managing the taiga (boreal) forest. (8 marks, ★★★★★)

Use a separate sheet of paper to write your answer to this question.

NAILIT!

Assess

The command word *assess* means that in your answer you must use evidence to show how significant something is. You must consider as many geographical factors as possible and identify which one (or ones) are most important. This is a harder type of question, so be prepared for it.

Consuming energy resources
Energy resources

(1) Define the term 'recyclable energy resource'. (1 mark, ★)

....

....

(2) Describe **two** possible environmental impacts of using uranium as a fuel source to create electricity. (2 marks, ★)

Impact 1: ....

....

Impact 2: ....

....

Study **Figure 1**, showing information about world geothermal energy capacity in 2015.

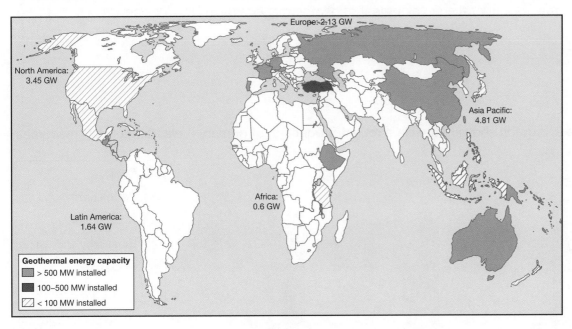

Figure 1

(3) Using **Figure 1**, and your geographical knowledge, describe the distribution of geothermal energy capacity in the world in 2015. (2 marks, ★)

....

....

....

....

NAILIT!

Knowing geographical terms, such as *sustainable* and *geothermal energy,* is important for the exam. It helps you understand questions, improve your answers and gain SPaG marks. The accompanying Edexcel GCSE Geography B Revision Guide contains a Glossary of terms like these.

DOIT!

Make sure that you understand the difference between the geographical terms 'location' and 'distribution'. *Location* is a precise position of something, while *distribution* is an amount and spatial arrangement (spread) of something. For distribution, use compass directions or names of regions if you can.

Study this student answer to Question 2. Give it a mark out of two and suggest how it could be improved.

The areas with most geothermal capacity are found on the left of the map, and there are some scattered across the centre of the map.

Make sure that you understand the meaning of the command word *suggest*. It means that there is more than one possible answer. For example, in **Question 1**, there are a number of possible reasons but you only have to present one.

④ Suggest **one** reason for the development of geothermal energy in New Zealand. (1 mark, ★)

....

....

Study **Figure 2**, a graph showing the UK's recent production of primary fuels from its own resources.

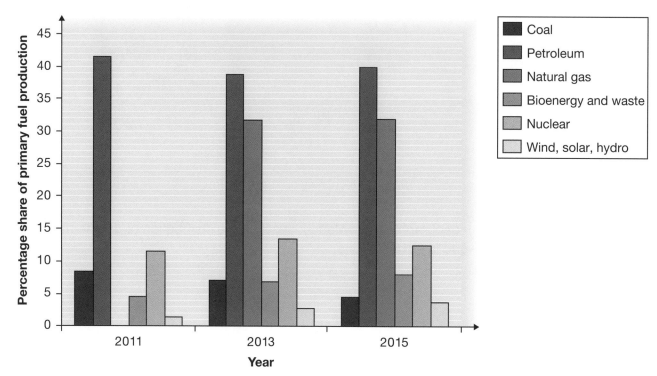

Figure 2

⑤ Using **Figure 2**, draw the bar for natural gas in 2011 to complete the graph using the following data:

2011 Natural gas   33% (1 mark, ★)

(6) State the increase in percentage share of primary fuel production of bioenergy and waste between 2011 and 2015.

Shade **one** circle only. (1 mark, ★)

A 3.5% ◯

B 4.4% ◯

C 6.7% ◯

D 7.9% ◯

> Remember, answering multiple-choice questions should be quick. In the exam, aim to spend no more than one minute to work out your answer.

Study **Figure 3**, a map showing energy access and security for countries in 2015.

EA&S percentile ranking
- High energy security (80–100%)
- Moderate energy security (60–79%)
- Low energy security (40–59%)
- Moderate energy insecurity (20–39%)
- High energy insecurity (0–19%)
- Not covered

0   3 000 km

Figure 3

(7) Using **Figure 3**, state the energy access and security performance level of China in 2015.

Shade **one** circle only. (1 mark, ★)

A 0–19% ◯   C 40–59% ◯

B 20–39% ◯   D 60–79% ◯

(8) Using **Figure 3**, describe the distribution of energy access and security performance levels in South America in 2015. (2 marks, ★)

....

....

....

....

NAILIT!

- Remember to identify the **command word** or **phrase** in a question. In **Question 9**, this is *explain*. 'Explain' means to set out the reasons.
- Identify the **key geographical ideas** in a question. In **Question 9**, these are *impacts of energy insecurity* and *poorer people*.
- Circle both the command words or phrases and the key geographical ideas in questions to help keep you on track.

(9) Explain how the impacts of energy insecurity cause difficulties for poorer people. (4 marks, ★★★)

....

....

....

....

....

....

....

(10) State and explain **two** reasons why energy consumption is increasing in the world. (4 marks, ★★★)

Reason 1: ....

....

....

....

Reason 2: ....

....

....

....

WORKIT!

Study **Figure 4**, a table showing the top five consumers of energy per capita in 2014.

Country	Energy consumption per capita (kg of oil equivalent per year)
Iceland	17 916
Canada	7874
UAE	7769
Indonesia	5122
New Zealand	4560

Figure 4

Using **Figure 4**, identify which of the following is the correct ratio of energy consumption between Iceland and New Zealand. (1 mark, ★)

A 1:0.26 ○

B 1:0.46 ○

C 1:0.86 ○

D 1:1.36 ○

While multiple-choice questions are usually easier questions, it is important not to rush them and make silly mistakes. Look at each option (A, B, C and D) carefully and compare each with the resource provided. You could put a cross over the wording of the incorrect answers as you rule them out – but never put any mark in the box at the end of the option. Only cross the box of the answer that you are sure is correct. In this question you must recall your numerical skills, specifically how **ratios** are calculated.

Oil

Study **Figure 5**, a table showing the top five producers and consumers of oil in 2016.

Oil production		Oil consumption	
Country	% of world	Country	% of world
Saudi Arabia	13.4	USA	19.5
USA	13.4	China	13.1
Russia	12.2	India	4.8
Iran	5.0	Japan	4.2
Iraq	4.8	Saudi Arabia	3.8

Figure 5

(1) Using **Figure 5**, compare the 2016 oil production and consumption patterns. (2 marks, ★★★)

....

....

....

....

NAILIT!

The command word **compare** is sometimes used in exam questions. 'Compare' means that you need to consider two or more things and look for **similarities** and **differences** between them. In **Question 1**, you need to compare the countries in the two lists.

(2) Evaluate the role of unstable international relations and conflicts in determining the world price of oil. (8 marks, ★)

Use a separate sheet of paper to write your answer to this question.

(3) Assess the advantages of the extraction of conventional fossil fuel resources in sensitive environmental areas. (8 marks, ★)

Use a separate sheet of paper to write your answer to this question.

(4) Assess the disadvantages of the extraction of unconventional fossil fuel resources in sensitive environmental areas. (8 marks, ★)

Use a separate sheet of paper to write your answer to this question.

Strategies to reduce energy demand

(1) State and explain **two** ways in which house design can help to create sustainable energy supplies. (4 marks, ★★★)

Way 1: ....

....

....

....

Way 2: ....

....

....

....

(2) Compare the problems of using hydrogen and solar as renewable energy resources. (4 marks, ★★★)

....

....

....

....

....

....

> Make sure that you do not muddle 'small-scale schemes' with 'large-scale schemes'. Also, make sure you know what is meant by the term 'sustainability'.

> Often in geography we consider *benefits* and *problems*, but an exam question may just ask for one of these. Make sure that you stick to the question and just write about the one stated.

WORKIT!

Explain how small-scale renewable energy schemes can create sustainable energy supplies. (4 marks, ★★★)

How to tackle this 'explain' question:

- Recall examples of a sustainable small-scale local schemes using renewable energy resources that you have studied. In the accompanying Edexcel GCSE Geography B Revision Guide, the case study is Chambamontera in Peru.

- Bring in a variety of relevant ways of achieving sustainable energy supplies through small-scale schemes.

- Make clear links between the features of the small-scale schemes and how they bring about sustainability.

- Sustainability points may include: ensuring a reliable energy supply; low set-up and maintenance costs for local people; low energy costs for local people; use of renewable energy sources that minimise negative impacts on the local and wider environment; and improvements in health levels through lower pollution.

(3) Define what is meant by the term 'carbon footprint'. (2 marks, ★★★)

....

....

....

....

Study **Figure 6**, a map showing total energy consumption by country in 2015 measured in Mtoe (millions of tonnes of oil equivalent).

Below 50   50 to 100   100 to 500   500 to 2000   Above 2000

Figure 6

(4) What was the total energy consumption for India in 2015?

Shade **one** circle only. (1 mark, ★)

A 50 to 100 Mtoe   ◯   **C** 500 to 2000 Mtoe   ◯

B 100 to 500 Mtoe   ◯   **D** above 2000 Mtoe   ◯

(5) Using **Figure 6**, describe the distribution of energy consumption in South America. (2 marks, ★)

....

....

....

....

(6) Explain why some people in developed countries believe that the energy mix of the country should not change. (4 marks, ★★★)

....

....

....

....

....

....

....

Study **Figure 7**, a graph showing the change in UK electricity generation from renewable sources.

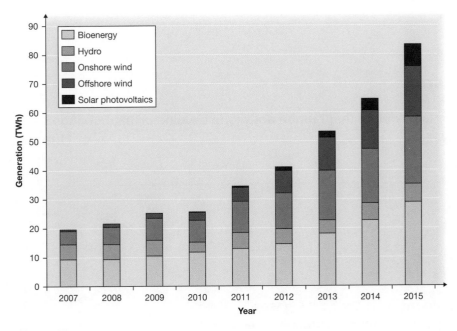

Figure 7

(7) Using **Figure 7**, suggest why the use of renewable energy sources in the UK is increasing.
(4 marks, ★★★)

....

....

....

....

....

....

....

....

(8) There are proposals to link Iceland to the rest of Europe via a network of undersea electricity cables. Explain why this is considered to be important for providing sustainable energy supplies to Europe in the future. (4 marks, ★★★)

....

....

....

....

....

....

....

Paper 1: Global geographical issues
Section A: Hazardous Earth

Answer **all** questions in this section.

Question 1: Hazardous Earth

1 (a) (i) Which of the following is evidence that human activity is causing climate change?
Shade **one** circle only.   **[1 mark]**

    A Volcanic eruptions ◯

    B Sea level rise ◯

    C Ice cores ◯

    D Historical sources ◯

    (ii) Human activities are producing greenhouse gases.
Which of the following are examples of greenhouse gases?
Shade **two** circles only.   **[2 marks]**

    A Methane ◯

    B Oxygen ◯

    C Hydrogen ◯

    D Nitrogen ◯

    E Carbon dioxide ◯

(b) Explain **two** natural causes of climate change.   **[4 marks]**

....

....

....

....

(c) Explain how atmospheric circulation redistributes heat energy around Earth.
[4 marks]

....

....

....

....

....

....

Study **Figure 1**, a map showing the track of Hurricane Katrina in 2005.

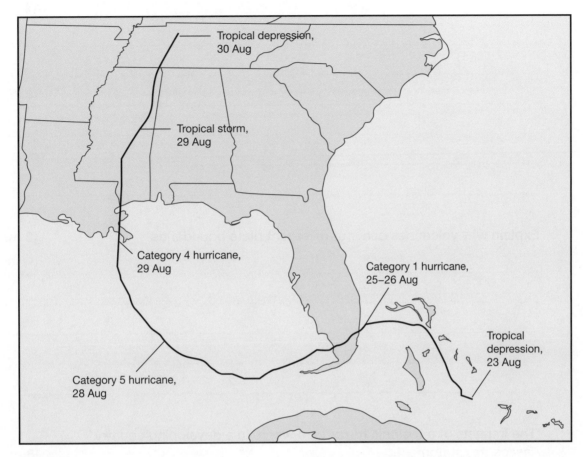

Figure 1

(d)   Describe the direction of the track of Hurricane Katrina in **Figure 1**.   **[2 marks]**

....

....

....

....

(e)   Identify the most appropriate technique to accurately measure the impact of
a tropical cyclone on people and the environment.   **[1 mark]**

A Seismometer   ◯   C Saffir Simpson scale   ◯

B Satellite images   ◯   D Line graph   ◯

(f)   Identify the most effective way for a country to prepare for a tropical cyclone. **[1 mark]**

A Weather forecasting   ◯   C Satellite image   ◯

B Saffir Simpson scale   ◯   D Lava diversion channels   ◯

(g)   Explain why some countries are more vulnerable to tropical cyclones than others.

[4 marks]

....

....

....

....

....

....

(h)   Explain why volcanoes occur at divergent plate boundaries   [3 marks]

....

....

....

....

....

(i)   'The impacts of a tectonic hazard are worse in a developing country.'
Assess this statement.   [8 marks]

....

....

....

....

....

....

....

....

....

....

Section B: Development dynamics

Answer **all** questions in this section.

Question 2: Development dynamics

2 (a)   (i)   Which of the following is the definition of the Human Development Index?   **[1 mark]**

        A   The amount of money made within a country divided by the total population.   ◯

        B   The average number of years that a new born child can be expected to live.   ◯

        C   The measure combining economic and social factors.   ◯

        D   The measure of the quality of decision making and government.   ◯

(ii)   Explain **one** way in which the adult literacy rate can be used to measure development of a country.   **[2 marks]**

....

....

....

....

Study **Figure 2**, a world map showing life expectancy in countries of the world in 2015.

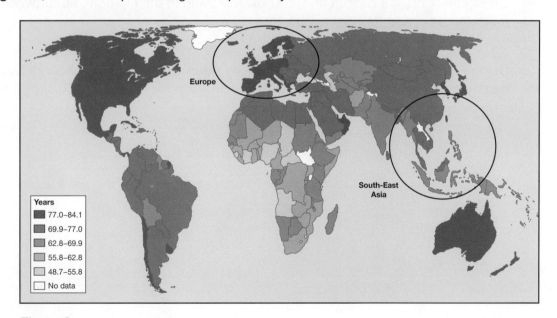

Figure 2

(b)   Using **Figure 2**, compare the life expectancies in Europe with those in South-East Asia.
[2 marks]

....

....

....

....

Study **Figure 3**, a scatter graph showing GNI per capita (person) and infant mortality rates for selected countries in 2015.

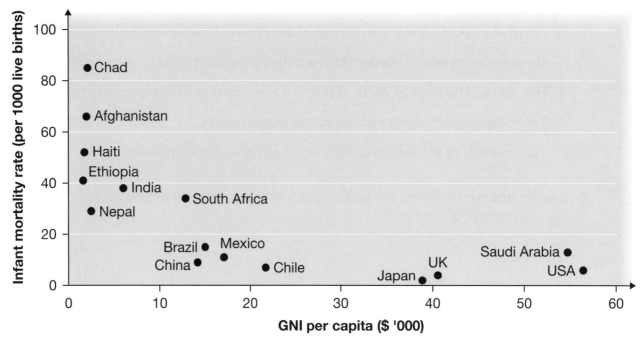

Figure 3

(c) (i) On **Figure 3**, draw a best-fit line to show the trend in the relationship between infant mortality rates and GNI per capita.   **[1 mark]**

(ii) Using **Figure 3**, explain how infant mortality rates can be used to show differences in quality of life between countries.   **[4 marks]**

....

....

....

....

....

....

Study **Figure 4**, a population pyramid for India in 2017.

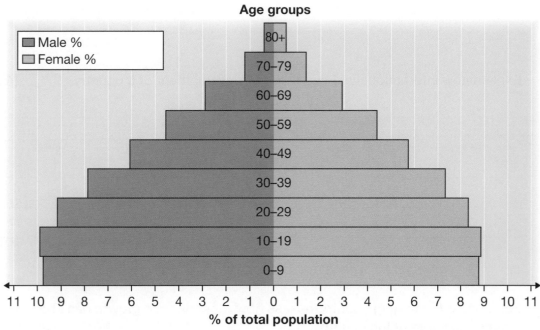

Figure 4

(d)   (i)   Using **Figure 4**, state the population size of the female age group 20–29 years of age
              in India in 2017.   **[1 mark]**

    A 7.32 per cent   ◯   C 8.86 per cent   ◯

    B 8.32 per cent   ◯   D 9.16 per cent   ◯

    (ii) Using **Figure 4**, describe the population structure of India in 2017.   **[2 marks]**

    ....

    ....

    ....

    ....

    (iii) Using **Figure 4**, suggest two population problems that India faces now and
          in the future.   **[4 marks]**

    ....

    ....

    ....

    ....

    ....

    ....

(e)   State **one** feature of Rostow's modernisation theory.   **[1 mark]**

....

....

(f)   Explain how international aid can help the development of a country.   **[4 marks]**

....

....

....

....

....

....

(g)   For a named emerging country, assess how far economic growth has changed the
         international role of the country.   **[12 marks]**
         Use a separate sheet of paper to write your answer to this question.
         State your chosen emerging country at the start of your answer.

In this question, **four** of the marks awarded will be for your spelling, punctuation and grammar and your use of specialist terminology.

Section C: Challenges of an urbanising world

Question 3: Challenges of an urbanising world

3 (a)   Study **Figure 5**, which shows the urban and rural populations of the world.

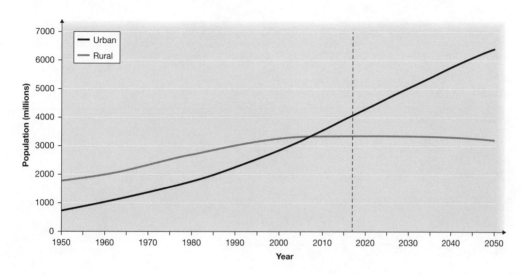

Figure 5

(i)   Calculate the predicted increase in the urban population from 1950 to 2050.   **[1 mark]**

....

....

(ii) Describe the pattern of growth shown.   **[2 marks]**

....

....

....

....

(b)   (i)   Define the term 'urbanisation'.   **[1 mark]**

....

....

(ii) Explain **one** reason for the rapid growth of cities in the developing world.   **[2 marks]**

....

....

....

....

(c)   Study **Figure 6**, a satellite image of Reading. Identify the land use marked X.   **[1 mark]**

Figure 6

....

....

(d)   Explain **one** reason why counter-urbanisation occurred.   **[3 marks]**

....

....

....

....

(e)   For a named megacity, explain **two** ways in which land use changes across the city.
    [4 marks]

....

....

....

....

....

....

(f)   Explain **two** differences between the formal and informal economy.   **[4 marks]**

....

....

....

....

(g)   Explain **two** advantages of bottom-down development for improving the lives of
people in developing cities.   **[4 marks]**

....

....

....

....

....

....

(h)   Assess the social and environmental impacts of rapid population growth.   **[8 marks]**

....

....

....

....

....

....

....

....

....

....

....

Paper 2: UK geographical issues
Section A: The UK's evolving physical landscape

Question 1: The UK's physical landscape

Study **Figure 1**, a photograph of a river in the UK.

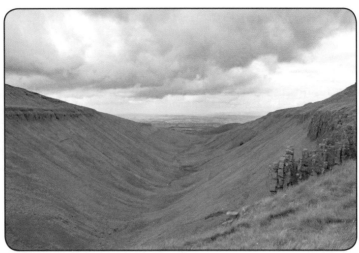

Figure 1

1 (a)   Identify the main geographical feature shown in Figure 1.

Shade **one** circle.   [1 mark]

A A V-shaped valley formed by a glacier   ◯

B A U-shaped valley formed by a glacier   ◯

C A landslide caused by an event of high rainfall ◯

D A gorge caused by abrasive erosion   ◯

(b)   Identify from the following list the main post-glacial process that has formed the landscape.

Shade **one** circle.   [1 mark]

A Soil creep   ◯

B Chemical weathering due to acid rain   ◯

C Biological weathering   ◯

D Freeze-thaw weathering   ◯

(c)   Explain **one** way in which geology has affected the UK's physical landscape.
                                                              [2 marks]

....

....

....

....

Question 2: Coastal change and conflict

Study **Figure 2**, a photograph of Old Harry Rocks, Dorset.

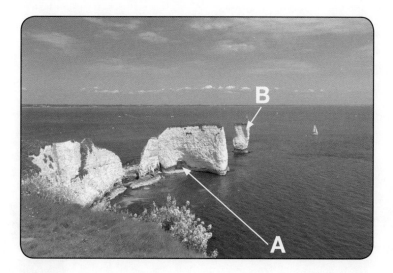

Figure 2

2 (a)   Using **Figure 2**, identify the coastal features shown at **A** and **B**.   **[2 marks]**

Feature A: ....

....

Feature B: ....

....

(b)   Explain how weathering can influence the rate of coastal retreat.   **[2 marks]**

....

....

....

....

....

....

(c)   Explain the formation of a spit.   **[4 marks]**

....

....

....

....

....

....

Question 3: River processes and pressures

Study **Figure 3**, showing a section of a river.

3 (a)   Name the stage of the river's long profile shown
          in **Figure 3**.   **[1 mark]**

....

....

....

....

Figure 3

(b)   Explain **two** causes of river flooding.   **[4 marks]**

Cause 1: ....

....

Cause 2: ....

....

(c)   Describe how human activities can affect storm hydrographs   **[2 marks]**

....

....

....

....

Question 4: Investigating a UK geographical issue

Analyse **Figure 4**, which shows the mean erosion rates along the Norfolk coastline.

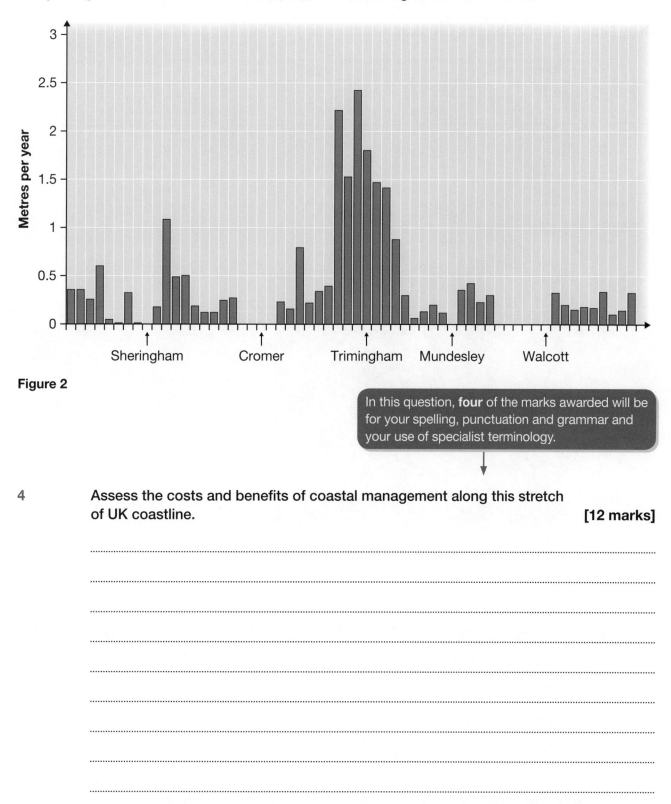

Figure 2

> In this question, **four** of the marks awarded will be for your spelling, punctuation and grammar and your use of specialist terminology.

4   Assess the costs and benefits of coastal management along this stretch of UK coastline.   **[12 marks]**

....

....

....

....

....

....

....

....

....

....

....

....

Answer all questions in this section.

Question 5: The UK's evolving human landscape

Study **Figure 5**, a map showing UK population density.

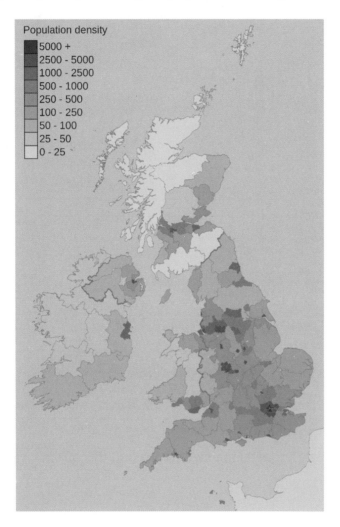

Population density

5000 +
2500 - 5000
1000 - 2500
500 - 1000
250 - 500
100 - 250
50 - 100
25 - 50
0 - 25

Figure 5

(a)   Using **Figure 5**, which of the following statements is correct about the
       distribution of areas with high levels of economic activity?   **[1 mark]**

       A Mostly in rural areas   ◯

       B Mostly in Scotland   ◯

       C Mostly in South East England   ◯

       D Mostly in South West England   ◯

(b)   State **one** reason why the area labelled **A** on the map has a high
       population density.   **[1 mark]**

       ....

       ....

Study **Figure 6**, a table comparing two London boroughs in 2015.

	Richmond upon Thames	Newham
Life expectancy	83 years	77 years
Unemployment	3.8%	8.5%
Pupils achieving 5 A*–C grades at GCSE	70%	57%
Average household income	£46 000	£28 000

Figure 6

(c)   Using **Figure 6**, compare the quality of life between the two boroughs.   **[4 marks]**

....

....

....

....

....

....

(d)   Explain reasons for the differences in life expectancy between Richmond
and Newham.   **[4 marks]**

....

....

....

....

....

....

6   Study Figure 7, a map showing the location of Exeter.

Figure 7

(a)   Explain why accessibility is an important factor for businesses to be successful.

[2 marks]

....

....

....

....

(b)   Using **Figure 7**, give **two** problems that accessible rural areas like Exeter might face due to economic growth.   **[2 marks]**

....

....

....

....

Study **Figure 8**, which is a photograph of a farm shop in Cornwall.

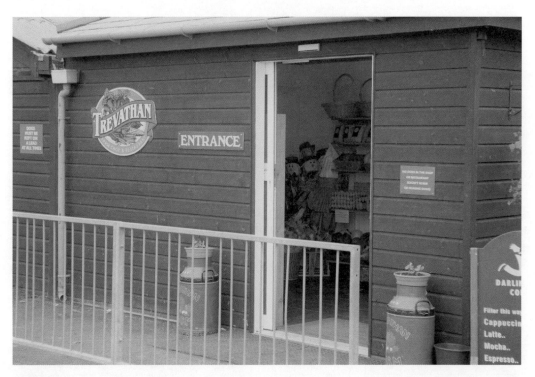

Figure 8

(c)   Explain why diversification projects are needed in rural communities to improve the local economy.   [4 marks]

....

....

....

....

....

....

(d)   Which of the following is the correct definition for 'urban sustainability'?

Shade **one** circle only.   [1 mark]

A   Rural areas with an over-reliance on urban areas nearby.   ◯

B   The need for urban areas to consume as much energy and resources as they need to function.   ◯

C   Cities organised without an over-reliance on rural areas surrounding them and using renewable energy.   ◯

D   Urban and rural areas both consume energy and resources to provide for the population living there.   ◯

(e)   Describe **two** features of a sustainable urban community.   **[2 marks]**

....

....

....

....

....

....

(f)   Evaluate the success of strategies aimed at making urban communities
more sustainable.   **[6 marks]**

....

....

....

....

....

....

....

....

....

....

....

....

Answer EITHER Question 8 OR Question 9 in this section.

Question 8: Coastal change and conflict

8 (a)   As part of an enquiry collecting primary physical geography data, a student measured the size of pebbles on the beach at Dawlish Warren at six different sites.

The results are shown in **Figure 9**.

Size	1	2	3	4	5	6
Pebble size 1 (mm)	44	48	52	97	88	74
Pebble size 2 (mm)	23	52	85	64	56	72
Pebble size 3 (mm)	61	68	65	77	65	70
Mean pebble size (mm)	42.67	56.00	67.33	79.33	69.67	

Figure 9

(i)   Calculate the mean pebble size for Site 6.

Show your working in the space below.   **[2 marks]**

....

(ii) Complete the scatter graph shown in **Figure 10** below using the data for the cross-sectional area for Sites 3 and 6.   **[2 marks]**

Figure 10

289

(iii) Describe **two** of the possible risks of measuring pebble size on a beach.   [2 marks]

....

....

(iv) Describe the data shown on the scatter graph in **Figure 10**.   [4 marks]

....

....

....

....

....

....

(b)   You have carried out your own fieldwork investigating a coastal location.

Name your coastal environment fieldwork location:

....

Assess how successful your primary data collection was in helping you complete your investigation.   [8 marks]

....

....

....

....

....

....

....

....

....

....

....

Question 9: River processes and pressures

9 (a)   As part of an enquiry collecting primary physical geography data, a student measured the width and depth of the River Horner at six different sites.

The results are shown in **Figure 11a**.

Site	1	2	3	4	5	6
Channel width (m)	1.22	1.19	3.28	4.45	5.08	8.01
Mean depth (m)	0.03	0.07	0.08	0.1	0.22	0.17
Cross-sectional area (m²)	0.04	0.08	0.26	0.45	1.12	

Figure 11a

The cross-sectional area of a river is calculated using the following formula:

channel width ✕ mean depth = cross-sectional area

(i) Calculate the cross-sectional area of the Rover Horner for Site 6.

Show your working in the space below.   **[2 marks]**

....

(ii) Complete the scatter graph shown in **Figure 11b** below using the data for the cross-sectional area for Sites 3 and 6.   **[2 marks]**

Figure 11b

(iii) Describe **two** of the possible risks of measuring the width and depth of a river.

[2 marks]

....

....

(iv) Describe the cross-sectional data shown on the scatter graph in **Figure 11b**.

[4 marks]

....

....

....

....

....

....

(b)   You have carried out your own fieldwork investigating rivers.

Name your river environment fieldwork location:

....

Assess how successful your primary data collection was in helping you complete your investigation.

[8 marks]

....

....

....

....

....

....

....

....

....

....

....

Section C2: Fieldwork in a human environment

Answer EITHER Question 10 OR Question 11 in this section.

Question 10: Investigating dynamic urban areas

10   You have carried out you own fieldwork investigating environmental quality in an inner-city environment.

Title of fieldwork investigation

....

....

(a)   (i)   Describe **one** of the primary data collection methods used for your fieldwork investigation.   **[2 marks]**

....

....

....

....

(ii)   Explain how you presented the primary data collected in your fieldwork investigation.   **[4 marks]**

....

....

....

....

....

....

(iii) Assess how successful your primary data collection was in helping you complete your fieldwork investigation.   **[4 marks]**

....

....

....

....

....

....

(b)   A group of students chose to investigate how and why there are variations in the quality of life within Hounslow (West London). They decided to use a questionnaire (**Figure 12**) at three different places along the High Street using a random sampling method for one hour on a Friday morning.

Age:	0–16	17–31	32–47	48–59	60+
Gender:	Male			Female	
Where do you live in Hounslow? (Street or Area)					
4. How would you rate living there? (with 10 being the best)					
5. Quality of life overall? (with 10 being the best)					
6. Quality of the houses? (with 10 being the best)					
7. Access to services? (with 10 being the best)					

Figure 12

Questions were asked by selecting a person to interview at random as they walked past.

Assess the suitability of the student's questionnaire and sampling method to investigate the variations in the quality of life in Hounslow.   **[8 marks]**

....

....

....

....

....

....

....

....

....

....

....

Question 11: Investigating changing rural areas

11   You have carried out you own fieldwork investigating environmental quality in a
          rural area.

          Title of fieldwork investigation:

          ....

          ....

(a)   (i)   Describe **one** of the primary data collection methods used for your
            fieldwork investigation.   **[2 marks]**

            ....

            ....

            ....

            ....

      (ii) Explain how you presented the primary data collected in your fieldwork investigation.
                                                                                        [4 marks]

            ....

            ....

            ....

            ....

            ....

            ....

      (iii) Assess how successful your primary data collection was in helping you complete
            your fieldwork investigation.   **[4 marks]**

            ....

            ....

            ....

            ....

            ....

            ....

            ....

(b)   A group of students chose to investigate how and why there are variations in the quality of life in three different villages in South Devon. They decided to use a questionnaire (**Figure 13**) in each of the different villages for an hour on a Friday morning.

Age:	0–16	17–31	32–47	48–59	60+
Gender:	Male			Female	
Where do you live in Devon? (Street or Area)					
4. How would you rate living there? (with 10 being the best)					
5. Quality of life overall? (with 10 being the best)					
6. Quality of the houses? (with 10 being the best)					
7. Access to services? (with 10 being the best)					

Figure 13

Questions were asked by selecting a person to interview at random as they walked past.

Assess the suitability of the student's questionnaire and sampling method to investigate the variations in the quality of life in the three villages in South Devon.

[8 marks]

Use a separate sheet of paper to write your answer to this question.

Resources for Paper 3 People and environment issues – Making geographical decisions

---

The issue: Resource conflicts in Canada

- Canada is located next to the USA. The USA is the second largest consumer of energy in the world and had a quarter of the world's GDP in 2017.

- Canada has an extensive taiga (boreal) forest biome, which provides a valuable timber resource and supports wildlife.

- Canada has an indigenous population, such as the Athabascan Indians. The indigenous peoples and their lands are under threat from the modern way of life.

- Canada's economy was the tenth largest in the world in 2017. This economy is supported by exports of timber and oil (which is partly extracted from oil sands).

Introduction

- In 2017 Canada had a population of 36.6 million people and a total GDP of US$1600 billion. The GDP per capita was approximately US$43 700 (or £32 400) in 2017.

- Canada is a huge country, stretching over 5000 km east to west from the Atlantic Ocean to the Pacific Ocean.

- The majority of the population live in the south of the country, close to the border with the USA, including the large cities of Toronto, Montreal and Vancouver. Northern areas are sparsely populated.

- Northern parts of Canada consist of Arctic and sub-Arctic climatic conditions, with tundra and permafrost. To the south of these areas there is an extensive boreal forest that extends from east to west across the whole country and some prairie grasslands bordering the USA.

- Canada's oil consumption has shown a small decrease between 2010 and 2016 from 102.3 million tonnes to 100.9 million tonnes; while its oil production has increased in the same time period from 162.8 million tonnes to 218.2 million tonnes. Canada has 10 per cent of the world's proven oil reserves.

- Canada's boreal forests provide timber and non-timber products, food and renewable raw materials for Canadians. Over 211 000 people are employed in the forestry industry, which contributed over US$18 billion to GDP in 2016. Canada is the world's largest exporter of softwood timber and newsprint paper, mostly to the USA, and 7 per cent of all Canada's exports are from the forestry industry.

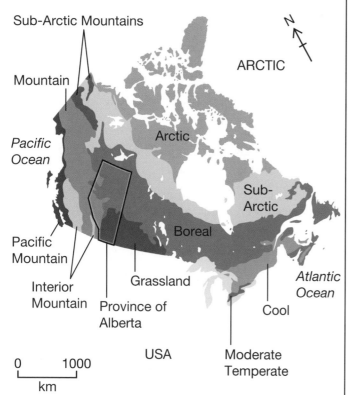

Key to eco-climatic regions of Canada

ARCTIC: Tundra with dwarf willow, saxifrage, mosses and dryads.

SUB-ARCTIC: Tundra with mosses and spruce trees.

BOREAL (TAIGA): Forests of spruce, fir and birch trees.

COOL TEMPERATE: Mixed forest of maple, beech, birch, spruce, pine and aspen trees.

MODERATE TEMPERATE: Forest of maple, beech, tulip and chestnut trees.

GRASSLAND: Prairie grasses with aspen trees.

SUB-ARCTIC MOUNTAIN: Alpine tundra with low spruce trees.

MOUNTAIN: Lichens, sedges and grasses with aspen, spruce, birch, willow, fir and pine trees.

INTERIOR MOUNTAIN: Grassland with spruce, fir and pine.

PACIFIC MOUNTAIN: Tundra with sedges, cotton grass and low shrubs with fir, birch, willow and hemlock trees.

Figure 1 Map showing location of biomes in Canada

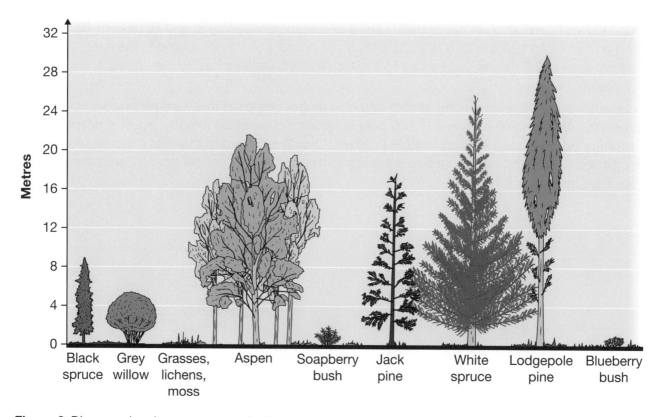

Figure 2 Diagram showing structure and selected vegetation types in the boreal forest of Alberta, Canada

Athabascan Indians have lived in the boreal climatic zone for thousands of years and over this period of time adapted to live in harmony with the natural environment, with much of their culture based on this lifestyle. An example is their belief in animal spirits which is linked to animal behaviours and the success of hunting. They see that all parts of the environment are closely linked together and that alterations to one part may affect other parts. 70 per cent of the Indian population lives in the boreal forest, and they own 2 per cent of it.

Figure 3 Athabascan Indian culture

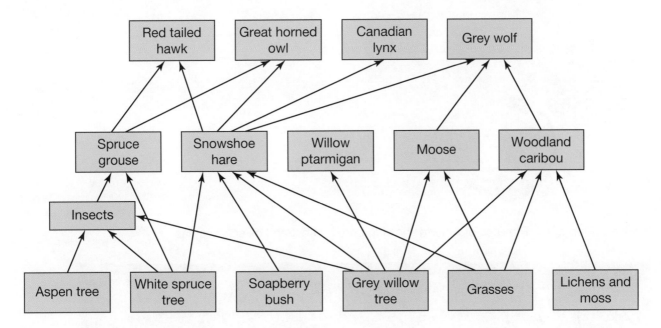

Figure 4 Part of a boreal (taiga) food web in Canada

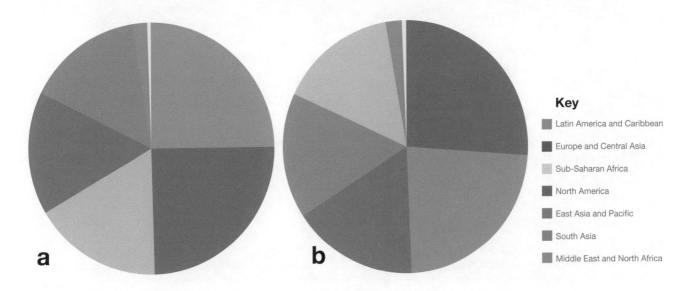

Figure 5 Forest area by world region **a** in 1990 and **b** in 2015

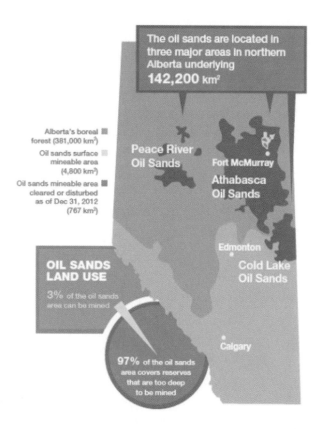

Figure 6 Map of the Province of Alberta showing boreal forest and oil sands areas

Figure 7 Satellite image of oil sands mining in the Athabasca area of Alberta 2016

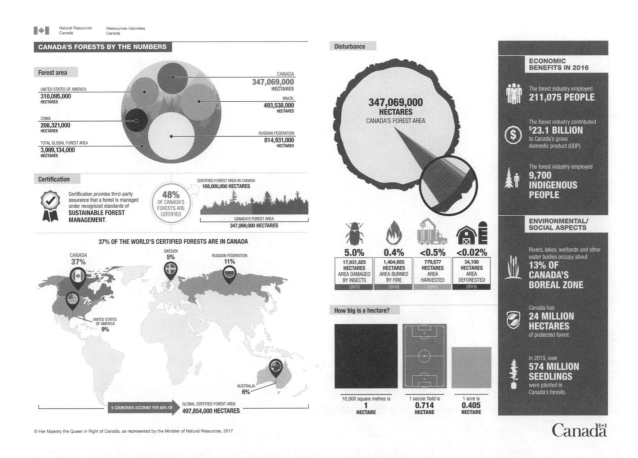

Figure 8 Canada's forest by the numbers (2016) (Note: financial data in Canadian dollars)

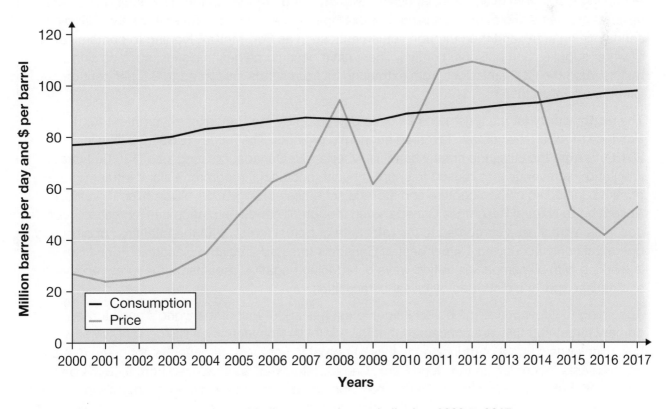

Figure 9 Graph showing change in world oil consumption and oil price, 2000 to 2017

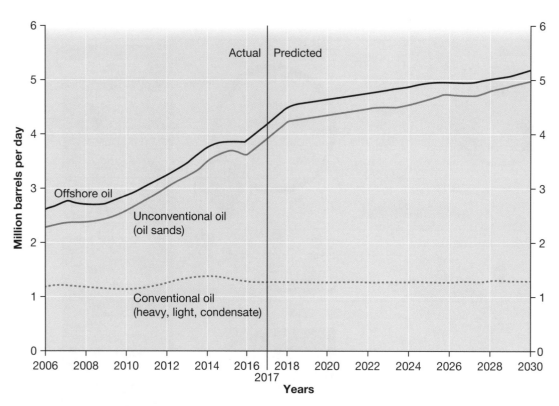

Figure 10 Conventional and unconventional oil production in Canada (2006 to 2030)

There are growing threats to both the Athabascan Indians and the boreal environment, many of which are linked to the extraction of oil sands (sometimes known as tar sands). This involves extracting water from rivers, the disposal of wastes, accommodation for thousands of workers, removal of forests and open-pit mining. For example, the Athabascan River flows through oil sands mining areas and then through settlements such as Fort McKay, leading to contamination of water supplies and poisoning of fish. There have been some health issues, such as skin rashes. Also the CO2 emissions from extracting oil from sands amounted to 8.5 per cent of Canada's total in 2015.

The responsibility for management has been delegated by the Canadian government to the Province of Alberta, who have favoured economic projects. The money (US$1.2 billion in 2016–17) from the oil sands greatly benefits Alberta and Canada, creating jobs (136 000 direct jobs) and tax revenue that is used to support health and social programmes and infrastructure projects, including carbon capture and storage schemes costing US$1 billion over 15 years. According to Natural Resources Canada, even though oil sands extraction has increased, it only occupies a small area compared to the total area of boreal forest, with the total area of oil sands operations only occupying 1.4 per cent of Canada's forested area. The Canadian Forest Service is working with oil companies to find ways of reducing negative impacts on the forest ecosystem and reclaim the land disturbed by oil sands activities.

According to Greenpeace the boreal (taiga) forest has about half of the world's undisturbed primary forest and they are concerned that the 2010 UN Convention on Biological Diversity, which includes a target of reducing the loss of boreal forest by 50 per cent, is not being met by governments. According to the World Bank, Canada's forested area reduced from 3.48 million km^2 in 1990 to 3.47 million km^2 in 2015. The Canadian government claim that 170 million hectares of forest are classified as sustainably managed.

Figure 11 Views and attitudes about the extraction of oil sands in Alberta's boreal forest

Paper 3: People and environment issues
Section A: People and the biosphere

Use the Resource Booklet to answer the questions on this paper. Answer **all** questions in this section.

Question 1: Hazardous Earth

1 (a)   Study **Figure 1**, a map of biomes in Canada. Describe the distribution of the boreal (taiga) biome in Canada.   **[2 marks]**

....

....

....

(b)   Study **Figure 2**, which shows the structure of the boreal forest in the Canadian province of Alberta.

(i)   Identify the height of the White Spruce tree.

Shade **one** circle only.   **[1 mark]**

A 10 metres   ◯

B 20 metres   ◯

C 25 metres   ◯

D 30 metres   ◯

(ii)   Calculate the difference in height between the Grey Willow tree and the Soapberry bush.   **[2 marks]**

....

(iii)   State **two** resources that people may obtain from the boreal forest in Canada.   **[2 marks]**

Resource 1: ....

Resource 2: ....

(c)   Study **Figure 4**, which shows part of the food web in the Canadian boreal forest. Explain the role of the Aspen tree in this food web.   **[2 marks]**

....

....

....

Section B: Forests under threat

2 (a)   Study **Figures 5a** and **5b**, which show the share of world forest in 1990 and 2015.

(i)   Name the world region with the smallest amount of forest in 1990.   **[1 mark]**

....

(ii)   Suggest why this world region had the smallest amount of forest in 1990 and 2015.

[2 marks]

....

....

....

(iii)   Between 1990 and 2015, two world regions had a decrease in their share of world forest. Name **one** of these countries.   **[1 mark]**

....

(iv)   Suggest **one** reason why this world region has had a decrease in its share of world forest area.   **[1 mark]**

....

....

(b)   Study **Figures 6, 7, 8** and **11**, which show information about activities in Canada's boreal forest. Explain what is happening to the boreal forest in Alberta and Canada.

[4 marks]

....

....

....

....

....

....

(c)   Study **Figure 8**, an infographic showing information about the timber industry in Canada. Describe how Canada's forests are being looked after so that they are more sustainable.   **[2 marks]**

....

....

....

Section C: Consuming energy resources

3 (a)   Study **Figure 9**, a graph showing oil consumption and price in the 21st century.

(i)   Describe the trend of world oil consumption between 2000 and 2017.   **[2 marks]**

....

....

....

....

(ii)   Assess the extent to which the world price of oil has affected the world consumption of oil between 2000 and 2017.   **[8 marks]**

....

....

....

....

....

....

....

....

....

....

....

....

....

(b)   Study **Figure 10**, which shows the production of conventional and unconventional oil in Canada between 2006 and 2017, and predictions up to 2030.

(i)   Define the term 'unconventional oil'.   [1 mark]

....

....

(ii)   Explain why a large increase is predicted for the future production of oil from oil sands in Canada.   [4 marks]

....

....

....

....

....

....

(iii)   Which percentage of Canada's oil production came was from unconventional oil (oil sands) in 2017?   [1 mark]

A 6 per cent   ◯

B 31 per cent   ◯

C 63 per cent   ◯

D 94 per cent   ◯

(c)   Use a separate sheet of paper to write your answers to these questions.

Study **Figure 11**, which shows different views about the extraction of oil from the oil sands in Alberta, Canada.

(i)   Explain two negative impacts on people caused by developing the oil sands in Alberta.   [4 marks]

(ii)   Assess the reasons why some people and groups are in favour of increasing the extraction of oil from the oil sands found in Canada.   [8 marks]

Section D: Making geographical decisions

In this question, 4 of the marks awarded will be for your spelling, punctuation and grammar and your use of specialist terminology.

4　　　Study the three options below for how to manage the boreal forest zone in the Province of Alberta.

Option 1: Allow Canadian companies to fully develop the oil sands to help the economy of Alberta and Canada.	**Option 2:** Allow limited development of the oil sands and at the same time help Athabascan Indian communities and the boreal forest ecosystem achieve sustainability.	**Option 3:** Stop any further development of the oil sands and concentrate instead on sustainable forestry and ecotourism.

　　　Select the option that you think would be the best long-term plan for the use of the boreal forest zone in the Province of Alberta. Justify your choice.

　　　Use information from the Resource Booklet and knowledge and understanding from the rest of your geography course to support your answer.　　　**[16 marks]**

　　　Use a separate sheet of paper to write your answer to this question. State your chosen emerging country at the start of your answer.

Exam Practice Answers

	Hazardous Earth: Climate change	
Q	Marking guidance	Marks
1	One mark for a reason and the second mark for an extension: volcanic ash can block sunlight. This leads to a reduction in temperatures in the short term.	2
2	One mark each for two of the following: ice cores; tree rings; historical sources.	2
3	One mark for how atmospheric circulation redistributes heat and further three marks for development of point: warm air rises at the equator creating an area of low pressure (1) due to the air expanding and becoming lighter (1). Colder, dense air sinks creating areas of high pressure (1). Air moves from high to low pressure (1).	4
4	One mark for what the enhanced greenhouse effect is and three further marks for explaining how it arises: the enhanced greenhouse effect is the added amount of greenhouse gases to the atmosphere through human activity (1). More carbon dioxide has been added to the atmosphere through burning fossil fuels (1) and increased transportation and/or deforestation (1). Methane has been added to the atmosphere through more intense farming such as rice farming and/or cattle ranches (1).	4
5	One mark for each natural cause of climate change and a further mark for explaining how it arises, up to a maximum of four marks. Natural causes and explanations include: • (Earth's) orbital changes (1) such as: eccentricity, which causes the (elliptical) path of Earth to change, so that Earth receives more energy from Sun, rising average temperature (1); precession, where the Earth 'wobbles' on its axis, changing seasonal distribution of the Sun's energy (1); tilt, where the angle of the Earth's axis changes, changing seasonal distribution of the Sun's energy (1). • Increase in solar energy linked to sunspots (1), the more sunspots there are the more energy is given out, increasing the average temperature on Earth (1). • Volcanic ash (1) can block out sunlight, reducing average temperatures (1). • Volcanic eruption of sulfur dioxide (1) mixes with water to produce sulfuric acid, this reflects the Sun's radiation, reducing temperatures (1). • Asteroid collisions (1), which blast large amounts of ash and dust into the atmosphere, blocking sunlight and reducing temperatures (1).	4
6	One mark for the first statement then one mark for each reason/explanation, up to a maximum of four marks in total: the result of human activity that contributes most to climate change is the rise in levels of carbon dioxide in the atmosphere, increasing average temperatures (1). This is brought about by: burning fossil fuels for industry and in power stations to generate electricity (1); burning fossil fuels for transport (1); deforestation that reduces the amount of carbon dioxide taken up by plants and stored (1). Also, intensive agriculture (cattle and rice farming) has contributed an increase in levels of methane, another greenhouse gas (1).	4
Workit!	**Indicative content** AO2 • Temperatures will rise between 1.1 and 6 °C • Sea levels will rise between 30 cm and 1 m AO3 • It is uncertain what the population of the world will be and therefore the amount of carbon dioxide emitted in the future is hard to predict. • The amount of fossil fuels being used is hard to predict and they could have been replaced by renewable methods that reduce the amount of carbon dioxide emissions. • People may change their lifestyles in the future by recycling, working from home instead of commuting, and using public transport more to reduce carbon dioxide emissions. **Level 0, no marks** • No relevant response. **Level 1 (Basic) 1–3 marks** • Demonstrates isolated elements of understanding of concepts and the interrelationship of places, environments and processes. (AO2) • Attempts to apply understanding to deconstruct information but understanding and connections are flawed. • An unbalanced or incomplete argument that provides limited synthesis of understanding. Judgments are supported by limited evidence. (AO3) **Level 2 (Clear) 4–6 marks** • Demonstrates elements of understanding of concepts and the interrelationship of places, environments and processes. (AO2) • Applies understanding to deconstruct information and provide some logical connections between concepts. • An imbalanced argument that synthesises mostly relevant understanding but not entirely coherently, leading to judgments that are supported by evidence occasionally. (AO3)	8

Q	Marking guidance	Marks
	Level 3 (Detailed) 7–8 marks • Demonstrates accurate understanding of concepts and the interrelationship of places, environments and processes. (AO2) • Applies understanding to deconstruct information and provide logical connections between concepts throughout. • A balanced, well-developed argument that synthesises relevant understanding coherently, leading to judgments that are supported by evidence throughout. (AO3)	

	Hazardous Earth: Weather hazards	
Q	Marking guidance	Marks
1	One mark for each correct answer: B Tropical cyclones form above warm oceans (27 °C or above). D The conditions in the eye of the cyclone are calm.	2
2	For each of two points, one mark for correctly identifying a way to prepare and one mark for development of point. Correct points include: windows, doors and roofs reinforced (1) to strengthen buildings to withstand strong winds (1); houses constructed on stilts (1) so that a storm surge will pass beneath (1); educating people (1) to be prepared for tropical cyclones (1).	4
3	Severe damage and a large number of people may die due to a storm surge (1). People are made homeless due to strong winds damaging homes (1).	2
4	One mark for each cause of tropical cyclones and one mark for the further development of each point, up to a maximum of four marks. • Ocean surface temperatures of at least 26.5 °C (1) cause a warm body of air to develop and rise up, allow more air to replace it, warm and rise (1). • Rising water vapour from the ocean condenses (1), which releases heat energy and powers the cyclone (1). • A strong Coriolis force (1) causes rising currents of air to spiral around the centre of the cyclone (1). • Heat and moisture (1) from the ocean continue to be added to the cyclone as it moves from its source and this feeds more energy into the system (1). • Strong winds in the troposphere (1) cause warm air to be drawn up rapidly from the ocean's surface (1).	4
5	**Indicative content** AO2 • Number of people killed. • Number of people made homeless. • The impact on agriculture: crops and animals. • Financial loss of families who have lost homes. • Destruction of embankments built to stop flooding. • People lost their jobs when businesses were destroyed. AO3 • Judgment about how severe the impacts were, e.g. social vs economic impacts. • Comment on the difference between developed and developing countries. • Reaching a conclusion about which impacts were most severe, social or economic, and explaining why. • Judgment about why the impacts were/were not severe, e.g. the country lacked money to improve defences, people there are poor so did not have mobile phones and did not know to evacuate. **Level 0, no marks** • No relevant response. **Level 1 (Basic) 1–3 marks** • Demonstrates isolated elements of understanding of concepts and the interrelationship of places, environments and processes. (AO2) • Attempts to apply understanding to deconstruct information but understanding and connections are flawed. • An unbalanced or incomplete argument that provides limited synthesis of understanding. Judgments are supported by limited evidence. (AO3) **Level 2 (Clear) 4–6 marks** • Demonstrates elements of understanding of concepts and the interrelationship of places, environments and processes. (AO2) • Applies understanding to deconstruct information and provide some logical connections between concepts. • An imbalanced argument that synthesises mostly relevant understanding but not entirely coherently, leading to judgments that are supported by evidence occasionally. (AO3) **Level 3 (Detailed) 7–8 marks** • Demonstrates accurate understanding of concepts and the interrelationship of places, environments and processes. (AO2) • Applies understanding to deconstruct information and provide logical connections between concepts throughout. • A balanced, well-developed argument that synthesises relevant understanding coherently, leading to judgments that are supported by evidence throughout. (AO3)	8

Q	Marking guidance	Marks
6	**Indicative content** **AO2** • Weather forecasts and warnings issued on TV and radio are used to warn people about cyclones. • Developed countries can afford to operate many satellites. **AO3** • Judgment about how effective the weather forecasts are, e.g. using evidence to say how many people are likely to see them, the problems with ageing satellites. • How effective other warning methods are, e.g. mobile phones, including data about mobile phone ownership. • Assessment of the National Hurricane Centre warning methods and their effectiveness in reducing severe impacts. • Reaching a conclusion about which method is more useful – prediction or warning – and explaining why. **Level 0, no marks** • No relevant response. **Level 1 (Basic) 1–3 marks** • Demonstrates isolated elements of understanding of concepts and the interrelationship of places, environments and processes. (AO2) • Attempts to apply understanding to deconstruct information but understanding and connections are flawed. • An unbalanced or incomplete argument that provides limited synthesis of understanding. Judgments are supported by limited evidence. (AO3) **Level 2 (Clear) 4–6 marks** • Demonstrates elements of understanding of concepts and the interrelationship of places, environments and processes. (AO2) • Applies understanding to deconstruct information and provide some logical connections between concepts. • An imbalanced argument that synthesises mostly relevant understanding but not entirely coherently, leading to judgments that are supported by evidence occasionally. (AO3) **Level 3 (Detailed) 7–8 marks** • Demonstrates accurate understanding of concepts and the interrelationship of places, environments and processes. (AO2) • Applies understanding to deconstruct information and provide logical connections between concepts throughout. • A balanced, well-developed argument that synthesises relevant understanding coherently, leading to judgments that are supported by evidence throughout. (AO3)	8

Hazardous Earth: Tectonic hazards

Q	Marking guidance	Marks
1	One mark for each point: earthquakes are found along plate boundaries (with an example given) (1); earthquakes are mostly found along convergent plate boundaries (1).	2
2	One mark for a reason and the second mark for an extension: earthquakes happen where tectonic plates subduct more (1); such as a convergent plate boundary, where the oceanic plate subducts underneath the continental plate (1).	2
3	One mark for a reason and the second mark for an extension, up to a maximum of two reasons and four marks: a convergent plate margin is where two plates are moving towards each other (1); the denser oceanic plate is subducted beneath the lighter continental plate (1); as the oceanic plate moves downwards it melts due to friction and heat from the mantle (1); less dense magma is created which breaks through to the surface to form steep sided composite volcanoes (1); the volcanic eruptions are often very violent and explosive (1).	4
4	One mark for a reason and the second mark for an extension, up to a maximum of two reasons and four marks: buildings and bridges can be constructed to resist the ground shaking associated with an earthquake (1); ·Wwalls can be reinforced with steel and concrete to reduce movement (1); shock absorbers can absorb ground shaking (1); there are open areas where people go for easy evacuation (1); automatic shutters come down over windows to prevent broken glass falling (1); rolling weights on a roof can counteract shock waves (1).	4
5	**Indicative content** **AO2** • Primary impact is that many buildings collapse, which can cause injuries and fatalities. • A secondary impact of buildings being damaged is economic, because businesses using those buildings may be affected, in turn affecting people's jobs. • Transport and communication can be disrupted, e.g. roads, bridges, airports and ports closed, meaning it could be difficult for aid to reach the area. • The water supply system could be destroyed. **AO3** • Judgment about how severe the impacts are in developed countries and whether the primary or secondary impacts are worse. • Comments about which impacts were more severe in developing countries and whether the primary or secondary impacts were worse. • Judgment about whether primary or secondary impacts are worse, and reasons why.	8

Q	Marking guidance	Marks
6	**Level 0, no marks** • No relevant response. **Level 1 (Basic) 1–3 marks** • Demonstrates isolated elements of understanding of concepts and the interrelationship of places, environments and processes. (AO2) • Attempts to apply understanding to deconstruct information but understanding and connections are flawed. • An unbalanced or incomplete argument that provides limited synthesis of understanding. Judgments are supported by limited evidence. (AO3) **Level 2 (Clear) 4–6 marks** • Demonstrates elements of understanding of concepts and the interrelationship of places, environments and processes. (AO2) • Applies understanding to deconstruct information and provide some logical connections between concepts. • An imbalanced argument that synthesises mostly relevant understanding but not entirely coherently, leading to judgments that are supported by evidence occasionally. (AO3) **Level 3 (Detailed) 7–8 marks** • Demonstrates accurate understanding of concepts and the interrelationship of places, environments and processes. (AO2) • Applies understanding to deconstruct information and provide logical connections between concepts throughout. • A balanced, well-developed argument that synthesises relevant understanding coherently, leading to judgments that are supported by evidence throughout. (AO3)	8
6	**AO2** • Impacts are worse because of high vulnerability in developing countries. • Economic impacts in developed countries can be worse. • Impacts can be worse in developing countries because of low capacity to cope. • Countries on plate boundaries may be on different plate boundaries and therefore may be affected by different tectonic hazards (at different levels of severity). • Hazards also happen away from boundaries/have different areas of extent, e.g. coastal locations (tsunami) or hillslopes (landslides), possibly hotspots/ global effects of volcanoes (ash clouds). **AO3** • Judgment about whether impact is measured by economic or social loss. • Judgment about long-term vs short-term impact. • Judgment about whether impact on the environment compared to people. • Judgment about whether the impact is higher because of magnitude or vulnerability. • Judgment about whether impact is worse because of physical environment, e.g. plate boundary location or human environment (vulnerability). **Level 0, no marks** • No relevant response. **Level 1 (Basic) 1–3 marks** • Demonstrates isolated elements of understanding of concepts and the interrelationship of places, environments and processes. (AO2) • Attempts to apply understanding to deconstruct information but understanding and connections are flawed. • An unbalanced or incomplete argument that provides limited synthesis of understanding. Judgments are supported by limited evidence. (AO3) **Level 2 (Clear) 4–6 marks** • Demonstrates elements of understanding of concepts and the interrelationship of places, environments and processes. (AO2) • Applies understanding to deconstruct information and provide some logical connections between concepts. • An imbalanced argument that synthesises mostly relevant understanding but not entirely coherently, leading to judgments that are supported by evidence occasionally. (AO3) **Level 3 (Detailed) 7–8 marks** • Demonstrates accurate understanding of concepts and the interrelationship of places, environments and processes. (AO2) • Applies understanding to deconstruct information and provide logical connections between concepts throughout. • A balanced, well-developed argument that synthesises relevant understanding coherently, leading to judgments that are supported by evidence throughout. (AO3)	8

Development dynamics: Development and inequalities

Q	Marking guidance	Marks
1	One mark for each similarity or difference between South America and Africa, up to a maximum of two. Similarities/differences include: • Africa has many more developing countries than South America (1). • South America only has two developing countries while Africa has many (1). • Neither continent has any developed countries (1). Credit relevant reference to named countries. No credit for descriptions of other continents or global pattern. Answer must also offer a comparison.	2

Exam Practice Answers

Q	Marking guidance	Marks
2	Credit one advantage only. One mark for a basic statement, such as: it shows how wealthy people are (1); it shows what people are getting paid for their work (1). Two marks for a developed idea, such as: it shows the wealth of people and to what extent they can improve their lives by spending money on their homes or services (2); it shows how much money people are earning and therefore how much taxes the government could be getting to spend on improving infrastructure (2).	2
3	Credit one disadvantage only. One mark for basic statement, such as: it only considers social and economic indicators (1); it does not use equality (1). Two marks for developed idea, such as: it does not take into account the state of the natural environment, which if damaged would make development unsustainable (2); the social factors that it includes do not consider the gender inequalities or other inequalities such as wealth and ethnicity (2).	2
4	Award one mark for correctly identifying an aspect of physical geography and climate, and up to a further three marks for development and explanation of that aspect, such as: • Climate influences development over a long period of time (1), with greater development in cooler wetter areas (temperate zones) (1). • Where it is not too hot and not too cold with enough rain crops grow better (1), so there is more food for people (1). • There are fewer fatal diseases in cooler areas (1) as these thrive where it is hot, like the tropics where many people die or are weakened so that they cannot work as well (1). • Hot and cold environments and drier climates are more difficult to work in (1), the human body cannot operate in extremes and therefore work is less efficient (1).	4
5	**C** 7 per cent	1
6	Haiti = 200 per 100 000 people. USA = 3 per 100 000 people. So 200 − 3 = **197** per 100 000 people. Must show working to get second mark.	2
7	The answer must give reasons for differences; there is no credit available for description of the graph on its own. **Indicative content** • The graph shows that developed countries have the lowest TB cases and developing countries have the highest, except for South Africa which is the highest (1). • Developed countries have a lot of money and have invested in health care systems, medicines and doctors, which keep the population healthier (1). • Developing countries are poor and do not have the money to invest in medical care and so people catch diseases more easily and are often not treated (1). • In developing countries people live in poor conditions, such as the lack of safe clean water, which allows TB to exist and spread (1). • South Africa may classify as an economically emerging country, but it is a country that has not invested in social infrastructure to improve people's lives at work and at home (1). • Developing and emerging countries may not be able to help people in more remote rural areas where TB rates can be higher (1).	4
8	One mark for each of two reasons, such as: • People are not strong enough to work efficiently on farms, this creates lower food supplies, which weakens people further (1). • People are not strong enough to work efficiently in factories, so productivity goes down and less money is made (1). • Children may not develop properly and cannot contribute to the economy as adults (1). • If people are unable to work properly and earn money they cannot pay taxes, the government has less money to invest in infrastructure and services (1). No credit for vague statements such as: too weak to work; health is poor; low-paid jobs.	2
9	Explanation needed, not just description. **Indicative content** • Rostow believed that countries progress through stages of development (1). • From traditional societies, countries develop a supporting infrastructure that is needed to enable manufacturing industries to develop (1). • Industries make money and employ people, creating an industrial revolution with rapid economic development (1). • Later there are modifications to industries and new ones emerge to keep economic progress going (1), especially supported by wealthier people who become consumers buying lots of goods (1).	4

	Development dynamics: Development strategies	
Q	Marking guidance	Marks
1a	Responses must focus on the comparison for two marks. Statement may be backed by fact. • FDI outflows have increased greatly from Developing Asia, while from Europe they have declined (2). • Developing Asia increased by $133b, while Europe declined by $60b (2).	2

Q	Marking guidance	Marks
1b	Transition = $63b and Africa = $13b. 63 − 13 = **$50b**. Must show working for two marks.	2
2	Credit one way only. One mark for basic statement, such as: FDI provides jobs (1); FDI helps the multiplier effect (1). Two marks for developed idea, such as: FDI brings investment into a country, which governments usually direct at higher unemployment areas to provide jobs and therefore income into the communities (2); FDI may bring factories into the country that will encourage the growth of linked industries, e.g. suppliers and services (2).	2
3	One expanded reason should be given, such as: • FDI may not reduce poverty because the amount of investment is too small to have a large impact, such as only employing a few people on low wages. • FDI may not reduce poverty because the TNC may take the profits made out of the country and not re-invest it to create economic growth locally. • FDI may not reduce poverty because the TNC uses components and supplies from abroad and so does not support local businesses and industries. No credit for vague statements such as: • Doesn't make people richer. • Profits disappear. • Government gives too much money.	2
4	**B** Better prices and working conditions directly supporting farmers and workers.	1
5a	2015 tourists = 3.69m and 2009 tourists = 2.75m. 3.69 − 2.75 = **0.94m** (allow 0.9m to 1.0m). Must showing working for two marks.	2
5b	Responses must focus on the comparison. Statement may be backed by fact. Only one fully developed response required. • Tourist arrivals increased steadily between 2009 and 2015 with minor fluctuations, while the income fell between 2009 and 2011 before increasing slowly after 2012. • Tourist income was highest in 2009 when arrivals were at their lowest, then as arrivals increased, income decreased until after 2012, the gap between arrivals and income has been increasing.	2
6	Credit one way only. One mark for basic statement, such as: tourism provides jobs for people (1); tourists spend money in the country (1). Two marks for a developed idea, such as: • Tourists from developed countries buy goods and spend money in the developing country's hotels, which gives the government tax money that it can spend on improving services such as education. With better education people can work better and so help the country develop (2). • Tourism provides many jobs and so gives people wages, these people then spend money in local shops and for local services which gives more people wages, which they can then spend on other things. In this way wealth and development is spread (2).	2

	Development dynamics: Rapid economic development and change	
Q	Marking guidance	Marks
1a	2004 = 2350 thousand barrels per day, 2016 = 1750 thousand barrels per day. 2350 − 1750 = **600** thousand barrels per day. (Allow 575 to 625.) Must show working to get two marks.	2
1b	Response must focus on the comparison. Statement may be backed by fact. Only one response required, such as: • Between 2004 and 2007 oil production increased to a peak and then declined sharply to a lower level, while between 2007 and 2010 there was a steep decline followed by a rise. • Both time periods have fluctuations but most of the 2004 to 2007 time period is at a high level (over 2400 thousand barrels per day) while 2007 to 2010 has a sharp decline – even dipping below 1700 thousand barrels per day.	2
2	No explanation needed. Describe two ways in which a named emerging country is linked to other countries. The example in the Edexcel GCSE Geography B Revision Guide is India. **Indicative content** • Trade links – especially exports to USA, UAE, China, UK and Singapore. • Migrants – moved to other countries and send remittances home. • Commonwealth – leading member of the British Commonwealth group of countries. • NDB – jointly set up New Development Bank. • International groups – member of UN, G20 and SAARC. • Cricket – plays cricket against many other countries.	2
3	Credit one factor only. Can be social or cultural. Should be linked to a named emerging country. India is the example used in the Edexcel GCSE Geography B Revision Guide. One mark for basic statement, such as: India has social/cultural divisions based on the caste system (1); India has extreme poverty but also billionaires (1); India has a lack of equality (1). Two marks for developed idea, such as:	2

Q	Marking guidance	Marks
	• India has several levels in its caste system with Brahmins at top and Shudras and Dalits at bottom. Historically, there has been social division between the higher castes and lower castes that has kept a lot of people at a disadvantage in terms of job opportunities and access to services such as a good level of education. This has held back improvements to the quality of life (2). • India has big businesses, such as Tata Steel, but 20 per cent of the population live in poverty with high infant mortality rates and an adult literacy rate of only 69 per cent (2).	
4	One mark for each reasoned step, up to a maximum of four marks. **Indicative content** • India has changed from a country producing agricultural products to an expansion of secondary industries manufacturing goods, especially between 1980 and 2006. Services have expanded since 2000 (1). • The contribution to GDP has changed: In 1960, Agriculture contributed 42 per cent, Services 38 per cent and Manufacturing 19 per cent, by 2010 the contributions were Services 55 per cent, Manufacturing 28 per cent per cent and Agriculture 18 per cent. • Since independence, India has tried to develop using its agricultural advantages at first, until about 1970, including the development of a textile industry based on cotton farming. • Due to the colonial legacy, India has a lot of English-speaking people, which has helped to develop business and trading links around the world. This has included the development of call centres. • Traditional industries were able to use local raw materials and imports, such as steel manufacturing, machinery and coal mining. Some, like TATA Steel, developed into large TNCs. • Recently, India has developed high technology industries, which includes space technology and nuclear energy. • The Indian government have promoted exports, which has encouraged the growth of secondary and tertiary businesses. • Both GDP and GNI have doubled since 1990.	4
5	**AO2 (4 marks) / AO3 (4 marks)** **Indicative content** (Assess how far …) AO2 • The Indian government has been supporting the export of goods and services to bring money into the country. • The government has invested in infrastructure development (especially transport and communications) within and between the large cities. Also developed port facilities to help exporting of goods. These have helped economic development. • The government has allowed FDI from USA and aid from the UK to help support economic projects. • There are other factors that have been important to helping economic development in India, such as the large workforce for all sectors of the economy. • There has been considerable corruption and weakly enforced regulations that have reduced the effectiveness of economic development. AO3 • Foreign trade is encouraged and a target has been set by the government to double exports (by value) by 2020. Trade links have been made with USA, UAE, UK and Singapore so there is access to these large markets to bring money into India. India was ranked seventh in terms of GDP in 2016 and by 2030 could be in third position. • Infrastructure development is important to help India to progress through the industrial revolution stage and then get its industries to mature. However, rural areas are being seriously neglected. • The government controls investment and finances within the country, which has reduced the Economic Freedom Index to the 'mostly unfree' category in 2017. This has restricted investment in new ideas and industries. • The government influence is important, sometimes helping and sometimes hindering economic development. There are also other factors that could be regarded as equally or more important, such as: geographical position (half-way between east Asia and the Middle East/Europe); remittances from migrants totalling $62.7 billion in 2016; 2008 recession holding back development. • HDI is not improving relative to other countries and 20 per cent of the population remain in poverty, especially in rural areas and the 17 per cent of the population that live in shanty towns. **Level 0, no marks** • No relevant response. **Level 1 (Basic) 1–3 marks:** • Demonstrates isolated elements of understanding of concepts and the interrelationship of places, environments and processes. (AO2) • Attempts to apply understanding to deconstruct information but understanding and connections are flawed. An unbalanced or incomplete argument that provides limited synthesis of understanding. Judgments are supported by limited evidence. (AO3) **Level 2 (Clear) 4–6 marks:** • Demonstrates elements of understanding of concepts and the interrelationship of places, environments and processes. (AO2) • Applies understanding to deconstruct information and provide some logical connections between concepts. An imbalanced argument that synthesises mostly relevant understanding but not entirely coherently, leading to judgments that are supported by evidence occasionally. (AO3)	8

Q	Marking guidance	Marks
	Level 3 (Detailed) 7–8 marks: • Demonstrates accurate understanding of concepts and the interrelationship of places, environments and processes. (AO2) • Applies understanding to deconstruct information and provide logical connections between concepts throughout. A balanced, well-developed argument that synthesises relevant understanding coherently, leading to judgments that are supported by evidence throughout. (AO3)	
5 SPaG	**SPaG 0 No marks awarded** • Learners write nothing. • Learner's response does not relate to the question. • Learner's achievement in SPaG does not reach the threshold performance level, for example, errors in spelling, punctuation and grammar severely hinder meaning. **SPaG 1 (Threshold performance) 1 mark** • Learners spell and punctuate with reasonable accuracy. • Learners use rules of grammar with some control of meaning and any errors do not significantly hinder meaning overall. • Learners use a limited range of specialist terms as appropriate. **SPaG 2 (Intermediate performance) 2–3 marks** • Learners spell and punctuate with considerable accuracy. • Learners use rules of grammar with general control of meaning overall. • Learners use a good range of specialist terms as appropriate. **SPaG 3 (High performance) 4 marks** • Learners spell and punctuate with consistent accuracy. • Learners use rules of grammar with effective control of meaning overall. • Learners use a wide range of specialist terms as appropriate.	4

Challenges of an urbanising world: Trends in urbanisation		
Q	**Marking guidance**	**Marks**
1	One mark for each correct answer: **B** The population of the world experienced a rapid growth from 1960. **C** Global population is predicted to rise to 9 billion by 2050.	2
2	**C** A city with a population of more than 10 million.	1
3	Most megacities are found in the developing world, mostly in Asia (1). There are few in developed countries (1).	2
4	Rural to urban migration (1) occurs when people move from the countryside to the city in search of a better quality of life (1). Natural increase when the birth rate exceeds the death rate (1) due to a large number of migrants being of child-bearing age (1).	4

Challenges of an urbanising world: Changing cities over time		
Q	**Marking guidance**	**Marks**
1	Award one mark for each aspect of the city's site given, up to a maximum of two. Award one further mark for each expansion/explanation of the aspects, up to a maximum of two. Answers will vary depending on city chosen; typical site features and reasons include: coastal location (1) makes trade easier (1). Flat land (1) allows building development (1). Location near a river (1) to provides water or trade (1). Fertile land (1) for growing food (1). Access to other countries and settlement (1) for trade (1).	4
2	**C** Squatter settlements	1
3	Work that is done unofficially with no workers' rights.	1
4	One mark per stage of explanation given, up to a maximum of three marks, including: workers have no rights (1); work longer hours (1); no paid holiday (1); no taxes paid (1); may be subject to exploitation (1); may be dismissed/sacked with little or no warning (1).	3
5	One mark per annotation, up to a maximum of four marks, including: open sewers lead to contaminated water and spread of diseases (1); waste is tipped freely with no collections, which encourages the spread of pests and diseases (1); overcrowded and high-density housing leads to rapid spread of disease and fire (1); poor quality buildings made from wood and other salvaged materials can catch fire easily, collapse or not protect occupants from bad weather (1); closeness to unscreened/unprotected transport routes (e.g. railway lines) leads to high risk of accidents or deaths (1).	4
Workit!	One mark overall for naming example(s). One mark for each benefit stated and explained, up to a maximum of three marks. One mark for each cost stated and explained, up to a maximum of three marks. One mark for including a statement about the success or otherwise of the strategy. The example in the Edexcel GCSE Geography B Revision Guide is Vision Mumbai. **Indicative content** **Benefits**: Cleared dangerous and dirty slum housing (1). Provided people with new homes with access to sanitation and running water (1). 45 000 new homes built (1). New trains and platform safety at stations (1). Wealthier residents are happy to remove eyesore of the Dharavi slum (1).	8

Exam Practice Answers

Q	Marking guidance	Marks
	Costs: Local people don't like the demolition aspect, they would rather have piped water and sanitation where they are (1). Living in flats has broken up communities (1). Businesses that are run out of people's homes, such as recycling, had to move out as those buildings got knocked down (1). Authorities have not listened to the local people and community (1). Conclusion: Students' answers will vary in saying whether the project was a success or a failure. Any reasoned conclusion based on the evidence given should be rewarded.	

	The UK's evolving physical landscape: Coastal change and conflict	
Q	**Marking guidance**	**Marks**
1	Spit	1
2	Longshore drift	1
3	One mark for description of a feature or process, one further mark for developing the description, such as: building settlements/villages/towns/cities (1) and including coastal defences (sea walls, groynes, etc.) to protect houses that may affect the coastline elsewhere (1); developing harbours (1) with the impact of construction of harbour walls, port facilities, etc. (1); tourism (1) leading to pollution and/or sea defences such as groynes to protect beaches (which impacts the natural development of coastline nearby) (1); agriculture (1) which changes the growth of vegetation and may encourage erosion (1).	2
4	One mark for naming a type of soft engineering and one mark for the explanation of how it works, such as: beach nourishment (1) where sand or shingle is added to a beach to maintain or increase its width (1); reprofiling (1) where the beach has materials added or taken away to re-shape the beach (1); dune regeneration (1) where marram grass is planted to help stabilise sand dunes and/or fencing is erected to reduce the numbers of people trampling the dunes and causing erosion (1).	2
5	**Indicative content** • Constructive waves are gently sloping whereas destructive waves are steep. • Constructive waves have a strong swash, which helps to build up beaches whereas destructive waves have a strong backwash, which removes beach material. • Constructive waves have a long wavelength/are far apart but destructive waves have a short wavelength/are close together. **Level 0, no marks** • No relevant response. **Level 1 (Basic) 1–2 marks** • Shows limited understanding of the difference between constructive and destructive waves. (AO2) • Demonstrates application of knowledge and understanding to make limited interpretations of the processes that cause constructive and destructive waves. (AO3) **Level 2 (Clear) 3–4 marks** • Shows clear understanding of why constructive and destructive waves are different. (AO2) • Demonstrates application of knowledge and understanding to make full interpretation of the processes that cause constructive and destructive waves. (AO3)	4
6	The answer must give reasons for differences; there is no credit available for description of the two types of coastline on their own. **Indicative content** • A discordant coastline is where the geology alternates between layers (strata) of hard rock and soft rock (1), whereas a concordant coastline has the same type of rock (hard or soft) along its length (1). • Concordant coastlines, as a result of their structure, tend to have fewer bays (1) and headlands (1) than discordant coastlines.	4
7	The answer must relate sub-aerial processes to the formation of particular coastal landscape features; there is no credit available for description of the processes without context. **Indicative content** • Sub-aerial processes include weathering (of several types) and mass movement (1). • Freeze-thaw weathering causes water to freeze and expand in cracks within rock, which may cause cliffs to break up or arches in headlands to collapse and form stacks (1). • Chemical weathering occurs when slightly acidic rainwater dissolves particular types of rock such as chalk or limestone, which may cause cracks or reshaping of the coastline (1). • Biological weathering occurs when plants and animals move or disturb the soil or rock, causing cracks and other features to develop on a coastline (1). • Mass movement such as rockfalls or landslides may cause coastal cliffs to collapse or subside into the sea (1).	4
8	**Indicative content** • A large crack forms in the headland at a point of weakness. • The crack is enlarged by the process of hydraulic action and abrasion to form a notch. • Waves make the crack larger over time to form a cave. • Two caves form back-to-back over time. • These will eventually cut through the headland to form an arch.	4

Q	Marking guidance	Marks
	Level 0, no marks • No relevant response. **Level 1 (Basic) 1–2 marks** • Shows limited understanding of how an arch is formed. (AO2) • Application is limited with basic interpretation of processes involved. (AO3) **Level 2 (Clear) 3–4 marks** • Shows clear understanding of how an arch is formed. (AO2) • Application is sound with clear interpretation of processes involved. (AO3)	
9	The answer must describe both costs and benefits, including explanation of each point made. Only four marks are available so only one or two types of hard engineering need be described. **Indicative content** • Sea walls: costs – very expensive (1), can be visually unappealing (1), can restrict access to a beach (1); benefits – effective at reflecting the energy of the sea (1), can last for many years if well maintained (1), can be developed into a positive feature such as a promenade (1), do not affect the movement of sediment (1). • Rock armour: costs – rocks used are taken from other coastlines or abroad (1), does not fit in with the local geology (1), usually visually unappealing (1); benefits – relatively cheap (1), structure is easy to build and maintain (1), can last for many years if well maintained (1). • Gabions: costs – look very unattractive in the short term (1), cages last for a few years only before rusting (1); benefits – cheap (1), easy to build (1), can improve cliff drainage to reduce landslip (1), vegetation will grow over them in the long term (1). • Groynes: costs – can look unattractive (1), interrupt longshore drift, starving areas further down the coast of sediment (1); benefits – cheap (1), create a wider beach more attractive to tourists (1), can last a long time if well maintained (1).	4
10	Answers should not just describe or state, but should include assessment and refer to sustainability wherever possible. **Indicative content (Assess the extent …)** • Areas of coastline should be identified as examples, such as concordant and discordant coastline in Dorset. • The range of coastal management techniques employed or available should be explained, including some reference to both suitability for particular areas or types of coastline, and their relative sustainability. • Integrated Coastal Zone Management (ICZM) should be described as a sustainable approach to hard and soft engineering. • Do nothing – leaves the coastline to natural forces but has zero cost and may be the most sustainable approach in some circumstances. • Hold the line – maintain the existing shoreline by building defences (range of sustainable and less sustainable options). • Managed realignment – manage and direct the process of natural change with a combination of soft and hard engineering (range of sustainable and less sustainable options). • Advance the line – build new defences on the seaward side to protect and grow the existing coastline features (can be sustainable but often is not). • Hard engineering – usually expensive but can be sustained over a long time after initial investment, with annual maintenance, including sea walls, rock armour, groynes and gabions. • Soft engineering – usually less expensive but may need to be repeated on a regular (annual?) basis, so may be less sustainable in the long run, including beach nourishment, reprofiling and dune regeneration. • Managed retreat – coastline is allowed to change naturally but land may be sacrificed; often a sustainable option. • Judgment on costs and sustainability of the different methods described. • Consideration of evidence from existing examples. **Level 0, no marks** • No relevant response. **Level 1 (Basic) 1–3 marks** • Demonstrates isolated elements of understanding of concepts and the interrelationship of places, environments and processes. (AO2) • Attempts to apply understanding to deconstruct information but understanding and connections are flawed. An unbalanced or incomplete argument that provides limited synthesis of understanding. Judgments are supported by limited evidence. (AO3) **Level 2 (Clear) 4–6 marks** • Demonstrates elements of understanding of concepts and the interrelationship of places, environments and processes. (AO2) • Applies understanding to deconstruct information and provide some logical connections between concepts. An imbalanced argument that synthesises mostly relevant understanding but not entirely coherently, leading to judgments that are supported by evidence occasionally. (AO3) **Level 3 (Detailed) 7–8 marks** • Demonstrates accurate understanding of concepts and the interrelationship of places, environments and processes. (AO2) • Applies understanding to deconstruct information and provide logical connections between concepts throughout. A balanced, well-developed argument that synthesises relevant understanding coherently, leading to judgments that are supported by evidence throughout. (AO3)	8

Q	Marking guidance	Marks
10 SPaG	**SPaG 0 No marks awarded** • Learners write nothing. • Learner's response does not relate to the question. • Learner's achievement in SPaG does not reach the threshold performance level, for example, errors in spelling, punctuation and grammar severely hinder meaning. **SPaG 1 (Threshold performance) 1 mark** • Learners spell and punctuate with reasonable accuracy. • Learners use rules of grammar with some control of meaning and any errors do not significantly hinder meaning overall. • Learners use a limited range of specialist terms as appropriate. **SPaG 2 (Intermediate performance) 2–3 marks** • Learners spell and punctuate with considerable accuracy. • Learners use rules of grammar with general control of meaning overall. • Learners use a good range of specialist terms as appropriate. **SPaG 3 (High performance) 4 marks** • Learners spell and punctuate with consistent accuracy. • Learners use rules of grammar with effective control of meaning overall. • Learners use a wide range of specialist terms as appropriate.	4

The UK's evolving physical landscape: River landscapes in the UK

Q	Marking guidance	Marks
1a	Lag time is the length of time between the peak rainfall and the river's peak discharge.	1
1b	Peak discharge – peak rainfall = 6.8 – 3.5 = 3.3 hours (allow range between 3.0 and 3.5)	1
2	As it runs from source to mouth, the cross-section of a river becomes wider (1) and deeper (1).	2
3	Hydraulic action is a process of erosion caused by the force of the water (1) hitting the river bank and river bed (1).	2
4	One mark for each of any two points from the following: • Warmer, wetter climates produce rivers that carry large volumes of water, so rivers are typically wider and deeper with a faster flow. • Rivers in drier climates may be seasonal (i.e. they slow to a trickle or disappear completely in the drier months, but form fast-running rivers in the wet season). • Rivers in temperate climates produce fast-running, shallow courses in the upper profile, and slower, more meandering courses in the lower profile. • Rivers in drier and temperate climates have increased risk of flooding after heavy and/or prolonged rainfall.	2
5	**Indicative content** • There will be larger and more angular sediment in the upper course. • The sediment will be considerably smaller and rounder in the lower course. • Sediment will be rounder and smoother as sediment is transported and eroded as it is moved downstream. • Erosion processes of hydraulic action, attrition and abrasion are key in reducing the size of sediment as it moves downstream. **Level 0, no marks** • No relevant response. **Level 1 (Basic) 1–2 marks** • Shows limited understanding of how size of sediment changes from source to mouth. (AO2) • Application is limited with basic interpretation of processes involved. (AO3) **Level 2 (Clear) 3–4 marks** • Shows clear understanding of how and why sediment changes from source to mouth. (AO2) • Application is sound with clear interpretation of processes involved. (AO3)	4
6	One mark for each statement of a social impact, one further mark for an explanation of that impact. Two impacts only to be marked, with a maximum of four marks available. **Indicative content** • Disruption to daily life (1), with property damaged by dirty floodwater (1) and access to local facilities limited (1). • Evacuation of people from properties (1) when a property is flooded and for months afterwards while the property is repaired (1). • Reduced property value (1) due to a history of flooding putting buyers off (1) or a difficulty in securing insurance for a property (1). • Change in make-up of local population (1) due to wealthier people being able to move away from flood risk areas and poorer people moving in to take advantage of cheaper property (1). • Risk of disease and other problems (1) during the time of flooding, due to little or no sanitation and the likelihood of sewage and other waste being present in floodwater (1).	4

Q	Marking guidance	Marks
7	One mark for one physical factor only, one mark for one human factor only. **Indicative content** Physical factors • Precipitation – heavy rainfall can lead to flash flooding or a long period of rain can lead to flooding (1). • Geology – impermeable rock increases surface run-off, which increases rate at which water reaches a river (1). • Saturated soil – waterlogged soil does not allow water to infiltrate (1). Human factors • Deforestation – decreases the amount of interception so rainfall can get to rivers quicker (1). • Urbanisation – increases impermeable surfaces which increase speed at which water reaches rivers (1).	4
8	**Indicative content** • The thalweg is the fastest line of velocity in a river. It swings from the outside of one bend to the outside of the next bend (1). • The faster velocity on the outside of a river bend causes more erosion on the outside of the bend (1). • The slower velocity on the inside of a river bend causes deposition on the inside of the bend (1). • The combination of erosion on the outside of a bend and deposition on the inside causes the bend to become more pronounced, so the river moves (meanders) across the valley floor (1).	4
9	One mark for each statement of a human process, one further mark for an explanation of that process. Two processes only to be marked, with a maximum of four marks available. **Indicative content** • Deforestation (1) in which people cut down trees along river banks, leading to faster erosion (1), or on land from which water drains into the river, leading to faster runoff and the potential of flooding further down the river (1). • Urbanisation (1) in which the area of impermeable surfaces is increased, increasing the speed at which water reaches rivers (1). • Building flood defences (1) in which water courses are stabilised or altered in order to prevent rivers from overflowing into settlements or other areas of land (1). • Tourism and other boat traffic (1), which can affect river banks through excessive erosion (1). • Construction of canals or drainage (1), which can affect or divert rivers, or significantly alter river flow (1).	4
10	Answers should not just describe or state, but should include assessment and refer to the scale and nature of flood risk wherever possible. **Indicative content (Assess the extent …)** • Areas of land or rivers should be identified as examples. • The range of human activities that affect rivers directly, or indirectly e.g. by affecting water catchment areas upstream, should be described and assessed. • Human activities with positive effects on flooding, e.g. building flood protection or managing water levels, should be included as well as the more usual activities that have negative effects. • Settlements and building of new developments – often introducing hard, impermeable surfaces into areas that previously soaked up water, causing higher risk of flooding and less chance of excess water soaking away. • Agricultural and other activity in the surrounding areas that may affect both drainage lower down the river, and accelerate runoff into the upstream areas of the river (causing higher risk of flooding). • Deforestation along river banks and in upstream catchment areas reduces the amount of water taken up by plants, leading to more rapid runoff and increased flooding risk. • Dredging of rivers through urban areas increases river flow rate but may sometimes increase the risk of flooding as a result. • Sheep and cattle grazing uplands, or closely cropping or burning vegetation on hillsides, accelerates runoff and may cause flooding further downstream. • Afforestation improves take-up of water upstream and reduces flooding risk. • Allowing different areas of land to flood may divert flooding from sensitive areas. • Land zoning, such as building high-cost housing and industry away from floodplains, reduces cost of flooding. • River restoration to a more natural state, including the surrounding land, reduces flood risks. • Judgment on scale of the different risks described. • Consideration of evidence from existing examples. **Level 0, no marks** • No relevant response. **Level 1 (Basic) 1–3 marks** • Demonstrates isolated elements of understanding of concepts and the interrelationship of places, environments and processes. (AO2) • Attempts to apply understanding to deconstruct information but understanding and connections are flawed. An unbalanced or incomplete argument that provides limited synthesis of understanding. Judgments are supported by limited evidence. (AO3)	8

Q	Marking guidance	Marks
10 SPaG	**Level 2 (Clear) 4–6 marks** • Demonstrates elements of understanding of concepts and the interrelationship of places, environments and processes. (AO2) • Applies understanding to deconstruct information and provide some logical connections between concepts. An imbalanced argument that synthesises mostly relevant understanding but not entirely coherently, leading to judgments that are supported by evidence occasionally. (AO3) **Level 3 (Detailed) 7–8 marks** • Demonstrates accurate understanding of concepts and the interrelationship of places, environments and processes. (AO2) • Applies understanding to deconstruct information and provide logical connections between concepts throughout. A balanced, well-developed argument that synthesises relevant understanding coherently, leading to judgments that are supported by evidence throughout. (AO3) **SPaG 0 No marks awarded** • Learners write nothing. • Learner's response does not relate to the question. • Learner's achievement in SPaG does not reach the threshold performance level, for example, errors in spelling, punctuation and grammar severely hinder meaning. **SPaG 1 (Threshold performance) 1 mark** • Learners spell and punctuate with reasonable accuracy. • Learners use rules of grammar with some control of meaning and any errors do not significantly hinder meaning overall. • Learners use a limited range of specialist terms as appropriate. **SPaG 2 (Intermediate performance) 2–3 marks** • Learners spell and punctuate with considerable accuracy. • Learners use rules of grammar with general control of meaning overall. • Learners use a good range of specialist terms as appropriate. **SPaG 3 (High performance) 4 marks** • Learners spell and punctuate with consistent accuracy. • Learners use rules of grammar with effective control of meaning overall. • Learners use a wide range of specialist terms as appropriate.	4

The UK's evolving human landscape: Changing people and places		
Q	**Marking guidance**	**Marks**
1a	One mark for each reasoned statement up to a maximum of two, such as: • Highest population densities are found in major urban areas such as London, Birmingham, cities of the North-West, Edinburgh and Glasgow (1). • Lowest population densities are found in inaccessible rural areas such as the Highlands of Scotland and remote islands (1). • A trend of higher population density towards the South-East of England, with lower density in mid-Wales, the far North of England and much of rural Scotland and Northern Ireland (1).	2
1b	One mark for each point stated and one further mark for a developed point, up to a maximum of two points and four marks. Points include: • Areas to the North and West tend to be more mountainous and much less accessible (1), reducing the availability of housing and facilities (1). • Urban areas have developed with strong pull factors (1) such as significant employment opportunities, better facilities, better transport links and better housing (1). • The South-East of England is closer to continental Europe (1) which historically led to better trade and movement opportunities (1) and also has led to a concentration of better transport and other facilities (1). • The availability of natural resources such as rivers and coal (1) historically led to the development of urban areas such as those in the North of England, where the Industrial Revolution was centred (1).	4
2	One mark for each point stated and one further mark for a developed point, up to a maximum of two points and four marks. Points include: • Immigration (1) from countries within the EU due to freedom of movement and from countries outside the EU due to historical factors (e.g. Commonwealth) (1) and pull factors arising from the UK being a centre of international business (1) with high standards of living (1). • Natural growth (1) due to an increased birth rate and increased life expectancy (1), in turn due to immigrant population being largely in their 20s and 30s and so more likely to have children (1).	4
3	Predominantly white (65%) with 49% white British (1). Other races make up 35% of the population, with 13% South Asian, 14% black and other and mixed race making up the remaining 8% (1).	2
4	One mark for an advantage, one mark for a disadvantage. Possible advantages: brings in specialist workers (1); increases birth rate where indigenous population is ageing (1); improves cultural diversity (1); increases trade (1); brings in more tax income (1). Possible disadvantages: increases pressure on local services such as healthcare and education (1); requires more support for a range of different languages (1); increases demand for housing (may push up prices) (1).	2

Q	Marking guidance	Marks
5	One mark for each statement of change, up to a maximum of two, from: significant reduction in primary sector, particularly mining (1); de-industrialised/secondary sector decline (less manufacturing output) (1); increased service/tertiary sector (1); increased IT/law/finance quaternary sector (1); more export-driven (1); increase in consumer/shopping demand (1).	2
6	De-industrialisation is a stage in economic development where manufacturing industries decline and close down, while service industries grow.	1
7	One mark for each of up to two features stated, such as: growth of hi-tech investment and industries (1); growth of knowledge-intensive service sector such as education, communications and information (1); growth in demand for higher skilled workers/university degrees (1); more global due to increased communications and connectivity (such as broadband) (1); higher levels of automation in production processes (1).	2
8	One mark for each statement of an impact of globalisation, one further mark for an explanation of that impact. Statements must be accompanied by explanations. **Indicative content** • Growth of 'free trade' (1), which is trade without tariffs or taxes so as to provide an economic boost to producer and consumer countries (1). • Increased flows of raw materials, products, services and workers between countries (1), which are necessary to produce and sell goods on a global basis (1). • Sourcing of manufacturing and extraction of raw materials from overseas (1), which occurs either because the source countries have a more readily available supply or because materials and/or labour are cheaper (1). • Reduction of prices (1) due to materials or products being sourced from countries where raw materials and/or labour are cheaper (1). • Growth of transnational corporations (1) which are needed to link countries providing raw materials, manufacturing and labour with countries carrying out design, assembly and sales (1). • Growth of foreign direct investment (FDI) (1) where investors from developed countries or TNCs have wealth to invest in other, less developed countries that have raw materials and workers (1). • Growth of privatisation (1) where privately- or shareholder-owned companies are more able to invest internationally than state-owned enterprises (1).	4

The UK's evolving human landscape: Dynamic UK cities		
Q	**Marking guidance**	**Marks**
1a	Using London as the example (students may provide other examples with other valid points): large areas of relatively flat land (1) for development (1); positioned along major river (1) that facilitates provision of services such as transport, water, access to trade (1); land near to river was fertile (1) so historically better for growing crops (1).	2
1b	Using London as the example (students may provide other examples with other valid points): geographically close to continental Europe (1) enabling easier trade and travel (1); location globally is in time zone equally spaced between Asia (5 to 7 hours ahead) and North America (5 to 8 hours behind) (1) which is beneficial for the overlap of daily activity in financial markets and other trade (1); good connectivity (1) via major hub airports such as Heathrow, enabling international travel for residents and visitors (1), and via rail and road networks within the UK enabling access to the rest of the UK economy (1).	2
2	One mark for each characteristic stated (no full description or explanation needed), up to a maximum of two, such as: oldest part of the city (1); highest density of buildings in the city (1); most expensive land/property values (1); used for offices, retail, financial services, government, some leisure and entertainment (1); poor environmental quality due to overcrowding and traffic congestion (1).	2
3	Areas to the north and east of the city centre, closer to the centre, tend to be more deprived/poorer (1), whereas areas to the south and west, further away from the centre/in the suburbs tend to be less deprived/wealthier (1).	2
4	Gentrification is the process by which wealthier people move into, renovate, and restore housing and sometimes businesses in inner cities or other deteriorated areas formerly home to poorer people.	1
Workit!	A student should evaluate a scheme using a named case study, e.g. London or Bristol, and explain the strategies used. Examples described here are London and Bristol, but similar features will apply to other UK cities. **Indicative content** This will vary depending on the example chosen but could include: • integrated transport network linking all different transport methods together • more frequent public transport services • crime reduction schemes • conversion of abandoned industrial buildings or sites into desirable residential accommodation • 'clean-up' of area to remove industrial contamination and re-site e.g. waste disposal sites	8

Q	Marking guidance	Marks
	• investment to improve connectivity and technology access such as high-speed broadband • development of retail and leisure facilities • development of parks and other open spaces to improve leisure facilities and environment. Problems or failures of the schemes: • crowding on public transport • housing still expensive due to continuing rise in land and property values (due to increased demand from residents and investors) • a degree of gentrification where wealthier families/individuals move into regenerated areas, displacing poorer existing residents • major retail parks may lead to closure of traditional 'high street' shops • success is dependent on companies relocating, hiring office space or providing retail outlets; if demand is not sustained, office and residential spaces may lie empty. **Level 0, no marks** • No relevant response. **Level 1 (Basic) 1–3 marks** • Demonstrates some knowledge of strategies to redevelop an area. (AO1) • Shows limited geographical understanding of how successful different schemes have been and may not give a suitable example. (AO2) **Level 2 (Clear) 4–6 marks** • Demonstrates specific and accurate knowledge of two or more different strategies to manage redevelopment. (AO2) • Shows clear geographical understanding to evaluate the success of schemes using at least one specific example. (AO3) **Level 3 (Detailed) 7–8 marks** • Demonstrates thorough application of knowledge and understanding to give detailed evaluation of the strategies to regenerate an area. (AO3) • Shows full understanding of a variety of schemes and gives named examples. Clearly shows the benefits and problems of such schemes. (AO3) • Offers a conclusion.	
Workit! SPaG	**SPaG 0 No marks awarded** • Learners write nothing. • Learner's response does not relate to the question. • Learner's achievement in SPaG does not reach the threshold performance level, for example, errors in spelling, punctuation and grammar severely hinder meaning. **SPaG 1 (Threshold performance) 1 mark** • Learners spell and punctuate with reasonable accuracy. • Learners use rules of grammar with some control of meaning and any errors do not significantly hinder meaning overall. • Learners use a limited range of specialist terms as appropriate. **SPaG 2 (Intermediate performance) 2–3 marks** • Learners spell and punctuate with considerable accuracy. • Learners use rules of grammar with general control of meaning overall. • Learners use a good range of specialist terms as appropriate. **SPaG 3 (High performance) 4 marks** • Learners spell and punctuate with consistent accuracy. • Learners use rules of grammar with effective control of meaning overall. • Learners use a wide range of specialist terms as appropriate.	4

People and the biosphere: Biomes		
Q	**Marking guidance**	**Marks**
1	**D** Tropical rainforest	1
2	Do not credit just an example. A biome is a world-scale ecosystem in balance with the climate.	1
3	The boreal biome is mostly found in the northern hemisphere. It exists in a band around the Earth between the colder polar climate and the warmer temperate climate. It is mostly found in the continents of North America and Asia.	2
Workit! 4	Credit statements about the conditions using information in the diagram, such as: • there is hot humid air at the equator (1) • the hot humid air rises upwards at the equator (or ITCZ) between the two Hadley Cells (1) • the rising humid air condenses as it rises leading to a large amount of rainfall (1) • temperatures are high, at least 25 °C all year round (1) • planetary winds blow westwards towards the equator and TRF areas (1). No credit for simply listing conditions (e.g. hot, wet).	2
4	**C** Large temperature range during a year (−20 °C to +14 °C) and low precipitation (approximately 500 mm a year). No credit if two or more statements are shaded.	1

Q	Marking guidance	Marks
5	**C** 29 °C No credit if two or more statements are shaded.	1
6	One mark for the correct answer: **7 mm**. (Units should be given).	1
7	**Indicative content** • Examples of any biome(s) should be used as a reference point for the answer, such as tropical rainforests, hot deserts and/or boreal (taiga) forests. • The question requires consideration of the extent to which the interactions between the living and non-living parts of biomes/global ecosystems create a balance in the ecosystem. • Answers may describe the balance that exists in biomes/global ecosystems. • Answers may focus on assessing specific examples within generalisations such as climate which determines plant growth (producers) at the base of trophic levels through heat, rain and sunlight; soils providing nutrients for plant growth and humus being added by plants (nutrient cycle); the supply of water for plants and animals. • Answers may consider factors that upset the balance such as climate change. • Answers must consider natural processes and decide whether interactions between biotic and abiotic components do create a balance and whether they are the only factors influencing the balance. **Level 0, no marks** • No relevant response. **Level 1 (Basic) 1–3 marks** • Demonstrates isolated elements of understanding of concepts and the interrelationship of places, environments and processes. (AO2) • Attempts to apply understanding to deconstruct information but understanding and connections are flawed. An unbalanced or incomplete argument that provides limited synthesis of understanding. Judgments are supported by limited evidence. (AO3) **Level 2 (Clear) 4–6 marks** • Demonstrates elements of understanding of concepts and the interrelationship of places, environments and processes. (AO2) • Applies understanding to deconstruct information and provide some logical connections between concepts. An imbalanced argument that synthesises mostly relevant understanding but not entirely coherently, leading to judgments that are supported by evidence occasionally. (AO3) **Level 3 (Detailed) 7–8 marks** • Demonstrates accurate understanding of concepts and the interrelationship of places, environments and processes. (AO2) • Applies understanding to deconstruct information and provide logical connections between concepts throughout. A balanced, well-developed argument that synthesises relevant understanding coherently, leading to judgments that are supported by evidence throughout. (AO3)	8
8	Must explain and not just describe. One mark for basic explanation with second mark for extended explanation. Answers may include examples. **Indicative content** • As altitude (the height of land above sea level) increases the temperatures become cooler so that vegetation must have adaptations for the colder conditions such as coniferous trees with needles and resin, while deciduous trees are found at a lower height. • As altitude increases so does the amount of precipitation, usually a higher amount is experienced (relief rainfall) so at lower heights often grasses are found as they tolerate changes from dry to wet while higher up trees will be found as there is plenty of water.	2
9	**C** Soil gets nutrients from decomposition of litter.	1
10	Credit statements about what water does in the nutrient cycle using information in the diagram, such as: • Washing of nutrients deep into a soil (leaching) (1) • Rain runs over the ground and carries nutrients away (1) • Rain supplies some dissolved nutrients (1) • Moisture helps the decomposition process (1) • Water dissolves nutrients so that plants can absorb them through their roots (1) No credit for simply listing parts of the water or nutrient cycles.	2
11	**D** −9.9 °C	1
12	Student task. Use precipitation scale to draw an accurate top to a bar to represent 20 mm in January (it may be quickly and neatly shaded in).	1

People and the biosphere: Biosphere resources and regulation		
Q	**Marking guidance**	**Marks**
1	No mark just for an example, but a definition may include an example. **Indicative content** A biosphere resource is something provided by an ecosystem that can be used by people, this could be a plant that provides berries for food or an animal that is hunted for its meat or wood from trees for building.	1

Exam Practice Answers

Q	Marking guidance	Marks
2	Answer must have genuine explanation. Up to two marks for basic explanation, with further two marks available for extended explanation. Description on its own should not be credited. **Indicative content** • The world population is larger than it used to be, so with each person needing a certain amount of resources the total used is much larger. • On average people are wealthier no than they used to be, so people today can afford to buy and use more biosphere resources than people did in the past. • A long time ago people just used nature to get what they needed, a subsistence existence, but now people want lots of things such as medicines or tropical hardwoods for furniture or biofuels so there is a lot more use.	4
3	**Indicative content** • The lack of water means that even plants that have adapted find it difficult to survive (1) as shown by the dead trees in Figure 6 (1). • Any water or lakes that form may evaporate quickly (1) as shown by the cracked ground in the photo (1). • It is often dry for long periods of time with clear skies (as shown in Figure 6) (1) so plants and animals have difficulty finding shade (1).	2
4	Only description needed not explanation. One mark for each correct problem. Expect some factual content. **Indicative content** • Problem 1: Deforestation, such as the tropical rainforest in Brazil or the taiga forest in Russia, has removed the largest plants from the biomes changing the structure and removing habitats for animals and birds. • Problem 2: Climate change is partly taking place because of human activities (burning fossil fuels), this changes the balance between climate and biomes that has existed for thousands of years, and plants and creatures unable to adapt or move will die.	2
5	Working must be shown to get second mark. **102** days. (1977 = 315, 2017 = 213. 315 − 213 = 102). Allow between 100 and 104 days.	2
6	Answer must evaluate and not just describe and explain. **Indicative content** • Malthus predicted that the Earth's resources would at some point be unable to support the world population size. • Malthus predicted that as the population size reached the carrying capacity of the Earth there would be natural and man-made checks on the population. • Malthus predicted that there would be a population crash as resources and population numbers returned to a balance. • Evidence to support his ideas includes famines, wars, disease epidemics and pandemics, mass migrations. Examples of places should be given. • However, he was writing a long time ago and no major worldwide population crash has yet occurred. • In contrast Boserup suggested that as the balance between resources and population numbers neared a crisis point humanity would find solutions, such as the Green Revolution, renewable energies, aid and birth control. • Judgment on the extent to which Malthus was successful. **Level 0, no marks** • No relevant response. **Level 1 (Basic) 1–3 marks** • Attempts to apply understanding to deconstruct information but understanding and connections are flawed. An unbalanced or incomplete argument that provides limited synthesis of understanding. Judgments are supported by limited evidence. (AO3) • Demonstrates isolated elements of understanding of concepts and the interrelationship of places, environments and processes. (AO2) **Level 2 (Clear) 4–6 marks** • Applies understanding to deconstruct information and provide some logical connections between concepts. An imbalanced argument that synthesises mostly relevant understanding but not entirely coherently, leading to judgments that are supported by evidence occasionally. (AO3) • Demonstrates elements of understanding of concepts and the interrelationship of places, environments and processes. (AO2) **Level 3 (Detailed) 7–8 marks** • Applies understanding to deconstruct information and provide logical connections between concepts throughout. A balanced, well-developed argument that synthesises relevant understanding coherently, leading to judgments that are supported by evidence throughout. (AO3) • Demonstrates accurate understanding of concepts and the interrelationship of places, environments and processes. (AO2)	8
Workit!	See 'key ideas' for answer.	8

Forests under threat: Tropical rainforest

Q	Marking guidance	Marks
1	**D** Biodiversity is high with a complex food web.	1
2	One mark for basic description, second mark for more detail. Explanations not required. **Indicative content** • Majority of nutrients are stored within the biomass (trees and vegetation). • There are few nutrients stored in the litter or the soil.	2
3	One mark for basic explanation, second mark for extended explanation. **Indicative content** • The movement of nutrients in the tropical rainforest is very fast due to the heat and the amount of moisture. • The heat and moisture accelerate chemical and biological breakdown of litter. • Heavy rainfall leaches nutrients deeper into the soil.	2
4	One mark for each correct label on photograph. Labels could include: buttress roots (to stabilise tall trees); tall trees (to get to sunlight); shallow roots (to get nutrients before they are washed away); broad leaves (to capture as much sunlight as possible).	2
5	One mark for basic explanation, second mark for extended explanation. **Indicative content** There are two main canopy layers within the tropical rainforest and the leaves from these treetops blocks sunlight from reaching the ground. Therefore plants at ground level find it difficult to photosynthesise and can only grow when a large tree falls and creates a gap.	2
6	Answers should concentrate on causes. Up to two marks for basic explanations, and a further two marks for extended explanations. **Indicative content** • One cause of deforestation is the desire of poor people in a developing country to have somewhere to live and land to farm. They often cut down the forest using a 'slash and burn' method which removes the natural forest. • One cause of deforestation is the desire of logging and timber companies to make money. They may clear large areas of forest to get valuable hardwoods such as mahogany. • One cause of deforestation is a government's desire to generate cheap electricity for its people and industries by building dams for HEP. These dams and linked infrastructure remove the forest and large areas of forest may be flooded. Accept any other relevant answer.	4
7	French Guiana. No credit for Guiana or any other country.	1
8	Four/4 (countries).	1
9	Credit one value only. Value must be to people (humans), not to the natural environment. One mark for stating a value, including: source of valuable resources (1); place to live and make a living (1); provision of oxygen (1); store carbon (1); biodiversity (1). Second mark for developing the point, including: • Resources in the forest such as foods, timber, medicines or under the forest, such as coal, oil, metals, can be used to provide jobs and make money for people and countries (1). • As populations grow people need living space and ways of farming to get their own food or products to sell (1). • People need oxygen to breathe, which is produced by plants and the greatest number of trees is in the TRF (1). • Climate change is and will greatly affect people, the TRF stores carbon and stops some CO_2 getting into the atmosphere to create more warming (1). • The huge biodiversity provides chemicals and substances which people may be able to use to create medicines and other beneficial products (1).	2
10	Credit one impact only. The answer must focus on a negative impact of deforestation of a TRF and should be referenced to one area (e.g. Malaysia or SE Asian rainforest). One mark for stating a negative impact, including: reduction of biodiversity (1); erosion of soils (1); increased rate of climate change (1); local area becomes drier (1); water and air pollution increase (1); reduction of eco-tourism (1). Second mark for a developed explanation, including: • If biodiversity is reduced the wildlife may be made extinct, loss of a resource to nature (food web unbalanced) and people (source of medicine) (1). • Erosion and degradation of soils means that the forest or crops will not grow and natural resources are lost (1). • Climate change threatens natural ecosystems by making them hotter or drier, which then reduces resources to support people (1). • Drier climate damages trees and causes dieback and further forest loss (1). • Pollution damages the conditions in which trees and plants live and also the health of people (1). • A damaged forest does not appeal to people for their holidays and so income is lost (1).	2

Q	Marking guidance	Marks
11	Credit one way only. The answer must focus on education of people and sustainability of the TRF. One mark for stating an aspect of education, such as: value of the TRF (1); ways of looking after TRF (1); rates and types of damage (1); ways of reducing damage to TRF (1); alternative ways of making money (1). Second mark for a developed explanation, such as: • If people appreciate the need for biodiversity and the benefits from TRF products then they are less likely to cut it down (1). • Understanding of the role of national parks, biosphere reserves, nature reserves so that their designation is recognised by people (1). • Understanding of the rapid loss and the consequences for local people, countries and the world would make people appreciate the need to look after TRF (1). • Sustainable logging practices, agroforestry rather than clearance, shifting cultivation help maintain forest structure and biodiversity (1). • Instead of cutting down TRF for money things like eco-tourism can provide income based on an undamaged TRF (1).	2
12	Answer must evaluate and not just describe and explain. **Indicative content** • Area or region of tropical rainforest must be identified e.g. Amazonia. • The range of human threats faced by a tropical rainforest, such as climate change and various reasons for deforestation. • An assessment of the seriousness of each human activity through the impacts that each could have on the tropical rainforest, such as loss of biodiversity, change to local climate, extinction of species, soil erosion, sediments in rivers. • The range of human activities that benefit the tropical rainforest such as national parks, wildlife reserves, conservation organisations, debt-for-nature swaps. • An assessment of the extent to which some human activities are beneficial. • Judgment on the extent to which human activities threaten, considering the balance of damaging and beneficial activities. • Consideration of data about the selected area or region of tropical rainforest. **Level 0, no marks** • No relevant response. **Level 1 (Basic) 1–3 marks** • Attempts to apply understanding to deconstruct information but understanding and connections are flawed. An unbalanced or incomplete argument that provides limited synthesis of understanding. Judgments are supported by limited evidence. (AO3) • Demonstrates isolated elements of understanding of concepts and the interrelationship of places, environments and processes. (AO2) **Level 2 (Clear) 4–6 marks** • Applies understanding to deconstruct information and provide some logical connections between concepts. An imbalanced argument that synthesises mostly relevant understanding but not entirely coherently, leading to judgments that are supported by evidence occasionally. (AO3) • Demonstrates elements of understanding of concepts and the interrelationship of places, environments and processes. (AO2) **Level 3 (Detailed) 7–8 marks** • Applies understanding to deconstruct information and provide logical connections between concepts throughout. A balanced, well-developed argument that synthesises relevant understanding coherently, leading to judgments that are supported by evidence throughout. (AO3) • Demonstrates accurate understanding of concepts and the interrelationship of places, environments and processes. (AO2)	8
WorkIt	See 'key ideas' for answer.	8

Forests under threat: The taiga biome

Q	Marking guidance	Marks
1	**B** Pine and spruce trees dominate the vegetation.	1
2	One mark for basic description, second mark for more detail. Explanations not required. **Indicative content** • Majority of nutrients are stored within the litter (dead leaves and twigs on the ground). • There are few nutrients stored in the biomass with least in the soil.	2
3	One mark for basic explanation, second mark for extended explanation. **Indicative content** • The movement of nutrients in the tropical rainforest is slow due to the cold temperatures and limited precipitation. • The lack of heat and moisture slows the chemical and biological breakdown of litter. • Some nutrients are lost due to run-off.	2
4	One mark for each correct label on photograph. Labels could include: Thick fur (to keep warm); white colouring (to hide in the winter); large antlers (for protection and digging up roots in hard ground); bears omnivorous (to get any food when it is available in harsh climate).	2

Q	Marking guidance	Marks
5	One mark for basic explanation, second mark for extended explanation. **Indicative content** • Winters are very cold with a lot of snow cover, and food is difficult to find, so many animals hibernate (sleep through the harshest months) or migrate to warmer areas where there is food. • In summer it is warmer and there is enough grazing and plenty of food, so animals migrate northwards, feed themselves ready to get through the next winter and raise their young.	2
6	Up to two marks for basic explanation, with a further two marks available for extended explanation. **Indicative content** • The lack of liquid water for part of a year means that even plants that have adapted find it difficult to survive (1) as shown by low plants and evergreen trees (1). • Snow and ice can cover the ground for a long time making it difficult for plants to grow through (1) leaving just the short summer for growth (1). • The cold conditions are made worse by wind chill, so plants have to grow close to the ground to survive (1), changes in climate can quickly affect plant growth (1). • All growth is very slow (1) and it is difficult for the plants to recover from any damage (1). • Animals depend on the ability to migrate to find food (1) and if this is not available or they are unable to move they have difficulties surviving (1). Accept any other relevant responses.	4
7	One mark for each suggestion (up to a maximum of two) that shows understanding of the benefits of taiga biomes for people. Must be biome related. **Indicative content** • timber supply (softwoods for construction or paper making) • diversity for scientific study of wildlife and adaptations to climate change • recreation and tourism to experience and appreciate the wildlife • water regulation (interception and absorption) by forests. Do not credit vague statements such as 'see animals' or 'go on holiday to'. Accept any other relevant answer.	2
8	Answers should concentrate on causes. Up to two marks for basic explanations, and a further two marks for extended explanations. **Indicative content** • One cause of deforestation is wildfires caused by natural lightning strikes, or artificial fires caused by people camping in the taiga. • One cause of deforestation is the desire of logging and timber companies to make money. They may clear large areas of forest to get valuable softwoods such as pine. • One cause of deforestation is a government's desire to obtain cheap energy for its people and industries by extracting oil and gas from the land under the taiga forest. Accept any other relevant answer.	4
9	Answer must evaluate and not just describe and explain. **Indicative content** • Area or region of taiga forest should be identified e.g. Canada, Russia. • The range of threats faced by a taiga forest from climate change should be explained. • An assessment of the seriousness of each threat through their impacts should be included, such as loss of biodiversity, change to local climate, extinction of species, increased storm damage, increase in number of wildfires, spread of pests and diseases, melting of sporadic permafrost areas. • The range of human activities that benefit the tropical rainforest such as national parks, wildlife reserves, conservation organisations, debt-for-nature swaps. • An assessment of the extent to which some threats may be beneficial. • Judgment on the extent to which threats are serious, considering the balance of short-term and long-term damage and change. • Consideration of data about the selected area or region of taiga forest. **Level 0, no marks** • No relevant response. **Level 1 (Basic) 1–3 marks** • Attempts to apply understanding to deconstruct information but understanding and connections are flawed. An unbalanced or incomplete argument that provides limited synthesis of understanding. Judgments are supported by limited evidence. (AO3) • Demonstrates isolated elements of understanding of concepts and the interrelationship of places, environments and processes. (AO2) **Level 2 (Clear) 4–6 marks** • Applies understanding to deconstruct information and provide some logical connections between concepts. An imbalanced argument that synthesises mostly relevant understanding but not entirely coherently, leading to judgments that are supported by evidence occasionally. (AO3) • Demonstrates elements of understanding of concepts and the interrelationship of places, environments and processes. (AO2)	8

Exam Practice Answers

Q	Marking guidance	Marks
10	**Level 3 (Detailed) 7–8 marks** • Applies understanding to deconstruct information and provide logical connections between concepts throughout. A balanced, well-developed argument that synthesises relevant understanding coherently, leading to judgments that are supported by evidence throughout. (AO3) • Demonstrates accurate understanding of concepts and the interrelationship of places, environments and processes. (AO2) Answer must assess and not simply describe. **Indicative content** • Responses must present management methods and rate their success or potential success. • There should be evidence that the candidate knows Taiga forest locations and specific ways of managing this forest area. • Methods should be clear and specific, showing understanding, such as: National parks (e.g. Banff), wilderness area designations, wildlife reserves (e.g. Arctic National Wildlife Reserve in Alaska, USA); agreeing to international Arctic treaties or developing new international agreements to protect Arctic areas; practising sustainable forestry; laws and regulations of countries and provinces. • Comparison of the different management methods and a judgment on their relative success. • Evidence must be used to support judgments made. **Level 0, no marks** • No relevant response. **Level 1 (Basic) 1–3 marks** • Demonstrates isolated elements of understanding of concepts and the interrelationship of places, environments and processes. (AO2) • Attempts to apply understanding to deconstruct information but understanding and connections are flawed. An unbalanced or incomplete argument that provides limited synthesis of understanding. Judgments are supported by limited evidence. (AO3) **Level 2 (Clear) 4–6 marks** • Demonstrates elements of understanding of concepts and the interrelationship of places, environments and processes. (AO2) • Applies understanding to deconstruct information and provide some logical connections between concepts. An imbalanced argument that synthesises mostly relevant understanding but not entirely coherently, leading to judgments that are supported by evidence occasionally. (AO3) **Level 3 (Detailed) 7–8 marks** • Demonstrates accurate understanding of concepts and the interrelationship of places, environments and processes. (AO2) • Applies understanding to deconstruct information and provide logical connections between concepts throughout. A balanced, well-developed argument that synthesises relevant understanding coherently, leading to judgments that are supported by evidence throughout. (AO3)	8

	Consuming energy resources: Energy resources	
Q	Marking guidance	Marks
1	One mark for correct definition, do not credit example on its own. **Indicative content** A recyclable energy resource is one that can be reused, perhaps after processing or renewing, and so lasts longer. An example is biofuels where the plants used are replanted and regrown.	1
2	One mark for each correct environmental impact, up to a maximum of two marks. **Indicative content** • Radioactivity released by an accident at a nuclear power station. • Scars in the landscape for mining the uranium ore. • Radioactivity leaks from nuclear waste storage sites. • Cooling water is returned to natural areas at a much higher temperature, harming wildlife.	2
3	Must be a description of distribution. Credit observations based on the map provided. One mark for basic description, such as: • More in northern hemisphere. • Most in areas with volcanoes. Second mark for developed point using detail from the map, such as: • Northern hemisphere areas such as USA, Iceland, Italy, Japan have a lot of geothermal energy, while South America and most of Africa have little. • Countries and regions with destructive plate boundaries such as New Zealand and SE Asia have geothermal energy. • Countries and regions with constructive plate boundaries such as Iceland and Kenya have geothermal energy.	2
4	One valid reason should be given, such as: • New Zealand is on a plate boundary so magma is near the surface to provide heat. • New Zealand is an HIC and therefore has the money and technology available to develop geothermal energy. No credit for vague statements such as: has volcanoes; is a rich country.	1

Q	Marking guidance	Marks
5	One mark for correctly drawn bar. Shading not essential to gain mark.	1
6	**A** 3.5% No credit if two or more answers are shaded.	1
7	**C** 40–59% No credit if two or more answers are shaded.	1
8	The focus of the question is on where the distribution of energy access and security is high and where it is lower in South America. One mark for basic description from the map, such as: • There are some countries with high and some with low. • There is a random distribution pattern from high to quite low. Second mark for developing a point with detail from the map, such as: • There is one country (Colombia) in the high category over 80%, and three countries in each of the other categories apart from the lowest (0–19%) where there are none. • The countries are split evenly between the categories with no distinct geographical pattern. There are three between 60–79% (e.g. Brazil), three between 40–59% (e.g. Peru), and three between 20–39% (e.g. Venezuela). Only one country in the high category. Names of countries not expected. No credit if wrong continent used or just listing of countries.	2
9	Two marks for basic explanation, with two further marks for extended explanation. **Indicative content** • An understanding of energy insecurity and its impacts should be indicated in the answer. Impacts include removing people, environmental damage, food production, industrial output, disputes/conflict and social unrest. • Responses should focus on the difficulties caused for poorer people by a selection of impacts. • Expect some development of at least one situation where there have been energy insecurity issues for poorer people. • As energy runs out there are pressures to expand exploration, extraction and production. Some of the locations chosen for this impact on poorer people, such as the Inuit in the Arctic or the Nanti in Peru. Poorer people may be forced to move from their homes because of flooding behind an HEP dam, or gas pipeline construction. • When there are energy shortages prices go up and poorer people cannot afford to buy enough energy for their needs. This affects the quality of their life and small businesses such as workshops and crafts. • Factories may be forced to close if they do not have energy to operate; people lose their jobs and have no money. • Energy is regarded by many as a modern essential and there is a lot of money involved so people may fight over it, often it is the poor people who are caught in the middle of conflicts (e.g. Iraq).	4
10	One mark for each reason given, one further mark for each expanded explanation, up to a maximum of two reasons (four marks). **Indicative content** • World population has grown and so therefore more energy is needed (e.g. for cooking, heating). • People are getting wealthier, even in developing countries and especially in emerging countries, and therefore people are demanding more energy for different purposes in their homes and lives (e.g. appliances, gadgets, cars). • Industries and businesses are expanding as the world develops economically and all of these need energy for factories, offices and transport.	4
Work It!	**A** 1:0.26	1

	Consuming energy resources: Oil	
Q	Marking guidance	Marks
1	One mark for basic comparison, two marks for extended comparison. Expect some data to be used from Figure 6. **Indicative content** • Saudi Arabia and USA appear in both top 5 lists, so they not only produce a lot of oil but they also use a lot, although Saudi Arabia uses much less than it produces while it appears that USA uses more than it produces. • Three of the top 5 producing countries are from the Middle East (Saudi Arabia, Iran and Iraq) while the top 5 consumers are spread throughout the world – North America, Middle East, South Asia and 2 from East Asia. • Russia produces a large percentage of oil (12.2%) but does not appear in the top 5 consumers and so must use less than 3.8% of the world total oil consumption. Accept any other relevant responses.	2

Q	Marking guidance	Marks
2	Answer must evaluate and not just describe and explain. **Indicative content** • Examples of unstable international relations and/or conflicts which have affected oil prices should be included within answer (e.g. Gulf Wars). • The range of instability and conflict situations, such as how frequent and how serious they need to be to have an effect. • An assessment of the role of instability and conflict on oil prices, such as the time delay in change, the recovery time and the amount of change. • The economic processes that lead to a range of price changes from decreases to increases, including the role of OPEC. • Judgment on the extent to which instability and conflict threaten oil supplies and prices, considering the trends over time. • Consideration of data about oil reserves, locations, supply and demand and the nature of oil as a finite fossil fuel. • Comparison of instability and conflict with other influences of world oil prices, such as economic recession and boom cycles. **Level 0, no marks** • No relevant response. **Level 1 (Basic) 1–3 marks** • Attempts to apply understanding to deconstruct information but understanding and connections are flawed. An unbalanced or incomplete argument that provides limited synthesis of understanding. Judgments are supported by limited evidence. (AO3) • Demonstrates isolated elements of understanding of concepts and the interrelationship of places, environments and processes. (AO2) **Level 2 (Clear) 4–6 marks** • Applies understanding to deconstruct information and provide some logical connections between concepts. An imbalanced argument that synthesises mostly relevant understanding but not entirely coherently, leading to judgments that are supported by evidence occasionally. (AO3) • Demonstrates elements of understanding of concepts and the interrelationship of places, environments and processes. (AO2) **Level 3 (Detailed) 7–8 marks** • Applies understanding to deconstruct information and provide logical connections between concepts throughout. A balanced, well-developed argument that synthesises relevant understanding coherently, leading to judgments that are supported by evidence throughout. (AO3) • Demonstrates accurate understanding of concepts and the interrelationship of places, environments and processes. (AO2)	8
3	Answer must assess and not simply describe. **Indicative content** • Responses must present conventional extraction methods and rate their advantages compared to the disadvantages of operations in environmentally sensitive areas. • There should be evidence that the candidate knows locations where conventional extraction is taking place in sensitive areas (such as the Alaskan Arctic). • Advantages should be clear and specific, showing understanding, such as: most accessible oil and natural gas has been found and exploited already; demand in an economically developing world is increasing; exports and foreign currency earnings can be made from new resources; new long-term reserves can be developed; new jobs created along with linked services in remote areas. • Comparison of the different advantages and a judgment on their relative importance, considering the potential damage to sensitive areas. • Evidence must be used to support judgments made. **Level 0, no marks** • No relevant response. **Level 1 (Basic) 1–3 marks** • Demonstrates isolated elements of understanding of concepts and the interrelationship of places, environments and processes. (AO2) • Attempts to apply understanding to deconstruct information but understanding and connections are flawed. An unbalanced or incomplete argument that provides limited synthesis of understanding. Judgments are supported by limited evidence. (AO3) **Level 2 (Clear) 4–6 marks** • Demonstrates elements of understanding of concepts and the interrelationship of places, environments and processes. (AO2) • Applies understanding to deconstruct information and provide some logical connections between concepts. An imbalanced argument that synthesises mostly relevant understanding but not entirely coherently, leading to judgments that are supported by evidence occasionally. (AO3) **Level 3 (Detailed) 7–8 marks** • Demonstrates accurate understanding of concepts and the interrelationship of places, environments and processes. (AO2) • Applies understanding to deconstruct information and provide logical connections between concepts throughout. A balanced, well-developed argument that synthesises relevant understanding coherently, leading to judgments that are supported by evidence throughout. (AO3)	8

Q	Marking guidance	Marks
4	Answer must assess and not simply describe. **Indicative content** • Responses must present unconventional extraction methods and rate their disadvantages compared to the advantages of operations in environmentally sensitive areas. • There should be evidence that the candidate knows locations where unconventional extraction is taking place in sensitive areas (such as the Athabascan oil (tar) sands). • Disadvantages should be clear and specific, showing understanding, such as: fracking damages local and area water quality through contamination; fracking causes small earthquakes and creates ground instability; open pit mining removes large areas of natural vegetation; open pit mining removes a lot of topsoil; accidental spillages damage wildlife; large scale water abstraction. • Comparison of the different disadvantages and a judgment on their relative importance, considering the potential damage to sensitive areas. • Evidence must be used to support judgments made. **Level 0, no marks** • No relevant response. **Level 1 (Basic) 1–3 marks** • Demonstrates isolated elements of understanding of concepts and the interrelationship of places, environments and processes. (AO2) • Attempts to apply understanding to deconstruct information but understanding and connections are flawed. An unbalanced or incomplete argument that provides limited synthesis of understanding. Judgments are supported by limited evidence. (AO3) **Level 2 (Clear) 4–6 marks** • Demonstrates elements of understanding of concepts and the interrelationship of places, environments and processes. (AO2) • Applies understanding to deconstruct information and provide some logical connections between concepts. An imbalanced argument that synthesises mostly relevant understanding but not entirely coherently, leading to judgments that are supported by evidence occasionally. (AO3) **Level 3 (Detailed) 7–8 marks** • Demonstrates accurate understanding of concepts and the interrelationship of places, environments and processes. (AO2) • Applies understanding to deconstruct information and provide logical connections between concepts throughout. A balanced, well-developed argument that synthesises relevant understanding coherently, leading to judgments that are supported by evidence throughout. (AO3)	8

Consuming energy resources: Strategies to reduce energy demand		
Q	**Marking guidance**	**Marks**
1	Two ways explained with two marks available for each; within each one mark for basic explanation and second for extended explanation. Do not credit only descriptive listing. **Indicative content** • Insulation within walls and in foundations of houses prevents heat loss from homes, so reducing the amount of energy needed and used to heat homes in the winter months. • Energy efficient appliances, from washing machines to light bulbs, reduces the amount of electricity used and makes supplies more sustainable and less electricity needs to be generated. Accept any other relevant response.	4
2	Up to two marks for basic comparison, with a further two marks for extended comparison. Must compare and not just list problems. **Indicative content** • Hydrogen has been suggested as a future renewable energy source but its main problem is that the hydrogen gas still needs an initial energy source to create it, and if this energy source consists of fossil fuels then it is still creating a carbon footprint which damages the environment. • One of solar energy's main problems also damages the environment, for example some of the materials used in its construction are toxic, such as mercury, lead and cadmium. • Solar energy needs a lot of space to be able to produce efficient electricity, this uses up farmland or fragile environments, while hydrogen uses up less space it has the problems of being flammable and technologies for safe storage and use. Accept any other relevant response.	4
WorkIt!	See 'key ideas' for answer.	4
3	One mark for basic definition, two marks for full definition. **Indicative content** The amount of carbon that someone puts into the atmosphere (1). A measurement of the carbon dioxide (and other greenhouse gases) that an individual, family, business or country emits into the atmosphere through their activities (2).	2
4	**C** 500 to 2000 Mtoe	1

Exam Practice Answers

Q	Marking guidance	Marks
5	One mark for basic description, with a further mark for extended description with reference to figures. **Indicative content** • Peru/Chile/Ecuador / western area of South America are low consumers of energy, below 50 Mtoe, while eastern area (particularly Brazil) are higher consumers of energy, between 100 and 500 Mtoe. • Brazil as an emerging economy is a much higher consumer of energy compared to developing economies such as Peru and Chile. Accept any other relevant response.	2
6	Up to two marks for basic explanation, with a further two marks for extended explanation. **Indicative content** • People in developed countries use a lot of energy and therefore wish for energy security, if their supplies are regular and relatively inexpensive then they would not want to risk change that may lead to energy shortages ('business as usual' scenario). • People in developed countries are relatively wealthy and use a lot of transport based on oil, such as cars and aeroplanes, they would not want their lifestyle to change as they like to have the freedoms associated with private transport and they like to fly to go on holidays. • Governments may be concerned with maintaining economic growth, and therefore want reliable affordable energy which means using tried and trusted technologies and energy supplies. Accept any other relevant response.	4
7	Up to two marks for basic reasoning, with a further two marks for extended reasoning. **Indicative content** • There is concern about the production of CO_2 through burning fossil fuels, so one way to reduce emissions is to increase production of electricity from renewable energy sources such as wind and solar. • The UK government have provided incentives for the development of renewable sources, such as offshore wind farms, and more of these facilities have been installed. • Renewable technologies have improved a lot and it is now more feasible to produce cheap electricity from sources such as solar and wind, therefore these are taking over from more conventional energy production methods. Accept any other relevant response.	4
8	Two marks for basic reasons behind the suggestions, with two further marks for extended reasoning. **Indicative content** • Candidates should demonstrate their knowledge and understanding of the energy debate to emphasise the role of sustainable energy supplies. Use should be made of the Figure. • Icelink involves undersea electricity cables directly from Iceland to the UK, Norway and Germany. Iceland produces electricity by using geothermal energy (over 500 MW installed) – a renewable and sustainable source. • The energy mix of most European countries, such as the UK, only includes a small proportion of renewable energy sources and still is heavily dependent on fossil fuels. There needs to be a greater diversification into renewables for the future for the benefit of the natural environment but also to achieve energy security. • Countries like Norway and the UK have depended on North Sea oil and natural gas and energy diversification is needed. Most northerly European countries have more limited opportunities for solar energy, but do use wind energy. A geothermal energy source would be an important addition to the future energy mix. • Energy demands have been increasing in countries such as Germany due to growth of tertiary industries and consumers as more electrical gadgets are being used. • Imports of energy from Iceland would avoid some of the negative issues associated with developing renewable energy sources in the UK such as bioenergy and solar farms using up cropland, wind turbines spoiling the scenery and causing deaths of birds.	4

Paper 1: Global geographical issues

Section A: Hazardous Earth		
Q	**Marking guidance**	**Marks**
1 a (i)	**C** Ice cores	1
1 a (ii)	**A** Methane **E** Carbon dioxide	2

1 b	One mark for a natural cause of climate change and one further mark for expanding on the point, up to a maximum of two points and four marks. Natural causes of climate change include:
	• Changes in the orbit of Earth (1) over long periods of time, such as:
	  • eccentricity, where the orbit shape changes from circular to elliptical; more elliptical orbits may cause ice ages (1)
	  • precession, the natural wobble of the Earth on its axis, which may change the length of the seasons in different parts of the globe (1)
		4

Q	Marking guidance	Marks

	• tilt, where the angle of the Earth's axis of rotation to the Sun changes, meaning parts of the Earth may have changes in the amount of the Sun's energy that falls on them (1).
	• Changes in the output of the Sun (1), linked to the number of sunspots that appear, which changes over an 11-year period, meaning the Earth may be warmer or cooler over this cycle (1).
	• Volcanic activity (1), either:
	  • because ash from volcanic eruptions can stay in the atmosphere for a long time and may partially block sunlight, changing temperatures (1)
	  • or sulfur dioxide emitted by volcanic eruptions mixes with water in the air to form sulfuric acid, which reflects the Sun's radiation and may reduce temperatures (1).
	• Asteroid collisions (1), which can cause large amounts of ash and dust to be thrown into the atmosphere, blocking sunlight and affecting temperatures (1).	

1 c	Warm air rises at the equator, creating an area of low pressure (1) due to the air expanding and becoming lighter (1). Colder, denser air sinks, creating areas of high pressure (1). Air moves from high to low pressure, carrying heat energy with it (1).	4
1 d	Answer must be purely descriptive and use direction in answer, such as: Hurricane Katrina initially travelled northwards, then travelled in a westerly direction before heading northwards again. Hurricane Katrina travelled in a westerly direction before heading northwards.	2
1 e	**C** Saffir Simpson scale	1
1 f	**A** Weather forecasting	1
1 g	Reasons should include both a statement of a difference between countries, and how that difference affects their responses to a tropical cyclone. **Indicative content** • Tropical cyclones only form in the tropics, so tropical countries are more vulnerable (1). • Tropical cyclones gain strength over the sea and lose strength as they travel over land, meaning that islands and coastal countries are most vulnerable (1). • Developed countries tend to have better systems and technology for predicting tropical cyclones, so they are likely to be better prepared than developing countries (1). • Developed countries have better communications and transport infrastructure than developing countries, so are more likely to evacuate or protect people from a tropical cyclone (1). • Developed countries are wealthier than developing countries, so usually can more effectively protect from or recover from the effects of a tropical cyclone (1).	4
1 h	At a divergent plate margin, two plates are moving apart (1). As the two plates move apart, magma rises up through the gap forming between the two plates (1). In some places, the magma breaks through the crust to form a volcano (1).	3
1 i	**Indicative content** AO2 • Impacts are worse because of high vulnerability in developing countries. • Economic impacts in developed countries can be worse because infrastructure is more expensive to replace. • Impacts can be worse in developing countries because of low capacity to cope. • Countries on plate boundaries may be on different plate boundaries and therefore maybe affected by different tectonic hazards (at different levels of severity). • Hazards also happen away from boundaries/have different areas of extent, e.g. coastal locations (tsunami) or hillslopes (landslides), possibly hotspots/ global effects of volcanoes (ash clouds). AO3 • Judgment about whether impact is measured by economic or social loss. • Judgment about long-term vs short-term impact. • Judgment about whether impact on the environment compared to people. • Judgment about whether the impact is higher because of magnitude or vulnerability. • Judgment about whether impact is worse because of physical environment, e.g. plate boundary location or human environment (vulnerability). **Level 0, no marks** • No acceptable response. **Level 1 (Basic) 1–3 marks** • Demonstrates isolated elements of understanding of concepts and the interrelationship of places, environments and processes. (AO2) • Attempts to apply understanding to deconstruct information but understanding and connections are flawed. • An unbalanced or incomplete argument that provides limited synthesis of understanding. Judgments are supported by limited evidence. (AO3)	8

Q	Marking guidance	Marks
	Level 2 (Clear) 4–6 marks • Demonstrates elements of understanding of concepts and the interrelationship of places, environments and processes. (AO2) • Applies understanding to deconstruct information and provide some logical connections between concepts. • An imbalanced argument that synthesises mostly relevant understanding but not entirely coherently, leading to judgments that are supported by evidence occasionally. (AO3) **Level 3 (Detailed) 7–8 marks** • Demonstrates accurate understanding of concepts and the interrelationship of places, environments and processes. (AO2) • Applies understanding to deconstruct information and provide logical connections between concepts throughout. • A balanced, well-developed argument that synthesises relevant understanding coherently, leading to judgments that are supported by evidence throughout. (AO3)	

Section B: Development dynamics		
Q	Marking guidance	Marks
2 a (i)	**C** The measure combining economic and social factors.	1
2 a (ii)	Credit for one way only. **Indicative content** • Adult literacy rate reflects the way of life of the population; if the country is still developing then children are usually expected to help the family or work from a young age and not go to school. • Adult literacy reflects the amount of money invested by a country in education (schools). A low adult literacy rate perhaps reflects a poor country still trying to develop economically. • Adult literacy rate reflects how well educated the workforce of a country is, and this shows how well they can help the businesses and industries of a country grow to make money and help a country develop.	2
2 b	Responses should focus on the differences (or similarities) between Europe and SE Asia in respect of life expectancies. There must be a comparison. Expect statements backed by data from the map. • Life expectancy is generally higher in Europe than SE Asia. • Many countries in Europe have life expectancies over 77 years while SE Asia they are mostly between 62.8 and 77. • Europe has a west-east divide (longer life expectancy in west) while SE Asia has a north/centre-south/periphery divide (longer in north/centre). No credit for statements about other parts of the world. Credit reference to countries within Europe and SE Asia.	2
2 c (i)	Student task: A best-fit line should bisect the points so that there are roughly equal numbers on each side.	1
2 c (ii)	**Indicative content** • Responses must make links between IMR levels and quality of life. • Developed countries tend to have low infant mortality rates because there are better living conditions, such as hygiene levels, which mean that babies are not affected by diseases as much. Developing countries have high infant mortality rates partly because hygiene levels are lower due to lack of understanding and so quality of life is lower. • Developed countries have lower infant mortality rates because money is spent on health care systems, which ensure that more babies are born healthy and medicines are available in case they get ill. Developing countries have less money available for health care and medicines and so babies are not as well looked after due to the lower quality of life. • Education levels are higher in developed than developing countries and therefore mothers/parents understand basic health care and the need for clean water and hygiene in developed countries and this lowers the infant mortality rate.	4
2 d (i)	**B** 8.32 per cent	1
2 d (ii)	No explanation required; credit description and use of Figure 3. • The population pyramid for India in 2017 is wider near the base than at the top, with a slight narrowing in the 0–9 age group. Sometimes called a 'bell shape'. It is widest in the 10–19 age group, which has just under 19 per cent of the total population. Numbers decrease quite rapidly after the 30–39 age group.	2
2 d (iii)	**Indicative content** Suggestions may include: • Very large population size, especially amongst the working population, so people will have problems finding jobs and there may be problems feeding the population. • There will be an ageing population because people are living longer as health and living conditions improve. So there will be a lot of people that need supporting by families or the government. • There is a gender imbalance, with more males and females in the younger age groups and working age groups, for example, nearly a 1 per cent difference in the 10–19 age group. This will make it difficult for men to get married and may cause a cultural change, and even tensions, violence or a large-scale emigration of males (or perhaps female immigration).	4

Q	Marking guidance	Marks
2 e	Countries go through stages of development, for example, 'take-off', **or:** All countries will develop to the final stage; they are just at different stages now.	1
2 f	**Indicative content** Two points well developed. International aid can help a country to develop by: • Providing finance for large-scale or small-scale schemes, such as infrastructure projects (e.g. HEP dams) so that local industries and businesses can grow. • Providing expertise to help with development of businesses and industries to be able to use latest technologies and increase efficiency or with services such as health care and schools to produce a healthier and better educated workforce. • Providing money for schemes aimed at improving the quality of life of the population, such as provision of primary schools, advice on birth control, advice on gender equality, provision of health care (including vaccinations and medicines). • Expect the multiplier effect to be mentioned.	4
2 g	**AO2 (4 marks)/AO3 (4 marks)** **Indicative content** (Assess how far…) AO2 – Demonstrate understanding • India has increased its geopolitical influence due to economic growth and potential. • India is surrounded by six other countries, although historically it has not had close ties with these due to religious differences and sometimes wars (e.g. with Pakistan), economic development has enabled India to recently dominate in South Asia and lead economically. • India's new wealth has turned it into a provider of aid, such as to Sri Lanka and Nepal. • India is a member of the UN and the G20 group that tries to resolve world economic issues. • India has become a major trading partner of other countries, such as the USA with whom it also has a defence agreement. • Since independence, India has been a member of the Commonwealth. Economic growth has increased its political power and enabled it to become a leader within the Commonwealth, representing developing countries. AO3 – Apply knowledge and understanding • India was ranked seventh in terms of GDP in 2016 and is predicted to be only behind China and the USA by 2030. This wealth has enabled it to work with other BRICS countries to set up the New Development Bank, which aims to help developing countries with loans for eco-friendly technologies and transport projects. It also plays a key role in the South Asian Association for Regional Cooperation (SAARC). • India has always had a key position between Europe and East Asia, and with new expanded ports (e.g. Kandla) it has increased its international trading (exports were $262 billion in 2015–16). Indian TNCs now operate around the world (e.g. Tata Steel, which employs 46 000 people abroad). Other Indian companies have provided FDI to other countries, such as Ireland, Netherlands, Belgium and Canada. • But there are other factors besides economic growth that influence India's international role. Such as having an English-speaking population, which has enabled greater involvement internationally, especially as this is the language used in business, industry and a lot of politics. Also the emigration of Indians over many decades, such as to the UK, in search of higher paid jobs and better quality of life has spread links and influences around the world. **Level 0, no marks** • No acceptable response. **Level 1 (Basic) 1–3 marks** • Demonstrates isolated elements of understanding of concepts and the interrelationship of places, environments and processes. (AO2) • Attempts to apply understanding to deconstruct information but understanding and connections are flawed. An unbalanced or incomplete argument that provides limited synthesis of understanding. Judgments are supported by limited evidence. (AO3) **Level 2 (Clear) 4–6 marks** • Demonstrates elements of understanding of concepts and the interrelationship of places, environments and processes. (AO2) • Applies understanding to deconstruct information and provide some logical connections between concepts. An imbalanced argument that synthesises mostly relevant understanding but not entirely coherently, leading to judgments that are supported by evidence occasionally. (AO3) **Level 3 (Detailed) 7–8 marks** • Demonstrates accurate understanding of concepts and the interrelationship of places, environments and processes. (AO2) • Applies understanding to deconstruct information and provide logical connections between concepts throughout. A balanced, well-developed argument that synthesises relevant understanding coherently, leading to judgments that are supported by evidence throughout. (AO3)	8

Exam Practice Answers

Q	Marking guidance	Marks
2 g SPaG	**SPaG 0, no marks** • Learners write nothing. • Learner's response does not relate to the question. • Learner's achievement in SPaG does not reach the threshold performance level, for example, errors in spelling, punctuation and grammar severely hinder meaning. **SPaG 1 (Threshold performance) 1 mark** • Learners spell and punctuate with reasonable accuracy. • Learners use rules of grammar with some control of meaning and any errors do not significantly hinder meaning overall. • Learners use a limited range of specialist terms as appropriate. **SPaG 2 (Intermediate performance) 2–3 marks** • Learners spell and punctuate with considerable accuracy. • Learners use rules of grammar with general control of meaning overall. • Learners use a good range of specialist terms as appropriate. **SPaG 3 (High performance) 4 marks** • Learners spell and punctuate with consistent accuracy. • Learners use rules of grammar with effective control of meaning overall. • Learners use a wide range of specialist terms as appropriate.	4

	Section C: Challenges of an urbanising world	
Q	**Marking guidance**	**Marks**
3 a (i)	800 000 – 6 300 000 = 5 500 000 Accept a range from 5 200 000 to 5 700 000	1
3 a (ii)	The population of urban areas increased at a slow rate from 1950 until 1980, when it started to increase rapidly from 2 million to 4 million by 2015. From 1980, the rural population started to decline slowly.	2
3 b (i)	The increase in proportion of people living in urban areas.	1
3 b (ii)	Rural-urban migration: people migrating into cities from rural areas (1). Natural increase: higher birth rates than death rates due to migrants being young and starting families (1).	2
3 c	Commercial / central business district	1
3 d	One mark for stating general point and up to two further marks for development of the point, such as the following. • Desire for more living space (1), as inner cities become crowded (1) and as people's wealth develops, so does desire for higher standard of living outside the inner city (1). • Desire to find cleaner/less polluted area in which to live (1), as the busy inner cities attract more vehicles causing pollution (1) and people leaving waste behind (1). • Greater wealth of some workers (1) means they can afford to buy bigger properties/more land (1) that is usually found in the suburbs/away from the inner city (1).	3
3 e	Must have named megacity, e.g. Mumbai or New York. Can be developed or developing. Ideas from: Mumbai CBD based at the tip of the peninsula, near the main port. Industrial areas surround the port with wealthy residential areas near to the CBD, edge of the city has sprawling squatter settlements. Navi Mumbai is a new suburban area on the outskirts of Mumbai.	4
3 f	One mark for statement of each difference, one further mark for expansion of the point, up to a maximum of two points, four marks. Any ideas from: formal workers pay tax (1) because employers are formally registered e.g. companies (1); formal workers have workers' rights (1) such as set working hours, holiday and sick pay but informal workers do not (1); formal workers receive a regular, predictable wage (1) but informal workers receive money only after a particular job has been completed (1).	4
3 g	Meets the needs of the local communities, small scale approach, involves local people in decision making, low cost, low technology, trickle-down effect, e.g. clean water pump, means less time collecting water, less disease and therefore able to work or go to school.	4
3 h	**Indicative content** Social effects • Growth of squatter settlements on edges of cities. • Rapid increase in population creating demand for housing and services. • Problems created in squatter settlements such as poor-quality housing, poor sanitation, open sewers, lack of water and electricity. • Increase in informal sector jobs with low pay and lack of workers' rights. • Pressure on employment in city with high rates of unemployment or increase in sweatshops. • Some improvements in education and access to health care better than rural areas.	8

Q	Marking guidance	Marks
	Environmental effects • Issues of increased population creating waste. • More people driving cars means more air pollution. • More people wanting jobs in factories leads to more waste dumped in rivers. • Waste from squatter settlements dumped into the rivers. **Level 0, no marks** No acceptable response = 0 marks. **Level 1 (Basic) 1–3 marks** • Demonstrates some knowledge of effects of rapid population growth in cities. (AO1) • Shows limited geographical understanding of the different social or environmental effects. Likely to be more negative than positive. (AO2) **Level 2 (Clear) 4–6 marks** • Demonstrates specific and accurate knowledge of social and environmental effects of rapid population growth. (AO2) • Shows clear geographical understanding of both social and environmental effects but may be more focused on one. May recognise the benefits also created. (AO3) **Level 3 (Detailed) 7–8 marks** • Demonstrates thorough application of knowledge and understanding to give detailed explanations of social and environmental effects of population growth on a named city. (AO3) • Shows full understanding of social and environmental effects. Will give some explanation of challenges and benefits created by rapid growth and offer a conclusion. (AO3)	

Paper 2: UK geographical issues

	Section A: The UK's evolving physical landscape	
Q	**Marking guidance**	**Marks**
1 a	**B** A U-shaped valley formed by a glacier.	1
1 b	**D** Freeze-thaw weathering.	1
1 c	One mark for a reason and the second mark for an extension, from the following: • Igneous rocks are more resistant rocks (1), which cause upland areas in North West England and Scotland (1). • Weaker sedimentary rock e.g. clay is more easily eroded (1) and creates lowland areas in south east England (1).	2
2 a	One mark each. Feature A: Arch Feature B: Stack	2
2 b	One mark for a reason and the second mark for an extension. **Indicative content** • Sub-aerial processes such as freeze thaw weathering weaken the cliff (1) which can cause mass movement (1). • Rain water saturates into permeable rock (1) this adds weight to the rock making it too weak to support itself (1).	2
2 c	One mark for key point on formation (longshore drift) and up to three further marks for explanation of point. **Indicative content** • Longshore drift carries sediment along the coastline (1) to a place where there is a change in the shape of the landscape, for example a headland or a river estuary, which changes speed or direction of flow causing deposition (1). • Deposition rates are faster than erosion and a sandy neck forms as a spit (1). • The spit will stop growing where deposition is in balance with erosion (1).	4
3 a	Upper course.	1
3 b	One mark for a reason, one further mark for a developed explanation. Maximum two reasons, four marks. **Indicative content** • Continuous heavy rainfall can lead to flash flooding (1) as the ground becomes saturated and surface runoff increases (1). • Impermeable rock increases surface runoff (1), which increases the rate at which water reaches a river (1). • Waterlogged soil doesn't allow water to infiltrate (1), which increases surface runoff (1). • Deforestation decreases the amount of interception (1), so rainfall can get to rivers quicker (1). • Urbanisation increases the amount of impermeable surfaces (1), which increases speed at which water reaches rivers (1).	4
3 c	One mark for a reason and the second mark for an extension. • Land use change can replace fields with buildings and roads (1), which increases runoff and reduces the lag time (1). • Deforestation reduces infiltration and interception (1) which can increase peak discharge (1) and/or reduce the lag time (1).	2

Q	Marking guidance	Marks
4	**Indicative content** AO2 • Coastal management will protect coastlines from retreat. • Not everywhere will be protected, so some areas will benefit but others lose out by not being protected and paying tax for coastal management. • It is an expensive process. • Some areas will not be protected because it is not cost effective. AO3 • Coastal erosion could increase in the future due to climate change so coastal management will become more expensive. • Understanding of which areas are more likely to not be protected, e.g. areas of low land value. **Level 0, no marks** • No acceptable response. **Level 1 (Basic) 1–3 marks** • Attempts to apply understanding to deconstruct information but understanding and connections are flawed. An unbalanced or incomplete argument that provides limited synthesis of understanding. Judgments that are supported by limited evidence. (AO3) • Uses some geographical skills to obtain information with limited relevance and accuracy, which supports few aspects of the argument. (AO4) **Level 2 (Clear) 4–6 marks** • Applies understanding to deconstruct information and provide some logical connections between concepts. An imbalanced argument that synthesises mostly relevant understanding, but not entirely coherently, leading to judgments that are supported by evidence occasionally. (AO3) • Uses geographical skills to obtain accurate information that supports some aspects of the argument. (AO4) **Level 3 (Detailed) 7–8 marks** • Applies understanding to deconstruct information and provide logical connections between concepts throughout. A balanced, well-developed argument that synthesises relevant understanding coherently leading to judgments that are supported by evidence throughout. (AO3) • Uses geographical skills to obtain accurate information that supports all aspects of the argument. (AO4)	8
4 SPaG	**SPaG 0, no marks** • Learners write nothing. • Learner's response does not relate to the question. • Learner's achievement in SPaG does not reach the threshold performance level, for example, errors in spelling, punctuation and grammar severely hinder meaning. **SPaG 1 (Threshold performance) 1 mark** • Learners spell and punctuate with reasonable accuracy. • Learners use rules of grammar with some control of meaning and any errors do not significantly hinder meaning overall. • Learners use a limited range of specialist terms as appropriate. **SPaG 2 (Intermediate performance) 2–3 marks** • Learners spell and punctuate with considerable accuracy. • Learners use rules of grammar with general control of meaning overall. • Learners use a good range of specialist terms as appropriate. **SPaG 3 (High performance) 4 marks** • Learners spell and punctuate with consistent accuracy. • Learners use rules of grammar with effective control of meaning overall. • Learners use a wide range of specialist terms as appropriate.	4

	Section B: The UK's evolving human landscape	
Q	Marking guidance	Marks
5 a	**C** Mostly in South-East England.	1
5 b	Ideas such as: High levels of economic activity means lots of jobs (1); closest area to the capital city means lots of entertainment and leisure (1).	1
5 c	Richmond has a higher quality of life and a lower level of deprivation than Newham. People in Richmond live to 83 on average compared to 77 in Newham, which indicates differences in health and lifestyle between Richmond and Newham. A higher percentage of pupils get A*–C grades in Richmond at 70 per cent compared to 57 per cent in Newham due to quality of the schools in Richmond.	4
5 d	Higher life expectancy in Richmond due to increased wealth means money spent on a healthier lifestyle such as gym membership and healthier food and diet. More likely to work in professional / tertiary sector rather than manufacturing or manual labour. Less likely to smoke.	4
6 a	Accessibility is important for goods to come in and out of the business (raw materials in for processing and finished product out for selling), employees able to easily access work by road or rail, access for external customers or clients to come into the business.	2

Q	Marking guidance	Marks
6 b	Pressure on housing as more people means more demand for new housing, which means developing new land for housing. Increased demand leads to rises in prices. Pressure on services such as schools and health care or leisure facilities with an increase in people.	2
6 c	Decline in traditional primary industry: closure of mines and quarries means a decline in local employment opportunities (1). Most employment is now in tourism, which can be seasonal and low paid (1). Farming is declining with problems with falling prices of food (1). Farms need to look for alternative ways to make money by developing new businesses on the farm such as shops or tourist accommodation (1).	4
6 d	**C** Cities organised without an over-reliance on rural areas surrounding them and using renewable energy.	1
6 e	One mark for each of any two points described from the following. Environmental sustainability: more renewable energy or energy efficiency, more recycling of waste, more use of public transport, more green spaces. Social sustainability: more community projects, more affordable housing. Economic sustainability: more employment opportunities for people, more flexible working.	2
6 f	Must use a suitable case study, e.g. London. Needs to extend points and give a judgment overall as to the level of success. Add data as evidence where possible. **Indicative content** • London introduced a congestion charge that resulted in a 6 per cent increase in bus passengers, raising funds for developing public transport. • Employers have been urged to let staff work from home, leading to a potential for reduction in congestion at peak journey times, however, there are issues with many employers wanting to do this or being able to. • Housing projects introduce affordable housing with new developments including housing for low income or key workers, however, these are still often too expensive. • More green spaces to improve quality of life for those living in London however, increased demand for developing land to provide affordable homes. • Those strategies that have been more successful than others and why. The limits to a city like London being entirely sustainable. **Level 0, no marks** • No acceptable response. **Level 1 (Basic) 1–2 marks** • Demonstrates some knowledge of effects of sustainable strategies in a named city. (AO1) • Shows limited geographical understanding of the different sustainable strategies in a named city. Likely to be more negative than positive, with a lack of judgment or development of points. (AO2) **Level 2 (Clear) 3–4 marks** • Demonstrates specific and accurate knowledge of sustainable strategies in a named city. (AO2) • Shows clear geographical understanding of sustainable strategies in a named city. May recognise the benefits created and some level of success or failure. (AO3) **Level 3 (Detailed) 5–6 marks** • Demonstrates a thorough application of knowledge and understanding to give detailed explanations of sustainable strategies in a named city. (AO3) • Shows full understanding of the strategies and how they are sustainable. Will give some explanation of sustainable strategies, make a judgment and offer a conclusion. (AO3)	6

	Section C1: Fieldwork in a physical environment	
Q	Marking guidance	Marks
8 a (i)	(74 + 72 + 70) / 3 = 72.00 mm Units of measurement must be included to gain both marks.	2
8 a (ii)	One mark awarded per correct point added to the scatter graph. 	2

Q	Marking guidance	Marks
8 a (iii)	One mark for each point described. There could be a range of answers, but most are likely to focus on the dangers of working in or near the sea and the associated possible risks of injury or drowning, and the risk of injury from tripping or falling on pebble/rock beaches.	2
8 a (iv)	**Indicative content** Answer must demonstrate understanding of the scatter graph. Answer may refer to: pebble size; position on beach; increase in size of the cross-sectional area. **Level 0, no marks** • No appropriate response. **Level 1 (Basic) 1–2 marks** • Demonstrates limited application of knowledge and understanding of scatter graphs in describing and interpreting the mean pebble size and its relationship to location. (AO3) • Basic use of data shown on the scatter graph. (AO4) **Level 2 (Clear) 3–4 marks** • Demonstrates clear application of knowledge and understanding of scatter graphs in describing and interpreting the mean pebble size and its relationship to location. (AO3) • Clear reference made to the data shown on the scatter graph. (AO4)	4
8 b	The title of the of fieldwork enquiry will depend on the specific fieldwork completed by the student. **Indicative content** The command word is 'assess', so candidates must provide an informed judgement relating to the overall effectiveness of their presentation technique(s) by examining the constituent primary data collection methods involved. Evaluative comments leading to the overall judgements are credited at levels 1 and 2. Actual content will depend on the physical geography fieldwork investigation undertaken and the technique(s) used. Answers may refer to: • Type(s) of primary data collection method(s) used. • Data collected. • Variables involved and how collected, such as surveys, counts and measurements. • Features within the primary data collection method(s) will be discussed in terms of success in helping you complete the fieldwork enquiry. • Overall judgements in relation to the features and the effectiveness of method(s) used will be very clear and substantiated. **Level 0, no marks** • No relevant content. **Level 1 (Basic) 1–3 marks** • Evaluative comments relating to specific primary data collection methods are limited and vague. (AO3) • Evaluation of primary data collection methods in terms of success is generic or incomplete. Example(s) of method(s) may not be provided. (AO3) **Level 2 (Clear) 4–6 marks** • Specific components of named primary data collection methods are evaluated with clear statements addressing their success. (AO3) • Evaluation of named primary data collection methods in terms of success is made using clear statements. (AO3) **Level 3 (Detailed) 7–8 marks** • Demonstrates a developed and balanced appreciation of the effectiveness of primary data collection methods in helping to complete the fieldwork enquiry. (AO3) • Provides a substantiated overall assessment of the success of the primary data collection methods and their part in helping to complete the fieldwork enquiry. (AO3)	8
9 a (i)	$8.01 \times 0.17 = 1.36 \text{ m}^2$ Units of measurement must be included to gain both marks.	2
9 a (ii)	One mark awarded per correct point added to the scatter graph. 	2
9 a (iii)	One mark for each point described. There could be a range of answers, but most are likely to focus on the dangers of working in or near a river and the associated possible risks of injury or drowning.	2

Q	Marking guidance	Marks
9 a (iv)	**Indicative content** Answer must demonstrate understanding of the scatter graph. Answer may refer to: width of the river; depth of the river; increase in size of the cross-sectional area. **Level 0, no marks** • No appropriate response. **Level 1 (Basic) 1–2 marks** • Demonstrates limited application of knowledge and understanding of scatter graphs in describing and interpreting the cross-sectional area. (AO3) • Basic use of data shown on the scatter graph. (AO4) **Level 2 (Clear) 3–4 marks** • Demonstrates clear application of knowledge and understanding of scatter graphs in describing and interpreting the cross-sectional area. (AO3) • Clear reference made to the data shown on the scatter graph. (AO4)	4
9 b	The title of the fieldwork enquiry will depend on the specific fieldwork completed by the student. **Indicative content** The command word is 'assess', so candidates must provide an informed judgement relating to the overall effectiveness of their presentation technique(s) by examining the constituent primary data collection methods involved. Evaluative comments leading to the overall judgements are credited at levels 1 and 2. Actual content will depend on the physical geography fieldwork investigation undertaken and the technique(s) used. Answers may refer to: • Type(s) of primary data collection method(s) used. • Data collected. • Variables involved and how collected, such as surveys, counts and measurements. • Features within the primary data collection method(s) will be discussed in terms of success in helping you complete the fieldwork enquiry. • Overall judgements in relation to the features and the effectiveness of method(s) used will be very clear and substantiated. **Level 0, no marks** • No relevant content. **Level 1 (Basic) 1–3 marks** • Evaluative comments relating to specific primary data collection methods are limited and vague. (AO3) • Evaluation of primary data collection methods in terms of success is generic or incomplete. Example(s) of method(s) may not be provided. (AO3) **Level 2 (Clear) 4–6 marks** • Specific components of named primary data collection methods are evaluated with clear statements addressing their success. (AO3) • Evaluation of named primary data collection methods in terms of success is made using clear statements. (AO3) **Level 3 (Detailed) 7–8 marks** • Demonstrates a developed and balanced appreciation of the effectiveness of primary data collection methods in helping to complete the fieldwork enquiry. (AO3) • Provides a substantiated overall assessment of the success of the primary data collection methods and their part in helping to complete the fieldwork enquiry. (AO3)	8

Section C2: Fieldwork in a human environment		
Q	**Marking guidance**	**Marks**
10 a (i)	The title of the fieldwork investigation will depend on the specific fieldwork completed by the student. Only one data collection method is required. Accept any reasonable method that may have been used for the investigation. One mark for stating the method and a second for describing how the method was carried out.	2
10 a (ii)	Answers need to identify the data presentation method that was used for one mark and explain how the data was presented and why it was presented in that way for a further three marks.	4
10 a (iii)	The answer will depend on the specific fieldwork completed by the student. **Indicative content** The command word is 'assess', so candidates must provide an informed judgement relating to the overall effectiveness of their presentation technique(s) by examining the constituent primary data collection methods involved. Evaluative comments leading to the overall judgements are credited at levels 1 and 2. Actual content will depend on the physical geography fieldwork investigation undertaken and the technique(s) used. Answers may refer to:	4

Q	Marking guidance	Marks
	• Type(s) of primary data collection method(s) used. • Data collected. • Variables involved and how collected, such as surveys, counts and measurements. • Features within the primary data collection method(s) will be discussed in terms of success in helping you complete the fieldwork enquiry. • Overall judgements in relation to the features and the effectiveness of method(s) used will be very clear and substantiated. **Level 0, no marks** • No relevant content. **Level 1 (Basic) 1–2 marks** • Evaluative comments relating to specific primary data collection methods are limited and vague. (AO3) • Evaluation of primary data collection methods in terms of success is generic or incomplete. Example(s) of method(s) may not be provided. (AO3) **Level 2 (Clear) 3–4 marks** • Specific components of named primary data collection methods are evaluated with clear statements addressing their success. (AO3) • Evaluation of named primary data collection methods in terms of success is made using clear statements. (AO3)	
10 b	**Indicative content** • Answers should provide explanations of the questionnaire and sampling method. • Answers should suggest strengths and weaknesses of the questionnaire and sampling method. • A judgment of the suitability of the questionnaire and sampling method to the investigation should be made. **Level 0, no marks** • No relevant content. **Level 1 (Basic) 1–3 marks** • Provides a basic set of strengths and weaknesses of questionnaire and sampling method. (AO3) • Provides a basic justification of the assessment of strengths and weaknesses. (AO3) • Any judgment as to the suitability of the questionnaire and sampling method will be weak and generic. (AO3) **Level 2 (Clear) 4–6 marks** • Provides a clear explanation of strengths and weaknesses. (AO3) • Provides a clear justification of the assessment of strengths and weaknesses. (AO3) • Makes a judgment as to the suitability of the questionnaire and sampling method. (AO3) **Level 3 (Detailed) 7–8 marks** • Provides a detailed explanation of strengths and weaknesses. (AO3) • Fully justifies the assessment of strengths and weaknesses. (AO3) • Makes an informed judgment as to the suitability of the questionnaire and sampling method. (AO3)	8
11 a (i)	The title of the fieldwork investigation will depend on the specific fieldwork completed by the student. Only one data collection method is required. Accept any reasonable method that may have been used for the investigation. One mark for stating the method and a second for describing how the method was carried out.	2
11 a (ii)	Answers need to identify the data presentation method that was used for one mark and explain how the data was presented and why it was presented in that way for a further three marks.	4
11 a (iii)	The answer will depend on the specific fieldwork completed by the student. **Indicative content** The command word is 'assess', so candidates must provide an informed judgement relating to the overall effectiveness of their presentation technique(s) by examining the constituent primary data collection methods involved. Evaluative comments leading to the overall judgements are credited at levels 1 and 2. Actual content will depend on the physical geography fieldwork investigation undertaken and the technique(s) used. Answers may refer to: • Type(s) of primary data collection method(s) used. • Data collected. • Variables involved and how collected, such as surveys, counts and measurements. • Features within the primary data collection method(s) will be discussed in terms of success in helping you complete the fieldwork enquiry. • Overall judgements in relation to the features and the effectiveness of method(s) used will be very clear and substantiated.	4

Q	Marking guidance	Marks
	Level 0, no marks • No relevant content. **Level 1 (Basic) 1–2 marks** • Evaluative comments relating to specific primary data collection methods are limited and vague. (AO3) • Evaluation of primary data collection methods in terms of success is generic or incomplete. Example(s) of method(s) may not be provided. (AO3) **Level 2 (Clear) 3–4 marks** • Specific components of named primary data collection methods are evaluated with clear statements addressing their success. (AO3) • Evaluation of named primary data collection methods in terms of success is made using clear statements. (AO3)	
11 b	**Indicative content** • Answers should provide explanations of the questionnaire and sampling method. • Answers should suggest strengths and weaknesses of the questionnaire and sampling method. • A judgment of the suitability of the questionnaire and sampling method to the investigation should be made. **Level 0, no marks** • No relevant content. **Level 1 (Basic) 1–3 marks** • Provides a basic set of strengths and weaknesses of questionnaire and sampling method. (AO3) • Provides a basic justification of the assessment of strengths and weaknesses. (AO3) • Any judgment as to the suitability of the questionnaire and sampling method will be weak and generic. (AO3) **Level 2 (Clear) 4–6 marks** • Provides a clear explanation of strengths and weaknesses. (AO3) • Provides a clear justification of the assessment of strengths and weaknesses. (AO3) • Makes a judgment as to the suitability of the questionnaire and sampling method. (AO3) **Level 3 (Detailed) 7–8 marks** • Provides a detailed explanation of strengths and weaknesses. (AO3) • Fully justifies the assessment of strengths and weaknesses. (AO3) • Makes an informed judgment as to the suitability of the questionnaire and sampling method. (AO3)	8

Paper 3: People and environment issues

Section A: People and the biosphere		
Q	**Marking guidance**	**Marks**
1 a	The boreal forest biome covers a very large part of Canada, reaching from the Atlantic coast in the east approximately 5600 km to the mountain zone in the west. In the south it borders the USA and stretches to the Sub-Arctic biome to the north (about 750 km).	2
1 b (i)	**C** 25 metres	1
1 b (ii)	Calculation must be shown to get two marks. Grey Willow tree = 6 metres; Soapberry bush = 2 metres. So 6 – 2 = 4 metres difference in height.	2
1 b (iii)	Two resources only required, such as: • Timber (or lumber) for buildings. • Berries for food (blueberries and soapberries). • Wood for fuel. • Timber for telegraph poles.	2
1 c	**Indicative content** • The Aspen tree is a producer, using nutrients from soil and photosynthesis to produce leaves, flowers, fruit and seeds for insects. Insects are then food for the Spruce Grouse, which may get eaten by the Red-tailed Hawk or Great Horned Owl. So the Aspen tree supports a significant part of the food web in the boreal forest.	2

Section B: Forests under threat		
Q	**Marking guidance**	**Marks**
2 a (i)	1990 = Middle East and North Africa	1
2 a (ii)	The Middle East and North Africa world region has a drier climate than other regions, being semi-arid or hot desert (1). Therefore, there is not enough precipitation to support large plants like trees; only plants that have adapted to dry conditions would survive (1).	2
2 a (iii)	**Either** Latin America and the Caribbean **or** Sub-Saharan Africa	1

Exam Practice Answers

Q	Marking guidance	Marks
2 a (iv)	• **Latin America and Caribbean**: Tropical rainforests in this world region are under threat in developing or emerging countries because they want land space and resources to help them develop (e.g. farming, timber, oil and gas). • **Sub-Saharan Africa**: There is a dry climate in many parts of this world region (e.g. Sahel), which creates difficulties for trees to grow. Also, an increasing population (mostly poor) need fuelwood daily for cooking and so trees are cut down.	1
2 b	**Indicative content** • In Alberta the boreal forest is under threat from three major areas of oil sands extraction (e.g. Athabasca) (Fig. 6), with 767 km2 cleared or disturbed by 2012. This is clearly shown in Fig. 7 by the large scars in the landscape, cutting across the dark green areas of boreal forest. • Natural Resources Canada estimate that 1.4 per cent of Canada's forested area has been damaged by oil sands operations (Fig. 11). • As well as oil sands extraction, nearly 780 000 hectares of forest is harvested in Canada for timber (Fig. 8) and farming also accounts for a very small amount of loss. • Around 7 per cent of all Canada's exports are from the forestry industry, amounting to a GDP contribution of US$18 billion in 2016. • Overall, making money from these economic activities is a priority for the provincial and federal governments in Canada.	4
2 c	**Indicative content** • Some of Canada's forests are being managed sustainably. For example, the Athabascan Indians live in harmony with the boreal forest but only own 2 per cent of it. • The forest is mostly managed by the provincial and federal governments: Canada does have the most 'certified' forest in the world (37 per cent), which is nearly half of Canada's total forested area; this is sustainable forest management because it is checked to see that it meets internationally recognised criteria. • In total, Canada has 24 million hectares of protected forest, and, in 2015, 574 million new trees were planted.	2

Section C: Consuming energy resources		
Q	**Marking guidance**	**Marks**
3 a (i)	No explanation required. The trend in world oil consumption is a steady increase from just under 80 million barrels per day in 2000 to just under 100 million barrels a day in 2017. There was a small dip in 2008–09.	2
3 a (ii)	**A03 (4 marks)/A04 (4 marks)** Answers will compare trends but then assess the correlation between these trends. **Indicative content** A03 • World oil consumption showed a steady increase between 2000 and 2017. • World oil price was variable during the same time period. • There appears to be no correlation between the price of oil and oil consumption. No matter what the price, the consumption trend has been consistent on a slow upward trend. • Both price and consumption dipped in 2008–09, but this was due to the world financial collapse (recession) that reduced demand for oil as it is an expensive fuel. • There must be other factors influencing world consumption, such as countries trying to develop or consumers having a lifestyle where they cannot easily do without oil. A04 • Oil consumption increased from around 80 million barrels per day in 2000 to around 100 million barrels in 2017. • The oil price increased rapidly between 2000 and 2007, from $26 to $95 a barrel. There was a sudden drop up to 2009 to about $60 a barrel. The price recovered to about $110 a barrel in 2012 before declining rapidly to about $40 a barrel in 2016. • China is one country that has been rapidly developing and using a lot of oil to support its industrial growth and the demand from an increasingly wealthier population. **Level 0, no marks** • No acceptable response. **Level 1 (Basic) 1–3 marks** • Attempts to apply understanding to deconstruct information but understanding and connections are flawed. An unbalanced or incomplete argument that provides limited synthesis of understanding. Judgments are supported by limited evidence. (AO3) • Uses some geographical skills to obtain information with limited relevance and accuracy, which supports few aspects of the argument. (AO4)	8

Q	Marking guidance	Marks
	Level 2 (Clear) 4–6 marks • Applies understanding to deconstruct information and provide some logical connections between concepts. An imbalanced argument that synthesises mostly relevant understanding but not entirely coherently, leading to judgments that are supported by evidence occasionally. (AO3) • Uses geographical skills to obtain accurate information that supports some aspects of the argument. (AO4) **Level 3 (Detailed) 7–8 marks** • Applies understanding to deconstruct information and provide logical connections between concepts throughout. A balanced, well-developed argument that synthesises relevant understanding coherently, leading to judgments that are supported by evidence throughout. (AO3) • Uses geographical skills to obtain accurate information that supports all aspects of the argument. (AO4)	
3 b (i)	Definition must be more than an example. Unconventional oil is oil that is extracted from the ground by using techniques other than traditional onshore or offshore wells. Usually heavier oil (bitumen) that needs more complex processing. An example is oil sands (sometimes known as tar sands).	1
3 b (ii)	There are several reasons for the predicted increase in production from Canadian oil sands (from about 2.6 million barrels per day in 2017 to 3.7 million barrels per day in 2030): • Offshore and onshore conventional supplies are static and are not predicted to increase, but the world demand for oil continues to increase, so more oil is needed. Canada has 10 per cent of the world's oil reserves when oil sands are included. • Canada, and Provinces such as Alberta, want to raise money to help develop the country economically, and maintain its top 10 world position, and improve the quality of life for Canadians. Alberta raised US$1.48 billion in 2016–17. • There is a large demand for oil from the USA, a main trading partner and neighbour, and selling oil to the USA will continue to provide jobs for Canadians (136 000 direct jobs in 2017).	4
3 b (iii)	**C** 63 per cent	1
3 c (i)	Two negative impacts needed, each explained. **Indicative content** • Athabascan Indians, 70 per cent of whom live in the boreal forest (Fig. 7), have their culture and lifestyle disrupted when the boreal forest is removed or polluted. • Rivers, such as the Athabasca, may be polluted by oil mining activities that contaminate the water supplies for settlements, such as Fort McKay where people have had skin rashes. • The extraction of oil from the oil sands needs a lot of energy and this puts CO2 emissions into the atmosphere, adding to global warming. This changes the climate of the boreal forest, altering the ecosystem on which Indians and forest workers depend.	4
3 c (ii)	**A03 (4 marks)/A04 (4 marks)** Answers will compare reasons and determine their significance. **Indicative content** A03 • People living in the remote parts of the boreal forest zone, such as northern Alberta, may be in favour because it would provide jobs in areas where there are few except forestry. • The Canadian government is in favour because it supplies important revenues from the taxes paid by the oil companies and export duties, and they want to keep the country wealthy. The oil sands only take up a small area of total land. • The Alberta Provincial government would be in favour because the revenues can be used to improve the quality of life for people in the province. • Canadian people and businesses using oil wish to ensure that they have enough oil in the future. World demand is slowly increasing, especially in the USA close to Canada so there is a market for oil companies. • Oil companies are in favour because they can make a profit from extracting and selling the oil. • The most significant reasons revolve around making money, at a government level, business level and for individuals. A04 • The oil sands industry currently provides 136 000 direct jobs. • The GDP per capita of Canada was US$43 700 in 2017 and the Canadian government want ways of keeping it high. • Oil sands only occupy 1.4 per cent of Canada's forested area (Figure 11) and only 3 per cent of the oil sands area can be mined (Figure 6). • The production of conventional oil in Canada is stagnant (Figure 10) so the future potential is in unconventional oil sands. • The Albertan oil sands made US$1.2 billion in 2016–17 and this revenue can be used for health and social programmes and infrastructure projects. **Level 0, no marks** • No acceptable response.	8

Q	Marking guidance	Marks
	Level 1 (Basic) 1–3 marks • Attempts to apply understanding to deconstruct information but understanding and connections are flawed. An unbalanced or incomplete argument that provides limited synthesis of understanding. Judgments are supported by limited evidence. (AO3) • Uses some geographical skills to obtain information with limited relevance and accuracy, which supports few aspects of the argument. (AO4) **Level 2 (Clear) 4–6 marks** • Applies understanding to deconstruct information and provide some logical connections between concepts. An imbalanced argument that synthesises mostly relevant understanding but not entirely coherently, leading to judgments that are supported by evidence occasionally. (AO3) • Uses geographical skills to obtain accurate information that supports some aspects of the argument. (AO4) **Level 3 (Detailed) 7–8 marks** • Applies understanding to deconstruct information and provide logical connections between concepts throughout. A balanced, well-developed argument that synthesises relevant understanding coherently, leading to judgments that are supported by evidence throughout. (AO3) • Uses geographical skills to obtain accurate information that supports all aspects of the argument. (AO4)	

Section D: Making geographical decisions

Q	Marking guidance	Marks
4	**AO2 (4 marks)/AO3 (4 marks)/AO4 (4 marks)** In order to fully justify a choice, the candidate must consider all three options and establish a clear argument based on 'long-term' plan. There is no preferred option. Any option can be justified. The balance of points will depend on which option is chosen; advantages and disadvantages of each option should be considered, supported with evidence. **Option 1** can be justified by suggesting that the revenues and income from the extraction of oil from oil sands are the most important factor, as this give money to the country and province that can be used to maintain a high standard of living for the citizens. In addition many jobs are provided. Also the area damaged or disturbed is relatively small. **Option 2** can be justified by suggesting that the oil is important for providing revenues that can improve the quality of life in the country, province and local areas, but that there are negatives for the natural environment and Athabascan Indians. So to keep a sustainable balance help needs to be given to protect the forest and Indians through investment and good management. **Option 3** can be justified by suggesting that the oil sands extraction is extremely damaging and destructive to the local environment, areas downstream and even global pollution. Therefore, alternative ways of making money in these remote areas need to be found, sustainable forestry already exists and is an important export and could be expanded, and the natural beauty and wildlife of the forest provides opportunities for tourism that provides an experience of nature but also teaches the need to conserve the forest. **Indicative content** AO2 Understanding demonstrated as follows. • Forest ecosystems, how they operate and their sensitivity to change. • Economic processes such as trade and revenues. • Political processes such as decision making at different government levels and pressure groups. • Socio-cultural processes linked to lifestyles and environmental concerns. • Climate change processes and impacts on natural environments. • Exploitation of natural resources has long-term impacts on the environment, which then affects social and economic development. • Different groups have different views and opinions of geographical situations and issues, and view things on different time scales. AO3 Apply knowledge and understanding as follows. • Athabascan Indians live in harmony with nature and respect the boreal forest environment. • Boreal forest food web is fragile due to extreme climate, links could be easily broken if trees are removed. • Oil sands are mined through open techniques on the surface, this removes any vegetation cover. • Canada has the most certified forests in the world and a lot of sustainable forest management. • Oil demand is slowly increasing and when the oil price is high a lot of money can be made. • Health concerns for people living near or downstream of the oil sands activities.	12

Q	Marking guidance	Marks
	• Governments favour the economic development of oil sands to make money, supporting projects to improve the lives of citizens (health, social programmes and infrastructure). • Canadian Forest Service is working with oil companies to reduce negative impacts on forest ecosystem and ensure that mined areas are reclaimed. • Greenpeace claim that Canada are not meeting their requirement to reduce loss of boreal forests by 50 per cent. AO4 Skills and techniques demonstrated as follows. • USA is the second largest consumer of energy and is located next to Canada (Intro page). • Forestry and oil industries support Canada's economy (Intro page). • Northern parts of Canada have a more difficult environment for people to make a living in (Intro). • Surplus of oil available to export (117.3 million tonnes in 2016) (Intro). • 211 000 people employed in forestry, contributed US$18 billion to GDP in 2016 and 7 per cent of exports (Fig. 8 and Intro). • 136 000 employed directly in oil sands, Albertan oil sands made US$1.2 billion in 2016–17 (Fig. 11). • Alberta has 381 000 km^2 of boreal forest and the mineable oil sands area is 4800 km^2 (Fig. 6). • Open pit mining leaves scars on the land surface and run-off may contaminate rivers (Fig. 7). • 48 per cent of Canada's forests are sustainably managed and in 2015 574 million seedlings were planted (Fig. 8). • Over 60 per cent of Canada's current oil production is from oil sands and there will be a dependence on this in the future (Fig. 10). • Contamination of water supplies and fish, which affects the health of people (e.g. skin rashes at Fort McKay) (Fig. 11) • US$1 billion over 15 years of the oil sands revenue is being used for carbon capture and storage schemes, reducing CO_2 emissions. • World Bank data shows that between 1990 and 2015 the amount of forest area in Canada reduced by a small amount (0.01 million km^2) (Fig. 11). **Level 0, no marks** • No acceptable response. **Level 1 (Basic) 1–4 marks** • Attempts to apply understanding to deconstruct information but understanding and connections are flawed. An unbalanced or incomplete argument that provides limited synthesis of understanding. Judgments are supported by limited evidence. (AO3) • Few aspects of the enquiry process are supported by the use of geographical skills to obtain information, which has limited relevance and accuracy. Communicates generic fieldwork findings and uses limited relevant geographical terminology. (AO4) **Level 2 (Clear) 5–8 marks** • Applies understanding to deconstruct information and provide some logical connections between concepts. An imbalanced argument that synthesises mostly relevant understanding but not entirely coherently, leading to judgments that are supported by evidence occasionally. (AO3) • Some aspects of the enquiry process are supported by the use of geographical skills. Communicates fieldwork findings with some clarity, using relevant geographical terminology occasionally. (AO4) **Level 3 (Detailed) 9–12 marks** • Applies understanding to deconstruct information and provide logical connections between concepts throughout. A balanced, well-developed argument that synthesises relevant understanding coherently, leading to judgments that are supported by evidence throughout. (AO3) • All aspects of the enquiry process are supported by the use of geographical skills. Communicates enquiry specific fieldwork findings with clarity and uses relevant geographical terminology consistently. (AO4)	

Exam Practice Answers

Q	Marking guidance	Marks
4 SPaG	**SPaG 0, no marks** • Learners write nothing. • Learner's response does not relate to the question. • Learner's achievement in SPaG does not reach the threshold performance level, for example, errors in spelling, punctuation and grammar severely hinder meaning. **SPaG 1 (Threshold performance) 1 mark** • Learners spell and punctuate with reasonable accuracy. • Learners use rules of grammar with some control of meaning and any errors do not significantly hinder meaning overall. • Learners use a limited range of specialist terms as appropriate. **SPaG 2 (Intermediate performance) 2–3 marks** • Learners spell and punctuate with considerable accuracy. • Learners use rules of grammar with general control of meaning overall. • Learners use a good range of specialist terms as appropriate. **SPaG 3 (High performance) 4 marks** • Learners spell and punctuate with consistent accuracy. • Learners use rules of grammar with effective control of meaning overall. • Learners use a wide range of specialist terms as appropriate.	4

Revision Guide Acknowledgements

Illustrations by York Publishing Solutions Pvt. Ltd: p. 9 F3, p. 16 F6 & F7, P. 21 F11, p. 22 F13, p. 23 F14 & F15, p. 24 F16, p. 29 F19, p. 32 F2 (Redrawn from http://hdr.undp. org/en/countries), p. 34 F3, p. 37 F5, p. 39 F6, p. 41 F8, p. 43 F10 (Redrawn from Microfinance Market Outlook, 2016, responsibility), p. 55 F3 (Data source UN 2002), p. 72 F4, F5 & F6, p. 73 F7 & F8, p. 74 F9 & F10 (Adapted from image by yefi/Wikimedia Commons), p. 75 F11 (Adapted from image at http://www.bbc.co.uk/education/guides/z3ndmp3/revision/3), p. 76 F12 (Adapted from diagram by Anna Bozzo, https://102coastsgroup2.wikispaces.com, Creative Commons SA 3.0 licence) & F13, p. 77 F14 (Adapted from diagram at https://www.geocaching.com/geocache/GC4KF9W_gold-coast-seawaywho-gives-a-spit?guid=d6d89c9a-de21-4fc6-a23b-7d374bf245f), p. 83 F15 & F16, p. 84 F17, p. 85 F18 & F19, p. 86 F21 & F22, p. 87 F23 & F24, p. 88 F25, p. 121 F1 (Redrawn from Soil climate map, USDA-NRCS, Soil Science Division, World Soil Resources, Washington DC), p. 122 F2, p. 123 F3, p. 124 F4 & F5, p. 127 F7 & F8, p. 128 F9, p. 135 F2, p. 136 F3, p. 140 F5 & F6 (Redrawn from map by UN Environment, sources: Brazilian Institute for Geography and Statistics; La déforestation en Amazonie), p. 144 F8, p. 156 F2, p. 157 F3 (Adapted from BP Statistical Review of World Engergy 2015), p. 159 F4, p. 180 F1, p. 181 F2, p. 182 F3

Illustrations by Dave Morris and Andrew Pagram: p. 21 F10, p. 25 F17, p. 35 F4, p. 40 F7, p. 46 F11, p. 48 F12 & F13, p. 54 F1, p. 55 F2, p. 57 F4, p. 59 F5, p. 60 F6 & F7, p. 61 F8, p. 62 F9, p. 65 F11, p. 71 F2 & F3, p. 92 F1, p. 93 F2, p. 94 F3, p. 96 F4, p. 98 F5 & F6, p. 103 F9, p. 104 F10, p. 109 F14, p. 130 F10, p. 132 F11, p. 136 F4, p. 146 F9, p. 147 F11, p. 148 F12, p. 161 F7, p. 167 F8, p. 176 F13

Other image acknowledgements: p. 8 F1 Jamilia Marini/Shutterstock.com, p. 9 F2 Designua/Shutterstock.com, p. 13 F4 daulon/Shutterstock.com, p. 15 F5 Image by Robert A. Rohde, Global Warming Art, Creative Commons Attribution-Share Alike 3.0 Unported license, p. 15 F8 Source: JTWC. Background image from NASA, p. 20 F9 Ellen Bronstayn/Shutterstock.com, p. 22 F12 Peter Hermes Furian/Shutterstock.com, p. 25 F18 udaix/Shutterstock.com, p. 31 F1 World Bank Databank 2016, p. 43 F9 Fairtrade Foundation, p. 50 F14 Jenny Matthews / Alamy Stock Photo, p. 68 F1 Bardocz Peter/Shutterstock.com, p. 86 F20 Dave Head/Shutterstock.com, p. 99 F7 CBD & inner city: ZGPhotography/Shutterstock.com; Suburbs: Vittorio Caramazza/Shutterstock.com, p. 100 F8 PhotoLondonUK/Shutterstock.com, p. 104 F11 Paul White Aerial views / Alamy Stock Photo, p. 105 F13 https://twitter.com/atkinsglobal/status/626710263333552128, p. 110 F15 Jürgen Matern / Wikimedia Commons, p. 125 F6 NASA Goddard Space Flight Center Image by Reto Stöckli (land surface, shallow water, clouds). Enhancements by Robert Simmon (ocean color, compositing, 3D globes, animation). Data and technical support: MODIS Land Group; MODIS Science Data Support Team; MODIS Atmosphere Group; MODIS Ocean Group Additional data: USGS EROS Data Center (topography); USGS Terrestrial Remote Sensing Flagstaff Field Center (Antarctica); Defense Meteorological Satellite Program (city lights), p. 134 F1 Frontpage/Shutterstock.com, p. 142 F7 Global Warming Images / Alamy Stock Photo, p. 155 F1 NASA International Space Station program and the JSC Earth Science & Remote Sensing Unit, ARES Division, Exploration Integration Science Directorate, p. 160 F5 World Economic Forum and Accenture analysis, p. 161 F6 UN Data, p. 168 F9 © A Goldstein/ Survival, p. 169 F10 iStockphoto/dan_prat, p. 170 F11 NASA's Earth Observatory, p. 172 F12 DBEIS Data

Practice Book Acknowledgements

Illustrations by York Publishing Solutions Pvt. Ltd: p. 214 F3, p. 217 F1 (Data source World Bank), p. 218 F2 (Data source Wikipedia, Lord Toran), p. 219 F3 (Data source WTO), p. 220 F4, p. 222 F5 (Data source UNCTAD), p. 223 F6 (Data source Jamaica Tourist Office), p. 224 F7 (Data source www. tradingeconomics.com, Organisation of the Petroleum Exporting Countries), p. 227 F1, p. 235 F3 (Adapted from http://www.s-cool.co.uk/gifs/g-geo-rivers-dia15.gif), p. 240 F2, p. 244 F1 (Redrawn from Soil climate map, USDA-NRCS, Soil Science Division, World Soil Resources, Washington DC), p. 245 F2, p. 246 F3, p. 247 F4, p. 248 F5, p. 252 F1, p. 254 F4 (Data source Mongabay.com, © Rhett Butler 2017, data source: RAISG Amazon 2012 Protected Areas Indigenous Territories), p. 261 F1 (Main world map image: Geothermal Power Generation in the World 2010-2014 Update Report, Ruggero Bertani, Open Access, http://www.sciencedirect.com/science/journal/03756505/60), p. 262 F2 (Data: National Statistics: Energy Trends September 2016, United Kingdom Statistics Authority), p. 263 F3 (Data: World Economic Forum and Accenture analysis), p. 269 F7 (Department of Energy & Climate Change, UK Energy Statistics, 2015 & Q4 2015, Statistical Press Release, 31 March 2016, © Crown Copyright 2017 Open Government licence), p. 271 F1 (Data:Weather.gov, mapping by NASA WorldWind Open Government licence), p. 273 F2 (Life expectancy at birth, both sexes, 2015, http://gamapserver.who.int/mapLibrary/Files/Maps/Global_LifeExpectancy_bothsexes_2015.png, reprinted with permission of WHO), p. 274 F3 (Data WTO), p. 277 F5, p. 291 F11b

Illustrations by Darren Lingard: p. 229 F3, p. 275 F4, p. 278 F6, p. 283 F4, p. 289 F10, p. 298 F1, p. 298 F2, p. 299 F4, p. 299 F5, p. 301 F9, p. 302 F10

Illustrations by Dave Morris and Andrew Pagram: p. 250 F7, p. 257 F5

Other acknowledgements: p. 210 F1 DarwelShots/Shutterstock.com, p. 212 F2 Robert A. Rohde, Global Warming Art, Creative Commons Attribution-Share Alike 3.0 Unported license, p. 228 F2 Data: UN Population Division, 2005, p. 230 F4 flocu/Shutterstock.com, p. 231 F1 Permit Number CP18/047 British Geological Survey © UKRI 2018. All rights reserved, p. 232 F2 Mr. Nut / Alamy Stock Photo, p. 237 F4 Paul Briden/Shutterstock.com, p. 239 F1 Attribution: Contains Ordnance Survey data © Crown copyright and database right 2018, p. 241 F3 Petrafler/shutterstock.com, p. 243 F4 Alasdair Rae, p. 249 F6 Galyna Andrushko/Shutterstock.com, p. 253 F2 enciktat/ shutterstock.com, p. 253 F3 KYTan/Shutterstock.com, p. 258 F6 Ludmila Ruzickova/shutterstock. com, p. 259 F7 NASA's Earth Observatory, p. 265 F4 data from the World Bank (2014, 2017), p. 266 F5 data from BP Statistical Review 2017, p. 268 F6 Enerdata: www.enerdata.net, p. 280 F1 Harry Green/shutterstock.com, p. 281 F2 DavidYoung/Shutterstock.com, p. 282 F3 Dchauy/Shutterstock. com, p. 284 F5 Attribution: Contains Ordnance Survey data © Crown copyright and database right 2018, p. 286 F7 Contains OS data © Crown copyright and database right 2018, p. 287 F8 Photo Cornwall / Alamy Stock Photo, p. 300 F6 Government of Alberta (Alberta.ca), p. 300 F7 NASA's Earth Observatory, p. 301 F8 Source: State of Canada's Forests Report, Natural Resources Canada, 2017. Reproduced with the permission of the Department of Natural Resources, 2018